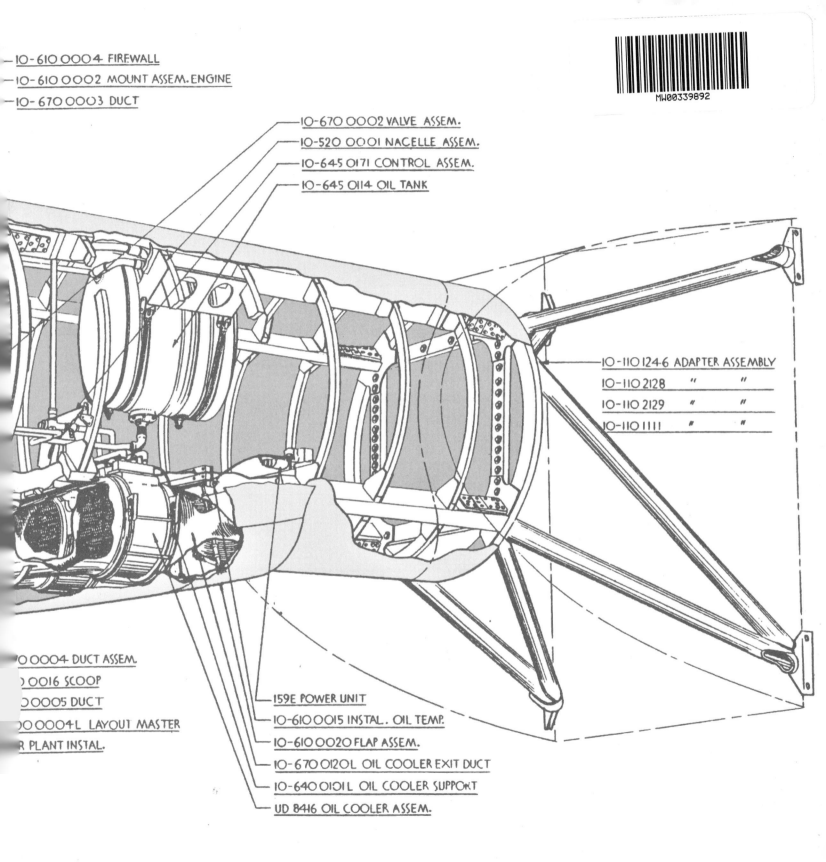

10-610 0004 FIREWALL
10-610 0002 MOUNT ASSEM. ENGINE
10-670 0003 DUCT

10-670 0002 VALVE ASSEM.
10-520 0001 NACELLE ASSEM.
10-645 0171 CONTROL ASSEM.
10-645 0114 OIL TANK

10-110 124-6 ADAPTER ASSEMBLY
10-110 2128   "   "
10-110 2129   "   "
10-110 1111   "   "

70 0004 DUCT ASSEM.
0 0016 SCOOP
0 0005 DUCT
0 0004L LAYOUT MASTER
R PLANT INSTAL.

159E POWER UNIT
10-610 0015 INSTAL. OIL TEMP.
10-610 0020 FLAP ASSEM.
10-670 0120L OIL COOLER EXIT DUCT
10-640 0101L OIL COOLER SUPPORT
UD 8416 OIL COOLER ASSEM.

Airframes and Powerplants a

America's Round-Engine Warbirds

Warbirds

Bill Yenne

The Close of the Military Prop Era

specialtypress
PUBLISHERS AND WHOLESALERS

specialtypress
PUBLISHERS AND WHOLESALERS

Specialty Press
6118 Main St.
North Branch, MN 55056
Phone: 651-277-1400 or 800-895-4585
Fax: 651-277-1203
www.specialtypress.com

Edit by Mike Machat
Layout by Monica Seiberlich

ISBN 978-1-58007-279-3
Item No. SP274

Library of Congress Cataloging-in-Publication Data Available

Written, edited, and designed in the U.S.A.
Printed in China
10 9 8 7 6 5 4 3 2 1

Unless otherwise noted, all illustrations in this book were images created prior to 1959 and are from the author's collection.

Frontispiece:

This purposefully surrealistic illustration, circa 1943, depicts a Wright R-1820 Cyclone 9-cylinder radial aircraft engine.

Title page:

In 1942, Alfred Palmer, a photographer with the Office of War Information, traveled to Southern California. While he was there, he visited several aircraft factories and took a number of Kodachrome transparencies of workers installing Wright Cyclones and Pratt & Whitney Wasps. (Photo Courtesy Library of Congress)

Table of contents page:

This cartoon of a 1943 Wright R-3350 Duplex Cyclone engine manual is deadly serious. It explains that these two fellows failed to read the manual and are attempting to remove a supercharger rear housing without first removing the fuel-pump driveshaft support, the rear fuel pump, the oil transfer tube, and other components.

DISTRIBUTION BY:

UK and Europe
Crécy Publishing Ltd
1a Ringway Trading Estate
Shadowmoss Road
Manchester M22 5LH England
Tel: 44 161 499 0024
Fax: 44 161 499 0298
www.crecy.co.uk
enquiries@crecy.co.uk

Canada
Login Canada
300 Saulteaux Crescent
Winnipeg, MB R3J 3T2 Canada
Tel: 800 665 1148
Fax: 800 665 0103
www.lb.ca

TABLE OF CONTENTS

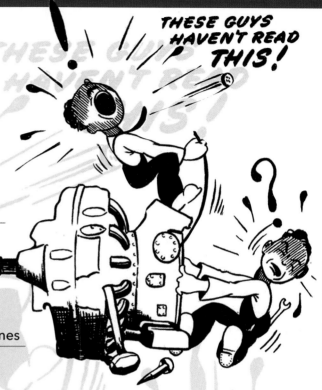

THESE GUYS HAVEN'T READ THIS!

INTRODUCTION

This book is about the power behind the American warbirds that became famous during World War II and those warbirds of the early Cold War, whose technical development began during World War II or evolved directly from wartime aircraft. Herein, these aircraft are viewed from the unique perspective of the powerplants that provided their muscle.

Specifically, this book features aircraft that were powered by air-cooled piston engines. Because the cylinders in these motors are located in a circular arrangement radiating from the shaft, they are known as radial, or "round," engines.

This is a narrative historical overview of the American engines and the aircraft they powered in that golden age of radial piston power that began between the world wars, reached its apogee from 1939–1946, and extended several fingers through the ensuing decades.

This is not an encyclopedic work because a truly encyclopedic work on this subject would, and should properly, consume a whole shelf—indeed a whole library—of books this size. Yet, having said this, many powerplants and a great many of the aircraft they powered are included. This book also features a great deal of nuanced technical and production data for these dozens of airplanes and engines.

This introduction begins with a briefing about piston aircraft engines. It delves into the types of engines and their technical distinctions. It looks at their origins and at the beginnings of aviation itself.

Founding Fathers

Sharing the piston engine field with radials throughout the history of aviation are water-cooled inline engines. Inline engines were state of the art during the early years of powered, heavier-than-air flight. The radial engine did not figure prominently until after World War I.

The inline engine as a standard powerplant for cars, trucks, tractors, and other land vehicles dates back to the 19th century. There are numerous patents for such engines scattered through the history

A woman worker demonstrates the finer points of installing a Pratt & Whitney R-1830 Twin Wasp as a fellow Douglas Aircraft Company employee looks on. This Kodachrome was taken by Alfred Palmer of the Office of War Information at the Douglas plant in Long Beach, California in October 1942. (Photo Courtesy Library of Congress)

of technology. They go back to that of steam engine pioneer John Stevens in 1798 and include that of Nicolaus Otto in Germany in 1864, who is considered by many to be the direct ancestor of modern gasoline engines. In 1886, Karl Benz, also in Germany, became the first to mass produce vehicles with internal combustion engines. In 1892, Rudolf Diesel produced the first compression ignition engine of the type that bears his name.

As seen in Chapter 1, the first operational aircraft engines were inline engines. Indeed, both Wilbur and Orville Wright as well as Glenn Curtiss (the founding fathers of powered flight) had all built and used inline internal combustion engines on the ground before they took to the air. Although the Wrights and Curtiss were rivals, their names came to be linked in 1929 (though none of them were still involved with their original companies) in the Curtiss-Wright Corporation. Discussed in detail in Chapter 2, Curtiss-Wright became one of the largest-ever manufacturers of round engines.

Meanwhile, there was a third type of piston engine that played an important role in aviation before the radial had its day. The rotary engine is similar in appearance to the radial engine, as the cylinders radiate from the crankshaft, and as such, it is also a "round" engine. However, while the radiating cylinders remain stationary in a radial engine, the entire cylinder block (with the propeller attached) rotates around a stationary crankshaft in a rotary engine.

In 1888, Felix Millet patented a rotary engine in France, and the engines were being used in motorcycles and automobiles by the turn of the century.

Rotary engines for aircraft originated in France. In 1905, Louis Seguin, a successful civil engineer, and his brother Laurent started Société des Moteurs Gnome, which later became the first company to mass produce rotary engines for aircraft.

Although its early development was a sideshow in the annals of early engine technology, the radial engine made its debut after the turn of the century. Many sources credit the invention of the radial engine to motorcycle builder Jacob Ellehammer of Denmark, who built a 3-cylinder radial during the winter of 1903–1904. However, as with many technical innovations, the time was right, and there were others with the same idea.

Another early pioneer in the development of the radial engine was the Englishman Samuel Dalziel Heron (see Chapter 2), whom is mentioned because of the part he played in American radial engine development in the 1920s. During World War I, he worked with Professor A.H. Gibson Herson at the Royal Aircraft Factory at Farnborough to conduct the first serious scientific study of air-cooled engine design.

In the United States, the first motor to power a heavier-than-air flying machine had been an inline engine that was built in the

Many inventors had worked on the internal combustion engine, but it was Karl Benz in Germany who first patented the two-stroke engine in 1880. He went on to patent the spark plug, the carburetor, the clutch, the gear shift, and other inventions.

Wright Brothers workshop, but that distinction almost went to a radial engine.

In 1903, even as the Wrights, those two obscure bicycle mechanics in Dayton, Ohio, were closing in on their first flight, another project was in motion. The US War Department was financing the efforts by the eminent scientist Samuel Pierpont Langley to fly the first powered heavier-than-air craft. As the secretary of the Smithsonian Institution in Washington, D.C., Langley had impeccable credentials and had conducted unmanned tests of his design.

To power his *Aerodrome*, Langley's chief engineer, Charles Matthews Manly, developed a 5-cylinder, 52-hp radial that was based on a rotary engine built by New York rotary engine pioneer Stephen Balzer. To make a long story short, the radial-engine-powered *Aerodrome* with Manly at the controls failed in two attempts to fly in late 1903. Manley survived, but Langley's dream did not. He blamed the launch mechanism for the two crashes, but they were actually due to his control system design and his failure to accurately calculate stress on the airframe.

The second failure, which resulted in Langley giving up, occurred on December 8, only nine days before the successful flights by the Wright Brothers.

Thanks to Seguin's Société des Moteurs Gnome and Louis Verdet's Société des Moteurs Le Rhône (with which it would merge in 1915 as Gnome et Rhône), rotary engines were well established in the aircraft industry in Europe by World War I. (In Germany, Motorenfabrik Oberursel licensed Gnome et Rhône technology and produced rotary engines through the war.)

However, inline engines were still predominant in wartime aircraft, and radial engine development lagged until after World War I. Indeed, it can be said that the single largest contribution by American industry to military aviation in World War I was an inline engine.

The Liberty L-12 was a 400-hp water-cooled engine with a displacement of 1,649 ci and 12 cylinders arranged in a "V" configuration. In May 1917, just a month after the United States entered the war, the federal Aircraft Production Board asked Elbert Hall of the Hall-Scott Motor Company of Berkeley, California, and Jesse Vincent of Detroit's Packard Motor Car Company to put their heads together to develop a powerful aircraft engine that would match or exceed anything being produced in Europe. A Liberty prototype built at Packard was ready by July, and it was approved in August.

The War Department ordered 22,500 Liberty engines, and by the time that production wound down after the Armistice of November 1918, 20,478 had been built by a consortium that included Ford, General Motors, Lincoln, and Packard. Few made it overseas to see combat, but they powered the trainers for American pilots who did see combat. In turn, they provided the power for postwar American military aircraft for many years and found a ready market in civilian aviation as surplus Liberties were sold off. They also helped ensure the dominance of inline aircraft engines in the early postwar years.

By the 1920s, rotary engines had faded from prominence because of technical limitations on fuel and airflow. At the same time, improvements in radial engine technology made them a practical, even more desirable competitor to inline engines. In 1920, the American National Advisory Committee for Aeronautics (NACA) confirmed that air-cooled radials could offer a high level of reliability and a better power-to-weight ratio because they did not need the added weight of the radiator and coolant required by liquid-cooled inline engines.

During the 1920s, radials were quickly moving to eclipse inlines as the principal aircraft engine type. By World War II, the production of radials outpaced that of inline engines by a ratio of more than 5:1.

The Le Rhône 9C was a popular 80-hp, 9-cylinder rotary aircraft engine produced in France by Louis Seguin's Société des Moteurs Le Rhône (later part of Gnome et Rhône). First run in 1916, it was used in numerous French and British military aircraft types during World War I.

In 1913, Louis and Laurent Seguin of Société Des Moteurs Gnome introduced their Monosoupape (single valve) rotary engines, which eliminated the inlet valve, replacing it with piston-controlled transfer ports similar to those of a two-stroke engine. Seen here is the 160-hp Gnome 9N Monosoupape, which was a 9-cylinder, single-row engine that they began marketing in 1917. It was used in such aircraft as the Sopwith Camel. (Photo Courtesy Stahlkocher, Licensed under Creative Commons)

Designations and Manufacturers

Round engines were designated accordingly by the United States armed forces with the letter "R." In these designations, the number to the right of this letter denoted the displacement of the particular engine in cubic inches, which was a number usually rounded off slightly so as to end with a "5" or "0."

The other principal type of piston engine commonly used in high-performance aircraft of this era was the water-cooled inline engine in which the cylinders were arranged in a "V" configuration (as with automobile engines). These were appropriately designated with a "V," although technically, this letter identified "vertical installation."

A much less common piston engine type was the "H" configuration, which was seen occasionally in the 1930s. In this powerplant, two separate flat engines with separate crankshafts were geared to the same output shaft. The two engine blocks looked like a letter "H" when seen from the front, hence the name.

While the major, high-performance, household-name American combat aircraft of this era originated with at least a dozen companies, the vast majority of the round engines originated with just two companies: Curtiss-Wright and Pratt & Whitney.

Likewise, almost all inline engines came from two sources, and they were of just two types. These were the V-1710 from the Allison Engine Company, which was a division of General Motors, and the V-1650 Merlin, which was designed in Britain by Rolls Royce and built under license in the United States by Packard Motor Car. Variants of the V-1710 were mainly used in just three aircraft types: the P-38, P-39, and P-40. With negligible exceptions, the Merlin was used only in the P-51 Mustang.

Parenthetically, lower-performance aircraft, especially trainers, used smaller engines, most of which were sourced from two other companies: Continental Aviation and Engineering of Muskegon, Michigan, and the Lycoming Foundry and Machine Company of Williamsport, Pennsylvania. Both produced a combination of radial engines and opposed-cylinder engines (designated "O").

Aside from the V-1650 and V-1710, most of the American military aircraft types from the World War II period had round engines, and both Curtiss-Wright and Pratt & Whitney produced a broad product line of engine types. This is the story of those aircraft and those engines.

The extent of production of radial engines during the halcyon years of American aircraft powerplants was impressive. The official USAAF (United States Army Air Forces) Materiel Command statistical recap of the period from July 1940 and August 1945 has the numbers.

Headquartered in East Hartford, Connecticut, Pratt & Whitney (along with its licensees) produced 355,985 radial engines. Wright Aeronautical of Patterson, New Jersey, the engine component of Curtiss-Wright, by itself and through its licensees produced 223,036 radials.

Then, there were the smaller makers of smaller engines: Continental, Lycoming, and Jacobs Aircraft Engine Company of Pottstown, Pennsylvania (see Chapter 6).

Continental produced 33,947 aircraft engines by the Materiel Command reckoning, but it also produced variants of the Wright Aeronautical R-975 radial engine for use in armored ground vehicles. This added 53,418 units to the Continental total, although these engines were not used in aircraft.

Among the other two manufacturers, Jacobs produced 32,119 engines (which included 11,614 Pratt & Whitney R-1340s), while Lycoming built 24,871 aircraft engines.

Among the leading makers of inline engines, the top two were Allison with 69,305 and Packard with 55,511. These numbers clearly show the relative significance of round engines.

This is the story of these manufacturers, their round engines, and the aircraft who flew with them.

Looking quite content in this photograph, Samuel Pierpont Langley imagined that he had developed the heavier-than-air craft that would make history's first powered, manned flight. He was a prominent astronomer and physicist who served for nearly two decades as the third secretary of the Smithsonian Institution. He did not succeed, however, in his aviation dream. (Photo Courtesy Smithsonian Institution Archives)

ABOUT THE AUTHOR

San Francisco–based author Bill Yenne has written more than two dozen books on military and historical topics. He is a member of the American Aviation Historical Society, and he has contributed to encyclopedias of both world wars. His work has been selected for the official Chief of Staff of the Air Force Reading List. In addition, he was presented with the Air Force Association's prestigious Gill Robb Wilson Award for his "most outstanding contribution in the field of arts and letters, [for his] work of over two dozen airpower-themed books, and for years of effort shaping how many people understand and appreciate airpower."

Walter J. Boyne, the former head of the Smithsonian National Air and Space Museum, has recommended Yenne's work.

"I can guarantee that you will be engaged by his master storytelling from his opening words to the very last page," Boyne wrote.

One of Yenne's most recent books, *Building the B-17: A Detailed Look at Manufacturing Boeing's Legendary World War II Bomber in Original Photos* is an exhaustive study of the conception, design, production, and technical nuances of this seminal warplane program.

His works on aviation and aerospace history include several meticulously detailed corporate histories of the Boeing Company that have been published over many years as well as acclaimed corporate histories of Convair, Lockheed, McDonnell Douglas, North American Aviation, and Rockwell International.

Aviation biographies penned by Mr. Yenne include *Hap Arnold: The General Who Invented the US Air Force*, and a dual biography of Dick Bong and Tommy McGuire titled *Aces High: The Heroic Saga of the Two Top-Scoring American Aces of World War II*, which was described by pilot and best-selling author Dan Roam as "the greatest flying story of all time."

Yenne has appeared in documentaries airing on the History Channel, the National Geographic Channel, the Smithsonian Channel, ARD German Television, and NHK Japanese Television. His book signings have been covered by C-SPAN.

Visit him on the web at BillYenne.com.

Bill Yenne is seen here seated at the executive dining table from the boardroom of the Douglas Aircraft Company. This table, constructed in 1953 for company founder Donald Douglas, featured an illuminated partial globe in the center and seated at least 15 people comfortably. It is seen here while on display at the Museum of Flying in Santa Monica, California.

Chapter 1

CURTISS-WRIGHT AND ITS WHIRLWINDS

Curtiss-Wright, one of the "Big Two" American radial engine manufacturers of the World War II era, originated in 1929 with a merger of companies: Curtiss of Buffalo, New York, and Wright Aeronautical of Patterson, New Jersey. They had as their namesakes the three former bicycle mechanics who had been the original names in American aviation. This trio included Wilbur and Orville Wright as well as Glenn Hammond Curtiss. However, by 1929, the three namesakes themselves had long since parted ways with the companies.

Wilbur and Orville, of course, had invented heavier-than-air flight in 1903 with their *Wright Flyer*, though there are earlier unproven claims. The Wrights went on to produce a series of aircraft over the next dozen years. The powerplant for the first Wright aircraft was an inline engine that was rough-sketched by them. It was refined and handmade by Charles Edward "Charlie" Taylor, a mechanic who worked in their bicycle shop. Taylor faced the challenge of keeping the weight down (a constant issue in engine design ever since) by casting his 4-cylinder engine block in an aluminum alloy (eight percent copper). At a time when 8-hp gasoline engines for automobiles weighed more than 200 pounds, Taylor delivered 12 hp at 180 pounds. Taylor built his own carburetor and used gravity feed to save weight and not require a fuel pump.

Glenn Curtiss of Hammondsport, New York, started out as a bicycle messenger, and like the Wrights, later had his own bike shop. By 1902, he was manufacturing both motorcycles and internal combustion engines of his own design. His first aircraft engines were built in 1904 for California exhibition pilot Tom Baldwin. Like Charlie Taylor, Curtiss created inline engines of the type being used for motorcycles and automobiles at the time.

In 1907, Curtiss caught the eye of the prolific inventor Alexander Graham Bell, whose list of credits ranged from the telephone and phonograph to the magnetic media that later evolved into the tape recorder and data drives. In 1907, Bell was heading the

USAAF test pilot Lieutenant Mike Hunter stands in front of a Wright R-2600-23 Twin Cyclone engine that is installed in a Douglas A-20C Havoc at the Douglas Aircraft plant in Long Beach, California, in October 1942. Curtiss-Wright was at the peak of prominence when thousands of its engines were flowing into the American aircraft industry.

Aerial Experiment Association (AEA), which was formed to create aeronautical innovations. Bell brought Curtiss aboard to design airplanes, the first of which was the *June Bug*, which made its debut in 1908 with Curtiss himself at the controls in the first pre-announced, public flight of a heavier-than-air craft.

Curtiss and the Wrights became bitter rivals. The Wrights filed suit, claiming that Curtiss and the AEA, in many of their aircraft, were violating Wright patents. In 1914, after years of legal wrangling—along with the dissolution of the AEA in 1909 and Wilbur's death in the typhoid epidemic of 1912—the US Court of Appeals finally ruled against Curtiss. By this time, the course of aviation history and the commercial interests of the parties involved had moved on.

Commercially, the Wrights never matched the success of Glenn Curtiss nor his entrepreneurial flair. The Wrights sold several of their aircraft to the US Army and set up a flying school near Dayton, where they trained a number of early Army pilots. However, a series of fatal crashes tarnished their image. Curtiss, meanwhile, sold aircraft to the US Navy and participated in a number of high-profile aviation events, including the Grande Semaine d'Aviation in France in 1909, and he won the Pulitzer Trophy for the first long-distance flight between American cities.

Curtiss began manufacturing both aircraft and aero-engines, merging these interests as the Curtiss Aeroplane and Motor Company in 1910, one year after the formal creation of the Wright Company. While Curtiss looked forward toward the development of newer aircraft, the Wright Company looked backward toward protection of the original patents.

In 1915, Curtiss began producing the ubiquitous JN-4 "Jenny" family of military trainers, of which more than 6,800 were built. Used as trainers during the war, they became a mainstay of American aviation in the early years after the war.

Pioneers Depart; Financiers Arrive

Orville, meanwhile, sold his patents and his interest in the Wright Company in 1915 to a syndicate of venture capitalists who merged it into the Wright-Martin Company that also briefly included the Glenn L. Martin Company. The Wright-Martin Company existed for just a short time, building Spanish Hispano-Suiza aircraft engines under license. In 1919, when Wright-Martin was liquidated, Glenn L. Martin himself continued in business in Baltimore, Maryland, and the Wright part of the short-lived entity evolved into the Wright Aeronautical Company of Patterson, New Jersey.

In 1917, meanwhile, Orville had also lent his name and expertise to another short-lived company called Dayton-Wright, whose bread and butter was manufacturing DeHavilland DH-4 biplane trainers for the US Army. Dayton-Wright was financed by a number of automotive industry leaders, headed by entrepreneur-inventor

This is a reconstruction of the engine that powered the first Wright Flyer in 1903. Because no existing automobile engine suited their needs, the Wrights turned to their friend Charlie Taylor, who built an engine from scratch. It was an inline 4-cylinder, water-cooled engine. Its crankcase was made of aluminum to reduce weight. (Photo Courtesy US National Park Service)

Charles Edward "Charlie" Taylor was an inventor and mechanic, and he was also the machinist who built the first engine used by the Wright brothers in 1903.

Charles Franklin "Ket" Kettering, who had previously founded Dayton Engineering Laboratories (DELCO).

In 1919, DELCO became the Delco Electronics component of General Motors, netting Kettering a substantial payday. Kettering earned an important footnote in aviation history for working with future USAAF Commanding General Henry "Hap" Arnold in 1918 to develop the US Army's "Kettering Bug," which is considered to be the ancestor of modern cruise missiles and Unmanned Combat Air Vehicles (UCAVs).

Also in 1919, General Motors bought Dayton-Wright, as the latter attempted to continue in business after the wartime orders for DH-4s ended. In 1923, General Motors liquidated the company and sold its designs and tooling, including those for the TW-3 basic trainer. The buyer was an entrepreneur named Reuben Hollis Fleet, who had just acquired the Gallaudet Aircraft Company in Rhode Island. He was on the verge of founding Consolidated Aircraft Company, which became one of the giants of the industry in the mid-20th century.

In 1916, meanwhile, Glenn Curtiss joined with John North Willys of the Willys-Overland Motor Company to take the Curtiss Aeroplane and Motor Company public. To advise them, they brought in investment banker Clement Melville Keys, who would become one of the significant aviation entrepreneurs of the Roaring Twenties. In 1920, with his usual deft touch for business, Glenn Curtiss cashed out. He sold his interests for $32 million (around $450 million today) and moved to Florida. He died in 1930.

Keys gradually built an impressive aviation empire. In 1928, he formed North American Aviation. Between 1937 and 1967, North American was one of America's foremost makers of military aircraft, but in the 1920s, it was just a holding company for companies acquired by Keys. These included such airlines as Eastern Air Transport (later Eastern Air Lines) and Transcontinental and Western Air (later TransWorld Airlines, TWA).

Wilbur Wright is pictured in 1905. (Photo Courtesy Library of Congress)

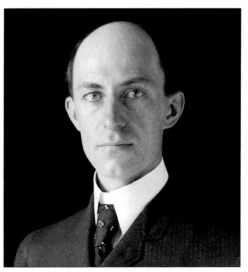

Orville Wright is pictured in 1905. (Photo Courtesy Library of Congress)

Also under North American's umbrella were Keystone Aircraft, the Curtiss Aeroplane and Motor Company, and Wright Aeronautical. In July 1929, the latter two name brands merged (along with a number of smaller companies) to become the Curtiss-Wright Corporation.

Curtiss-Wright continued to manufacture both aircraft and engines at separate locations. The "Curtiss" name was used for the aircraft, and the "Wright Aeronautical" name was used for powerplants.

Wright Aeronautical operated factories in Patterson, New Jersey, and Lockland, Ohio, while Curtiss aircraft were built mainly at the original facility in Buffalo, New York. During World War II, this operation was greatly expanded, and a new factory was built. The principal product produced here prior to World War II was the P-36 Hawk (Curtiss Model 75), of which more than 1,100 were built.

Going into the war years, the company's largest production product was the family of Curtiss Model 81/87 fighters that served the USAAF as the P-40 Warhawk and other air forces as the Tomahawk and Kittyhawk. Nearly 14,000 of these were built. In second place among Curtiss production aircraft was the US Navy's SB2C Helldiver (known in the USAAF as the A-25 Shrike), of which more than 7,100 were built. During World War II, additional airframe plants came online in Columbus, Ohio, and St. Louis, Missouri. A factory in Louisville, Kentucky, was added to build the C-76 Caravan, but it was converted to produce the C-46 Commando (Model CW-20) transport, of which more that 3,100 were built.

Rentschler, Lawrance and the Ascendancy of Radial Engines

Frederick Brant Rentschler was born in Hamilton, Ohio, about 40 miles south of Dayton. He was the son of George Adam Rentschler, who later became a partner in the Republic Motor Car Company in Ohio. Fred himself graduated from Princeton

The first powered, controlled, sustained airplane flight in history was on December 17, 1903. Orville Wright is at the controls of the Wright Flyer while Wilber stands by to pilot the second flight. (Photo Courtesy Library of Congress)

University in 1909 and worked at Republic until the United States entered World War I when he joined the US Army. Because of his expertise, he was assigned as an Army liaison to the Dayton-Wright Company, which was, among other projects, manufacturing 8-cylinder inline aircraft engines under license from Hispano-Suiza in Spain. These "Wright-Hisso" engines carried the Wright model designations A, E, and H.

His immersion in the world of engine technology persuaded young Captain Rentschler of the superiority of radials over their inline cousins. He also discovered his calling in life. When the war ended, Rentschler did as so many retiring military officers do—he went to work in the aviation industry. As the incoming president of Wright Aeronautical, Rentschler tried to chart a course toward a radial engine future, where more power could be had in a lighter-weight package.

Rentschler developed the Wright R-1 radial for the US Army, working with such men as Andrew Willgoos and George Jackson Mead. Educated at the Massachusetts Institute of Technology (MIT), Mead had started his engineering career with the Crane-Simplex Company, makers of automobiles with those brand names. He had come to Wright when Crane-Simplex was acquired by Wright-Martin in 1916.

Rentschler's route toward a radial engine future led through the uncertain shoals of new technology, as radial engines were still a work in progress and investment in research and development was a hard sell to the Wright Aeronautical board. The men at the top, their eyes on the bottom line, saw little reason to go out on a technological limb when the Wright-Hisso engines were still selling.

Charles Lanier Lawrance was a man of the times. It was the Roaring Twenties, a decade of high-flying (pun intended) financiers, and empire-building venture capitalists in the mold of Clement Melville Keys. Lawrance fit in with this crowd, being well placed in the upper crust of society. His father's second wife was the sister of Ava Willing, who had once been married to John Jacob Astor IV. His aunt married into British nobility, and his own half-sister married into Polish royalty. His great-grandfather was financier James F.D. Lanier, and his grandfather was an associate of J. Pierpont Morgan, *the* financier of the Gilded Age.

Yet, for being a child with a silver spoon in his mouth, Lawrance grew into a man with motor oil under his fingernails and a vision that brought him notoriety in his own right. He graduated from Yale in 1905, dabbled in the automotive industry designing race car engines, and later moved to Paris. While in Paris, he worked with Italian radial engine pioneer Alessandro Anzani and studied at the laboratory complex in which Gustave Eiffel (the same engineer who designed the tower of the same name) had built an early aeronautic wind tunnel.

Returning home on the eve of World War I, Lawrance rented a Manhattan loft where he designed opposed-twin radials and 3-cylinder engines, such as his 60 hp L-1 "Y-type" radial. In 1917, he formed the Lawrance Aero Engine Company, which outsourced production to small machine shops. Another early Lawrance project was the P-1 radial, a 1,652-ci, 9-cylinder engine that delivered 400 hp.

In 1920, Lawrance created his 788-ci, 200-hp J-1, which was a 9-cylinder radial that caught the eye of the US Navy, specifically its Bureau of Engineering, and later that of the new Bureau of Aeronautics (BuAer), which came into being in 1921 under Rear Admiral William Moffett.

The Navy liked the idea of radials because of the favorable power-to-weight ratio when compared to inline engines, which needed heavy radiators. It appreciated the potential reliability of air-cooled engines for over-water operations, especially for the fighters that would operate from the USS *Langley* (CV-1), its first aircraft carrier. In February 1921, Lawrance received his first Navy contract, calling for 50 engines to be delivered when the J-1 passed its 50-hour endurance test, which was a milestone achieved in January 1922.

Even as the Navy embraced the J-1, it feared that the Lawrance Aero Engine Company was too small to keep up with future orders. Lieutenant Commander Bruce Leighton at BuAer went so far as to urge Wright Aeronautical to acquire Lawrence's company.

Fred Rentschler resisted, calling Lawrance's business "a completely confused manufacturing operation," but the Curtiss-Wright board pressed on. Rentschler accepted the inevitable.

When the ink on the contracts dried in May 1923, Wright Aeronautical had a subsidiary that changed the course of its history and the Navy had a major industrial company with substantial resources to build its radial engines. Charles Lawrence came away with a deal worth around $8 million in today's money and the vice-presidency of Wright Aeronautical. When Rentschler left Wright in September 1924, Lawrance succeeded him as president.

The Wright Whirlwind

Wright Aeronautical had done as companies often do in lieu of research funding—it acquired another company that had the required expertise. Indeed, Charles Lawrance's J-1 engine was a technological milestone. Using aluminum cylinders with steel liners to conserve weight, it checked an important box for weight-conscious naval aviation while at the same time providing the reliability of a powerplant that operated for 300 trouble-free hours when 50 hours of endurance was considered normal.

Next in the series was the J-2, which was actually a pair of J-1s that were experimentally bored out with a slightly larger displacement. This variant never entered production, as it did not offer a substantial improvement over the J-1.

Introduced in 1923, the J-3 variant was similar to the J-1 but featured several design differences, including a stronger crankshaft

and other improvements. Whereas the J-1 had three synchronized carburetors, the J-3 had just one, eliminating the need for synchronization. Much of the early success of the J-series can be credited to Andy Willgoos and George Mead, who had been with the company since the Wright-Martin acquisition of Crane-Simplex.

As Wright had developed a family of inline engines under the "Tornado" brand name, the J-series radials, beginning in 1924 with the J-4 variant, were conferred with the brand name "Whirlwind." The emphasis now was on making the engine lighter, but overheating was the result of thinned-down cylinder walls. This as well as decreased fuel economy resulted in the modified J-4B Whirlwind.

The breakthrough design in the Whirlwind lineage came with the J-5, which incorporated an all-new, single-piece cylinder head design created by the British engineer Sam Heron, who had done important work on radial engine development at the Royal Aircraft Factory during World War I. After a short time at the firm of automaker John Davenport Siddeley, Heron immigrated to the States in 1921.

Glenn Hammond Curtiss was an aviation and motorcycle pioneer who gained prominence in the development of engines as well as aircraft. He is seen here in France in 1909 for the Grande Semaine d'Aviation air meet in Rheims.

The J-5 Whirlwind had a displacement of 788 ci, delivered around 200 hp, and had an empty weight of 520 pounds. In 1925, the military services assigned the designation R-790 to the J-5, making it the first Whirlwind with an "R" designation.

The R-790 was used in several US Navy biplane trainers, including the Boeing NB-1, the Curtiss N2C-1 Fledgling, the Naval Aircraft Factory N3N-1 Canary, and the Stearman NS-1. The Navy also used it in its Vought FU-1 convertible floatplane/landplane fighter and the UO-1 two-seat observation variant of the FU-1. Stearman used it in its C2 and C3 commercial biplanes.

Reuben Fleet's Consolidated Aircraft became a major customer, specifying the J-5/R-790 Whirlwind for its Model 2, of which the US Navy ordered 186 as NY-2. Meanwhile, Consolidated built 285 Model 2 aircraft for the US Army Air Corps as O-17 Courier observation planes and PT-3 trainers.

Fokker, the Dutch planemaker, and its American subsidiary, Atlantic Aircraft, used the J-5 in several variants of the F.VII

The Wright J-5 Whirlwind air-cooled 9-cylinder radial engine evolved from the Wright J-1, which was developed by Charles Lawrence. (Photo Courtesy USAF)

This is a 1917 photo of a Model V-2 aircraft engine from the Curtiss Aeroplane and Motor Corporation of Buffalo, New York. (Photo Courtesy National Archives)

The 2-cylinder Lawrance A-3 aircraft engine was designed by Charles Lawrance and produced by his Lawrance Aero Engine Company. This one, manufactured in 1916, is displayed in the Aviation Hall of Fame and Museum of New Jersey. (Photo Courtesy Ad Meskens, Licensed under Wikimedia Commons)

The Boeing NB-1 trainer, first flown on October 20, 1923, was powered by a Lawrance J-1 radial engine.

Charles Lanier Lawrance (left) was an American aeronautical engineer and an early proponent of air-cooled aircraft engines. He created the L-1 engine and helped to jump-start the Wright Aeronautical engine business with the J-1 developed from it. He is seen here in a lively discussion with Commander F.P. Forshew of the US Navy, while socialite John Jacob Astor IV and his wife (between them) sit by uncomfortably. The US Navy bought hundreds of Lawrance-designed powerplants. One of the world's richest men, Astor died a few years later in 1912 in the sinking of the Titanic. (Photo Courtesy Library of Congress)

The 3-cylinder Lawrance L-3 Y-Type radial engine was designed and built by the Lawrance Aero Engine Company in the early 1920s. This one is on display at the Steven F. Udvar-Hazy Center of the Smithsonian National Air and Space Museum. (Photo Courtesy Kogo, Licensed under the GNU Documentation License)

Trimotor transport. These included the C-2 and C-2A that served with the US Army Air Corps.

The most famous use of the J-5 in a non-military aircraft was in Charles Lindbergh's Ryan NYP, best known as the *Spirit of St. Louis*. On May 20, 1927, Lindbergh set out from Roosevelt Field on Long Island, New York, to become the first person to fly nonstop to Paris, a distance of around 3,600 miles. When he landed at LeBourget Field the following day, the J-5 Whirlwind had run continuously for 33 hours and 30 minutes. This was as much of a milestone of endurance as that which made Lindbergh an international celebrity and a role model for generation of young, air-minded future aviators.

Although Lindbergh stole hearts, minds, and headlines, other endurance flights with J-5 Whirlwinds soon followed. A month later, in June 1927, Clarence Chamberlin and Charles Levine flew nonstop from New York to Eisleben, Germany, in 42 hours and 30 minutes, using a single-engine WB-2 that Wright had commissioned from Bellanca Aircraft to showcase the Whirlwind. Also in June 1927, Albert Hegenberger and Lester Maitland flew a J-5-powered Fokker C-2 from Oakland, California, to Honolulu, Hawaii, in 25 hours and 50 minutes. A year later, in the course of making a several-leg first aerial crossing of the Pacific, Sir Charles Kingsford Smith made a 34 hour and 30 minute flight from Hawaii to Fiji in a Fokker Trimotor powered by three J-5s.

The Wright J-5 Whirlwind aircraft engine was developed by Charles Lanier Lawrance for the Wright Aeronautical Corporation from his earlier L-1 and J-1 engines. The J-5 produced 220 hp and was the first engine to have sodium-cooled exhaust valves and to be self-lubricating. It earned Lawrence the celebrated Collier Trophy for 1927. (Photo Courtesy Sanjay Acharya, Licensed under Creative Commons)

A partially-sectioned Wright Aeronautical J-4B engine is displayed at the Canada Aviation Museum in Ottawa. (Photo Courtesy Imnop88a, Licensed under Creative Commons)

In January 1929, the US Army Air Corps made a closed-course record endurance flight of 150 hours and 40 minutes in a Fokker C-2A named *Question Mark*, a flight that also showcased aerial refueling.

The 1927 endurance flights directed global attention to radial engines in general and to Wright Aeronautical in particular. In turn, Charles Lawrance, the company's president, was awarded the 1927 Collier Trophy for the radial engine, which was deemed by the US Aeronautic Association as the year's foremost achievement in aviation.

In 1928, Wright phased out the J-5/R-790 and began introducing additional Whirlwind family members (engines of similar design but with varying numbers of cylinders). The smallest Whirlwind, the 165- to 175-hp Model J-6-5, was a 5-cylinder radial designated as R-540 by the armed forces and used mainly in small general-aviation aircraft, such as the Curtiss Robin.

The Wright Cyclone

Developed in parallel with the Whirlwind family was the Cyclone series, whose name would rise to legendary status in World War II in the form of the R-1820 Cyclone and the R-2600 Twin Cyclone—among others. The Cyclone name was first assigned in 1925 to the 9-cylinder, 435-hp Wright P-2, which evolved from the P-1 that Lawrance built during World War I. Appearing in 1927, the 9-cylinder R-1750 was initially tested at 500 hp, which was later improved to 525 hp at 1,900 rpm.

In 1932, after the Curtiss-Wright merger, collaboration between the engineering teams of both

Charles Lanier Lawrance (right), president of the Wright Aeronautical Corporation, receives the 1927 Collier Trophy (center) for the development of the J-5 air-cooled radial engine from President Calvin Coolidge (left). US Army and US Navy aviation officials are in the background of this photo taken on the lawn of the White House in March 1928.

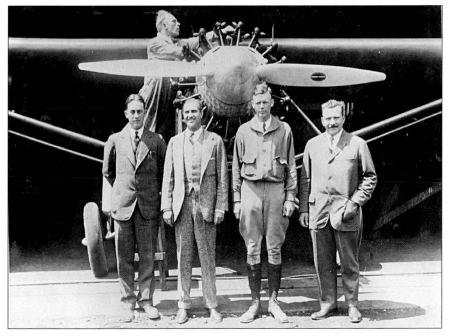

Used by Charles Lindbergh for his historic May 1927 Transatlantic flight, the Ryan NYP Spirit of St. Louis was powered by a Wright J-5C Whirlwind 9-cylinder air-cooled radial engine. Seen here from left to right are B.F. Mahoney, Harry Guggenheim, Lindbergh, and Charles Lawrance. Mahoney was the president of the Ryan Aeronautical Company of San Diego, which built the airplane. Guggenheim was a philanthropist and promoter of aviation. Lawrance designed the engine. (Photo Courtesy SDASM)

The Wright J-5 Whirlwind was designated as R-790 by the military services based on its displacement in cubic inches. This one is in the collection of the Smithsonian National Air and Space Museum. (Photo Courtesy Dane A. Penland, Licensed under Creative Commons)

This is a side view of a Wright R-790 (J-5) Whirlwind that is in the collection of the National Museum of the US Air Force. (Photo Courtesy Kogo, Licensed under the GNU Documentation License)

A US Navy Curtiss N2C-2 Fledgling is displayed at the National Museum of Naval Aviation in Pensacola, Florida. The N2C-2 was powered by a Wright R-760 (J-6-7) Whirlwind. (Photo Courtesy US Navy)

companies helped develop the Cyclone F. Based on experience gained in the R-1750 project, the new engine incorporated such advances as a forged crankcase, improved cylinder finning, and the capability of being mated with a Hamilton variable-pitch propeller. With a displacement of 1,823 ci, it was designated as the R-1820. This story resumes in Chapter 3.

Curtiss-Wright

The merger of Wright Aeronautical and the Curtiss Aeroplane & Motor Company on July 5, 1929, came at the threshold of the great radial engine renaissance in which Wright was perfectly positioned. The company was in the midst of rolling out one of its most significant products to date.

A US Navy Consolidated NY-2 is shown at the National Advisory Committee for Aeronautics at Langley, Virginia, in May 1928: The Consolidated NY series were powered by Wright R-760 (J-5) Whirlwinds. (Photo Courtesy NASA)

Built in 1932, this Curtiss Travel Air 16E has a Wright R-540 Whirlwind engine. The R-540 (J-6-5) was a series of about 500 5-cylinder air-cooled aircraft engines built by the Wright Aeronautical division of Curtiss-Wright between 1929 and 1937. This engine was photographed at the Historic Aircraft Restoration Museum in St Louis. (Photo Courtesy Tim Vickers, Released into the Public Domain)

A Naval Aircraft Factory N3N-3 primary trainer is on display at the National Air and Space Museum's Steven F. Udvar-Hazy Center in Chantilly, Virginia. The N3N-3 was powered by a 235-hp Wright R-760-2 Whirlwind engine. (Photo Courtesy Balon Greyjoy, Licensed under Creative Commons)

The J-6-7, designated as R-760 by the armed forces, was created specifically to supersede the J-5/R-790. Equipped with a gear-driven supercharger, it delivered 225 hp and was used in US Navy biplane trainers that were in the same lineage as aircraft that used the R-790 engine. These included the Curtiss N2C-2 Fledgling and the Consolidated NY-2 and NY-3 as well as the Naval Aircraft Factory N3N-3 Canary. There were 816 N3N-3s produced, with most of its engines built under license at the Naval Aircraft Factory.

The supercharged R-760 was gradually improved as production continued. The R-760E, rolled out in 1931, delivered 250 hp at 2,000 rpm, and the R-760E-2 of 1935 was rated at 350 hp at 2,400 rpm. The R-760 family continued in production through World War II with more than 1,400 built by Wright.

Wright's 9-cylinder Model J-6-9 with the military designation R-975 was produced in larger numbers than any other Whirlwind. With production beginning in 1929 and lasting into the 1950s, Wright built more than 7,000 of them, while the Continental Aircraft Engine Company division of Continental Motors built another 53,000 under license, mostly during World War II. The R-975 is discussed in greater detail in Chapter 6.

A US Army Air Corps flight crew in heavy leather flight suits stands in front of an Atlantic-Fokker C-2A. One C-2A that was known as the Question Mark was involved in a famous endurance demonstration in 1929. Powered by three R-760 (J-5) engines, it made a nonstop flight of 151 hours between January 1 and January 7, 1929, flying between San Diego and Los Angeles and being refueled in the air 37 times. Commanded by future USAF Chief of Staff Major Carl "Tooey" Spaatz, the crew included Ira Eaker, Elwood Quesada, Harry Halverson, and Roy Hooe. (Photo Courtesy USAF)

Chapter 2

PRATT & WHITNEY: THE WASP AND HORNET

Francis Pratt and Amos Whitney never saw an airplane. In 1860, when they started their machine tool company in Hartford, Connecticut, Nicolaus Otto in Germany was on the verge of building the first gasoline engine, but the use of such motors in practical aircraft was far in the future—an innovation that would be realized only by people not yet born.

Born in the innovative crest of the Industrial Revolution in America, the Pratt & Whitney Machine Tool Company produced precision tooling for factories that built products such as sewing machines. Meanwhile, the Civil War began in 1861, and there was a great deal of demand from the arms industry for tooling. Since Pratt and Whitney themselves had previously worked for pistol maker Samuel Colt in Hartford, they had the expertise to expand their business as government subcontractors.

Pratt & Whitney eventually became a component of the large industrial holding company Niles-Bement-Pond. By the early 1920s, the president of Niles-Bement-Pond was James K. Cullen, who was a friend of George Rentschler, who was the father of Frederick Brant Rentschler, who was president of Wright Aeronautical. Cullen had known Fred when he was a boy. Another principal in Niles-Bement-Pond as well as a George Rentschler associate was Colonel Edward Andrew Deeds, who was a one-time financier of Dayton-Wright and an associate of Charles Franklin "Ket" Kettering in the founding of Dayton Engineering Laboratories (DELCO). Industrial America was a small world.

All of these connections came into play when Fred Rentschler parted ways with Wright in 1924. He had been getting only lukewarm support from Wright's board for radial engines when the Navy

At the peak of its prominence as a radial engine maker, Pratt & Whitney is illustrated by this image from 1943 that shows a front view of an R-1830 Type C3 Twin Wasp 14-cylinder radial engine with the single ignition wire manifold, governor mounting pad, and rocker box scavenge sump.

A companion image to the one adjacent, this rear view of a Pratt & Whitney R-1830 Type C3 Twin Wasp 14-cylinder radial engine intermediate rear section displays the dual spring coupled blower intermediate drives and the generator drive gears.

Frederick Brant Rentschler was the engineer and aircraft engine designer who founded the Pratt & Whitney Aircraft Company. Its first engine, the 425-hp R-1340 Wasp, was completed in 1925 on Christmas Eve.

George Jackson Mead (left) and Frederick Rentschler were part of the team that created Pratt & Whitney. Mead and Rentschler left Wright Aeronautical with the plan to start their own aviation-related business. Mead was the head of engineering at Pratt & Whitney from 1925 to 1935 and later was president of the US National Advisory Committee for Aeronautics. (Photo Courtesy NACA)

coaxed the company into buying a stand-alone radial-engine company from Charles Lawrance. As Lawrance came aboard as Wright's vice president, Rentschler started looking for the door—but not just *any* door.

Noting that Pratt & Whitney was located in an area with a good skilled labor pool and a lot of engineering talent, Rentschler decided that Pratt & Whitney ought to have an aircraft engine division, and he started pitching the idea to James Cullen. In April 1925, he left Cullen's office just off Wall Street in New York City with a letter of introduction to Clayton Burt, the general manager of the Pratt & Whitney Machine Tool Company.

Burt showed him around and suggested that he might set up shop in a building on Capitol Avenue in Hartford that was being used to store tobacco. This was the former Pope electric automobile factory and now a part of the Pratt & Whitney campus. Rentschler pitched the aircraft engine business model to Cullen and Burt, and eventually, a deal was struck. With adequate funding promised by Cullen and Niles-Bement-Pond, Rentschler started putting his new company together. He lured a number of his old engineering colleagues, especially Andy Willgoos and George Mead, to leave Wright Aeronautical and come follow him. Andy's brother, Bill Willgoos, also joined the firm. On July 22, 1925, the Pratt & Whitney Aircraft Company opened for business.

Thanks to 1933 US Senate hearings into US Post Office air-mail contracts, the *Congressional Record* provides specific details of the Pratt & Whitney Aircraft Company's early corporate finances. Passing through the Pratt & Whitney Machine Tool Company, initial

The single-row, 9-cylinder Pratt & Whitney R-1340 Wasp was the company's first engine and the first of the legendary Wasp series. In 2016, it received the designation as a Historic Engineering Landmark from the American Society of Mechanical Engineers. (Photo Courtesy Sanjay Acharya, Licensed under Creative Commons)

funding for Pratt & Whitney Aircraft was $202,713. It increased to $1,030,413 in 1926 and was secured by shares of common stock in the Pratt & Whitney Aircraft Company. Of the 5,500 shares issued in July 1925, Rentschler and Mead had 1,375 shares each, and the rest went to Pratt & Whitney Machine Tool. Five months later, Rentschler sold 110 shares to Charles Deeds.

The Pratt & Whitney Wasp

As soon as the new Pratt & Whitney Aircraft Company was in business, Rentschler approached Rear Admiral William Moffett at the US Navy's Bureau of Aeronautics. The timing was right. Both the US Navy and the US Army Air Service were getting a boost in funding by a US Congress that was keen to establish the United States as a world power in aviation—at a time when most of the important speed and altitude records were being established in Europe. Meanwhile, the US Navy's second and third aircraft carriers, the USS *Lexington* (CV-2) and the USS *Saratoga* (CV-3), were being launched in 1925.

As naval aviation was expanding, Rentschler secured a $90,000 development contract for a new radial engine. BuAer was doing business with Wright for Whirlwind engines but was keen to encourage a second source for the sake of industrial competition.

Willgoos and Mead set to work in the detached garage at the Willgoos home in Montclair, New Jersey, while the tobacco was being cleared out of the Hartford building. Incorporating Sam Heron's steel-barrel Type M cylinder with sodium exhaust-valve cooling and a forged (not cast) crankcase, their new 9-cylinder radial had a displacement of 1,344 ci, delivered 400 hp at 1,800 rpm, and weighed 650 pounds. By comparison, the contemporary Wright J-5/R-790 Whirlwind displaced 788 ci, delivered 200 hp, and weighed 520 pounds.

Edward Deeds promised a turkey for every member of the team if the engine was ready by Christmas 1925, and the deadline was met. Unveiled on Christmas Eve, Pratt & Whitney's first engine was given the name "Wasp" by the company president's wife, Faye Belden Rentschler, as she and Evelyn Mead passed out the turkeys at the plant.

The assigned military designation for the Wasp was R-1340. In Navy qualification tests, which began in March 1926, the Wasp ran through the full-throttle, 50-hour test, registering an average of 415 hp. The first flight test came on May 5, 1926, in the debut flight of the Wright XF3W-1 Apache, a biplane used solely to test the Wasp. In 1928, Navy Lieutenant Carleton Champion took the world altitude record away from France by taking the Wasp-powered XF3W-1 up to 38,744 feet and secured the seaplane record of 37,955 feet with the aircraft fitted with pontoons. A year later, Lieutenant Apollo Soucek took the landplane Apache to 39,140 feet.

Commander Eugene Wilson, head of BuAer's Engine Section, commented that the Wasp "incorporates some of the finest engineering yet seen in aircraft engines, [and it is] considerably advanced over any other air-cooled engine of its class."

The Navy issued a purchase order for 200 R-1340 Wasps in October 1926. These were the first of 34,966 in a production run that lasted through the 1950s.

Among the first planemakers to notice the Wasp was Chauncey Milton "Chance" Vought, whose career had begun as an engineer working with Orville Wright. He started the first of a series of aircraft companies in 1917 and had been doing business with the US Navy. By 1926, he had a contract with the US Navy to build the Vought O2U-1 Corsair, a two-place observation biplane that was convertible as a floatplane or landplane. He told Rentschler that if the R-1340

Pratt & Whitney executives pose with the 1,000th Wasp engine in 1928. From left to right are George Mead, head of engineering; Fred Rentschler, president; Donald Brown, general manager; and William Willgoos, head of assembly and testing.

delivered the performance he needed, he would specify it for the Corsair. Rentschler delivered, and Vought kept his promise. Using the Wasp-powered Corsair, US Navy pilots set a series of speed and altitude records on the Hampton Roads speed course through the spring of 1927.

Including a pair of prototypes, the US Navy acquired 132 O2U-1 aircraft equipped with the 450-hp R-1340-88 variant of the Wasp. These were followed by 190 O2U-2 through O2U-4 Corsairs with 450-hp R-1340-B and R-1340-C Wasps.

With Charles Lindbergh's *Spirit of St. Louis* and the Wright J-5/R-790 Whirlwind, the notoriety of a single aircraft shone favorably upon its engine. Analogous to this was the Pratt & Whitney Wasp and the series of race planes built by Granville Brothers Aircraft of Springfield, Massachusetts. The brothers, Edward, Mark, Robert, Thomas, and Zantford, built only two dozen aircraft, but during their heyday in 1931–1933, the Gee Bee racers were household words in the aviation community.

The most famous Gee Bee was the Wasp-powered R-1 in which the legendary Jimmy Doolittle set a world speed record of 296 mph while winning the 1932 Thompson Trophy in the National Air Races.

The Pratt & Whitney Hornet

In 1926, with the Wasp performing in his fighters as desired, Admiral Moffett at the US Navy's BuAer turned to Pratt & Whitney for a more powerful radial engine to power his carrier fleet's offensive punch. The heavier, ordnance-laden bombers and torpedo bombers needed more power.

Specifically, Moffett had in mind the Martin T3M-1 torpedo bomber, which was considered underpowered for its weight with its 575-hp Wright T-3B inline engine, while the T3M-2 was overweight with its 770-hp Packard 3A-2500 inline engine. Martin was working on a successor torpedo bomber, designated as T4M-1, and the Navy turned to Pratt & Whitney for a radial engine to power it.

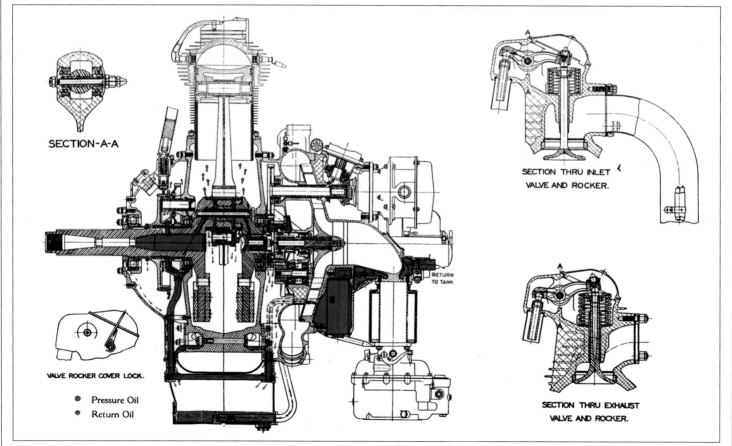

SECTION-A-A

VALVE ROCKER COVER LOCK.

● Pressure Oil
● Return Oil

RETURN TO TANK

SECTION THRU INLET VALVE AND ROCKER.

SECTION THRU EXHAUST VALVE AND ROCKER.

A side-view cutaway of a Pratt & Whitney Wasp engine from 1928 highlights the lubrication system.

Developed in the relatively short span of just two years, Pratt & Whitney's new single-row, 9-cylinder radial was a direct follow-on from the Wasp, having over half of its parts in common with the earlier engine. This pleased BuAer because it would simplify maintenance, especially aboard carriers, where space to store spare parts was at a premium.

In keeping with the snarling, aggressive insect naming convention, the Wasp's new stablemate was named Hornet. With its displacement of 1,690.5 ci, it was designated as R-1690. It had a pushrod-actuated valvetrain, a single-speed centrifugal supercharger, and a 2-barrel carburetor. It was 51 inches long and 54.4 inches in diameter.

The first Hornet was completed in June 1926 after six months of experimenting with geared and direct-drive radial designs. The Hornet passed its 50-hour qualification test in March 1927 with a rating of 525 hp.

Martin's engineers calculated that the R-1690-24 Hornet weighed 3,000 pounds less than the Packard 3A-2500 inline engine when installed in the XT4M-1. When the Navy verified this and performance details were confirmed, it awarded Martin with a contract for 102 R-1690-24 Hornet-powered T4M-1s.

As the T4M-1 served as the standard Navy torpedo bomber for most of the 1930s, Martin developed a smaller XT5M-1, of which 16 were completed as BM-1 dive bombers. They were powered by the R-1690-22 and R-1690-44 Hornets, respectively.

Wasps for Boeing

Pratt & Whitney's biggest military customer for the R-1340 Wasp and indeed the biggest external influence on Pratt & Whitney during its early days was the Boeing Airplane Company of Seattle. Indeed, the symbiotic relationship was such that Fred Rentschler was to enter into a far-reaching partnership with the Seattle company's founder in 1929.

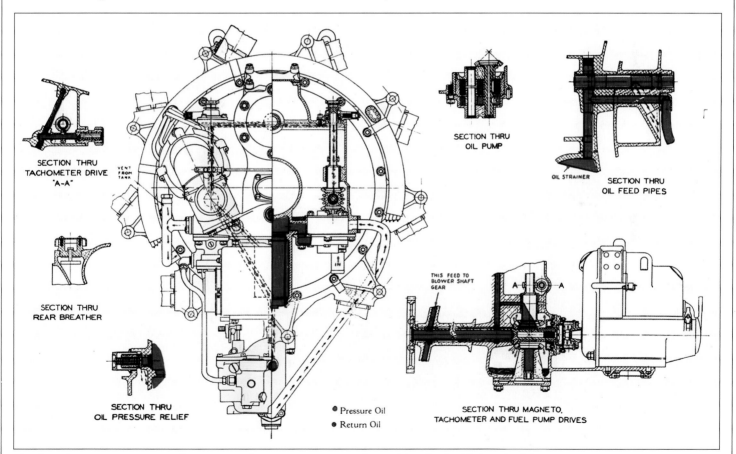

This front/rear view cutaway of a Pratt & Whitney Wasp engine from 1928 also highlights the lubrication system.

Edward Andrew Deeds was an engineer, inventor, and president of the National Cash Register Company. He also helped Charles "Ket" Kettering start the Dayton Engineering Laboratories Company (Delco). In addition, he was an investor in Pratt & Whitney and the man who promised a turkey to every member of the R-1340 team if it was completed by Christmas Eve 1925. Deeds bought a lot of turkeys that year. (Photo Courtesy Library of Congress)

During its tenure as a Pratt & Whitney R-1340-B Wasp testbed, the Wright XF3W-1 Apache is seen at the Langley Aeronautical Laboratory at Hampton, Virginia. A centerline float was attached, and the aircraft was tested on the Little Back River to validate the use of observation floatplanes aboard battleships. (Photo Courtesy NASA)

Before this came Boeing's emergence in the 1920s as an American leader in fighter aircraft development. Since World War II, Boeing has been synonymous with large multi-engine aircraft, and since the last quarter of the 20th century, it has emerged as America's signature builder of jetliners. In the 1920s, though, Boeing was known for its popular biplane fighter aircraft.

The first chapter in the story of Boeing fighters came with the company's Model 15, which was an inline-engine, single-seat biplane that served the US Navy under the FB designation and the US Army Air Service as the PW-9 (Pursuit, Water-cooled, Ninth). However, Boeing soon migrated to radial engines, specifically to variants of the R-1340 Wasp.

A new era began for the company on November 3, 1926, with the first flight of the Navy's F2B-1 (Boeing Model 69).

After 35 F2B-1s, Boeing first flew its prototype XF3B-1 (Model 74) in February 1928, and this was followed by 73 production F3B-1s (Model 77). Powered by the R-1340-80 Wasp, they were deployed as the front-line fighter aboard the Navy's three carriers: the USS Langley, the USS Lexington, and the USS Saratoga.

The F3B-1 was not on the front line for long. Boeing was already at work on a successor—actually, a vast extended family of visually-nearly-identical successors.

Initiated by Boeing as an in-house project, they were lighter and more nimble than the F3B but still had the power of an R-1340. They were built under numerous military subvariant designations and Boeing model numbers. Those for the US Navy were designated as F4B, and those for the US Army Air Corps were designated as P-12. Those built for export customers were referred to by their Boeing model numbers.

The program began in 1928 with the completion of the company-financed Model 83 and Model 89 prototypes; both were powered by Pratt & Whitney R-1340Bs and later designated

First flown in May 1926, the Wright XF3W-1 Apache was delivered to the US Navy with a Wright P-1 Simoon engine. However, the Navy re-engined it with a Pratt & Whitney R-1340-B and used the XF3W-1 as a testbed for the Pratt & Whitney engine until 1930, during which time the aircraft set several records.

This shows a Vought O2U-1 Corsair of Observation Squadron VO-3S aboard the USS Raleigh, circa 1926. O2U-1s were powered by Pratt & Whitney R-1340-88 engines. (Photo Courtesy US Navy)

Powered by a Pratt & Whitney R-1340-C engine, this is a US Navy Vought SU-1 Corsair scout plane. This one was photographed circa 1933–1934 while operating with Scouting Squadron VS-1. (Photo Courtesy US Navy)

as XF4B-1 by the US Navy. From this point, through the last delivery of the P-12F (Model 251) to the Air Corps in May 1932, the F4B/P-12 family included 579 individual aircraft—a very large number for the threshold of the Great Depression. Aviation historian Ray Wagner called it the "height of traditional biplane design" for American fighter aircraft.

The definitive naval variant was the F4B-4 (Model 235), of which 99 were built. These were powered by Pratt & Whitney R-1340-16 Wasps, delivering 550 hp at 6,000 feet.

This Vought O2U Corsair of the Argentine Navy was powered by a Pratt & Whitney R-1340-88 Wasp in October 1933. (Photo Courtesy SDASM)

The Curtiss SOC-1 Seagull scout-observation aircraft, seen here in July 1939, was powered by a 600-hp Pratt & Whitney R-1340-18 Wasp. The subsequent land-based SOC-2 had a Pratt & Whitney R-1340-22 Wasp.

The principal US Army variants were the P-12B (Model 102), of which 96 were built; the P-12C (Model 222), of which 99 were built; and the P-12E (Model 234), of which 110 were built. The P-12B used the R-1340-7 Wasp, which was rated at 450 hp at 5,000 feet; the P-12C was powered by the R-1340-9 Wasp, which was rated at 450 hp at 8,000 feet; and the P-12E used the fuel-injected R-1340-17 Wasp, which was rated at 500 hp at 7,000 feet.

Some of the P-12s were redesignated and used as testbeds for experimental Pratt & Whitney Wasp variants. The XP-12G tested the 575-hp R-1340-15 with a side-mounted supercharger. The XP-12H evaluated the experimental geared GISR-1340E. The XP-12Ks were fitted with fuel-injected SR-1340Es, and one of these was in turn fitted with an F-2 supercharger.

Boeing also used the R-1340 Wasp in several of its commercial aircraft, including the Model 40A airliner in 1926. The Wasp was 200 pounds lighter than the Liberty inline engine that was used in the earlier Model 40. This greatly improved performance, especially in flights over Western mountain ranges.

In 1932, Boeing, Pratt & Whitney, and the US Army Air Corps took a small step into the future of military aviation. March 20 of

The Pratt & Whitney R-1690 Hornet single-row, 9-cylinder, air-cooled radial engine was first flown in 1927 and remained in production until 1942. This example is displayed at the Deutsches Museum in Munich. (Photo Courtesy Jaypee, Licensed under Creative Commons)

A Martin T4M-1 of Torpedo Squadron VT-2B snags the arrestor cable aboard the aircraft carrier USS Saratoga, circa 1931–1932. The T4M-1s were powered by Pratt & Whitney R-1690-24 Hornets. (Photo Courtesy US Navy)

that year marked the debut flight of the Boeing P-26 Peashooter, which was the first all-metal fighter and the first monoplane fighter to enter squadron service with the Air Corps. There were 151 of these open-cockpit aircraft built for the Air Corps and three export countries (China, Spain, and the Philippines) and a few were around to see combat early in World War II.

A Pratt & Whitney R-1690 Hornet single-row, 9-cylinder engine with its chamber walls cut away shows its internal workings. This display can be seen at the Pacific Aviation Museum at Pearl Harbor in Hawaii. (Photo Courtesy J. J. Messerly, Licensed under Creative Commons)

The Martin XT5M-1 torpedo bomber, first flown in May 1929, was intended as a smaller follow-on to the Martin T4M-1. Instead, the US Navy ordered them as BM-1 and BM-2 dive bombers. The BM-2 seen here flew with Torpedo Squadron VT-2B in the early 1930s. The Martin XT5M-1 was powered by a 525-hp Pratt & Whitney R-1690-22 Hornet, while the dive bombers had the more powerful R-1690-44 engine. (Photo Courtesy US Navy)

Three Boeing F2B-1 fighters belonging to the US Navy aerobatics team, the Three Seahawks, are shown in flight over NAS Pensacola in Florida in 1928. The F2B-1 was powered by a Pratt & Whitney R-1340B Wasp. (Photo Courtesy US Navy)

The Peashooter prototype (Model 266) was powered by an R-1340-21 Wasp delivering 525 hp at 6,000 feet, while the production-series P-26As (Model 266), which was first flown in January 1934, used the R-1340-27 rated at 600 hp at 6,000 feet.

The P-26B series was intended to be powered by fuel-injected, 600-hp R-1340-33s, but the fuel injection systems were not available, and only two P-26Bs were built. The remainder of 25 intended P-26Bs were completed with R-1340-27s and designated as P-26Cs. The R-1340-33 Wasps caught up to the Peashooter program in August 1934 in time for the Model 281 export variant. A dozen were built for China, and one was diverted to Spain.

In 1934, in the midst of the Peashooter program, Boeing dabbled with the idea of an improved monoplane fighter that was company-designated as Model 264. It differed from the P-26 in that it had an enclosed cockpit and retractable landing gear. The power-plant was an R-1340-31 or R-1340-39, delivering 550 hp at 10,000 feet. The Air Corps ordered and evaluated three Model 264s under the YP-29 designation, and the US Navy acquired one similar Model 273 as XF7B-1.

Meanwhile, Boeing also ordered Hornets from Pratt & Whitney. These included 30 Hornets to power 10 of its Model 80A tri-motor, enclosed-cockpit, biplane airliners and 25 Hornets for its single-engine Model 95 mailplane.

United Aircraft & Transport Corporation

William Edward Boeing was part of a generation of visionary industrialists who had big dreams and acted upon them in a big way. In 1914, he took an airplane ride, decided to build his own

This is the company-financed Boeing Model 89 fighter prototype with its Pratt & Whitney R-1340B Wasp engine in July 1928.

A Boeing F4B-1 (Model 99) is powered by a Pratt & Whitney R-1340-8 Wasp during carrier operations. (Photo Courtesy US Navy)

airplane, and wound up starting one of America's greatest aircraft companies. His company was born in 1916 as the Pacific Aero Products Company and became the Boeing Airplane Company in 1917.

In 1927, Bill Boeing started an airline: Boeing Air Transport (BAT). A year later, he acquired Pacific Air Transport (PAT) and created the Boeing Airplane & Transport Corporation (BATC) as a

A trio of Boeing F4B-4 (Model 235) aircraft is powered by Pratt & Whitney R-1340-10 Wasps during flight operations. (Photo Courtesy US Navy)

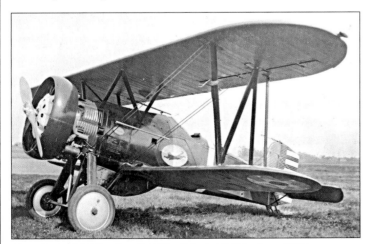

Here is 1 of 35 Boeing P-12Ds (Model 227), circa 1931, powered by a Pratt & Whitney R-1340-17 Wasp engine.

holding company for BAT and PAT as well as the Boeing Airplane Company. Through 1931, he acquired several new manufacturing and airline subsidiaries and united all of his airlines into an entity called United Air Lines.

In 1929, Bill Boeing joined forces with Fred Rentschler at Pratt & Whitney Aircraft, as the latter company disassociated itself from the Pratt & Whitney Machine Tool Company. The tool company later evolved into Pratt & Whitney Measurement Systems, which still exists to this day.

The two men decided to form the United Aircraft and Transport Corporation (UATC), an aviation conglomerate on a scale not yet seen in the American aviation industry. It would manufacture engines and airframes together with makers of other components as well as of the airlines that put the hardware to work.

Rentschler brought Pratt & Whitney into the fold, and Boeing brought his airplane company and all of his airlines and the company's air-mail contracts. In turn, the two men "united" a number of other companies under a new corporate umbrella.

These included planemakers that were still managed by the household-name aviation pioneers who founded them—companies such as Sikorsky Aviation Company, owned by Igor Sikorsky, and Vought Aircraft, owned by Chance Vought, whose order for Wasps helped to launch Pratt & Whitney. Lloyd Stearman's Stearman Aircraft Company in Wichita, Kansas, also became part of UATC.

Two propeller makers, the Hamilton Aero Manufacturing Company of Milwaukee and the Standard Steel Propeller Company of Pittsburgh, were acquired by UATC and merged as Hamilton Standard. UATC was a potential powerhouse that was seen by some as anti-competitive, and Congress agreed. In June 1934, the antitrust

A Boeing P-12B (Model 102), circa 1929, is powered by a Pratt & Whitney R-1340-7 Wasp engine.

This is 1 of 110 Boeing P-12Es (Model 234) powered by a Pratt & Whitney R-1340-17 Wasp engine. This restored P-12E is in the collection of the National Museum of the United States Air Force. (Photo Courtesy USAF)

One of three Boeing-financed Model 248 (XP-936) prototypes is shown in March 1932. When accepted by the Army Air Corps, these Pratt & Whitney R-1340-21 Wasp-powered aircraft became Y1P-26s (later P-26s) and the foundation of the P-26 Peashooter lineage.

mood in Congress led to the passage of the Air Mail Act, under which companies were forbidden to own both airlines and planemakers, and UATC was broken up into three parts.

United Air Lines spun off as an independent entity, and UATC's manufacturing was divided geographically. The Boeing Airplane Company was reorganized as a corporate holding company to hold the manufacturing subsidiaries of UATC, which included Boeing, Stearman, and Boeing Aircraft of Canada.

A new company, the United Aircraft Corporation, was formed in Connecticut in 1934 as the corporate parent of Vought, Sikorsky, Hamilton Standard, and Pratt & Whitney. Fred Rentschler became its first president and later served as chairman.

Bill Boeing, disgusted by the breakup of UATC, handed the presidency of his namesake company to Clairmont "Claire" Egtvedt, whom he had hired as a young engineer in 1917 and had been vice president since 1926. In 1934, he left the building—and the aviation industry entirely. He never looked back.

This close-up view of the Boeing P-26A Peashooter (Model 266) is in the collection of the National Museum of the United States Air Force. The Peashooter was the first American production all-metal fighter aircraft and the first pursuit monoplane to enter squadron service with the Army Air Corps. (Photo Courtesy USAF)

This restored and flyable Boeing P-26A, seen in markings of the 95th Pursuit Squadron, belongs to the Planes of Fame Air Museum in Chino, California. It is seen here on a moody day in 2014 at the Flying Legends air show at the Imperial War Museum facility at Duxford in England. (Photo Courtesy Tony Smith, Licensed under Creative Commons)

Chapter 3

THE WRIGHT CYCLONE AND THE FLYING FORTRESS

The 9-cylinder Wright R-1820 Cyclone and the 14-cylinder Pratt & Whitney R-1830 Twin Wasp (both radial engines) represented the first generation of engines that helped define American military aviation in World War II. The aircraft for which the R-1820 would do much of this defining was the Boeing Model 299, which is better known under its military designation as the B-17 Flying Fortress.

More than 120,000 R-1820 Cyclones were built over three decades. An amazing 64,093 of them were the R-1820-97 variant and were produced (according the Wright Aeronautical records) between July 1942 and October 1943. This was the engine used in the Boeing B-17F and B-17G variants of the Flying Fortress, which utilized 48,340 R-1820-97s for their initial deliveries alone (nevermind the spares that later flowed out to the operational squadrons).

The R-1820 Cyclone family began in 1932 with the Cyclone F and gradually evolved through the 1930s to the F-50 series. It found a ready market in such applications as the DC-series airliners of the Douglas Aircraft Company. The Cyclone F-50 was introduced in 1935 in several variants that were rated at more than 600 hp. For example, the Cyclone F52 variant was rated at 890 hp for takeoff.

Introduced in 1937 and subsequently produced in many variants, the Cyclone G was the definitive R-1820 of the World War II era.

Both the F- and G-series R-1820 Cyclones had a diameter of 54.25 inches and were 43.25 inches long. They weighed roughly between 1,000 and 1,200 pounds, depending on the variant. Each had a bore of 6.125 inches and a stroke of 6.875 inches.

The Cyclone G incorporated a single-speed General Electric centrifugal-type supercharger with improved oil seals, and it had a Stromberg PD-12K10 carburetor with an automatic mixture control. It had two overhead valves for each cylinder and was cooled by sodium-filled exhaust valves.

Other improvements that came with the Cyclone G included automatic valve gear lubrication through an integral system without external lines or tubes, a dynamic damper counterweight to reduce vibration at all crankshaft speeds to extend the operational range, full pressure baffling on all nine cylinders, and induction systems to increase altitude performance. The cooling-fin area of the Cyclone G was increased to 2,800 square inches compared to 1,000 square inches in the earlier Cyclone.

At the Wright factory in New Jersey, five large nitriding furnaces were installed. This and improved foundry procedures allowed casting the cooling fins on the Cyclone G cylinder head "as closely spaced as the teeth on a comb" and nearly 2 inches in depth over the combustion chamber. The cylinder barrels were cast of Nitralloy steel that was nitrided to obtain a cylinder bore with a wear resistance improved three-fold over a normally heat-treated cylinder.

With its Hamilton Standard propellers balanced nicely on its Wright R-1830 Cyclones, this B-17F is ready to emerge from Boeing's Plant 2 in Seattle. (Photo Courtesy Andreas Feininger, Library of Congress)

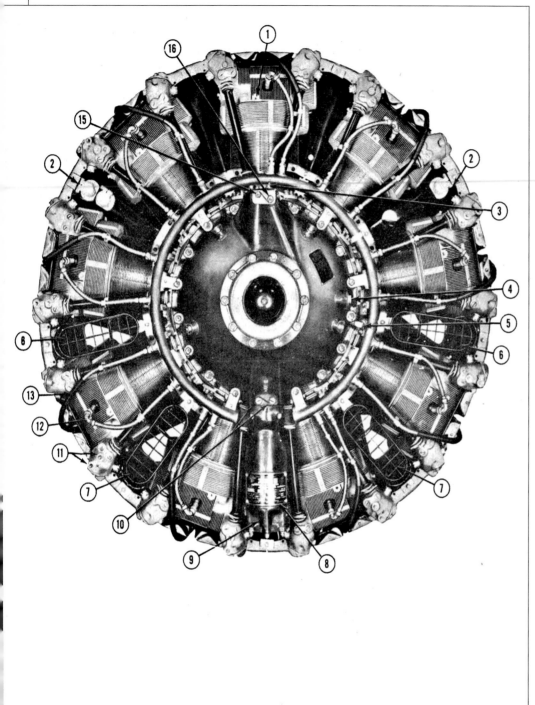

1. Rocker Roller Hub and Pin
2. Rocker Roller Hub and Rocker Roller
3. Rocker Roller Hub and Rocker Arm
4. Rocker Roller and Rocker Arm
5. Rocker Box
6. Bearing Race and Rocker Bolt
7. Bearing Race and Rocker
8. Rocker Box and Cylinder Head
9. Valve Guide and Valve Intake Center Ends
10. Valve Guide and Valve Exhaust Center Ends
11. Cylinder Head and Intake Valve Guide
12. Cylinder Head and Exhaust Valve Guide
13. Piston Pin Bushing and Piston Pin
14. Piston Pin and Piston
15. Piston Pin and Piston Pin Plug
16. Piston Pin Bushing and Master Rod
17. Crankpin Bearing and Crankpin
18. Crankpin Bearing and Crankpin
19. Master Rod and Bearing
20. Articulated Rod and Knuckle Pin Bushing
21. Master Rod and Knuckle Pin Bushing
22. Master Rod and Knuckle Pin Both Ends
23. Knuckle Pin and Bushing
24. Cylinder Barrel and Piston Center of Skirt
25. Piston Ring and Piston No. 1 Ring (Top)
26. Piston Ring and Piston No. 2 Ring
27. Piston Ring and Piston No. 3 Ring
28. Piston Ring and Piston No. 4 Ring
29. Piston Ring and Piston No. 5 Ring (Bottom)
30. Valve Tappet Guide and Crankcase Front Section
31. Valve Tappet and Guide
32. Valve Tappet Roller Pin and Valve Tappet
    and Roller
33. Crankcase Main and Intersection
34. Crankcase Main Front Section and Front Bearing
    Ring
35. Crankshaft Front Roller Bearing and Ring
36. Crankcase and Rear Bearing Ring
37. Crankcase Rear Bearing Ring and Bearing
38. Crankshaft and Roller Bearing
39. Crankshaft Rear and Ball Bearing
40. Crankshaft and Thrust Bearing
41. Crankcheek and Cap Screw
42. Front Crankcase and Cover and Ball Bearing
43. Cam Hub Bearing and Adapter
44. Cam Bearing Adapter and Cam Hub
45. Cam and Cam Drive Pinion Backlash
46. Cam Drive Pinion and Bushing
47. Cam Drive Gear Shaft and Bushing
48. Cam Drive Gear and Shaft
49. Cam Driving Gear and Cam Drive Gear Backlash
50. Cam Driving Gear and Cam Drive Gear Oiling
    Bracket
51. Impeller and Supercharger Housing
52. Impeller and Diffuser Plate
53. Impeller Shaft Oil Seal Front and Rear Sleeve
    and Supercharger Housing Front and Rear Sleeve
54. Supercharger Housing Front and Rear Sleeve
    and Impeller Shaft Bearing Support and Super-
    charger Rear Housing
55. Starter Shaft Bushing and Supercharger Housing
    Rear Cover
56. Accessory Driveshaft and Bushing
57. Accessory Driveshaft Coupler and Accessory
    Driveshaft
58. Accessory Driveshaft and Impeller Shaft Bushing
59. Impeller Driveshaft and Impeller Shaft Front
    and Rear Bushing
60. Impeller Shaft Thrust Ring and Impeller Shaft
    Retainer
61. Accessory Driveshaft
62. Supercharger Rear Housing and Impeller Clutch
    Shaft

This is a longitudinal section schematic drawing of a direct-drive Wright R-1820F Cyclone 9-cylinder radial engine (1935).

63. Supercharger Rear Cover and Impeller Clutch Shaft
64. Impeller Clutch Shaft and Bushing
65. Impeller Drive Pinion and Bushing
66. Impeller Clutch Weight and Impeller Clutch Band
66. Impeller Drive Ring Gear
67. Impeller Clutch Assembly
68. Impeller Clutch Gear and Impeller Driveshaft Gear Backlash
69. Impeller Drive Pinion and Accessory Drive Gear and Generator Drive Gear Backlash
70. Generator Gear
71. Generator Gear and Bushing
72. Supercharger Rear Cover and Accessory Bushings
73. Packing Retaining Ring and Supercharger Rear Cover
74. Pump Driveshaft in Oil Pump Body
75. Oil Pump Body and Gears
76. Pump Drive Gear End Clear
77. Pump Drive Gear and Bushing
78. Idler Gear and Idler Gear Shaft
79. Oil Pump Gears and Body End Clear
80. Oil Strainer and Supercharger Housing Rear Cover
81. Magneto Driveshaft Gear and Synchronizer Drive Gear Backlash
82. Magneto Driveshaft End Clear
83. Magneto Driveshaft and Bushing
84. Supercharger Rear Cover and Magneto Driveshaft Bush
85. Magneto Drive Gear and Pump Drive Gear Backlash
86. Accessory Drive and Pump Drive Gear Backlash
87. Tachometer Drive Housing and Bushing
88. Tachometer Drive Gear Shaft and Bushing
89. Tachometer Drive Gear Shaft and Driveshaft Backlash
90. Tachometer Drive Gear and Housing
91. Tachometer Drive Gear Shaft End Clear
92. Synchronizer Driveshaft Bushing and Supercharger Housing Rear Cover
93. Crankcase Rear Main Bearing Ring and Crankcase Main Section
94. Crankcase Rear Main Bearing Ring and Ball Bearing
95. Crankcase Front Section and Crankcase Main Section
96. Crankcase Front Section and Ball Bearing
97. Propeller Shaft Ball Bearing Adapter and Ball Bearing
98. Reduction Driving Gear and Ball Bearing Retainer Backlash
99. Reduction Driving Gear and Reduction Gear Pinion Backlash
100. Reduction Gear Pinion and Bushing
101. Reduction Gear Pinion Bushing and Reduction Gear Spider
101. Reduction Gear Pinion Bushing and Reduction Gear Spider End Clear
102. Propeller Shaft and Reduction Gear Spider Spline
103. Propeller Shaft Ball Bearing Adapter and Propeller Shaft
104. Propeller Shaft and Propeller Shaft Ball Bearing Adapter Large
105. Propeller Shaft and Front Bushing
106. Propeller Shaft Front Bushing and Crankshaft
107. Propeller Shaft and Rear Bushing
108. Propeller Shaft Rear Bushing and Crankshaft
109. Crankshaft and Cam Drive Hub Spline
110. Cam Drive Hub and Reduction Driving Gear Spline
111. Cam Drive Hub and Cam Hub Bearing
112. Cam Drive Hub and Cam Hub
113. Crankshaft Breather Assembly and Breather Support
114. Breather Assembly and Propeller Shaft
115. Synchronizer Driveshaft Support and Bushings
116. Synchronizer Driveshaft and Bushings
117. Synchronizer Driveshaft End Clear
118. Synchronizer Cam and Roller (with Plunger in Locked Position)
119. Synchronizer Roller and Plunger
120. Synchronizer Roller and Plunger
121. Synchronizer Housing and Plunger
122. Synchronizer Plunger and Lower Housing
123. Crankshaft Thrust Bearing
124. Hydro Control Propeller Operating Valve and Crankcase Front Cover
125. Propeller Shaft Thrust Bearing Nut and Crankcase Front Cover
126. Propeller Shaft Oil Seal Ring Gap
127. Crankshaft Thrust Bearing Nut and Crankcase Front Cover

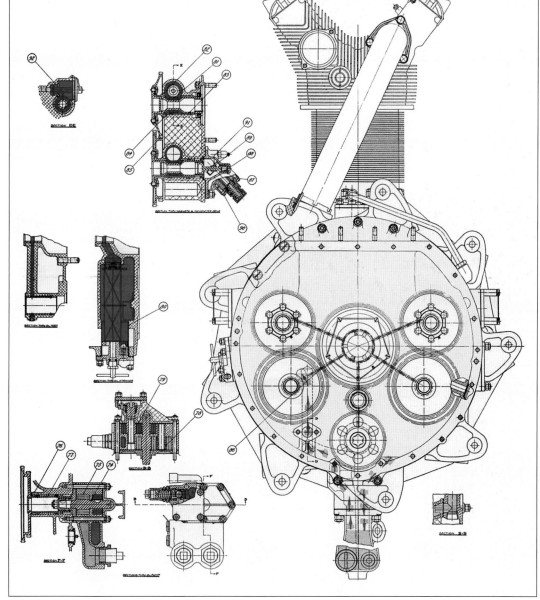

A front-view schematic drawing is shown of a direct-drive Wright R-1820F Cyclone 9-cylinder radial engine (1935).

The Cyclone F and G were both produced in both a direct-drive and a geared configuration. In the latter, a gearbox inserted between the engine and propeller permitted the option of the propeller rotating more slowly and more efficiently. The engines thus equipped were designated as GR-1820 and weighed about 100 pounds more than the direct-drive Cyclones. The highest horsepower rating among the geared Cyclones was in the GR-1820-G2, which delivered 1,000 hp for takeoff, 810 hp at sea level, and 850 hp at 5,500 feet.

The geared Cyclones were used mainly in transports, especially the Douglas DC-3 and its military derivatives (see Chapter 5) as well as prewar airliners, such as the Lockheed Super Electra, Lockheed Lodestar, and the Boeing 307.

The R-1820 Cyclone was also used in the Brewster F2A Buffalo monoplane fighter, which first flew in December 1937 and became operational with the US Navy in 1939. The US Navy received 11 F2A-1s, 43 F2A-2s, and 108 F2A-3s—the latter variants with 1,200-hp R-1820-40 engines.

Orders for Cyclone-powered Buffalos came in from Belgium in 1940, but most of these were delivered to the British after the German defeat of Belgium. Likewise, Buffalos ordered by the Netherlands for use in the Dutch East Indies were diverted to Australia as the Imperial Japanese Army invaded and occupied the Indies.

During the early days of World War II, the Buffalo performed badly for the Americans in the Pacific and for the British in Singapore

The Wright R-1820 Cyclone 9-cylinder, single-row radial engine entered production in 1931 with deliveries continuing into the 1950s. More than 120,000 were produced, including nearly 50,000 that went into initial factory deliveries of Boeing B-17F and B-17G Flying Fortresses. (Photo Courtesy Stahlkocher, Licensed under Creative Commons)

and Burma, taking a beating from the Japanese. However, Buffalos performed remarkably well in service with Finland against the Soviet Union. Top-scoring Finnish aces Ilmari Juutilainen and Hans Wind both scored many of their nearly 170 combined victories in Buffalos.

The R-1820 remained in production into the 1960s, as about 7,000 were built by Lycoming after World War II and nearly 300 made by Pratt & Whitney Canada. The largest single production block had 63,789 Cyclones being turned out during World War II by Studebaker in South Bend, Indiana.

Strategic Airpower and the Flying Fortress

The R-1820-powered Boeing B-17 and the P-1830-powered Consolidated B-24 were both part of a strategic doctrine that began during World War I as an idea, that of using airpower to reach beyond the battlefront and beyond the tactical use of aircraft to support ground troops. The idea was to reach deep into enemy territory to strike strategically at the opposition's ability to wage war by destroying factories and infrastructure, such as the railroads that moved men and materiel to the front lines.

The idea of strategic airpower or of a strategic bombing campaign had numerous parents, but insofar as the USAAF of World War II was concerned, the man with *the* vision was Colonel William Lendrum "Billy" Mitchell. He commanded the Air Service of the American Expeditionary Force (AEF). He had been developing plans to strike into Imperial Germany when World War I ended, and after the war, he continued to promote this idea within the US Army.

Most leaders, including General John J. "Blackjack" Pershing, commander of the AEF and later Chief of Staff, saw air power strictly as tactical ground support, while Mitchell saw the future of airpower as a strategic weapon. Mitchell was outspoken to the contrary, and strategic airpower became a passionate crusade for him—one that ultimately cost him his career.

By the 1930s, with Hitler in power in Germany and Imperial Japan on the rampage in China, many military planners thought it was prudent to prepare for the possibility of another world war. In the United States, the men who led the Army Air Corps, the same men who had been young officers back when Mitchell ran the Air Service, were in positions whereby they could implement his ideas. By 1935, the two men who would shape the strategic campaign against the Third Reich in World War II each moved up a notch. Ira Eaker became a major, and Carl "Tooey" Spaatz became a lieutenant colonel. Meanwhile, Henry Harley "Hap" Arnold, who would command the USAAF as it became the largest air force in world history, became a brevet brigadier general and assistant chief of the Air Corps.

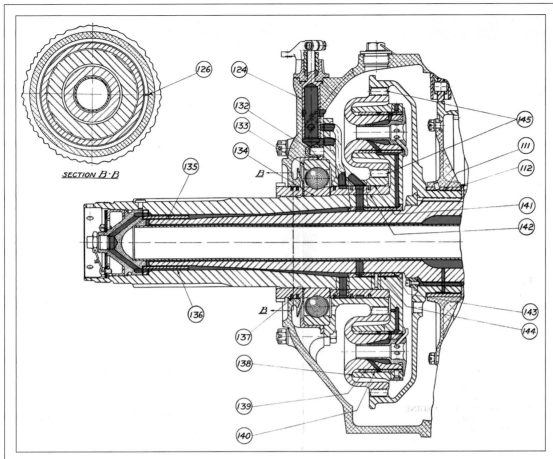

This is a longitudinal section schematic drawing of a geared-drive Wright GR-1820F Cyclone 9-cylinder radial engine (1935).

128. Crankcase Front Section and Crankcase Front Section Sleeve
129. Crankcase Front Section Sleeve and Cam Hub
130. Cam Bearing Adapter and Cam Hub Bearing
131. Cam Hub Bearing and Cam Hub
132. Propeller Shaft Thrust Bearing Retainer and Ball Bearing
133. Propeller Shaft Thrust Bearing
134. Propeller Shaft and Ball Bearing
135. Front End Crankshaft and Propeller Shaft Front Bushing
136. Propeller Shaft and Propeller Shaft Front Bushing
137. Propeller Shaft Thrust Bearing Nut and Crankcase Front Section
138. Propeller Shaft and Reduction Gear Drive Pinion
139. Reduction Gear Drive Pinion and Reduction Gear Drive Pinion Bushing
140. Propeller Shaft and Reduction Gear Drive Pinion Bushing
141. Cam Bearing Adapter and Stationary Reduction Gear
142. Cam Bearing Adapter and Propeller Shaft
143. Front End Crankshaft and Propeller Shaft Rear Bush
144. Propeller Shaft and Propeller Shaft Rear Bushing
145. Stationary Reduction Gear Reduction Driving Gear and Pinion Backlash

The first step on the road to strategic airpower was to develop aircraft (strategic heavy bombers) that could execute that doctrine if a world war came to pass.

In April 1934, the US Army General Staff approved Project A, a top-secret initiative that called for an aircraft with a range of 5,000 miles and a 1-ton payload capacity. As the designs were submitted by planemakers, the Air Corps assigned XBLR (Experimental Bomber, Long Range) designations to the aircraft, which were changed in July 1936 to "B-for-bomber" designations. Of these, only two were actually built: the Boeing XB-15 (formerly XBLR-1) and the Douglas XB-19 (XBLR-2). They were powered, respectively, by four R-1830-11s (see Chapter 4) and four R-3350-5s (see Chapter 12).

There was only one XB-15 and one XB-19 built. Because of the rapid acceleration of technical development and the march of history during that era, both aircraft, and especially the XB-19, were almost obsolescent relics of another era by the time they appeared. The XB-15 made its first flight in October 1937—27 months *after* the B-17.

The B-17 program evolved from a 1934 Air Corps design competition that called for a new "multi-engined" bomber to supersede its fleet of Martin B-10 twin-engine bombers. The speed requirements represented a modest improvement over the B-10, but increased endurance was the goal. The duration of flight was specified to be up to 10 hours with a range of 2,000 miles added in parentheses.

Both Boeing and Douglas entered the competition, which called for each company to construct a prototype at its own expense.

Boeing had just put into service its Model 247, which was a modern, all-metal, monoplane airliner with a passenger capacity of 10. It was powered by a pair of 500-hp Pratt & Whitney R-1340-S1H1-G Wasps, and Boeing was feeling good about its future in multi-engine aircraft. So too was Douglas. Its DC-2 airliner had just gone into service with Transcontinental and Western Air (TWA) between Chicago and Newark, and it was already proving itself. Powered by a pair of Wright GR-1820-F52 Cyclones, it was faster than the Boeing 247 and seated 14 passengers. As is known from hindsight, the DC-2 was the predecessor of the

The first Boeing Model 299 rolled out of the factory at Boeing Field in Seattle on July 17, 1935, powered by a Pratt & Whitney R-1690 Hornet and was nicknamed "Flying Fortress" by the media on the same day. The first flight came 11 days later. It had been unofficially named "XB-17" by Boeing, but the US Army Air Corps made this designation official when it accepted the aircraft.

"four." Four engines would give a Boeing proposal greater range and payload capacity than two.

At Boeing, a team of brilliant young engineers, notably Stanford-educated Edward Curtis Wells, went to work on the project and designed just such an aircraft. The Boeing Model 299 prototype was rolled out at Boeing Field in Seattle on July 17, 1935. Although the Model 299 was unarmed, Richard Williams of the *Seattle Times* called it a "Flying Fortress," and the name stuck. Boeing, meanwhile, had used the unofficial designation "XB-17," and this was later adopted by the Army.

The company-financed Model 299 production series was powered by four engines, but it wasn't with the Wright R-1820 Cyclones. Instead, the 9-cylinder R-1690-E Hornet radials from rival Pratt & Whitney were used.

However, Douglas, Boeing's main competitor for the "multi-engine" bomber contract did equip its Model DB-1 demonstrator with R-1820s—a pair of them. In August, both aircraft arrived at the Army Air Corps Materiel Division (Materiel Command after 1942) at Wright Field in Ohio for official evaluation by Major Oliver Echols, chief of engineering at Wright Field, and his team.

Both aircraft met all the criteria, although the 299 came out significantly ahead of the DB-1 when it came to range, which was the lead technical criteria in the competition. However, when it came to price, there was no contest. The Boeing aircraft was nearly twice the price of the Douglas aircraft. In January 1936, the War Department ordered 133 DB-1s under the B-18 designation and just 13 Flying Fortresses (plus a structural test airframe), which were now officially designated as B-17.

Douglas DC-3, which was first flown in 1935 and revolutionized global air travel.

At his namesake company in Santa Monica, when Donald Douglas looked at the line in the specifications that read "multi-engine," he assumed that it meant "two engines." Up in Seattle, Boeing's Claire Egtvedt looked at the work then being done by Boeing on four-engine aircraft and decided that "multi" could just as well mean

First flown in December 1936, the service test aircraft were designated as Y1B-17 (Model 299B) and powered by four Wright GR-1820-39 Cyclones, delivering 930 hp for takeoff.

Throughout 1936, Air Corps Chief of Staff, Major General Oscar Westover, pushed continually for more money for

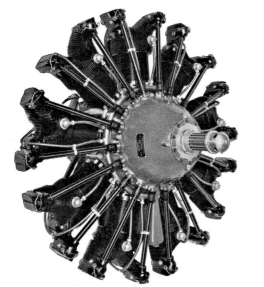

FAR LEFT: *This is a front three-quarter view of the GR-1820F geared drive variant of the F-series Wright Cyclone 9-cylinder radial engine (1935).*

LEFT: *A rear three-quarter view is shown of the R-1820F direct-drive variant of the F-series Wright Cyclone 9-cylinder radial engine (1935).*

The first of 13 Boeing Y1B-17 (Model 299B) Flying Fortresses made its debut flight on December 2, 1936. For these aircraft, Boeing made the switch from Pratt & Whitney Hornet to Wright Cyclone and never looked back. The Cyclone variant used in the Y1B-17 was the 930-hp R-1820-39. (Photo Courtesy USAF)

The Boeing B-17C (Model 299H) Flying Fortress made its first flight on July 21, 1940. The aircraft were powered by 1,200-hp Wright R-1820-65 Cyclones. (Photo Courtesy USAF)

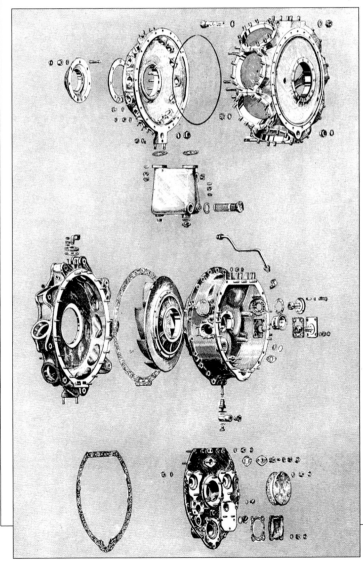

The Brewster F2A Buffalo made its first flight on December 2, 1937, a year to the day after Boeing's Y1B-17. Like Boeing's Flying Fortress, the Buffalo flew with a Wright Cyclone, a 1,200-hp R-1820-40. Seen here is an F2A-2 Buffalo undergoing testing at the NACA Langley Research Center in Hampton, Virginia, in 1943. (Photo Courtesy NASA)

Cylinder sections from a Wright R-1820 Cyclone 9-cylinder radial engine are shown in 1935.

The Boeing B-17E (Model 299-O) was the first Flying Fortress variant with the redesigned rear fuselage and the trademark rounded tail. First flown on September 5, 1941, the B-17Es were powered by 1,200-hp Wright R-1820-65 Cyclones.

The Boeing B-17F (Model 299P) incorporated the redesigned rear fuselage and the trademark rounded tail and introduced the one-piece blown-Plexiglas nose. First delivered on May 30, 1942, Wright R-1820-97 Cyclones became standard for more than 12,000 B-17Fs and B-17Gs.

long-range, four-engine bombers, but the accountants carried the day. However, in the fall of 1936, Westover's deputy (and in 1938, his successor), Brigadier General Hap Arnold, lobbied for additional Flying Fortresses, and an order for 39 B-17Bs (Model 299M) finally was issued in August 1937.

Superchargers

The Y1B-17 structural test airframe was made flyable and designated as Y1B-17A (later B-17A). It was first flown in May 1937 pow-

ered by GR-1820-51 Wright Cyclones. These were each augmented by turbosuperchargers to evaluate their use in future Flying Fortresses, especially the B-17B variant.

Invented by Alfred Büchli in Switzerland in 1915 and first used operationally a decade later, the turbosupercharger (known in the vernacular as a "turbo") was used in aircraft engines to overcome the loss of power at high altitude due to diminished air density.

At 18,000 feet, air pressure is half that of sea level, and the aerodynamic drag encountered by an airframe is halved. Because the air in the cylinders is pushed inward by air pressure, the engine

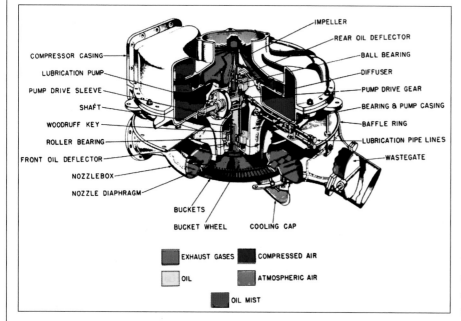

IMPELLER
REAR OIL DEFLECTOR
BALL BEARING
DIFFUSER
PUMP DRIVE GEAR
BEARING & PUMP CASING
BAFFLE RING
LUBRICATION PIPE LINES
WASTEGATE

COMPRESSOR CASING
LUBRICATION PUMP
PUMP DRIVE SLEEVE
SHAFT
WOODRUFF KEY
ROLLER BEARING
FRONT OIL DEFLECTOR
NOZZLEBOX
NOZZLE DIAPHRAGM
BUCKETS
BUCKET WHEEL   COOLING CAP

EXHAUST GASES   COMPRESSED AIR
OIL   ATMOSPHERIC AIR
OIL MIST

This is the basic General Electric B-2 turbosupercharger that was installed in early B-17 Flying Fortress variants. It was rated at 211,300 rpm.

This three-quarter cutaway view shows a General Electric B-2 turbosupercharger such as was installed in Wright R-1820 Cyclone engines installed in early variant B-17s (1943).

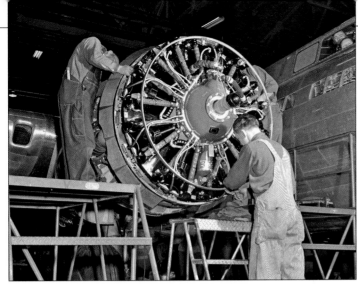

Adjustments are made to the cowling and the ignition wiring system of a Wright R-1820-97 Cyclone on the wing of a B-17F at Boeing's Plant 2 in Seattle. (Photo Courtesy Andreas Feininger, Library of Congress)

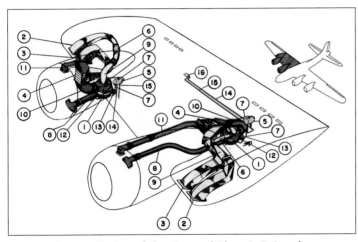

Here is the installation of the General Electric B-2 turbosuperchargers in the R-1820-65 engines of a Boeing B-17E (1943). Red indicates exhaust, dark blue indicates compressed air, light blue indicates atmospheric air, and yellow indicates oil flow.

1. Turbosupercharger
2. Carburetor Air-Intake Scoop
3. Intercooler Cooling-Air-Intake Scoop
4. Intercooler
5. Turbosupercharger Oil-Supply Tank
6. Induction Ducting Relief Valve
7. Turbosupercharger Oil Supply Lines
8. Engine Exhaust Stack to Nozzlebox Inlet
9. Air-Induction Ducting to Turbosupercharger Inlet
10. Air-Induction Ducting from Turbosupercharger to Intercooler
11. Air-Induction Ducting from Intercooler to Carburetor
12. Turbosupercharger Regulator
13. Turbosupercharger Waste Pipe
14. Air Vent for Turbosupercharger Oil-Supply Tank
15. Drain Line for Turbosupercharger Oil-Supply Tank
16. Vent Manifold, Bottom Side of Wing

produces half the power at full throttle as it does at sea level. The turbosupercharger maintains manifold pressure as altitude increases to compensate for the decreasing air density. The idea is to maintain the sea-level power output of the engine.

The use of the turbosupercharger in aircraft engines was refined by Dr. Sanford Moss of General Electric, who earned the 1940 Collier Trophy for this work. Working with Moss, Air Corps engineers at Wright Field developed superchargers for numerous aircraft before and during World War II, beginning with the F-14 supercharger in

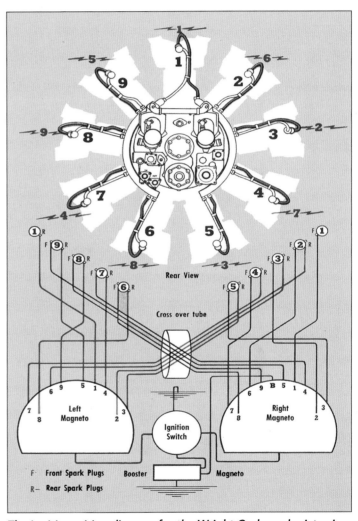

The ignition wiring diagram for the Wright Cyclone depicts nine numbers around the top drawing to indicate the firing order of the 9-cylinders. This colorful illustration was intended for the commercial market and the C9GC export variant of the R-1820-87 Cyclone that was used in the Brewster Model 339-16 Buffalo.

Rows of Wright Aeronautical R-1820-97 Cyclone 9-cylinder radial engines lined up on the factory floor at Boeing's Plant 2 in Seattle in December 1943 are prepared for installation into rows of B-17Gs.

This shows a good front view of the left inboard Wright R-1820-97 Cyclone of a Boeing B-17F with technicians reaching inside behind the cowling to fine tune the rear of the engine. (Photo Courtesy Andreas Feininger, Library of Congress)

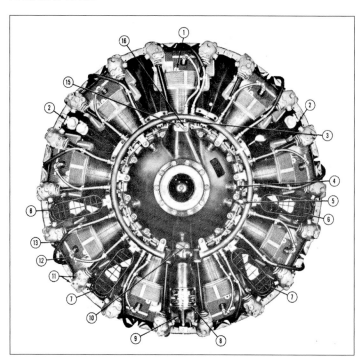

This is a full front view of a Wright R-1820 engine.

1. Detonation Indicator Connection
2. Magneto Air Blast Tube
3. Propeller Governor Mounting Pad
4. Timing Inspection Plug
5. External Hydro-Oil Line
6. Air Ducts for the Carburetor
7. Air Ducts for Oil Cooler
8. Engine Data Plate Attached to Sump
9. Sump Scavenge Pump Housing
10. Crankcase Front Section Oil Drain Plugs
11. Cowl Attaching Studs
12. Front Spark Plug Elbow
13. Rear Spark Plug Lead
14. [Reference Deleted in 1945 Revision]
15. Propeller High Oil Pressure Plug
16. Propeller Low Oil Pressure Plug

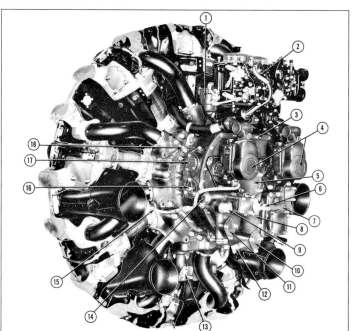

Here is a three-quarter left rear view of the Wright R-1820 engine.

1. Air-Maze Oil Separator
2. Carburetor
3. Manifold Pressure Connection
4. Right and Left Magnetos
5. Starter Mounting Pad
6. Mechanical Tachometer Drive
7. Upper and Lower Accessory Drive Mounting Pads
8. Generator Mounting Pad
9. Oil Pressure Relief Valve
10. Oil out Connection
11. Oil in Connection
12. Pump External Scavenge Oil Connection
13. Sump External Scavenge Oil Connection
14. Oil Check Valve
15. External Hydro-Oil Line
16. Oil Strainer
17. Gun Synchronizer Substituting Cover
18. Cabin Heater Connection

Barbara Scott, a worker at the Vega Aircraft Company in Burbank, California, is seen here working on a Wright R-1820-97 Cyclone engine for a B-17G. Vega built 500 B-17Fs and 2,250 B-17Gs.

the Y1B-17A. These were initially mounted atop each engine nacelle. However, when this configuration was first flown in April 1938, the turbosuperchargers proved to be problematic. Boeing initially installed the turbos on top of the engine, but as Mansfield recalled, this presented a serious stumbling block.

As the instruments recorded a 25-percent increase in power, the air speed indicator dropped, the aircraft began to shake, and the tail whipped violently.

It was back to the drawing board and on to the wind tunnel. The F-14s were moved to the bottom of the engine nacelle, and the problems were ironed out. At the time, the turbosupercharger was seen as the single most important new innovation to become standard in the B-17B. It was the feature that allowed the Flying Fortress to become the high-altitude strategic bombing platform that its advocates had long intended.

Early Flying Fortress Production

The B-17B first flew on June 27, 1939. Production-series deliveries started a month later and wrapped up in March 1940. Power for the B-17B was supplied by four 1820-51 Cyclones rated at 1,000 hp

One final touch is made before buttoning up the cowling on this Wright R-1820-97 Cyclone with its propeller already hung. (Photo Courtesy Andreas Feininger, Library of Congress)

A B-17F receives fuel for its delivery flight. This photograph taken at Boeing Field by Andreas Feininger of the Office of War Information provides a good look at the front and side of the Wright R-1820-97 Cyclones on the left wing. (Photo Courtesy Andreas Feininger, Library of Congress)

at 25,000 feet and 1,200 hp for takeoff. These were augmented for high-altitude operations with B-3 turbosuperchargers.

A pair of landmark events occurred for Boeing in September 1939, the same month that Germany invaded Poland and the world was plunged into World War II. First came the sought-after order from the Air Corps for 38 B-17Cs (Model 299H), and second was the return of Philip Gustav Johnson to the company.

Like Claire Egtvedt, Johnson had been hired by Bill Boeing in 1917 upon his graduation from the University of Washington engineering program. The two men were Boeing's right-hand men until 1934, when the company was reorganized and the founder departed. Egtvedt became president, and Johnson went on to the airline industry. However, in 1939, with orders coming in fast, Boeing Corporate Attorney Bill Allen suggested that Johnson, who was by most accounts a production genius, be lured back. Phil Johnson assumed the presidency, and Egtvedt became chairman.

A second order for B-17Cs came in April 1940, just eight days after the German assault on Western Europe that began with the invasion of Denmark and Norway. This batch of aircraft included so many internal detail changes that they were designated as B-17D (also Model 299H), although they were outwardly almost identical.

The powerplant for the 38 B-17Cs and 42 B-17Ds was the supercharged R-1820-65 Cyclone, which delivered 1,200 hp for takeoff

and 1,000 hp at 25,000 feet. The B-17C first flew in July 1940, and the B-17D did so in February 1941. Deliveries of all the aircraft were complete by April 1941.

The R-1820-65 Cyclone was retained in the B-17E variant, although there were major changes in the airframe design, most notably in the shape of the tail and the addition of a tail gunner.

In May 1940, as Hitler's fast moving blitzkrieg swept through the Netherlands and Belgium and continued into France, President Roosevelt went before Congress to ask for more money for military aircraft. His previous request for 3,000 had raised eyebrows. Now, the president took off the metaphorical gloves and proposed that Congress authorize funding for 50,000.

The B-17E (Model 299-O) was a high-priority part of this. Orders for the B-17E, issued in August and September 1940 and June 1941, totaled 512 aircraft. These were delivered between November 1941 and June 1942.

Definitive Variants

The definitive Flying Fortress variants were the B-17F and B-17G (both Boeing Model 299P). They were produced in very large numbers: 3,405 of the former and 8,680 of the latter. Outwardly, they are easily distinguished from each another by the incorporation of the

Bendix Chin Turret in the B-17G, but otherwise they appear almost indistinguishable in a cursory glance.

Both the B-17F and B-17G were standardized with turbosupercharged Wright R-1820-97 Cyclones that delivered 1,200 hp at 2,500 rpm for takeoff; 1,000 hp at 2,300 rpm at 25,000 feet; and had a war emergency power rating of 1,380 hp.

The R-1820-97 weighed 1,315 pounds, was 47.8 inched long, and had a diameter of 55.1 inches. It had a compression ratio of 6.7:1 and a supercharger ratio of 7:1.

Although data varies by source and subvariant, the cruising speed was between 160 mph and 182 mph, the top speed was rated at 300 mph at 30,000 feet, and it had a war emergency rating of 302 mph. The service ceiling was between 35,000 and 37,600 feet, depending on the source. The B-17G had a 2,000-mile range with 6,000 pounds of bombs and a maximum ferry range of 3,400 miles.

With the common engine type as a case in point, it can be noted that the B-17F and B-17G were so similar that both USAAF and Boeing serial numbers (S/N) for the last B-17F were only one digit removed from the first B-17G. However, in that lineage of 12,731 aircraft, so many changes were made that the first B-17Fs were vastly different than the later B-17Gs.

Again, the supercharger provides a case in point. The early 1820-97 Cyclones were equipped with the General Electric B-2 turbosupercharger, but during 1944, it was gradually upgraded to the B-22 type. The manual lists the B-2 with a governed speed of 23,400 rpm and the B-22 with a governed speed of 26,400 rpm.

Final lubrication of a Wright R-1820-97 Cyclone on this Flying Fortress takes one man to get his hands dirty and two to watch and provide advice. (Photo Courtesy Andreas Feininger, Library of Congress)

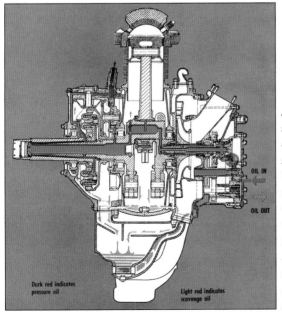

A left-side schematic drawing shows a Wright R-1820 Cyclone 9-cylinder radial engine and highlights the lubrication system.

OIL IN

OIL OUT

Dark red indicates pressure oil

Light red indicates scavenge oil

The need to manage each minute detail and change through the manufacturing of thousands of aircraft under wartime conditions was literally unprecedented. With this in mind, Major General Oliver Echols, the chief of the USAAF Materiel Division (Materiel Command after April 1942), introduced the block system.

Initiated in 1941, even before the United States entered World War II, the block system made both high rates of production and rapid change possible. It was applied not only to the Flying Fortress but also to virtually all of the aircraft production programs for the USAAF during the war.

Under the system, aircraft of a single variant were built in "blocks" of as few as a handful and as many as several hundred. The aircraft within the block were identical, but accumulated change orders were incorporated at the point of a block transition. This put the changes on a predictable schedule and gave individual aircraft a designation that could be traced through the mountains of paperwork surrounding the production.

As an example of how the block system worked, let's return to the example of the B-22 supercharger. Tracking of this change order was important because the mounting provisions for either the B-2 or B-22 were the same, but the oil and return lines had to be revised.

To add further to the complexity, the B-17Fs and B-17Gs were not all built by Boeing. In 1941, even before the United States entered World War II, Colonel (later General) Oliver Echols at the

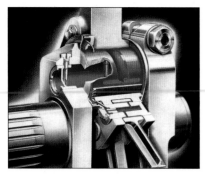

A cutaway drawing of the Master Rod Bearing (end seal type) in a Wright R-1820 Cyclone 9-cylinder radial engine.

Materiel Division decided that production on the scale that he saw coming required some logistical rethinking. An official postwar study of Echols and his command, observed that "as the production requirements continued to rise, it became apparent that multiple contractors would need to work together to meet the demands . . . the plane was Boeing's design, but because of the demands of the war, the company was willing to allow the other manufacturers to produce it."

With this in mind, Echols called together representatives of Boeing, the Douglas Aircraft Company, and the Lockheed Aircraft Company and worked out an arrangement to share production of the B-17F and B-17G. They would be made not only by Boeing in Seattle but also by Douglas in Long Beach, California, and by the Vega Aircraft subsidiary of Lockheed in Burbank, California. This new cooperative arrangement that was known as the Boeing-Douglas-Vega (BDV) Committee was managed by representatives of each

The practiced eye of the man with the screwdriver scans the left outboard Wright R-1820-97 in the Flying Fortress during final servicing. (Photo Courtesy Andreas Feininger, Library of Congress)

With all the inspections complete, the Wright R-1820-97 Cyclones of this Flying Fortress are run up at Boeing Field in Seattle one last time before it takes off for its delivery flight. (Photo Courtesy Andreas Feininger, Library of Congress)

This restored B-17G is seen during an appearance at the Chino Air Show in 2014. It was built by the Douglas Aircraft Company in Long Beach, California, as part of that company's Block 85 Flying Fortress production. Delivered to the USAAF in March 1945, it survived World War II and was used by the US Air Force for tasks such as air-sea rescue and drone directing until 1959. Restored to its wartime appearance, it is now operated by the Arizona unit of the Commemorative Air Force. (Photo Courtesy Airwolfhound, Licensed under Creative Commons)

The Vega XB-38 Flying Fortress was the result of a feasibility study of powering four-engine bombers with inline, rather than radial, engines. First flown on May 19, 1943, the XB-38 was actually a Boeing-built B-17E in which the Vega Aircraft Company removed the four Wright R-1820-65 Cyclone radials and replaced them with Allison V-1710-89 V-type inline engines similar to those used in aircraft like the Lockheed P-38. After evaluating the reengineered aircraft for possible production, the USAAF canceled the project.

company and of the Materiel Command. Boeing provided all necessary drawings, patterns and blueprints, and the three-company committee coordinated production among themselves and all of their subcontractors.

Each aircraft received a designation suffix that identified the factory where it was built. For example, a B-17G built in Seattle was a B-17G-BO, one from Douglas in Long Beach was a B-17G-DL, and one from Vega in Burbank was designated as B-17G-VE.

The BDV Committee became a template for diversified production of many other high-priority aircraft. For instance, as is seen in Chapter 4, the Consolidated B-24 Liberator heavy bomber was built by that company in San Diego but also at five other locations by four other aircraft manufacturers.

The B-22 supercharger is another example of multisource acquisition. By early 1944, just as there were three companies producing the Flying Fortress, there were three companies producing the B-22. These went to numerous factories for use in engines installed in many different engines that powered a variety of aircraft types. The B-22 was made by its originator, General Electric, which had a monthly output of 6,500 units; Allis-Chalmers, which had a capacity of 4,500; and Ford, which could turn out 3,500 a month.

The B-22s that flowed into the B-17G program were built mainly by General Electric as Part WW8456556. The B-22 was integrated into Vega's assembly line with B-17G-25-VE, which was first delivered on January 13, 1944. Douglas started with its Block 35 deliveries on January 17, and Boeing began with its own Block 35 on January 27.

An Inline-Engine Flying Fortress

Although the R-1820 Cyclone had been standardized for the Flying Fortress, the USAAF did consider the option of a possible variant with inline engines. In July 1942, the Materiel Command officially issued a contract to Vega to experimentally adapt a B-17E to be powered by four Allison V-1710-89 V-12, water-cooled inline engines. These were some of the V-1710s being used to power the P-38 Lightning fighters that were built across the ramp in Burbank from where Vega would potentially produce these new Flying Fortress aircraft under the B-38 designation.

The first XB-38 prototype was a modified Boeing B-17E that made its first flight in May 1943. A full comparison had not been completed when the sole XB-38 crashed a month later, and the project was abandoned.

Chapter 4

WRIGHT'S REMARKABLE R-1830 TWIN WASP

This is a rare color photo of a Consolidated PB2Y-5 Coronado. A conversion from the PB2Y-3, it was powered by four Pratt & Whitney R-1830-92 Twin Wasps, the same engine used in later Catalinas. Note the air-to-surface vessel (ASV) radome above the flight deck.

The Twin Wasp was probably the most produced American aircraft piston engine in history, as 173,618 units were manufactured. The development of this engine dates back to 1929, when work began under the direction of Leonard S. "Luke" Hobbs, a former research engineer with the Army Air Corps at Wright Field, whom George Mead (see Chapter 1) had recruited to work on twin-row radial designs. By 1934, when Fred Rentschler moved up to head parent company United Aircraft, Mead was running things at Pratt & Whitney. When Mead retired for health reasons a decade later, it was Hobbs who took over what the company described as "complete direction of all Pratt & Whitney engineering."

The idea behind a twin-row engine is to increase the total displacement of an engine without increasing its frontal area. In addition, the smaller cylinders being used allow for a greater crankshaft speed and more numerous power impulses to produce a smoother operation. After many experiments, Mead and Hobbs settled on the two designs: the R-1830 Twin Wasp and the R-1535 Twin Wasp Junior (see Chapter 6).

First unveiled in 1931, the R-1830 entered production in 1932 and gradually evolved into the R-1830 series C by 1936. This engine produced 1,050 hp at 2,700 rpm on takeoff compared to the rating of 750 hp at 2,300 rpm for the original Twin Wasp. Depending on variant, the horsepower rating for the Twin Wasp series generally ranged from 700 hp while cruising at 2,325 rpm to 1,200 hp at 2,700 rpm for takeoff.

The 14-cylinder R-1830 Twin Wasp displaced 1,829 ci, was 59 inches long, and had a diameter of 48 inches, which was about 6 inches less than the rival Wright Cyclone. The R-1830 weighed around 1,250 pounds depending on the variant.

The Twin Wasp had a forged aluminum crankcase with forged-steel cylinder barrels and cast-aluminum heads. It was equipped with a 2-barrel carburetor (see the "R-1830-43, R-1830-65, and Their Carburetors" subsection), a single-speed General Electric supercharger, and a valvetrain with two overhead valves. It had a bore of 5.5 inches and a stroke of 5.5 inches.

The characteristics that Pratt & Whitney promoted in the R-1830 included its automatic valve gear lubrication and automatic fuel mixture control. In promotional literature, the company highlighted its "patented pressure baffles for increased cooling" and spoke of the R-1830's increased fuel efficiency "over comparable engines," presumably meaning the rival R-1820.

Twin Wasp production was mainly outsourced to the massive assembly lines of the automotive industry. Of the total, 43 percent were built by Buick in Melrose Park, Illinois, and 33 percent were built by Chevrolet in Tonowanda, New York. Pratt & Whitney itself built 24 percent at its own East Hartford, Connecticut, plant.

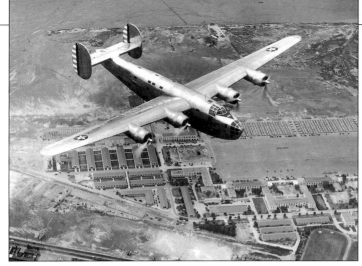

The Consolidated XB-24 is in flight near San Diego. Powered by four Pratt & Whitney R-1830-33s, it made its first flight on December 29, 1939.

While the Consolidated B-24 Liberator was the largest user of R-1830 Twin Wasps, the Grumman F4F Wildcat deserves prominent mention. Seen here in the blue-gray over light-gray scheme of early 1942, this is the F3F-3 variant, which was powered by a 1,200-hp R-1830-76 Twin Wasp. Wildcats were for a time the US Navy's top carrier-based fighter, but they achieved legendary status flying with outnumbered US Marine aviators in Guadalcanal.

The Twin Wasp and the Wildcat

While the story of the R-1830 is thoroughly intertwined with that of big, four-engine Consolidated aircraft, an important single-engine fighter that used the engine must be mentioned: the Grumman F4F Wildcat.

Leroy Grumman, along with several other veterans of the Loening Aircraft Engineering Company, struck out on their own and opened shop. The Grumman Aircraft Company opened its doors in Bethpage, Long Island, New York, on the second day of 1930. Within a few years, the company built such a reputation for solidly built naval aircraft that it came to be known as the "Grumman Iron Works."

The F4F Wildcat was Grumman's first monoplane fighter to enter production, although it was originally supposed to have been a biplane like its predecessor, the F3F, which used Pratt's R-1575 Wasp Junior. However, the design was reworked, and the XF4F-2 monoplane made its first flight on September 2, 1937, powered by a Pratt & Whitney R-1830-66. However, this prototype aircraft lost a US Navy production contract to the Brewster XF2A-1 Buffalo and its Wright R-1820-22 engine.

Undaunted, Grumman submitted its redesigned XF4F-3, which was powered by an XR-1830-76, in 1939 and won production contracts for 369 F4F-3 Wildcats with R-1830-76s. The first of these were in service with fighter squadron VF-4 aboard the USS *Ranger* by the end of 1940. Meanwhile, the British Royal Navy began receiving the first of 210 under the name Martlet. To these, an additional 902 were eventually added under the Wildcat name.

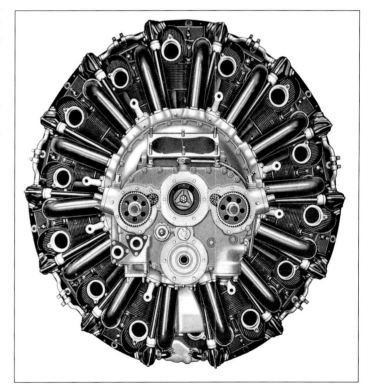

The Pratt & Whitney R-1830 Twin Wasp shows the rear case in place with the magneto, starter, and generator gears exposed.

The definitive production variant for the US Navy was the F4F-4, which was powered by the Pratt & Whitney R-1830-86 Twin Wasp. Grumman built 1,169 F4F-4s in Bethpage, but General Motors was also brought into the production pool for the Wildcat, just as it was for the Grumman TBF Avenger (see Chapter 8). GM had formed its Eastern Aircraft Division in early 1942 and began building Grumman-designed aircraft at the GM plant in Linden, New Jersey, which originally opened in 1937 for automobile production. Eastern went on to build 1,060 analogs of the F4F-4 (also powered by R-1340-86s) under the FM-1 designation. In turn, Eastern built 4,127 FM-2s after Grumman produced a pair of samples. A variety of R-1830-56 Twin Wasp subvariants were used in the FM-2.

Consolidated and the Twin Wasp

As Boeing had embraced Wright's R-1820 for its Flying Fortress, Consolidated Aircraft of San Diego adopted Pratt & Whitney's R-1830 Twin Wasp for all of its large production, multi-engine aircraft. Notably, these included the B-24 Liberator/PB4Y Privateer family of four-engine bombers and the PBY Catalina and PB2Y Coronado flying boats.

While Boeing, which had once been a sister company to Pratt & Whitney, chose a Wright engine, Consolidated turned to Pratt despite the fact that Consolidated's founder, Reuben Fleet, created his company through the acquisition of aircraft designs from Dayton-Wright.

In 1923, Fleet set up shop in Buffalo, New York, and began producing military aircraft for the US Army and US Navy. In 1927, Fleet hired the brilliant Wright Field Engineer Isaac Machlin "Mac" Lad-

Block 35 B-24D (B-24D-35-CO) bombers equipped with Pratt & Whitney R-1830-43 Twin Wasps near completion on the Consolidated Aircraft Corporation assembly line in San Diego, circa October 1942.

don away from the US Army. Laddon was, in turn, instrumental in Consolidated beginning to achieve success with seaplanes and flying boats. Because it is hard to test seaplanes in Buffalo during the winter when Lake Erie freezes over, Fleet and Laddon relocated the company to San Diego in 1933.

In 1941, Fleet left Consolidated, selling his 34-percent controlling interest to Errett Lobban Cord's Aviation Corporation (AVCO). Cord was the creator of the famous Cord automobile and

Reuben Hollis Fleet was an early pioneer in the American aviation industry. He founded the Consolidated Aircraft Company in 1923 in Buffalo, New York, and moved it west to San Diego a decade later. He built his company into one of the largest on the West Coast.

Isaac Machlin "Mac" Laddon became chief designer of large aircraft for the US Army Air Service Experimental and Engineering Test Center at McCook Field, Ohio, during World War I and joined Reuben Fleet's Consolidated Aircraft Company as chief engineer in 1927. He was responsible for developing the B-24 Liberator and the PBY Catalina.

A Pratt & Whitney R-1830 Twin Wasp 14-cylinder two-row radial engine is shown at the Imperial War Museum campus in Duxford, England. (Photo Courtesy Nimbus 227, Licensed under Creative Commons)

Cord's plan was to merge Vultee with Consolidated, but in December 1941, when the United States entered World War II, the necessity to gear up for wartime production took precedence over everything else. The housekeeping details for the merger were worked out over time, and in March 1943, stockholders gave their final approval. The Consolidated-Vultee Aircraft Corporation officially came into being.

The name "Convair" as a contraction for Consolidated-Vultee Aircraft Corporation was used informally. It would not be an official corporate name until after World War II. It is worth noting that the term "Consair" as an abbreviation for Consolidated Aircraft Company had also been in use *before* the merger. Both the Consolidated and Vultee components operated independently during the war, and these singular terms are used when referring to the respective operations in San Diego and Downey. Convair became a division of General Dynamics in 1954.

the owner of the Auburn Automobile Company. Cord created AVCO as his aviation holding company, and by 1941, when he brought Consolidated into it, AVCO holdings included the Vultee Aircraft Company of Downey, California, famous for its Vultee Valiant family of trainers. As Fleet departed, the Consolidated presidency went to Harry Woodhead, who previously presided over Cord's AVCO. However, Mac Laddon continued to run the show as vice president and general manager.

The B-24 Liberator

Consolidated's major project during World War II (and the main aircraft associated with the R-1830) was the B-24 Liberator, which was produced in greater numbers than any other American warplane ever.

The total varies depending on source. Aviation historian William Green lists 18,188 aircraft, probably excluding two prototypes. John Andrade's meticulously detailed accounting of production by

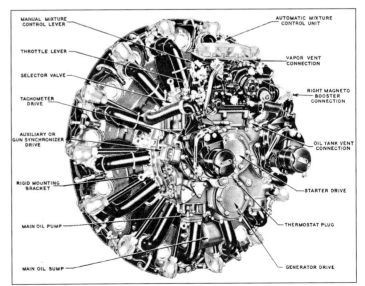

Front and rear views of the Pratt & Whitney R-1830 Twin Wasp 14-cylinder two-row radial engine are shown. Fleet and Laddon picked this powerplant for both the B-24 Liberator and the PBY Catalina, the two most-produced Consolidated aircraft.

Powered by Pratt & Whitney R-1830-43 Twin Cyclones, this B-24D was part of Block 7 delivered from Consolidated's headquarters plant in San Diego. (Photo Courtesy USAF)

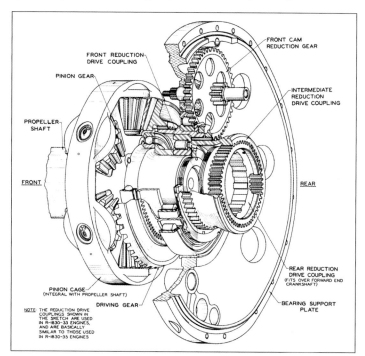

This spline-coupled, reduction-gearing, variable-speed clutch was originally used in the Pratt & Whitney R-1830-33 Twin Wasp engine. This engine powered the XB-24 Liberator prototype as well as the B-24A initial production series. This system later appeared in the R-1830-35.

each individual USAAF serial number yields a total of 18,190 plus 284 C-87 Liberator Express transport aircraft, which were unarmed Liberators produced in separate blocks with separate serial numbers in the same sequence as the B-24s.

Of the USAAF Liberator total, 977 of those built with USAAF serial numbers were transferred to the US Navy and designated as PB4Y-1. However, an additional production run of 736 similar but single-tailed aircraft was delivered to the Navy without USAAF serials and identified as PB4Y-2 Privateers. Finally, there were 59 Liberator Expresses built with Navy serials as RY-3 and transferred to Britain as Liberator C.IX. According to company records, 18,482 Liberators were manufactured, excluding the PB4Y-2s and RY-3s.

Adding them all up by serial numbers brings the overall total to 19,269. If this reckoning is accurate, the Liberator/Privateer program consumed 77,076 R-1830 radials (about 45 percent of all Twin Wasps that were made) just for the initial deliveries.

As the USAAF Materiel Command had established the BDV Committee to manage multisource production of the B-17 (see Chapter 3), a similar arrangement was done for B-24 production. Under this plan, Consolidated itself built 6,726 at its headquarters in San Diego and another 3,034 at a new government-owned facility that the company operated in Fort Worth, Texas, after 1942.

USAAF records show 984 B-24s produced by Douglas in Tulsa; 2,750 by Lockheed in Burbank; 966 by North American Aviation in Dallas; and 6,792 by the Ford Motor Company. The latter rolled out of Air Force Plant 31, a huge government-financed factory in Willow Run near Ypsilanti, Michigan.

The Liberator program began in January 1939 when Consolidated proposed its Model 32 to the Army Air Corps as a four-engine strategic bomber that was potentially superior to the B-17. The idea of having a second four-engine bomber in the pipeline appealed to the Army, and the prototype XB-24 was ordered in February. Orders for seven service test YB-24s followed in April and for 38 B-24As in August.

The XB-24 made its debut flight in December 1939, three months after the German invasion of Poland started World War II.

The XB-24, YB-24, and nine of the B-24As were equipped with the R-1830-33, delivering 1,200 hp for takeoff and 1,000 hp at 14,500 feet. When the speed of aircraft was clocked at 273 mph instead of the desired 311 mph, the XB-24 was re-engined with the supercharged R-1830-41 (commercially designated as R-1830-S3C4-G) engines, which had the same horsepower rating as the R-1830-33. Redesignated as XB-24B, this aircraft was delivered in August 1940.

In the meantime, with the war on, representatives of the French government visited San Diego to express an interest in an export variant that Consolidated had designated as LB-30. In April 1940, 175 LB-30MF (Mission Français) aircraft were ordered, but within

B-24D and B-24E Liberators are shown on the parallel assembly lines at Consolidated's Fort Worth factory. The first and third aircraft on the right are B-24E-25-CF S/N 41-29074 and 41-29075. The second aircraft is B-24D-10-CF S/N 42-63858. Note the distinctive paint scheme on the line of PB4Y-1s being assembled for the US Navy on the left. (Photo Courtesy US Air Force)

two months, France was defeated and occupied by the Germans. Britain's Royal Air Force (RAF) took over orders for 165 LB-30s, stipulating supercharged engines.

The Army Air Corps deferred its own first deliveries so that the first 26 Liberators could go to the RAF. These included six YB-24s that were delivered in December 1940 as LB-30As and 20 B-24A aircraft that were sent to Britain as LB-30B Liberator Is in March 1941.

The first B-24As, most with R-1830-41 engines, reached the Air Corps as it became the USAAF in the summer of 1941. The R-1830-41, equipped with General Electric B-2 turbosupercharger, was standard in the longer-nosed B-24C and the equivalent Liberator II export variant, where the engine carried the R-1830-S3C4-G commercial designation.

Building Factories to Build Bombers

How did factories such as those at Willow Run and Fort Worth come about? To facilitate the large-scale mass production of aircraft, the US government had gotten into the business of underwriting the expansion of the American aircraft industry through agencies such as the new Defense Plant Corporation. Under this plan, the government financed and owned the factories, but they were run by the aircraft companies.

Since most aircraft factories were then in coastal states (especially in southern California) the idea was for the government to

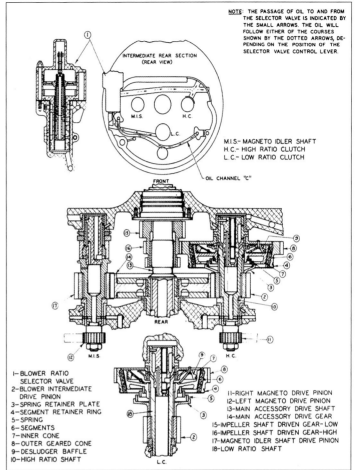

This impeller ratio selector valve and blower with variable-speed clutch mechanism was used on the R-1830-33, as installed in the B-24A. This system incorporated a control lever and linkage, piston, housing, and housing cover. The valve housing, which accommodated the piston, was installed in a large bore in the intermediate rear case. Oil ports were provided in the valve housing, in the hole in the intermediate rear case, and in the shaft, which was integral with the piston. The location of the ports in the piston shaft with respect to those in the valve housing and bore were governed by the position of the piston and regulated by the control lever and linkage. Manual operation of the control lever would cause the piston to move into either the high-ratio position or the low-ratio position. The selector valve directs engine oil pressure to a chamber between the gear and the cone of the clutch for the particular gear ratio selected. The oil pressure caused the cone to engage segments which, in turn, engaged the gear.

build satellite factories for the existing planemakers at inland locations. For the B-24 program, this involved Air Force Plant 4 at Fort Worth and Plant 31 at Willow Run.

Ground was broken for Plant 4 in May 1941 on 563 acres on the north side of Fort Worth. With its visually spectacular mile-long assembly line, the government-owned factory was operated entirely by Consolidated. The plant was completed in less than nine months, and the first B-24D rolled off the assembly line in April 1942.

Willow Run, on the other hand, was built and operated by the Ford Motor Company specifically to showcase the rapid production of Liberators using auto industry procedures. These were considered, especially by auto industry executives, to be more efficient than those of the aircraft industry. Indeed, Willow Run was of personal interest to the company founder, 78-year-old Henry Ford.

A much larger facility than the San Diego or Fort Worth plants, Willow Run attracted a great deal of media attention for its vast size and ambitious plans for the scale of production that was planned. The main building alone was the largest factory in the world under a single roof. It was 3,200 feet long with more than 2.5 million square feet of floor space—more than that of the prewar factories of Consolidated, Douglas, and Boeing combined.

When Willow Run opened in 1941, the *New York Sun* called it an "amazing bomber plant," and there was a flood of news reports telling of the flood of aircraft flowing from its doors. However, it was producing only subassemblies for other factories until 1942. The first complete finished aircraft was a B-24E in September 1942. During the

B-24E Liberators take shape on one of several assembly lines at Ford's big Willow Run factory near Ypsilanti, Michigan, in February 1943. Officially called Air Force Plant 31, but best known as "the Willow Run Bomber Plant," the complex included a main factory building that enclosed 2.5 million square feet. (Photo Courtesy National Archives)

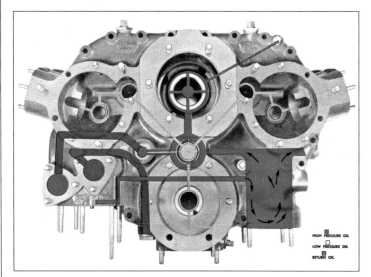

This schematic drawing shows the inner workings of the oiling system in the rear section of the Pratt & Whitney R-1830-43 and R-1830-65 Type C4G Twin Wasp engines.

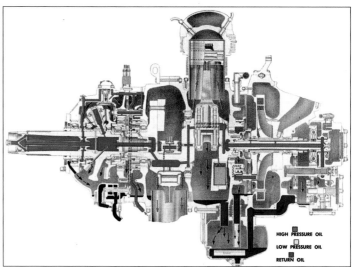

This schematic drawing shows the inner workings of the oiling system in the power and accessory section of the Pratt & Whitney R-1830-43 and R-1830-65 Type C4G Twin Wasp engines.

intervening year, there were considerable difficulties, including quality control, in adapting auto industry methods to building aircraft.

As David L. Lewis wrote in the September/October 1993 issue of *Michigan History* magazine, Willow Run in its first year was "in a state of turmoil as tools were received, fixtures set up, and supervisors and untrained employees tried coping with an alien undertaking. The task was aggravated by a severe housing shortage near the Willow Run vicinity and the length of time required—an hour or more each way—for Detroit workers to commute to and from their jobs . . . Willow Run's problems were ignored or glossed over in the hundreds of news stories and editorials about the huge plant in early 1942. Instead, the press dwelt on the size of the factory and the scope of its operations."

In the early years, the reality did not live up to the hype at Willow Run, but the increase in output was steady, During 1943, output increased from 31 Liberators in January to 190 in June and 365 in December.

Lewis wrote that "the plant entered a period of glory in 1944." The factory was running 24 hours a day, every day. The actual numbers were at last worthy of the promises of 1941. In April 1944, 100 bombers were produced in two days, most of them in two nine-hour shifts. The peak production month was August 1944, when 428 Liberators rolled out. It was calculated that a B-24 was delivered every 63 minutes. Willow Run's output in airframe weight was estimated to be half that of the entire aircraft industry of either Britain or Germany. Unit cost, meanwhile, went down. Lewis added that Ford could now "deliver Liberators to the government for $137,000 each in 1944, compared to $238,000 two years earlier."

By this time, however, the squadrons overseas that once had been starved for four-engine bombers, were becoming saturated.

In July 1943, photographer Jack Delano of the Office of War Information captured these USAAF Air Service Command technicians working on a Pratt & Whitney R-1830 Twin Wasp on the wing of a B-24 at Warner Robins Field in Georgia. (Photo Courtesy Library of Congress)

This is a left side view of the Pratt & Whitney R-1830-43/R-1830-65 Type C4G Twin Wasp engine.

Howard Hollem of the Office of War Information took this Kodachrome photograph of Ford workers installing a Pratt & Whitney R-1830-65 engine in a B-24E at Willow Run. (Photo Courtesy Library of Congress)

A recently-completed B-24E Liberator awaits its delivery flight at the Ford Willow Run Bomber Plant.

This B-24J-195-CO, the 5,000th Liberator built at the Consolidated San Diego plant was "autographed" by hundreds of factory workers and appropriately dubbed "V Grand." The aircraft later served in the Mediterranean with the USAAF Fifteenth Air Force.

This, and the desire of Hap Arnold and the USAAF command to focus production resources on the B-29 Superfortress, meant that Willow Run's production line slowed and never reached its estimated 650-unit monthly potential.

Official USAAF materiel Command records report that when the last Liberator moved off the assembly line on June 24, 1945, 6,792 completed aircraft had been built there, which was 36 percent of the overall total.

Variants and Their Powerplants

Large-scale mass production of the Liberator began with the B-24D, which was first ordered in August 1940 and first delivered in January 1942. Most of the Consolidated-built B-24Ds were manufactured in San Diego, while all of the similar Consolidated-built B-24Es were manufactured in Fort Worth.

Consolidated built 2,415 B-24D-COs in San Diego and completed 303 B-24D-CFs in Fort Worth. The latter factory rolled out 144

B-24E-CFs, while Douglas built 10 B-24D-DTs and 167 B-24E-DTs at Tulsa. The Ford factory in Willow Run came online with the B-24E, producing 490 aircraft. The Douglas aircraft were powered by Type C4G R-1830-43s, while those from Consolidated and Ford had the comparable Type C4G R-1830-65 installed.

The 430 examples of the B-24G variant were all built by North American Aviation in Dallas as the B-24G-NT. Initial production aircraft were equipped with the R-1830-43, but beginning with Block 10 and continuing through the end of production at Block 16, they were equipped with the R-1830-65.

The Stromberg PD-12F8/PD-12F12 injection carburetor is shown.

1. Boost Venturi Tube
2. Fuel Transfer Tube Mounting Flange
3. Automatic Rich Cut-out Valve
4. Manual Mixture Control Lever
5. Tube Assembly-Supercharger Pressures
6. Taper Seat Plug
7. Taper Seat Plug
8. Automatic Mixture Control Unit (This system responded to air pressure and temperature changes and automatically compensated for such changes, thus preventing natural enrichment at high altitudes.)
9. Vapor Vent Connections
10. Fuel Inlet (The fuel control unit contained fixed jets to limit the fuel flow

to provide the correct mixture at all airflows. As the airflow increased [throttle valve opened wider], the poppet valve opened wider, thus increasing the fuel pressure in the regulator which forced a greater flow through the fuel control unit and on to the fuel discharge nozzle.)
11. Primer Valve Fuel Line Connection
12. Throttle Balance (The throttle unit contained a throttle valve to control the airflow through the carburetor and venturi tube to measure the airflow.)
13. Fuel Strainer Assembly
14. Fuel Pressure Gauge Connection
15. Primer Valve Electrical Connection

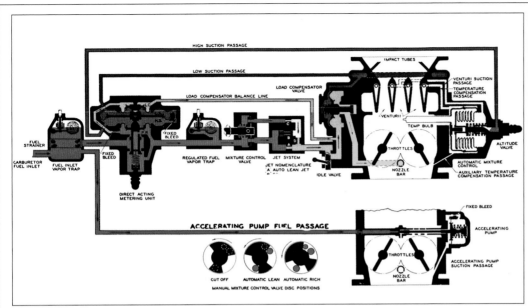

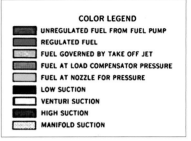

This schematic drawing shows the inner workings of the Chandler-Evans (CECO) Model 1900 CPB3-1 direct-metering carburetor installed and used in the Pratt & Whitney R-1830-65 engine. Its air meter measured airflow over the entire stream and therefore minimized the effect of air-scoop variations on the metering of the carburetor. A fuel metering unit was designed so that the fuel force against which the air forces act was equal to the metering head rather than the higher value that would result from using direct fuel inlet pressure alone.

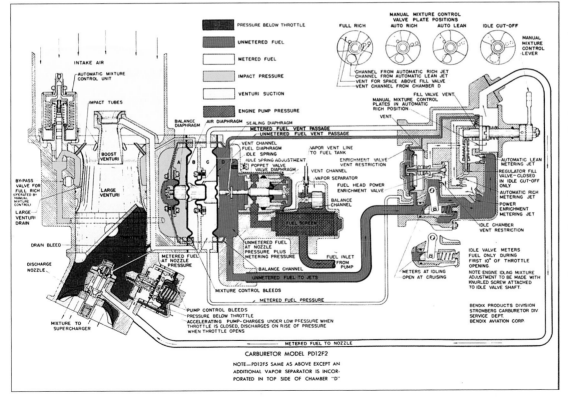

This schematic drawing shows the inner workings of the Stromberg PD-12F8-series injection carburetor used on the Pratt & Whitney R-1830-43 engine. It incorporated a "fuel head" enrichment valve, an automatic mixture control unit, and idle cut-off. A provision was made in the design of both carburetors for the attachment of the Stromberg electric primer valve, which was considered optional equipment. These carburetors were also equipped with a throttle balance, which reduced the tendency of the throttle valves to creep shut when the vacuum below the throttle valves was high.

Sporting their distinctive Emerson Nose Turrets, these Block 145 B-24J Liberators move down the assembly line at Consolidated's factory in San Diego. (Photo Courtesy SDASM)

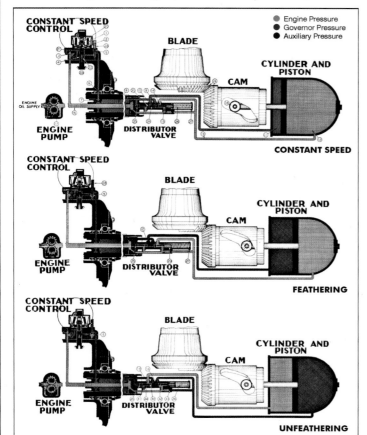

Powered by Pratt & Whitney R-1830-43 Twin Wasps, the C-87 Liberator Express was developed as the transport variant of the B-24D. Consolidated built 284 of them at Fort Worth.

The next very large mass-production run of Liberators came with the 3,100 aircraft of the B-24H series. This variant incorporated an Emerson Nose Turret and a retractable Sperry Ball Turret in the belly. Both of these features remained standard equipment in subsequent variants.

The R-1830-43 was installed in early B-24H production by Ford and by Consolidated in Fort Worth, but these two locations switched early to the R-1830-65. The Douglas factory in Tulsa used the R-1830-43 for all of its B-24H deliveries. The B-24J, as well as the B-24L and B-24M variants from all manufacturers, had the R-1830-65 with a B-22 supercharger installed.

More B-24Js, a total of 6,678, were built than any other Liberator variant. Of these, 2,792 were produced by Consolidated in San Diego and 1,558 in Fort Worth, with North American building 536. Ford, meanwhile, produced 1,587 complete aircraft at Willow Run as well as 205 unassembled kits for assembly by Douglas and 57 for assembly by Consolidated. Many of the B-24Js went to the Navy as PB4Y-1 Privateers.

This schematic drawing shows the inner workings of the propeller feathering systems of the Pratt & Whitney R-1830-43 and R-1830-65 Type C4G Twin Wasp engines.

1. Governor Flyweight
2. Governor Pilot Valve
3. Governor Pump
4. Hollow Driveshaft
5. Governor Cut-off Valve
6. Engine Shaft Oil Transfer Rings
7. Propeller Shaft Air Separator Plug
8. Propeller Shaft Oil Passage
9. Distributor Valve Port
10. Distributor Valve Port
11. Propeller Cylinder—Inboard End
12. Propeller Cylinder—Outboard End
13. Oil Supply Tube—Outboard Cylinder End
14. Distributor Valve Port
15. Distributor Valve Port
16. Engine Oil Pressure Supply Tube
17. Engine Pump Relief Valve
18. Cam Slot Rollers
19. Bevel Gears
20. Governor Control Spring
21. Governor Relief Valve
22. Governor Drain Port
23. Governor Drive Gear
24. Propeller Distributor Valve
25. Propeller Distributor Valve
26. Distributor Valve Spring
27. Distributor Valve Spring Housing
28. External High Pressure Oil Line
29. Distributor Valve (Outboard End)
30. Distributor Valve Land
31. Distributor Valve Port
32. Distributor Valve Land
33. Dome Pressure Relief Valve

The single-tail US Navy PB4Y-2 Privateer patrol bomber was powered by four Pratt & Whitney R-1830-94 engines. Consolidated delivered 977 twin-tailed PB4Y-1s that were produced under USAAF B-24D orders. The 736 PB4Y-2s were delivered directly to the US Navy.

The Consolidated PBY-3 was powered by a pair of Pratt & Whitney R-1830-66 Twin Wasps, delivering 900 hp at 10,000 feet.

The B-24L and B-24M variants, the last mass-produced Liberators, were distinguished from their predecessors by revised tail armament. The B-24L had a handheld .50-caliber mount, while the B-24M incorporated the lightweight Consolidated A-6B turret. This armament was installed at modification centers rather than at the factories.

Of the secondary manufacturing sources, only Ford participated in B-24L and B-24M production. Beginning in July 1944, Consolidated produced 417 B-24Ls in San Diego, with 1,250 coming from Willow Run. With deliveries starting in October 1944, Consolidated produced 916 B-24Ms in San Diego, while Ford manufactured 1,677. The last B-24M delivery, marking an end to Liberator production, came at San Diego in June 1945. By this time, Ford had tooled up to build the single-tail B-24N, but with the war coming to a close, only seven were produced.

The US Navy, meanwhile, ordered 660 single-tail PB4Y-2 Privateers powered by 1,350-hp R-1830-94 engines. After a first delivery in March 1944, the Navy sought to augment its fleet with a 710-ship second order in October 1944. The entire first batch was delivered, but only 76 of the latter were delivered when the second order was canceled.

R-1830-43, R-1830-65, and Their Carburetors

As seen earlier, two similar variants of supercharged Pratt & Whitney Type C4G Twin Wasp engines were used in the production of the mass-produced Liberators beginning with the B-24D and

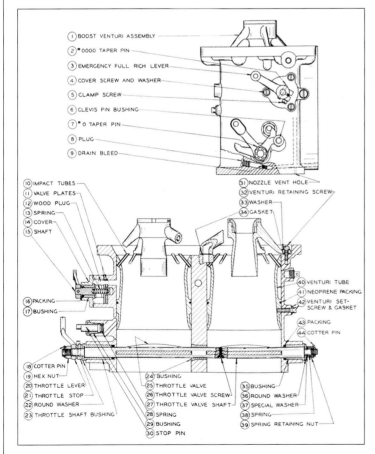

1. BOOST VENTURI ASSEMBLY
2. 0000 TAPER PIN
3. EMERGENCY FULL RICH LEVER
4. COVER SCREW AND WASHER
5. CLAMP SCREW
6. CLEVIS PIN BUSHING
7. 0 TAPER PIN
8. PLUG
9. DRAIN BLEED
10. IMPACT TUBES
11. VALVE PLATES
12. WOOD PLUG
13. SPRING
14. COVER
15. SHAFT
16. PACKING
17. BUSHING
18. COTTER PIN
19. HEX NUT
20. THROTTLE LEVER
21. THROTTLE STOP
22. ROUND WASHER
23. THROTTLE SHAFT BUSHING
24. BUSHING
25. THROTTLE VALVE
26. THROTTLE VALVE SCREW
27. THROTTLE VALVE SHAFT
28. SPRING
29. BUSHING
30. STOP PIN
31. NOZZLE VENT HOLE
32. VENTURI RETAINING SCREW
33. WASHER
34. GASKET
35. BUSHING
36. ROUND WASHER
37. SPECIAL WASHER
38. SPRING
39. SPRING RETAINING NUT
40. VENTURI TUBE
41. NEOPRENE PACKING
42. VENTURI SET-SCREW & GASKET
43. PACKING
44. COTTER PIN

This schematic drawing shows the inner workings of the throttle body assembly for the Pratt & Whitney R-1830-43 and R-1830-65 Type C4G Twin Wasp engines.

continuing through the B-24M. Both the R-1830-43 and R-1830-65 engines were rated at 1,200 hp and differed primarily in the type of carburetor that was used.

Another distinction with little difference between the R-1830-43 and R-1830-65 came with the 1830-43A and R-1830-65A designations. Again, the types were essentially the same, with the "A" suffix or lack thereof denoting the engine manufacturer. The 1830-43 designation identified an engine produced by Pratt & Whitney itself, while the R-1830-43A was produced by Buick or Chevrolet. To add to the complexity, Buick built both R-1830-65s and R-1830-65As, while Chevrolet manufactured R-1830-65As almost exclusively.

The use of the "A" suffix appears only in some (not all) technical documents and is not used in most general descriptions of the aircraft and engines. To avoid confusion, this convention is used in this book.

With its Pratt & Whitney R-1830-92 Twin Wasps generating 1,200 hp for takeoff, a Consolidated PBY-5 Catalina flying boat accelerates through the ocean spray.

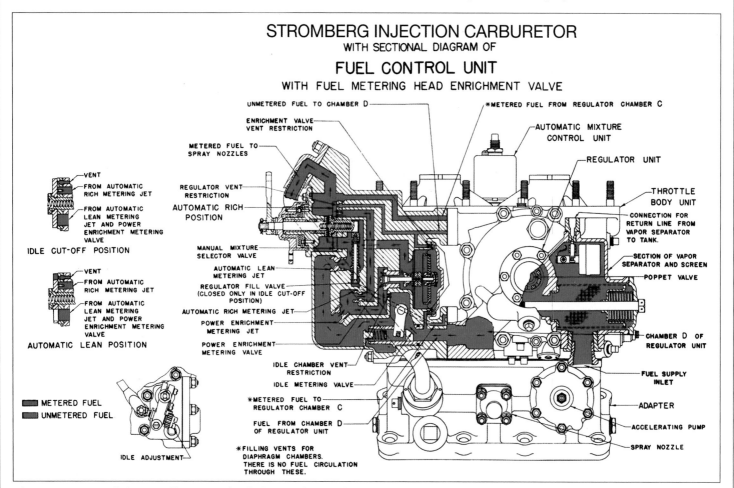

This 1944 sectional drawing illustrates the fuel control unit of the Stromberg PD-12F-series injection carburetor with the fuel metering head enrichment valve.

The R-1830-43 used the Stromberg Model PD-12F–series carburetor. As with the Stromberg PD-12K–series carburetors used in the Wright R-1820 Cyclone of the B-17, the PD prefix indicated a "double-barrel" carburetor.

Based in South Bend, Indiana, Stromberg was an original component of the Bendix Corporation, founded by inventor and auto parts maker Vincent Hugo Bendix in 1929. Ranked 17th among United States corporations in the value of wartime production contracts, Bendix moved its headquarters from South Bend to Detroit in 1942. In technical literature, the Stromberg component was occasionally, though not always, identified as "Bendix-Stromberg." Most of the time, it was simply "Stromberg," and this convention is used.

In 1942, the production urgency of the R-1830 and the B-24 programs led the USAAF Materiel Command to bring in a second source in the production of carburetors, and the R-1830-65 used the Model 1900 CPB-3 (also written as CPB3) carburetor from Chandler-Evans (CECO).

The lineage of Stromberg and Chandler-Evans was intertwined. Milton Chandler began his career as an engineer with the Stromberg Motor Devices in 1929 and had his name on carburetor patents by 1933. When Stromberg was acquired by Bendix, Chandler became vice president in charge of all carburetor engineering in a corporate division known as Bendix-Stromberg Carburetor. However, he had left the company in 1935 to go out on his own. Another twist in the intertwining of companies was that Milton Chandler had secured investment capital from Niles-Bement-Pond (the parent company of Pratt & Whitney) when he joined with Edward Evans of the Evans Appliance Company in 1938 to form CECO.

Both the PD-12F and the Model 1900 CPB-3 carburetors, like those of most high-performance American aircraft of the time, especially combat aircraft, were floatless pressure carburetors. This type utilizes pressure, rather than gravity, and can therefore operate when an aircraft is in any attitude, including upside down.

While float-type carburetors have a float chamber vented to atmosphere, the pressure ones had a closed system from the engine-driven fuel pump to the fuel discharge nozzle. The carburetor discharges fuel under positive pump pressure into the air stream to provide a combustible mixture to the engine. The components of this carburetor type were coordinated to measure and control the air and fuel flow to the engine to maintain the correct predetermined air-to-fuel ratio throughout the entire range of operation.

These carburetors can be considered a mechanical ancestor to modern electronic fuel control computers.

The Stromberg PD-12F8 and PD-12F12 injection carburetors used on the R-1830-43 engines incorporated a "fuel head" enrichment valve, an automatic mixture control unit, and idle cut-off. A provision was made in the design

OIL FROM SEL. VALVE

DRAIN

DRAIN OIL FROM LOW CLUTCH

OIL TO HIGH CLUTCH

ENGINE OIL PRESSURE

PART OF MAIN CIRCULATING SYSTEM–NOT FOR CLUTCH OPERATION.

DRAIN OIL TO SEL. VALVE WHEN SHIFTED FROM LOW TO HIGH CLUTCH

① HIGH RATIO CLUTCH
② BLOWER INTERMEDIATE DRIVE PINION.
③ MAGNETO DRIVE PINION
④ ACCESSORY DRIVE GEAR
⑤ IMPELLER SHAFT
⑥ ACCESSORY DRIVE SHAFT
⑦ LOW RATIO CLUTCH
⑧ CLUTCH SELECTOR VALVE
⑨ PISTON GUIDE
⑩ CHECK VALVE

HIGH PRESSURE OIL
LOW PRESSURE OIL
DRAIN OIL

The R-1830 impeller ratio selector valve incorporated a control lever and linkage, piston, housing, and housing cover. The valve housing, which accommodated the piston, was installed in a large bore in the intermediate rear case. Oil ports were provided in the valve housing, in the hole in the intermediate rear case, and in the shaft, which was integral with the piston. The location of the ports in the piston shaft with respect to those in the valve housing and bore were governed by the position of the piston, as regulated by the control lever and linkage. Manual operation of the control lever would cause the piston to move into either the high-ratio position or the low-ratio position. The selector valve directs engine pressure oil to a chamber between the gear and the cone of the clutch for the particular gear ratio selected. The pressure oil causes the cone to engage segments which, in turn, engage the gear. The selector valve was mounted in the upper left side of the intermediate rear case.

Seen here sporting prewar markings, the Consolidated PB2Y-2 Coronado was powered by four Pratt & Whitney R-1830-78 Twin Wasps.

of both carburetors for the attachment of the Stromberg electric primer valve, which was considered optional equipment.

The Stromberg carburetors were also equipped with a throttle balance, which reduced the tendency of the throttle valves to creep shut when the vacuum below the throttle valves was high. The only variation between the PD-12F8 and the PD-12F12 was that the latter had a throttle actuated accelerating pump that was installed on the center of the regulator unit.

The Chandler-Evans Model 1900 CPB-3 direct-metering carburetor was fully automatic and incorporated several innovative features. The company noted that it was "designed to give every possible consideration to durability, ease of maintenance and simplicity of calibration."

The air meter of the Model 1900 measured airflow over the entire stream and therefore minimized the effect of air scoop variations on the metering of the carburetor. A fuel metering unit was designed so that the fuel force against which the air forces acted was equal to the "metering head" rather than the higher value that would result from using direct fuel inlet pressure alone. In the November 1943 instructional manual for R-1830-43 and R-1830-65 engines, the term "metering head" is defined as "the force tending to close the valve [i.e.] Regulator pressure minus load compensator pressure."

These detail drawings illustrate three of the fuel pumps that were specified for incorporation into Pratt & Whitney R-1830-43 and R-1830-65 Type C4G Twin Wasp engines. Clockwise from top left, these were produced by the Chandler-Evans Company (CECO), Romec (later Lear Romec), and Pesco. The sequence indicated on the Romec drawing included the following: (A) A blade end in the displacement area is forced centrifugally against the rocker seal. (B) The mechanical force of the revolving rotor maintains a close fit of the blade and rocker as fuel pressure of the blade holds the rocker against the bore wall. (C) When passing the discharge port, hydraulic discharge pressure helps force the blade toward the inlet side. (D) The rocker maintains continuous contact with the bore wall. (E) The pump operates in either direction of rotation. In the clockwise rotation seen here, (H) is the inlet and (G) is the discharge.

With one of its Pratt & Whitney R-1830 Twin Wasps roaring to life, this PBY Catalina flying boat was photographed by Howard Hollem of the Office of War Information at Naval Air Station Corpus Christi in August 1942.

Fuel was pumped to the carburetor and into the inlet chamber at a pressure of 15 to 18 pounds. The inlet chamber was provided with a vapor trap that automatically liberated all vapor as the fuel then flowed through the fuel-regulator valve, the action of which was controlled by the three diaphragms in the metering unit. From the fuel-regulator valve, fuel flowed through a second vapor trap to the passage leading to the fuel mixture control. Holes in the mixture control disc were indexed with passages to the jets. If an engine used a constant mixture strength for all operating conditions, one jet would be sufficient, but it did not, so it was necessary to arrange a system using four jets.

As Chandler-Evans noted in its own literature, the Model 1900 Carburetor was "non-icing to the extent that was had no inherent tendency to create an icing condition."

The Catalina

In excess of 3,200 PBY Catalina flying boat patrol bombers were produced, which was more than any other Consolidated aircraft except the Liberator/Privateer family. The direct predecessor of the PBY was the XP2Y-1 Ranger, which was introduced in March 1932, but Consolidated already had a long history in flying boats. The Ranger was a sesquiplane—a biplane with one wing much shorter than the other. In the case of the P2Y, the top wing was similar to the high parasol wing familiar on the PBY, while the lower wing was very small. A total of 23 P2Y-1s and 23 P2Y-3s were delivered through May 1935, mainly to the US Navy. All were powered by Wright R-1820 Cyclone variants.

The Catalina first flew in March 1935 under the XP3D-1 designation, but given that the Navy had decided to use it as a long-range patrol bomber (rather than merely a patrol aircraft), the designation was changed to XPBY-1. The prototype was powered by a pair of 825-hp

Pratt & Whitney R-1830-58 radials, while the initial production-series PBY-1 and PBY-2 used R-1830-64 Twin Wasps rated at 900 hp for takeoff and 850 hp at 8,000 feet. There were 60 and 50 examples, respectively, of these variants.

The 66 PBY-3s were equipped with R-1830-66 Twin Wasps that delivered 1,050 hp at takeoff and 900 hp at 10,000 feet. The 33 Catalinas of the PBY-4 series had R-1830-72s rated at 1,050 hp at takeoff and 900 hp at 10,000 feet.

The PBY-5 was the definitive Catalina variant, being launched in December 1939 with an order for 200 aircraft, but this number, large for the time, would be dwarfed by things to come. Meanwhile, Consolidated received export orders for another 174 Catalinas to be delivered to Britain, France, Australia, and Canada.

Deliveries of PBY-5s and export Model 28-5Ms began in October 1940, with the US Navy aircraft equipped with R-1830-82 engines delivering 1,200 hp for takeoff and 1,050 hp at 5,700 feet. The export variants used the similar, commercially designated R-1830-S1C3G engines. Midway through PBY-5 production, the R-1830-92 engine was substituted.

The R-1830-92, rated at 1,200 hp for takeoff and 1,050 hp at 7,000 feet, was also used to power the PBY-5A and PBY-6As, which differed from earlier Catalinas in that they were fully amphibious, with tricycle landing gear to allow them to operate from runways. There were 803 PBY-5As and 332 PBY-6As produced.

The Navy's own Naval Aircraft Factory in Philadelphia used the R-1830-92 for its PBN-1, a Catalina variant with a redesigned tail, of which 155 were built.

Company records list a total of 3,281 Catalinas. Of these, Consolidated built 2,159 in San Diego, 235 in New Orleans and 1 in Buffalo. Among the remainder, Boeing Aircraft of Canada built 362 in Vancouver as PB2B-1s, and Canadian Vickers produced 369 in Montreal as PBV-1s. The Catalinas that served with the USAAF as OA-10s were all ordered under Navy serial numbers. There were 56 OA-10s ordered as PBY-5As, and 230 PBV-1As that became OA-10As.

The Coronado

Consolidated's four-engine Coronado (Model 29), which was slightly bigger than its twin-engine Catalina, was among a generation of four-engine, long-range flying boat types commissioned by the US Navy on the cusp of World War II. Others included the famous Martin PB2M Mars, which was equipped with four Wright R-3350s (see Chapter 13).

The Consolidated XPB2Y-1 made is debut flight in December 1937, and in 1939, it entered service as an executive transport, flying between California and Pearl Harbor. The first of only six PB2Y-2 production aircraft was finally delivered in December 1940, although the type was not in regular service until the end of 1941.

Beginning in June 1942, Consolidated delivered 210 examples of the PB2Y-3, which was the principal production type. Of these, 33 were set aside for the RAF as Coronado GR.I, although only 10 were actually delivered to the RAF.

The prototype XPB2Y-1 was powered by the same engine that Consolidated would use for the PBY-4, this being the Pratt & Whitney R-1830-72, which was rated at 1,050 hp at takeoff and 900 hp at 10,000 feet.

The PB2Y-2 used the R-1830-78, which delivered 1,200 hp at takeoff and 1,000 hp at 19,000 feet, while the first 169 PB2Y-3 production-series aircraft were equipped with the similar R-1830-88, which delivered 1,200 hp at takeoff and 1,000 hp at 19,500 feet.

As with all previous Coronados, the last 41 PB2Y-3s were built by Consolidated, but they were completed by the Rohr Aircraft Corporation in Chula Vista (12 miles away in San Diego Bay) and designated as PB2Y-3R. Rohr installed R-1830-92 engines, delivering 1,200 hp at takeoff and 1,000 hp at 7,000 feet.

There were two minor re-engined Coronado variants. The XPB2Y-4 variant was a single PB2Y-2 that was re-engined with four Wright R-2600 Twin Cyclones, while the PB2Y-5 designation went to several PB3Y-3s that had their R-1830-92s augmented by rocket-assisted takeoff equipment.

After the Liberator, Catalina, and Coronado, the next major large aircraft program from Consolidated was the Model 33/34 Dominator, which was powered by the Wright R-3350 (see Chapters 12 and 13).

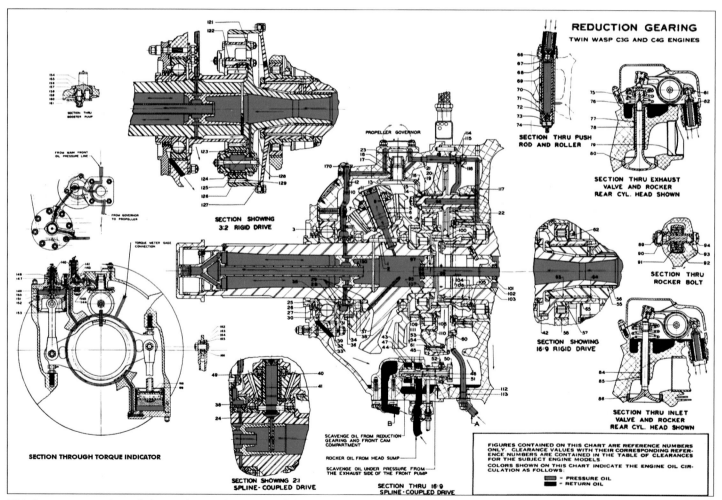

This is a cutaway view of the R-1830-43/R-1830-65 lubrication system and reduction gearing (October 1943).

1. Reduction Drive Pinion Shaft Retaining Pin—Propeller Shaft
2. Reduction Drive Pinion Shaft—Propeller Shaft
3. Governor Oil Transfer Pipe—Reduction Drive Fixed Gear Anchor
4. Reduction Drive Pinion Backlash—Reduction Drive Fixed Gear, and Reduction Drive Gear
5. Reduction Drive Pinion Bushing—Pinion
6. Reduction Drive Pinion Bushing—Pinion Shaft
7. Reduction Drive Pinion Thrust Bearing—Pinion
8. [Omitted]
9. Reduction Drive Pinion Shaft Oil Plug—Pinion Shaft
10. Governor Oil Transfer Upper Pipe—Governor Oil Transfer Lower Pipe
11. Reduction Drive Pinion Shaft—Pinion Cage
12. Governor Oil Transfer Pipe—Reduction Gear Housing
13. Reduction Drive Pinion—Pinion Cage
14. Governor Intermediate Drive Gear Splines—Front Cam Reduction Gear Splines
15. Governor Intermediate Drive Gear End Clearance
16. Governor Drive Gear Backlash—Governor Intermediate Drive Gear
17. Governor Drive Gear Bushing—Reduction Gear Housing
18. Governor Drive Gear Bushing—Governor Drive Gear
19. Front Cam Reduction Gear Front Bushing
20. Front Cam Reduction Gear Bushing—Support Plate
21. Governor Oil Feed Pipe—Reduction Gear Housing
22. Front Cam Reduction Gear Backlash—Front Cam
23. Governor Drive Gear Snap Ring Side Clearance
24. Reduction Drive Pinion Shaft Retaining Pin—Propeller Shaft
25. Propeller Shaft Thrust Bearing Oil Seal Ring Gap
26. Propeller Shaft Thrust Bearing Oil Seal Ring Side Clearance
27. Propeller Shaft Thrust Bearing Cover Liner—Cover
28. Propeller Shaft Thrust Bearing—Propeller Shaft
29. Governor Oil Transfer Seal Ring Carrier and Spacers Propeller Shaft
30. Propeller Shaft Thrust Bearing Spacer Pinch—Thrust Bearing Cover
31. Governor Oil Transfer Seal Ring Gap
32. Propeller Shaft Thrust Bearing Liner—Thrust Bearing Liner
33. Propeller Shaft Thrust Bearing Liner—Reduction Gear
34. Reduction Dive Fixed Gear Anchor Liner
35. Governor Oil Transfer Seal Ring Side Clearance
36. Reduction Drive Fixed Gear Anchor Splines—Fixed Gear Splines
37. Reduction Drive Fixed Gear Bearing—Propeller Shaft
37. Reduction Drive Gear Bearing—Propeller Shaft
38. Reduction Drive Fixed Gear Bearing—Fixed Gear (and Reduction Drive Gear Bearing—Drive Gear)
39. Reduction Drive Fixed Gear Anchor—Thrust Bearing Liner
40. Reduction Drive Pinion Thrust Bearing—Pinion
41. Reduction Drive Fixed Gear Liner—Fixed Gear (and Reduction Drive Gear Liner—Drive Gear)
42. Reduction Drive Gear Splines—Reduction Drive Gear Coupling Splines
43. Oil Scavenge Pump Gear End Clearance
44. Oil Scavenge Pump Gear Backlash
45. Oil Scavenge Pump Gear and Gear Shaft Keys
46. Oil Scavenge Pump Drive and Idler Gear Shafts—Oil Scavenge Pump Body Sections
47. Oil Scavenge Pump Gears—Oil Scavenge Pump Body Sections
48. Oil Scavenge Pump Drive Gear Shaft—Oil Pump Gears
49. Reduction Drive Pinion Thrust Bearing—Pinion Bushing
50. Oil Scavenge Pump Drive Gear Backlash—Intermediate Drive Gear
51. Oil Scavenge Pump Drive Gear End Clearance
52. Oil Scavenge Pump Rear Body—Support Plate
53. Oil Scavenge Pump Intermediate Drive Gear Bushing Support Plate
54. Oil Scavenge Pump Intermediate Drive Gear Bushing Gear
55. Propeller Shaft Rear Bearing—Crankshaft
56. Propeller Shaft Rear Bearing—Propeller Shaft
57. Reduction Drive Gear Coupling Bearing—Coupling
58. Reduction Drive Gear Coupling Bearing—Liner
59. Reduction Drive Gear Coupling Bearing Liner—Support Plate
60. Oil Scavenge Pump Intermediate Drive Gear Backlash Cam
61. Oil Scavenge Pump Intermediate Drive Gear End Clearance
62. Front Cam Reduction Gear Backlash—Crankshaft Front Gear
63. Reduction Drive Gear Coupling Splines—Crankshaft Splines
64. Crankshaft Front Gear Splines—Crankshaft Splines
65. Crankshaft Front Gear—Reduction Drive Gear Coupling
66. Push Rod Ball End-Socket
67. Valve Tappet Ball Socket—Tappet
68. Valve Tappet Guide Outer End—Crankcase
69. Valve Tappet—Valve Tappet Guide Outer End
69. Valve Tappet—Valve Tappet Guide Inner End
70. Valve Tappet Guide Inner End—Crankcase
71. Valve Tappet Roller Side Clearance—Valve Guide
72. Valve Tappet Roller Pin—Roller
73. Valve Tappet Roller Pin—Tappet
74. Valve Tappet Roller Side Clearance—Tappet
75. Inlet and Exhaust Valve Inner Spring Pressure at 1.5 inches/92 pounds max
76. Inlet and Exhaust Valve Outer Spring Pressure at 1.5 inches/102 pounds max
77. Exhaust Valve Guide—Valve
78. Exhaust Valve Guide—Cylinder Head
79. Exhaust Port Liner—Cylinder Head
80. Exhaust Valve Seat—Cylinder Head
81. Rocker Ball Socket—Rocker
82. Push Rod Ball End—Push Rod
83. [Omitted]
84. Inlet Valve Guide—Valve
85. Inlet Valve Guide—Cylinder Head
86. Inlet Valve Seat —Cylinder Head
89. Rocker Shaft Large Bushing—Cylinder Head
90. Rocker Shaft Large Bushing—Rocker Shaft
91. Rocker Bearing Rocker
92. Rocker Bearing Rocker Shaft
93. Rocker Shaft Small Bushing—Cylinder Head
94. Rocker Shaft Small Bushing—Rocker Shaft
95. Propeller Shaft Rear Bearing Spacer—Propeller Shaft
96. Propeller Shaft Rear Plug—Propeller Shaft
97. Propeller Shaft Rear Plug Oil Seal—Plug
98. Crankshaft to Propeller Shaft Oil Transfer Pipe Propeller Shaft Rear Plug
99. Reduction Drive Front Coupling Splines—Intermediate Coupling Splines
100. Front Cam Reduction Gear Backlash—Reduction Drive Intermediate Coupling
101. Crankshaft Front Plug Oil Seal—Plug
102. Crankshaft to Propeller Shaft Oil Transfer Pipe Crankshaft Front Plug
103. Crankshaft Front Plug—Crankshaft
104. Reduction Drive Rear Coupling—Crankshaft
105. Reduction Drive Rear Coupling Splines—Intermediate Coupling Splines
106. Reduction Drive Rear Coupling Splines—Crankshaft Splines
107. Propeller Shaft Rear Bearing—Propeller Shaft
108. Reduction Drive Front Coupling Bearing—Coupling
109. Propeller Shaft Rear Bearing Reduction Drive Front Coupling
110. Reduction Drive Front Coupling Bearing—Liner
111. Reduction Drive Gear Splines Front Coupling Splines
112. Front Main Crankcase Oil Transfer Pipe—Liner
113. Front Main Crankcase Oil Transfer Pipe Liner Crankcase
114. Governor Oil Feed Pipe—Bracket
115. Front Cam Bearing Oil Feed Pipe—Bracket
116. Front Main Crankcase Oil Transfer Pipe—Bracket
117. Front Cam Bearing Oil Feed Pipe—Crankcase
118–120. [Omitted]
121. Reduction Drive Pinion Cage—Propeller Shaft
122. Reduction Drive Pinion Cage Bolts—Cage
123. Reduction Drive Pinion End Clearance
124. Reduction Drive Pinion Shaft—Propeller Shaft and Pinion Cage
125. Reduction Drive Pinion Bushing—Pinion Shaft
126. Reduction Drive Pinion Bushing—Pinion
127. Reduction Drive Gear—Hub
128. Reduction Drive Pinion Backlash—Fixed Gear
129. Reduction Drive Pinion Backlash—Drive Gear
130. Propeller Oil Feed Pipe Rear Support—Pipe
131–139. [Omitted]
140. Booster Pump Relief Valve Spring Pressure and Torque Indicator Piston Bleed Valve Spring Pressure at 1.4375 inches/21 pounds max
141. Booster Pump Relief Valve—Pump Cover
142. [Omitted]
143. Booster Pump Cover Aligning Pin—Pump Body
144. Booster Pump Body Aligning Pin—Pump Body
145. Booster Pump Drive Gear Backlash—Intermediate Drive Gear
146. Torque Indicator Piston Bleed Valve—Valve Sleeve
147. Torque Indicator Piston Bleed Valve Sleeve Upper Cylinder Cover
149. Torque Indicator Cylinder Oil Transfer Thimble Cylinder Cover
150. Torque Indicator Cylinder Liner—Reduction Gear Housing
151. Torque Indicator Piston Cylinder Liner
152. Torque Indicator Piston Ring Gap
153. Torque Indicator Piston Ring Side Clearance
154. Booster Pump Cover—Reduction Gear Housing
155. Booster Pump Gear Backlash
156. Booster Pump Cover Reduction Gear Housing
157. Booster Pump Gear End Clearance
158. Booster Pump Gears Pump Body
159. Booster Pump Body Reduction Gear Housing
160. Booster Pump Drive and Idler Gear Shafts Body and Cover
161. Booster Pump Drive Gear Splines—Drive Gear Shaft Splines
162. Connecting Rod Bushing Torque Arm
163. Connecting Rod Bushing—Bushing Collar
164. Connecting Rod Bushing Collar Rod Bolt
165. Connecting Rod—Rod Bolt
166. Connecting Rod End Clearance
167. [Omitted]
168. Torque Indicator Piston Pin and Connecting Rod
169. Torque Indicator Piston Pin Plug Pin
170. Governor Oil Transfer Pipe Projection—Reduction Gear Housing

Chapter 5

ROUND ENGINES AT DOUGLAS: ROUND ONE

If there was one individual who stood out among the captains of American aircraft industry in the early 1940s, it was Donald Wills Douglas. In 1941, *Fortune* magazine wrote that "the development of the airplane in the days between the wars [the DC-3 transport] is the greatest engineering story there ever was, and in the heart of it is Donald Douglas."

Donald Wills Douglas, himself, had started his career at MIT, where he graduated two years ahead of schedule in 1914. Having worked for Glenn Martin, whose Los Angeles company was already one of America's premier airplane builders, Douglas struck out on his own in 1920. He built a wide variety of single-engine biplanes at his Santa Monica, California, factory before achieving global notoriety in 1924. In that year, his Douglas World Cruisers (DWC) became the first aircraft to completely circumnavigate the world. Under the power of World War I–vintage Liberty 12-cylinder inline engines, the 25,553-mile trip took six months.

The Douglas Aircraft Company was one of the largest producers of military aircraft in the world during World War II. The firm

A test pilot works his way through his checklist before a flight in an SBD-4 Dauntless dive bomber at the Douglas Aircraft plant in El Segundo, California, circa 1943. Both the SBD-3 and SBD-4 used Wright Aeronautical R-1820-52 Cyclones, but the SBD-4 had the Hamilton Standard propellers seen here. Note the bomb-slinging trapeze beneath the forward fuselage.

These are rows of new, recently delivered Pratt & Whitney R-1830 Twin Wasp engines on the factory floor of the Douglas Aircraft Company plant in Long Beach, California. (Photo Courtesy Douglas)

was first in total airframe weight, accounting for 15.3 percent of all American production, which was just ahead of Consolidated with 14.6 percent. With a total of 30,980 individual aircraft produced, Douglas was second only to North American Aviation, whose Mustangs, Mitchells, and AT-6/SNJ family of trainers (see Chapter 7) brought its total to 41,839.

Douglas operated California factories at Santa Monica (its headquarters), El Segundo, and Long Beach. Before the war was over, the company was operating at government-financed inland locations near Oklahoma City, Tulsa, and Chicago. Between 1940 and 1943, the Douglas workforce increased from 8,000 to nearly 170,000 in California alone, accounting for just over half of the aviation workforce in a state that accounted for around 2 out of every 5 pounds of finished American airframe weight.

Douglas aircraft used a variety of radial engines, and the first wartime generation was split mainly between the Wright R-1820 Cyclone and the Pratt & Whitney R-1830 Twin Wasp. This is the focus of the present chapter.

Douglas Military Transports

Although they were not combat aircraft, so many of the surviving examples of the legendary Douglas transports were built for military applications that they occupy an integral niche in the warbird legacy. Hence, they must be included in this book.

In the 1930s, Douglas completely revolutionized commercial air travel with the DC-2/DST/DC-3 series of large twin-engine monoplane propliners. However, by 1945, roughly 9 out of 10 of the aircraft in this lineage had been built as military aircraft.

One lone DC-1 first flew in 1933, and the DC-2 (essentially the production version of the DC-1) followed in 1934. The Douglas Skysleeper Transport (DST) first flew on December 17, 1935, and was designated as the DC-3 when configured as a day-use, non-sleeper. It offered luxury and reliability that could not have been imagined only a few years before. Beginning with the first flight of the DST and initial airline deliveries in 1936, Douglas produced 607 members of its revolutionary DST/DC-3 family of airliners for the civilian market.

Even before World War II began, the US Army Air Corps (USAAF after June 22, 1941) and the US Navy started to acquire DC-2s and DC-3s to satisfy their needs for transport aircraft.

The great California factories of the Douglas Aircraft Company were a hub of activity during World War II. A visit to Santa Monica, El Segundo, and Long Beach might involve watching the installation of R-1820s or R-2600s from Wright Aeronautical or Pratt & Whitney R-1830s or R-2000s. This woman, employed at Long Beach, was one of 167,000 Californians working for Douglas. (Photo Courtesy Library of Congress)

Donald Wills Douglas was an aviation pioneer and entrepreneur who came to preside over one of the largest and most successful aircraft manufacturing firms in the world. During World War II, his Douglas Aircraft Company had a greater output (measured in total airframe weight) than any other planemaker in the United States.

The 156 commercial DC-2s were powered by Wright Cyclone radials with variants ranging from the R-1820-F2 with 720 hp to the R-1820-F53 with 770 hp. Designated as DC-2As, two aircraft flew with two Pratt & Whitney R-1690-S2EG Hornets, and another pair

By 1943, Donald Wills Douglas (second from left cracking a joke) was one of the most important captains of industry in California. To his left, California Governor Earl Warren looks at Douglas admiringly. On Douglas's right is Frederic Warren "Ted" Conant, senior vice president at the Douglas Aircraft Company. Across the table is Ava Michael "Rocky" Rochlen, a former Los Angeles newspaper man who created the first public relations department for Douglas. During World War II, Rochlen served as director of industrial relations.

A pair of Pratt & Whitney R-1830-92 Twin Wasps roars to life as this Douglas C-47 is prepped for its delivery flight. It can be identified as a C-47 because the air scoop atop the nacelle is at the leading edge of the cowling. In the C-47A, it would be moved aft of the cowling.

was delivered to LOT Airlines in Poland with British-made 750-hp Bristol Pegasus VI radial engines.

A number of DC-2s served with the USAAF. One was factory-built as a 14-seat executive transport. Designated as XC-32, it was powered by a pair of 750-hp Wright R-1820-25 Cyclones. After World War II began, two dozen commercial DC-2s were commandeered under the designation C-32A. Two additional executive transports, analogous to the XC-32, were built for Secretary of War Henry Stimson's staff and designated as C-34s.

Meanwhile, 18 DC-2s were factory-built with R-1820-25s as transports for the Air Corps. Designated as C-33s, these had reinforced floors and large cargo doors.

Modifications involving combined DC-2 and DC-3 components resulted in several designations. The first one was a C-33 retrofitted with a DC-3-type tail section and 975-hp Wright R-1820-45 engines. Its designation changed several times: from C-33A to C-38 to C-39. A production series of 35 additional C-39s was built as 16-seat personnel transports with 975-hp Wright R-1820-55 engines.

The US Navy acquired five DC-2s under the designation R2D-1. These were powered by 710-hp R-1820-12 Cyclones.

The C-41 and C-42 designations lay on the cusp of the DC-2/DC-3 transition. The C-41 was a single C-39 hybrid that was re-engined with 1,200-hp Wright R-1820-21 Cyclone engines. The C-41A designation went to two DC-3 airframes that were powered by Pratt & Whitney R-1830-21 Twin Wasps and were 23-seat executive transports. The C-42 designation was assigned to three executive transport C-39s: one delivered in 1939 for use by the chief of the Army Air Corps, General Hap Arnold; and later, to two converted from C-39s in 1943.

Like the DC-2 (but unlike the later Twin Wasp–powered military DC-3 derivatives), the commercial DC-3s were powered by geared (rather than direct drive) variants of the G-series Wright Cyclone engines.

In 1935, the first DST was powered by the Wright SGR-1820-G5, rated at 1,000 hp for takeoff and 850 hp at 1,770 feet. A similar rating applied to the SGR-1830-G2 and SGR-1830-G2E engines that were installed in early-production DSTs and DC-3s.

The improved G100-series Cyclone engines that were introduced in 1937 offered a compression ratio increased from 6.45:1 to 6.7:1 plus improved cylinder cooling. In DC-3 production, these included the SGR-1830-G102A with a rating of 1,100 hp for takeoff and 900 hp at 6,700 feet.

In 1939, the G200-series Cyclones increased the cooling area of 2,800 square inches per cylinder to 3,500 inches. The SGR-1820-G202A Cyclone delivered 1,200 hp for takeoff and 1,050 hp at 7,500 feet.

Meanwhile, the parallel DST-A and DC-3A variants were delivered with Pratt & Whitney R-1830 Twin Wasp engines of various types. These ranged from the R-1830-SC-G (rated at 1,050 hp for takeoff and 900 hp at 11,000 feet) to the R-1830-S4C4-G (rated at 1,200 hp for takeoff and 900 hp at 15,400 feet).

As with the DC-2, there were numerous military DC-3 variants, although 99 percent of the more than 10,000 military DC-3s were C-47 Skytrains and C-53 Skytroopers built for the USAAF, many of which were transferred to the US Navy as R4Ds.

Aside from the C-41A, the first Air Corps order for a military DC-3 was for an initial batch of 147 C-47s, which was placed in September 1940. The US Navy, meanwhile, assigned the designation R4D-1, ordering 66 directly from Douglas and acquiring another 33 through the Air Corps.

Skytrain fuselage and inner wing sections are shown on the Douglas factory floor in Long Beach. The R-1830-92 engines have already been installed, but cowlings will come later.

The Office of War Information caption for this Kodachrome taken by Alfred Palmer in October 1942 reads "Flexible performance of C-47 transport planes is due in part to their two 1,200-hp [Pratt & Whitney R-1830 Twin Wasp] radial engines and to their three-blade, variable-pitch propellers, Long Beach, California. Picture taken at the Douglas Aircraft Company." (Photo Courtesy Library of Congress)

These aircraft differed from their commercial DC-3 cousins with the installation of large cargo doors at the rear fuselage, a reinforced floor for cargo, and the absence of airline-style seating. Passengers sat along the sides of the cabin, leaving a large open interior volume for cargo.

As with the DC-2, there were many other Air Corps/USAAF designations for small batches of military DC-3s. Most designations went to commercial DC-3s with airliner interiors that were commandeered by the USAAF, mainly at the start of World War II. Of these, there were 36 C-48s, 138 C-49s, 14 C-50s, 1 C-51, and 1 C-84. The Navy commandeered 2 airliners as R4D-2 and 17 as R4D-4. These aircraft were powered by Wright R-1820 Cyclone variants, except the C-48, which used the Pratt & Whitney R-1830-82 Twin Wasp. Two other USAAF designations went to commandeered DC-3s powered by Pratt & Whitney R-1830 Twin Wasp engines. There were 5 C-52s and 2 C-68s.

Beginning in December 1941, Douglas delivered 965 C-47 Skytrains from its Long Beach, California, factory. These were followed by 2,954 C-47A Skytrains built at Long Beach and 2,299 C-47As built by Douglas in Oklahoma City. These 6,218 aircraft accounted for 60 percent of all military DC-3 derivatives.

The C-47B variant was designed for high-altitude operations, such as the supply route between India and China across the "Hump" in the eastern Himalayas. As such, it was powered by a R-1830-90C Twin Wasp with two-stage blowers and improved heaters. It was rated at 1,200 hp for takeoff and 1,000 hp at 14,500 feet. Douglas built 300 C-47Bs in Long Beach and 2,932 in Oklahoma City.

A USAAF Douglas C-47 Skytrain flies over the pyramids at Giza in Egypt in 1942. The C-47 was the workhorse of the USAAF Air Transport Command, which established schedule routes across the Atlantic and Pacific, linking six continents and becoming the world's first truly global "airline."

This early C-47 wears the second wartime iteration of the USAAF insignia. The red spot in the center was dropped early in the war to avoid confusing with the JJJ insignia, and bars were added to the star in the summer of 1943.

This woman is reaching into a space between the cylinders to make adjustments to the air ducts for the carburetor of a Pratt & Whitney R-1830 Twin Wasp engine that has been installed on the wing of a C-47 Skytrain. (Photo Courtesy Library of Congress)

C-47As from production Block 75 (C-47A-75-DL) are shown near completion on the Long Beach assembly line. The R-1830-92s are already in place with the cowlings installed. The assembly line moves at 2:25. It could be early morning or afternoon. The work was around the clock.

There were 238 C-47As transferred to the US Navy as R4D-5s and 157 C-47Bs transferred as R4D-6s.

The C-53 Skytrooper, which was designed to transport paratroopers in airborne operations, was like the C-47 but with 28 fixed side seats and a smaller rear door. With production at Santa Monica, Douglas turned out 219 C-53s, 8 C-53Bs, 19 C-53Cs, and 159 C-53Ds. The C-47s, C-47As, and all the C-53s were equipped with Pratt & Whitney R-1830-92 Twin Wasps rated at 1,200 hp for takeoff and 1,050 hp at 7,500 feet.

The Dauntless and the Cyclone

Douglas began its DC-2/DC-3 commercial family with Wright Cyclones but shifted to Pratt & Whitney Twin Wasp powerplants for the military variants. With the company's single-engine monoplane bombers for the US Navy's aircraft carriers, the shift went the opposite way.

The TBD-1 Devastator torpedo bomber used the Pratt & Whitney R-1830 Twin Wasp, while the Douglas family of SBD Dauntless scout bombers was powered by Wright R-1820 Cyclones.

Seen here is a Douglas Block 30 TC-47B, one of an order for 133 navigational trainers that was placed in 1944. While most Skytrains were built in Long Beach, these were built at the Douglas factory in Oklahoma City. The TC-47B-DK aircraft were powered by Pratt & Whitney R-1830-90C Twin Wasps.

The Pratt & Whitney R-1830-92 Twin Wasp is prominent in this 2009 photo of the Douglas Block 20 C-47A that is preserved at the National World War II Museum in New Orleans. Built at the Douglas Aircraft plant in Oklahoma City, it was delivered to the USAAF in April 1944. Reaching England in May 1944, this aircraft carried 82nd Airborne Division pathfinders during the Normandy Invasion and later carried 101st Airborne pathfinders during Operation Market Garden. (Bill Yenne Photo)

This is an excellent close-up view of a 1,200-hp Wright R-1820-60 Cyclone engine installed in a restored Douglas SBD-5 Dauntless. Formerly with the US Navy, this Dauntless now serves with the Dixie Wing of the Commemorative Air Force. It was photographed at Falcon Field, also known as Atlanta Regional Airport, in Fayette County, Georgia. (Photo Courtesy Hawkeye UK, Licensed under Creative Commons)

This is a TBD-1 Devastator torpedo bomber shortly after it rolled out of the Douglas plant in Santa Monica, circa 1937. The TBD-1 was powered by a 900-hp Pratt & Whitney R-1830-64 Twin Wasp, while the XTBD-1 prototype used the 800-hp XR-1830-60.

For the operational TBD-1, it was an R-1830-64, rated at 900 hp for takeoff and 850 hp at 8,000 feet.

When the XTBD-1 Devastator first flew in 1935, it was a highly advanced aircraft with its enclosed cockpit, retractable landing gear, and hydraulically-operated folding wings. By the time of World War II, though, the Devastator was considered obsolete, and in its signature combat action at the Battle of Midway in June 1942, the operational TBD-1s were recipients of devastation rather than devastators. Of the 41 TBD-1s that were launched against the Japanese fleet, only 4 survived, and none achieved a torpedo strike on an enemy ship.

The Douglas Dauntless, on the other hand, proved to be the hero (among aircraft types) of the American victory at Midway. Three Dauntless squadrons, VB-6 and VS-6 from the USS *Enterprise*, and VB-3 from the USS *Yorktown*, successfully engaged the Japanese carriers, sinking all four of them. While the Devastators were withdrawn from service after Midway, the Dauntlesses continued to serve with distinction throughout the war.

The Dauntless had its roots in the Northrop BT-1. It should be noted that when the Northrop Corporation was formed in 1932, Jack Northrop himself was president, but Douglas owned 51 percent of the stock. When the company dissolved in 1937, Jack Northrop started his new Northrop Aircraft while the former Northrop Corporation Facilities in El Segundo, California, became the El Segundo Division of Douglas. The BT-1 was a product of this lineage.

A group of operational Douglas TBD-1 Devastator torpedo bombers are shown in flight in January 1941. The devastator showed promise as the US Navy's first all-metal, monoplane torpedo bomber, but the type failed disappointingly in its baptism of fire at Midway in June 1942 and was withdrawn from front-line service.

The XBT-1 US Navy bomber, itself based on the Northrop A-17 Army Air Corps attack aircraft, first flew in August 1935. The prototype was powered by a 700-hp Pratt & Whitney R-1535-66 Twin Wasp Junior, which was upgraded in the production BT-1s to an R-1535-94 rated at 825 hp for takeoff and 750 hp at 9,500 feet. One of the 54 production-series BT-1s was retrofitted with a Wright R-1820-32 Cyclone and redesignated as an XBT-2. This aircraft was heavily modified to become the XSBD-1 prototype.

The first SBD-1 production aircraft flew in May 1940, and deliveries of the SBD-2 began in November. Like the XBT-2/XSBD-1 prototype, these 144 aircraft were all powered by Wright R-1820-32 Cyclones.

Large-scale Dauntless production began with the improved SBD-3, which was delivered in March 1941. Douglas delivered 584 SBD-3s to the US Navy, and the type was present on all American carriers at the time the United States entered World War II. An additional 168

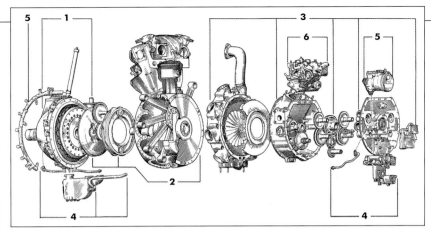

All 3,640 members of the SBD-5/A-24B group were powered by Wright R-1820-60 Cyclones rated at 1,000 hp for takeoff and 1,000 hp at 13,800 feet. The final Dauntless variant, of which 450 were delivered, was the SBD-6, which had no USAAF equivalent. It was powered by the 1,350-hp R-1820-66 Cyclone.

Dauntlesses served on practically every American carrier in the Pacific, fought in every battle where carrier air power played a role, and sunk numerous enemy ships—including six Japanese carriers and a battleship.

of the SBD-3-type aircraft were delivered to the USAAF under the designation A-24. Beginning in October 1942, these were followed by 780 SBD-4s for the Navy and 170 similar A-24As for the USAAF.

All of the aircraft in the SBD-3/SBD-4 series and their USAAF equivalents were powered by Wright R-1820-52s that delivered 1,000 hp for takeoff and 800 hp at 16,000 feet.

With deliveries beginning in February 1943, the largest production series of Dauntlesses was the SBD-5/A-24B group. There were 2,965 SBD-5s produced for the US Navy and an additional 60 SBD-5As that were originally on the USAAF order but were retained by the Navy and rerouted to the Marine Corps. The USAAF did receive 615 of this type under the A-24B designation. While the earlier A-24s had been built in El Segundo, this batch was produced at the Douglas plant in Tulsa.

The C-54 and the Pratt & Whitney R-2000

The Douglas C-54 Skymaster was the largest military transport acquired in large numbers by the USAAF in World War II. Just as the C-47 began as the civilian DC-3, the C-54 began as the civilian DC-4. On the eve of World War II, Douglas was about to revolutionize civilian air travel once again with the delivery of its long-range, four-engine DC-4A airliner to United Air Lines and Eastern Airlines.

This is an exploded schematic view of the engine propeller shaft and reduction gearing in a US Navy model Wright R-1820.

12. Lock, Propeller Shaft Hydro Oil Connection Cover Nut
13. Screw, Propeller Shaft Hydro Oil Connection Cover Lock
14. Washer, Propeller Shaft Hydro Oil Connection Cover Lock
15. Bushing, Reduction Gear Pinion
16. Pinion, Reduction Gear
17. Bolt, Reduction Gear Pinion
18. Nut, Reduction Gear Pinion Retaining
19. Carrier, Reduction Gear Pinion
20. Bolt, Reduction Gear Pinion Carrier to Propeller Shaft
21. Nut, Reduction Gear Pinion Carrier to Propeller Shaft Bolt
22. Bearing, Propeller Shaft Thrust Radial Ball
23. Spacer, Propeller Shaft Thrust Bearing
24. Ring, Propeller Shaft Thrust Bearing Spacer Oil Seal
25. Nut, Propeller Shaft Thrust Bearing
26. Ring, Propeller Shaft Thrust Bearing Nut Oil Seal
27. Gear, Stationary Reduction
28. Ring Reduction Gear Pinion Guard
29. Support and Sleeve Assembly, Stationary Reduction Gear
30. Sleeve, Stationary Reduction Gear Support
31. Plug, Stationary Reduction Gear Support Oil Retaining
32. Plug, Stationary Reduction Gear Support Oil Retaining
33. Pin, Stationary Reduction Gear Support Sleeve

1. Shaft and Bushing Machining Assembly, Propeller and Shaft
2. Sleeve, Propeller Shaft
3. Washer, Propeller Shaft Front Bushing
4. Bushing, Propeller Shaft Front
5. Bushing, Propeller Shaft Rear
6. Pin, Propeller Shaft Rear Bushing Lock
7. Adapter, Propeller Shaft Hydro Oil Connection
8. Gasket, Propeller Shaft Hydro Oil Connection Adapter
9. Cover, Propeller Shaft Hydro Oil Connection
10. Gasket, Propeller Shaft Hydro Oil Connection Cover
11. Nut, Propeller Shaft Hydro Oil Connection Cover

However, as the United States entered the war, the USAAF literally commandeered all two dozen DC-4As off the assembly line and put them into service as C-54s.

The idea behind the larger aircraft had been to offer the airlines a transport with greater range than the popular DC-3 and a capacity of up to about 50 passengers (depending on configuration). An experimental, triple-tail DC-4E version was first flown in June 1938. No subsequent prototype of the single-tail production-series DC-4A was flown before the first aircraft made its debut in February 1942 as a C-54.

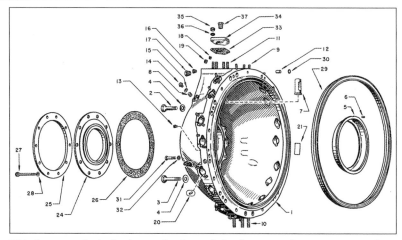

This is an exploded schematic view of the front crankcase section of the US Navy model Wright R-1820 engine.

1. Crankcase Front Section Studding Assembly
2. Bolt, Crankcase Front Section to Crankcase Main Front Section
3. Bolt, Crankcase Front Section to Crankcase Main Front Section
4. Washer, Crankcase Front Section to Crankcase Main Front Section Bolt
5. Retainer, Propeller Shaft Thrust Bearing
6. Pin, Propeller Shaft Thrust Bearing Retainer
7. Bushing, Governor and Distributor Drive Gear Shaft
8. Bushing, Spinner Afterbody Attaching Screw
9. Crankcase Front Section to Valve Tappet Guide
10. Stud, Crankcase Front Section to Oil Sump
11. Stud, Crankcase Front Section to Governor Drive Housing or Substituting Cover
12. Pin, Crankcase Front Section to Crankcase Main Section
13. Screw, Crankcase Front Section Puller
14. Plug, Spinner Afterbody Screw Bushing
15. Gasket, Spinner Afterbody Screw Bushing Plug
16. Plug, Governor Oil Line
17. Plug, Governor Oil Line
18. Plug, Governor Oil Line
19. Plug, Governor Oil Line
20. Pin, Valve Tappet Guide Locating
21. Decal, Valve Tappet Removal Caution
22. [Omitted]
23. [Omitted]
24. Flange, Crankcase Front Section
25. Spacer, Crankcase Front Section Flange
26. Gasket, Crankcase Front Section Flange
27. Screw, Crankcase Front Section Flange to Stationary Reduction Gear
28. Washer, Crankcase Front Section Flange to Stationary Reduction Gear Screw
29. Ring, Crankcase Front Section to Crankcase Main Section
30. Ring, Crankcase Front Section to Crankcase Main Section Locating Pin
31. Bolt, Crankcase Front Section to Stationary Reduction Gear
32. Washer, Crankcase Front Section to Stationary Reduction Gear Bolt
33. Gasket, Governor Substituting Cover
34. Cover, Governor
35. Nut, Governor Substituting Cover to Crankcase Front Section Stud
36. Washer, Governor Substituting Cover to Crankcase Front Section Nut
37. Plug, Governor Substituting Cover Dehydrating Substitute

This Douglas advertisement (circa early 1942, based on the insignia and the factory list) touts the hitting power of the Dauntless, claiming a "world record" that in all likelihood belonged at this time to Germany's Junkers Ju 87 Stuka. Note the dive brakes deployed on the Dauntless heading down.

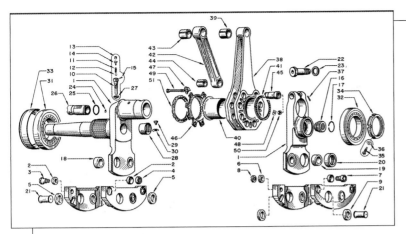

In a seemingly endless line, these SBD Dauntlesses, with their R-1820-92s installed, near completion at the Douglas factory in El Segundo, California. The picture can be dated to the summer of 1943, as the red outline on the national insignia was used only briefly around this time.

This is an exploded schematic view of the crankcase and connecting rods of the US Navy model Wright R-1820 Engine Connecting Cap.

1. Crankshaft Machining and Balancing Assembly
2. Cup, Counterweight Attaching Bolt Lock
3. Bolt, Counterweight Attaching Bolt
4. Nut, Counterweight Attaching Bolt
5. Bushing, Front Counterweight
6. Cup, Counterweight Attaching Bolt Lock
7. Bolt, Counterweight Attaching
8. Nut, Counterweight Attaching Bolt
9. Bushing, Rear Counterweight
10. Body, Piston Oil Check Valve
11. Spring, Piston Oil Check Valve
12. Ball, Piston Oil Check Valve
13. Nozzle, Piston Oil
14. Stop, Piston Oil Check Valve
15. Rivet, Piston Oil Check Valve Stop to Body
16. Coupling, Accessory Drive and Starter Shaft
17. Circlet, Accessory Drive and Starter Shaft Coupling
18. Bushing, Front Counterweight Crankshaft
19. Bushing, Rear Counterweight Crankshaft
20. Bearing, Rear Counterweight Crankshaft
21. Pin, Crankshaft Front and Rear Counterweight
22. Screw, Crankcheek
23. Washer, Crankcheek Screw
24. Pin, Reduction Driving Gear Aligning
25. Ring, Crankshaft Crankpin Sludge Retaining Plug Packing
26. Plug, Crankshaft Crankpin Sludge Retaining
27. Washer, Crankshaft Crankpin Sludge Retaining Plug Piston Check Valve
28. Plug, Crankshaft Breather
29. Screw, Crankshaft Breather
30. Lock Washer, Crankshaft Breather Plug Retaining Screw
31. Bearing, Crankshaft Main Front Roller
32. Bearing, Crankshaft Main Rear Roller
33. Ring, Crankshaft Main Front Bearing Retaining
34. Nut, Crankshaft Main Rear Bearing
35. Screw, Crankshaft Main Rear Bearing Nut Lock
36. Lock Washer, Crankshaft Main Rear Bearing Nut Lock Screw
37. Cotter Pin, Crankcheek Screw
38. Rod Assembly, Master Connecting
39. Bushing, Piston Pin
40. Bearing, Master Connecting Rod
41. Spacer, Master Connecting Rod Spacer
42. Rod, Articulated
43. Bushing, Piston Pin Split
44. Bushing, Knuckle Pin Split
45. Pin, Knuckle
46. Plate, Knuckle Pin Locking
47. Lock, Knuckle Pin
48. Lock, Knuckle Pin Retaining Bolt Nut
49. Bolt, Knuckle Pin Retaining
50. Nut, Knuckle Pin Retaining Bolt
51. Disc, Master Rod Oil Seal

The C-54 was powered by four Pratt & Whitney R-2000 Twin Wasp radial engines. This new engine was actually a larger variant of the R-1830 Twin Wasp created to emphasize fuel economy and ease of production. The latter was accomplished with front-mounted rather than rear-mounted magnetos and the use of ball bearings for the crankshaft rather than roller bearings.

The 14-cylinder, twin-row R-2000 had a displacement of 2,004 ci. It retained the 5.5-inch stroke of the R-1830, although the bore was increased to 5.75 inches. The engine was 61 inches long with a diameter of 49.49 inches, and it had a dry weight of 1,570 pounds. Equipped with a Stromberg carburetor, the R-2000 was rated at 1,300 hp at 2,700 rpm with 87 octane fuel; 1,350 hp with 100 octane; or 1,450 hp at 2,800 rpm with 130 octane fuel. It had a compression ratio of 6.5:1.

After the initial two dozen DC-4As were commandeered as C-54s, the USAAF ordered 252 additional C-54A aircraft with their floors strengthened for heavy cargo. Given the official name "Skymaster," 97 were built at the original Douglas plant at Santa Monica, and the rest were built at the new Douglas facility near Chicago that eventually evolved into today's O'Hare International Airport.

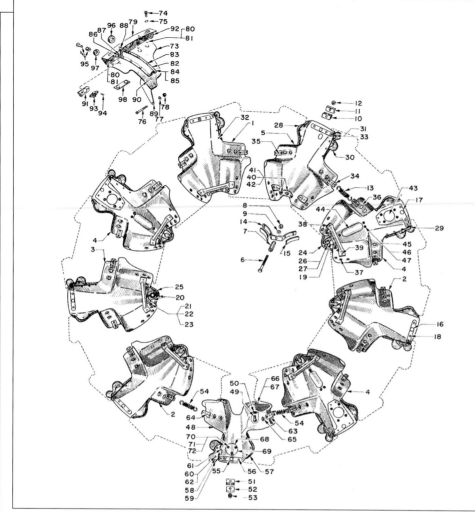

This schematic shows the inter-cylinder and cylinder head air deflectors for the US Navy model Wright R-1820 engine.

The final Douglas Dauntless variant was the SBD-6, seen here on April 11, 1944. With the Wright R-1820-66 Cyclone installed, 450 were built.

During 1942 and 1943, the USAAF placed a series of orders for C-54B aircraft that was similar to the C-54As but had provisions for stretcher racks that would be used for evacuating severely wounded personnel from the war zones to hospitals in the United States that had the facilities to treat their injuries.

The single VC-54C is of special note because of the "V" prefix, which indicated "Very Important Person." The executive that it was to carry was President Franklin Delano Roosevelt. Converted from a C-54A in 1944 and given the official nickname and call sign *Sacred Cow*, the VC-54C was America's first aircraft specifically designed for use by the President of the United States. It was the forerunner of today's Air Force One. The interior contained a presidential stateroom, a meeting room, and accommodations for the president's staff.

Douglas built 100 C-54B-DOs in Santa Monica and 120 C-54B-DCs in Chicago. Thereafter, all production was at the latter facility. This included 380 C-54D-DCs and 125 C-54E-DCs. Between

The C-54 Skymaster was the USAAF equivalent of the Douglas DC-4 commercial propliner. Widely used during World War II, it continued to be used up into the 1950s. This Block 5 C-54D was photographed in US Air Force markings in March 1949. Its powerplant was the Pratt & Whitney R-2000-11 Twin Wasp. The early variants were built in Santa Monica, but the C-54Ds were produced at the Douglas plant that became Chicago's O'Hare Airport.

The USAAF's Douglas A-24 Banshee could be quickly distinguished from the US Navy's SBD Dauntless by its olive drab, rather than blue and gray, paint scheme. The two aircraft were largely identical, although the aircraft carrier arresting hook was not installed in the A-24. Built at El Segundo, the A-24 was the equivalent of the SBD-3A, while the A-24A was an SBD-4 equivalent. They were powered by the Wright R-1820-52 Cyclone, but subsequent A-24Bs, built by Douglas in Tulsa, used the R-1820-60.

This is a left front view of a twin-row, 14-cylinder Pratt & Whitney R-2000 Twin Wasp radial, the powerplant used by Douglas in the C-54 Skymaster and the comparable DC-4 airliner. This engine was an enlarged version of the Pratt & Whitney R-1830 Twin Wasp, created to reduce production cost and adapted to use 87-octane fuel in case the availability of 100-octane fuel was compromised. (Photo Courtesy Kogo, Licensed under the GNU Free Documentation License)

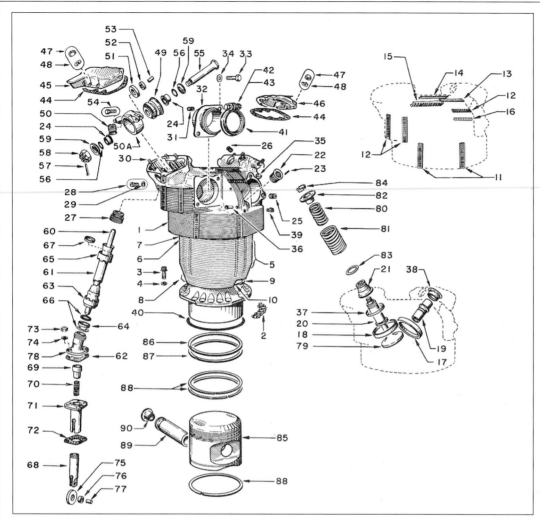

This shows the cylinder, valve mechanism, and piston of the US Navy model Wright R-1820 engine.

1. Cylinder Machining and Studding Assembly
2. Plate, Cylinder Hold Down Screw Locking
3. Screw, Cylinder Hold Down
4. Washer, Cylinder Hold Down Screw Spherical
5–8. Fin Assembly, Cylinder Barrel
9. Fin, Cylinder Barrel Deflector Attaching
10. Wire, Cylinder Barrel Deflector Attaching Fin Caulking
11. Brace, Cylinder Head Fin 13 Slots
12. Brace, Cylinder Head Fin 15 Slots
13. Brace, Cylinder Head Fin 19 Slots
14–15. Brace, Cylinder Head Fin
16. Spring, Cylinder Head Fin Damper

17. Seat, Intake Valve
18. Seat and Ring Assembly, Exhaust Valve
19. Guide, Intake Valve
20. Guide, Exhaust Valve (Used with Sleeve)
21. Sleeve, Exhaust Valve Guide Retainer
22. Insert, Spark Plug
23. Pin, Spark Plug Insert
24. Bushing, Rocker Arm Hub Bolt
25. Bushing, Intake Pipe Flange Bolt Screw
26. Bushing, Cylinder Head Air Deflector Screw
27. Connection, Push Rod Housing
28. Screw, Push Rod Housing Connection Upper Nut Locking
29. Washer, Push Rod Housing Connection Upper Nut Locking Screw
30. Stud, Cylinder to Rocker Box Cover
31. Insert, Exhaust Pipe Connection Screw
32. Connection, Exhaust Pipe
33. Screw, Exhaust Pipe Connection to Cylinder Head

34. Washer, Exhaust Pipe Connection to Cylinder Head
35. Stud, Cylinder to Nose Cowl
36. Spacer, Thermocouple and Deflector Attaching Bolt
37. Washer, Valve Spring Outer Lower
38. Washer, Valve Spring Inner Lower Intake, Cylinder and Piston Complete Assembly
39. Fitting, Cylinder Head Thermocouple
40. Ring, Cylinder Oil Seal 6100 In M Packing Supersedes
41. Clamp Assembly, Exhaust Pipe to Collector Ring
42. Nut, Exhaust Pipe to Front Exhaust Extension Clamp Bolt
43. Bolt, Exhaust Pipe to Front Exhaust Extension Clamp
44. Gasket, Rocker Box Cover Supersedes
45. Cover and Bushing Assembly, Rocker Box Exhaust

46. Cover and Bushing Assembly, Rocker Box Intake
47. Nut, Rocker Box Cover to Cylinder Head
48. Washer, Rocker Box Cover to Cylinder Head Nut (Arm Complete Assembly)
49. Bearing, Rocker Arm
50. Screw, Valve Clearance Adjusting (Arm Assembly, Intake Valve Rocker)
50a. Arm Assembly, Exhaust Valve Rocker
51. Roller, Rocker Arm
52. Hub, Rocker Arm Roller
53. Pin, Rocker Arm Roller Hub
54. Screw, Valve Clearance Adjusting Screw Lock
55. Bolt, Rocker Arm Hub and Bolt, Rocker Arm Hub Cylinder No. 1 Intake
56. Ring, Rocker Arm Hub Bolt Oil Seal
57. Cotter Pin, Rocker Arm Hub Bolt Nut
58. Nut, Rocker Arm Hub Bolt
59. Washer, Rocker Arm Hub Bolt Nut Spherical for Bolt
60. Rod Assembly, Push Rod, Push End, Push Rod Ball
61. Housing Assembly, Push Rod Housing, Push Rod, Sleeve, Push Rod Housing
62. Gasket, Push Rod Housing Adapter
63. Nut, Push Rod Housing Connection Lower
64. Ring, Push Rod Housing Packing
65. Nut, Push Rod Housing Connection Upper
66. Washer, Push Rod Housing Packing
67. Ring, Push Rod Housing Oil Seal
68. Tappet, Valve
69. Socket, Valve Tappet Ball
70. Spring, Valve Tappet Ball Socket
71. Guide, Valve Tappet Supersedes
72. Gasket, Valve Tappet Guide
73. Nut, Valve Tappet Guide Adapter to Crankcase Front Section
74. Washer, Valve Tappet Guide Adapter to Crankcase Front Section Nut
75. Roller, Valve Tappet
76. Bushing, Valve Tappet Roller
77. Pin, Valve Tappet Roller, Adapter, Valve Tappet Guide Intake
78. Adapter, Valve Tappet Guide Exhaust
79. Valve, Exhaust
80. Spring, Valve Inner
81. Spring, Valve Outer
82. Washer, Valve Spring Upper
83. Washer, Inner Lower Exhaust Valve Spring
84. Lock, Valve Spring Upper Intake and Exhaust, Piston and Ring Assembly, Cylinders No. 1, 2, 3, 8, and 9; Piston and Ring Assembly, Cylinders No. 4, 5, 6, and 7
85. Piston, Cylinders No. 1, 2, 3, 8, and 9; Piston, Cylinders No. 4, 5, 6, and 7
86. Ring, Piston Compression Groove
87. Ring, Piston Groove No. 2
88. Ring, Piston Grooves No. 3, 4 and 5
89. Pin, Piston
90. Plug, Piston Pin

The Pratt & Whitney R-2000-9 Twin Wasp clutches and selector valve are in high position.

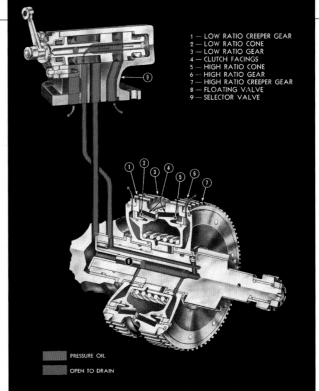

1 — LOW RATIO CREEPER GEAR
2 — LOW RATIO CONE
3 — LOW RATIO GEAR
4 — CLUTCH FACINGS
5 — HIGH RATIO CONE
6 — HIGH RATIO GEAR
7 — HIGH RATIO CREEPER GEAR
8 — FLOATING VALVE
9 — SELECTOR VALVE

PRESSURE OIL.

OPEN TO DRAIN

This vintage color image shows one of the first of nearly 200 C-54s that were transferred from the USAAF to the US Navy and redesignated as R5D. This R5D-1 (ordered as a C-54A) was powered by 4 Pratt & Whitney R-2000-7 Twin Wasp radials.

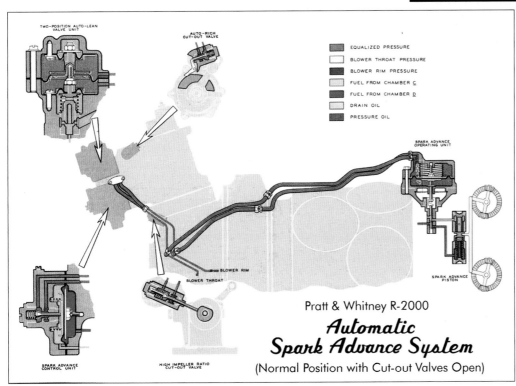

EQUALIZED PRESSURE
BLOWER THROAT PRESSURE
BLOWER RIM PRESSURE
FUEL FROM CHAMBER C
FUEL FROM CHAMBER D
DRAIN OIL
PRESSURE OIL

TWO-POSITION AUTO-LEAN VALVE UNIT

AUTO-RICH CUT-OUT VALVE

SPARK ADVANCE OPERATING UNIT

SPARK ADVANCE PISTON

BLOWER RIM

BLOWER THROAT

SPARK ADVANCE CONTROL UNIT

HIGH IMPELLER RATIO CUT-OUT VALVE

Pratt & Whitney R-2000
Automatic Spark Advance System
(Normal Position with Cut-out Valves Open)

A schematic view of the automatic spark advance system is shown in the Pratt & Whitney R-2000-9 Twin Wasp. When engine speed was increased into the cruising range, this system automatically shifted the spark advance from 25 degrees to 37 degrees before the piston was at top dead center. This provided more complete fuel economy during operation in the cruising power range. When power was increased above the cruising range, when the carburetor mixture control was placed in the auto-rich position, or when the impeller ratio selector valve was shifted to the high-ratio position, the system automatically shifted the spark back to the 25-degree or normal advance position, providing the normal fuel-air mixture.

1942 and 1945, the USAAF C-54 fleet averaged more than 20 flights a day across the rugged North Atlantic. By the end of the war in Europe, Skymasters successfully completed 79,642 transoceanic flights with only three ditchings, one of which was a test.

The C-54 was also one of the aircraft to benefit most from mass production in terms of its unit cost. When the DC-4s were commandeered off the assembly line after Pearl Harbor, they were one of the most expensive aircraft in the USAAF at $516,552 apiece. By 1943, with the development costs better amortized, the unit cost was down to $400,831, and in 1944, it cost the USAAF just $285,113 to buy a Skymaster.

In parallel with the use of the R-1820 and R-1830 by Douglas was the company's use of the larger Wright R-2600 in its A-20 Havoc series and the Pratt & Whitney R-2800 in its A-26 Invader. Details of those applications follow in Chapters 8 through 11.

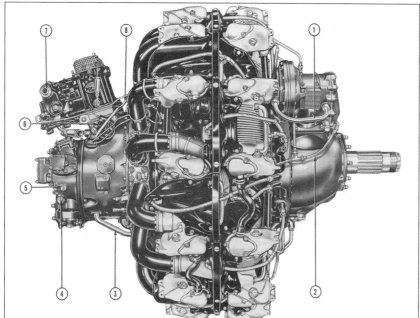

Chapter 6

MILITARY APPLICATIONS OF SMALLER ROUND ENGINES

While the emphasis of this book is on the powerful powerplants of first-line combat aircraft, the complete story must include smaller engines built for other military applications, especially those for primary training as well as light liaison aircraft. The numbers produced, in many cases exceeding the numbers produced for combat aircraft, make these engines impossible to ignore.

Both Wright Aeronautical and Pratt & Whitney had engines smaller than 1,000 ci in their product portfolios during World War II. Wright had its J-6 family of Whirlwind engines, including the R-760, as well as the R-975, which was mentioned in Chapter 1. Pratt & Whitney had its R-985 Wasp Junior as well as its R-1535 Twin Wasp Junior.

In the annals of American radial engines, the comparison and competition between the R-975 and R-985 is analogous to that between the respective companies and their larger radials: the R-1820 Cyclone and the R-1830 Twin Wasp.

It was in the field of smaller radial engines that smaller companies made their mark—with very large numbers. There are three such companies of particular note: Continental, Lycoming, and Jacobs.

The Continental Aircraft Engine Company was a division of Continental Motors of Muskegon, Michigan. During World War II, according to USAAF records, Continental produced 16,977 of its small 65–80 hp O-170 horizontally opposed engines, as well as 11,828 of its W670/R-670 radials. *The Curtiss Wright Historical Engine Survey* (1983) reports that that Continental also produced 53,000 Wright R-975 Whirlwinds under license.

Lycoming traces its roots to the Demorest Manufacturing Company, which turned from sewing machines and bicycles to automotive engines early in the 20th century. Based in Williamsport, Pennsylvania, it was acquired by auto magnate Errett Lobban Cord, whose Auburn, Cord, and Deusenberg automobiles used Lycoming engines. In 1939, Cord folded Lycoming into his Aviation Corporation (AVCO), which famously gained a controlling interest in Consolidated-Vultee in 1941. Lycoming produced 12,476 of its R-680s for the war effort, although this was slightly fewer than half of the total number of R-680s that Lycoming produced between 1930 and 1945. During the war, Lycoming also delivered 12,395 of its smaller horizontally opposed piston engines.

The Jacobs Aircraft Engine Company of Pottstown, Pennsylvania, which was founded in 1926, produced 5,759 of its 7-cylinder, 330-hp R-915s, and 14,746 of its 7-cylinder, 225-hp R-755s for the military services.

Stearman NS-1 Kaydet US Navy trainers fly out of NAS Pensacola during training of the first class of the Naval Aviation Cadet program in 1936. The NS-1 was powered by a Wright R-790-8 (J-5) radial engine. (Photo Courtesy US Navy)

Continental's W670/R-670

The Continental Motors Company opened for business in 1905, manufacturing four-stroke, 4-cylinder engines for independent automakers, including Durant Motors. When Durant went out of business in 1931 and the financiers who took over the factory failed a year later, Continental rather reluctantly became an automaker to keep its own auto engine business going. By 1934, this business had been phased out. In the meantime, the Continental Aircraft Engine Company division, started in 1929, was off to a good beginning with its first radial aircraft engine: the 170-hp A-70.

First run in 1934, the A-70's successor was the Continental W670—the engine that truly established the company as a major player in the industry. Given the military designation of R-670, it was a 7-cylinder, four-cycle radial aircraft engine that displaced 668 ci.

The W670/R-670 was 34.1873 inches long with a diameter of 42.5 inches and a dry weight of 450 pounds. It had a bore of 5.125 inches and a stroke of 4.625 inches, and it used a Stromberg NA-R6 carburetor.

The W670-K and W670-L each had a compression ratio of 5.4:1 and were rated at 225 hp. They differed in that the former used 65-octane fuel and had front exhausts, while the latter used 73-octane fuel and had rear exhausts. The W670-M and W670-N each had a compression ratio of 6.1:1, were rated at 240 hp, and used 80-octane fuel. The W670-M had front exhausts, and the W670-N had rear exhausts. The fuel-injected variants of each engine had the same ratings and specifications but were company-designated as W670-K1, W670-L1, W670-M1, and W670-N1.

The principal use of the W670/R-670, like that of the Lycoming R-680, was in the Stearman Model 75. Because of the intermingling of engine types, this aircraft is discussed in the next subsection.

It should be added that more W670/R-670 radial engines were used in tracked armored vehicles as well as in aircraft during World War II. Beginning in 1935, it was used in several combat cars and light tanks that were produced in small numbers as well as in 698 M2 light tanks, which saw limited use early in World War II.

The largest use of the W670/R-670 in tanks was in the M3 Stuart light tank. Named for Civil War cavalry commander J.E.B. Stuart, the 12-ton M3 entered production in March 1941 as a development of the M2A4 variant of the earlier M2. The fan-cooled W670/R-670 was used to power 8,936 M3 and M3A1 tanks as well as 3,427 improved M3A3s. The much-improved M5 Stuart light tank, which was developed from the M3, switched to a Cadillac V-8 automobile engine. Parenthetically, the M5 also used the General Motors Hydra-Matic transmission, which was introduced in 1939 as the first successful mass-produced automatic automobile transmission.

The Pratt & Whitney R-985 Wasp Junior 9-cylinder, air-cooled, radial aircraft engine was first run in 1929 but remained in production until 1953. Nearly 40,000 were built. (Photo Courtesy Bill Larkins, Licensed under Creative Commons)

This is a Continental-built R-670 7-cylinder 4-cycle radial engine installed in a Stearman PT-17 Kaydet primary trainer. (Photo Courtesy Nimbus227, Licensed under Creative Commons)

This is a restored 1944 Stearman PT-13D Kaydet at Keevil Airfield in Wiltshire, England, in 2006. PT-13s were produced with engines in the Lycoming R-680 series. (Photo Courtesy Adrian Pingstone, Released to the Public Domain)

Lycoming produced its first aircraft engine (the R-680) in 1929, and it remained in production until 1945. More than 26,000 were built, many being used in the Stearman PT-l3 Kaydet trainer of World War II. (Photo Courtesy Kogo, Licensed under GNU Documentation)

Lycoming's R-680

A contemporary and a direct competitor of Continental's 7-cylinder W670/R-670, the 9-cylinder Lycoming R-680 was first run in 1929. More than 26,000 units were produced before manufacturing wound down in 1945.

Displacing 680 ci, the R-680 was 37.5 inches long with a diameter of 43.5 inches and a dry weight of 515.46 pounds. The bore was 4.625 inches, and the stroke was 4.5 inches. It used a single-barrel carburetor, and its valvetrain had a single inlet and exhaust valve for each cylinder.

The engine was produced in a "B" and an "E" series. Horsepower ratings depended on the variant. The B-series R-680B4E was rated at 225 hp at 2,100 rpm, while the E-series R-680E3A was rated at 285 hp at 2,200 rpm. Among the military variants, the R-680-6 was rated at 245 hp, while the R-680-13 delivered 300 hp at 2,200 rpm.

An early customer for the R-680 was the Stinson Aircraft Company, which was founded by Edward Anderson "Eddie" Stinson. It was installed in Stinson's 10-passenger SM-6000 trimotor airliner. Coincidentally, both Stinson Aircraft and Lycoming were acquired by auto magnate Errett Lobban Cord, who eventually folded them into his Aviation Corporation (AVCO) conglomerate.

Stinson also used the R-680 on its O-49/L-1 Vigilant, of which 324 were built for the Army Air Corps as well as on several variants of the Stinson Reliant monoplane, of which 1,327 were built with 250 serving the Army Air Corps as the AT-19 advanced trainer. Curtiss used the R-680 for 792 of its AT-9 Fledgling trainers, while Beechcraft used it for 2,371 AT-10 trainers.

A major use of both the Lycoming R-680 and the Continental R-670 was in the Stearman Kaydet.

Stearman's Kaydet and Its Radial Engines

Lloyd Stearman started his Stearman Aircraft Company in Venice, California, in 1926; established his factory in Wichita, Kansas, in 1927; and sold out to United Aircraft (owned by Bill Boeing and Fred Rentschler) in 1929. When United was split up in 1934 and the Boeing Aircraft Company became independent again, Stearman became Boeing's Wichita Division, although the "Stearman" brand name remained in use.

First entering service in 1934, Stearman's most famous product was the Kaydet biplane primary trainer. More than 10,600 were built, mostly under the Model 75 company designation, although a few aircraft were identified as Model 73 or 76. In turn, they received a variety of military designations that were generally delineated by engine type (Continental, Lycoming, or Wright), although the aircraft were virtually identical.

The first military Stearman variant was the Model 73 that was powered by a 220-hp Wright R-J-5 (R-790-8), of which Stearman exported 17 and delivered 61 to the US Navy as NS-1s.

The Air Corps began ordering Kaydets in 1936 with 26 PT-17s (Model 75s) powered by 215-hp Lycoming R-680-5s, although the Air Corps had test flown the Model 75 prototype with a 225-hp Wright R-760E.

For the Army Air Corps/USAAF, the PT-13 designation identified Kaydets powered with Lycoming engines, PT-17 for those with

A restored Stearman PT-13D Kaydet is shown at the Dirgantara Mandala Museum hangar in Indonesia. The PT-13D, the standard USAAF/USN PT-13 trainer, was delivered with Lycoming R-680-17 engines. (Photo Courtesy Dirgantara Mandala, Licensed under Creative Commons)

A Boeing Stearman PT-17 Kaydet is shown at the Venezuelan Air Force's Aeronautics Museum in Maracay, Venezuela. The PT-17 Kaydets were variations on the PT-13 Kaydet that were powered by Continental R-670-series engines. (Photo Courtesy Carlos E. Perez SL, Licensed under Creative Commons)

Continental engines, and PT-18 for those with the 7-cylinder R-755 radial from the Jacobs Aircraft Engine Company.

Stearman produced 1,392 PT-13s, and most were the PT-13C variant with the 225-hp R-680-17 engine. There were 3,064 PT-17s built with the 220-hp R-670-5 engine and five lightly armed A75B4 export variants delivered to Venezuela with 320-hp Wright R-760-82 Whirlwind radials. There were 150 PT-18s with Jacobs R-755 radials.

In US Navy service, the Continental engine dominated. The 220-hp Continental R-670-4 equipped all 250 N2S-1s and the first of the 1,875 N2S-3s, although the 220-hp R-670-5 was introduced midway in the production of the latter variant. The 1,786 aircraft of the N2S-5 final production variant were standardized with the USAAF PT-13D, both being equipped with 220-hp R-760-17s.

The largest single block of Navy Kaydets were the 1,875 N2S-2s that used the 220-hp Lycoming R-680-8.

In the decades following World War II, many of the thousands of Kaydets that came onto the civilian market were gradually re-engined, and the Pratt & Whitney R-985 Wasp Junior was a popular choice for doing so.

Wright's R-760 Whirlwind

Wright introduced its J-6 Whirlwind family in 1928 with the 7-cylinder engine designated as R-760 by the military services. The R-760 series was intended to supersede the 9-cylinder R-790 of the

J-5 Whirlwind family as a powerplant with fewer and larger cylinders (see Chapter 1).

The supercharged, direct-drive R-760 displaced 756 ci and was rated at 225 hp at 2,000 rpm, although the R-760-E2 variant was rated at 350 hp at 2,400 rpm for takeoff, and 320 hp at 2,100 rpm in flight. By comparison, the R-790 was rated at 220 hp at 2,000 rpm.

The R-760 had a stroke of 5.5 inches and a bore of 5 inches. It had a compression ratio of 6.3:1 and a power-to-weight ratio of 0.56 hp per pound. The engine weighed 570 pounds and was 42.44 inches long with a diameter of 45 inches.

In addition to its use in Stearman Kaydets, the R-760 was used by several manufacturers of general aviation aircraft, including Beech, Cessna, and Stinson. Other military applications included a pair of US Navy primary trainer types; the Curtiss N2C Fledgling, of which 51 were built in two production variants; and the Naval Aircraft Factory N3N Canary, of which 996 were built in two production variants.

Pratt & Whitney's R-985 Wasp Junior

First run in 1929 and in service the following year, Pratt & Whitney's 9-cylinder Wasp Junior series remained in production until 1953, with 39,037 having been produced mainly during the war years. The Wasp Junior remains in service in the 21st century mainly for light and agricultural aircraft but also on the antique aircraft and warbird circuit. Many surviving Stearman Model 75 Kaydets that originally flew with Continental R-670s or Lycoming R-680s are today fitted with Wasp Juniors for ease of maintenance and increased power.

As the name suggests, the idea behind the creation of the Wasp Junior was for a smaller variant of the R-1340 Wasp to fill the market

This is a Stearman N2S-5 Kaydet on display at the Air Zoo at Kalamazoo/Battle Creek International Airport in Portage, Michigan. The R-670-powered N2S was the US Navy equivalent of the USAAF PT-17. (Photo Courtesy Michael Barera, Licensed under Creative Commons)

A restored Stearman N2S-3 Kaydet trainer is shown at the Military Aviation Museum in Virginia. The N2S-3 was delivered with Continental R-670-4 engines. (Photo Courtesy Michael Rehbaum, Licensed under Creative Commons)

tier that called for a smaller engine—albeit with many parts that were interchangeable with the Wasp. It had smaller cylinders than the Wasp with power boosted using a single-speed, gear-driven centrifugal supercharger. As indicated by its designation, the R-985 had a displacement of exactly 985 ci.

The Wasp Junior A variant (R-985-1) was rated at 300 hp. Horsepower increased with the B series, beginning with the Wasp Junior TB (including R-985-9, R-985-11, and R-985-21). Optimized for low altitude, it was rated at 420 hp at sea level and 440 hp for takeoff. The Wasp Junior SB series (including the R-985-13, R-985-17, R-985-23, and R-985-33) was optimized for higher altitudes and was more common. It was rated at 450 hp at 2,300 rpm for takeoff and 400 hp at 2,200 rpm up to 5,000 feet. Its compression ratio was 6.0:1, and it had a power-to-weight ratio of 0.625 hp per pound.

The general specifications of the Wasp Junior SB (as given in the FAA type certificate data sheet) show it to be 41.59 inches long with a diameter of 45.75 inches and a dry weight of 640 pounds. Characteristic of the Wasp in general, it had both a stroke and bore of 5.8125 inches. The Wasp Junior featured a General Electric single-speed gear-driven centrifugal supercharger, and its valvetrain consisted of two pushrod-actuated overhead valves in each cylinder.

In 1935, the Wasp Junior was used in Lockheed's Model 10 Electra, the company's first twin-engine airliner. This was also the aircraft

Good front and side detail views are shown of a Pratt & Whitney R-985 Wasp Junior 9-cylinder, radial engine. (Photo Courtesy Srvban, Licensed under Creative Commons)

that Amelia Earhart chose for her ill-fated round-the-world flight in 1937. Army Air Corps variants of the aircraft included an XC-35, a C-37, and 19 C-36s. The US Navy ordered one designated as XR2O-1 as an executive transport for Secretary of the Navy Claude Swanson.

Lockheed also used the Wasp Junior in its Model 12 Electra Junior, which was first flown in 1936. The Army Air Corps bought a dozen from Lockheed with the C-40-series designation. The US Navy acquired seven with the utility designations JO-1 through JO-3.

The largest numbers of Wasp Juniors produced for the Army Air Corps were used in several basic trainers, including 30 Seversky BT-8s with the 450-hp R-985-11 Wasp Junior TB and 251 North American Aviation BT-14 Yales with 450-hp R-985-25 Wasp Junior T1B2s.

These numbers were dwarfed by the Wasp Juniors that powered 7,832 Vultee BT-13 Valiants. The initial batch of 300 aircraft with

R-985-25 engines was followed by 6,407 BT-13As and 1,125 BT-13Bs with 450-hp R-985-AN-1 engines. Of the total, 2,000 Army Valiants were transferred to the US Navy as SNV-1 and SNV-2 scout trainers.

With both the North American Yale and Vultee Valiant, there were parallel variants where essentially the same airframe received an alternate designation because of an alternate engine. Earlier versions of the Yale powered by Wright R-975-7 Whirlwinds were designated as BT-9. There were an additional 1,693 Vultee Valiants produced under the BT-15 designation with the 450-hp Wright R-975-11 Whirlwinds.

Ultimately, the little Valiant was to be one of the most successful aircraft in American aviation history, as 11,538 were built before and during World War II. There was such a huge demand for trainers that sales of these small-but-ubiquitous craft helped to propel

Office of War Information photographer Jack Delano took this photo of Pratt & Whitney R-985 Wasp Junior engines being installed in a Vought OS2U Kingfisher aircraft at the Vought-Sikorsky Aircraft Corporation in Stratford, Connecticut, in November 1940. (Photo Courtesy Library of Congress)

The Pratt & Whitney R-1535 Twin Wasp Junior was introduced in 1932 as a 14-cylinder development of the 9-cylinder R-985. This one is on display at the Naval Aviation Museum in Pensacola, Florida. (Photo Courtesy Greg Goebel, Licensed under Creative Commons)

Vultee and North American Aviation into the top two slots among the companies within the American aircraft industry during World War II. At the end of 1943, it was reported that Vultee's Downey plant was working on the largest single unit order yet placed by the War Department.

Aside from the Valiants, the US Navy's largest use of Wasp Juniors was to power the Vought OS2U Kingfisher observation floatplane. After the prototype, there were 54 OS2U-1s with 450-hp R-985-48 Wasp Junior SBs; 158 OS2U-2s with 450-hp R-985-50 Wasp Junior SBs; 1,006 OS2U-3s with 450-hp R-985-AN-2 Wasp Junior SBs; and 300 OS2N-1s built at the Naval Aircraft Factory with 450-hp R-985-AN-2 Wasp Junior SBs.

This is a Wright Whirlwind R-975 9-cylinder radial as the powerplant for an M4 Sherman tank. (Released under the GNU Free Documentation License)

A Wright Whirlwind R-975 E-3 9-cylinder air-cooled radial aircraft engine is shown in the Aviation Museum of Central Finland. (Photo Courtesy MKFI, Released into the Public Domain)

Pratt & Whitney's Twin Wasp Junior

As the name indicates, the R-1535 Twin Wasp Junior was a twin-row derivative of the Wasp Junior that displaced 1,535 ci. It had 14 cylinders, compared to the 9 of the Wasp Junior. While the Wasp Junior used direct drive, the Twin Wasp Junior used epicyclical gearing.

The R-1535 was 53.27 inches long with a diameter of 44.13 inches and a dry weight of 1,087 pounds. Both its stroke and bore were 5.1875 inches. The engine featured a valvetrain with two overhead valves for each cylinder, a single-speed centrifugal supercharger, and a Stromberg 2-barrel carburetor.

Horsepower ratings began at 625 hp for the R-1535-44. The R-1535-11 and R-1535-13 variants were both rated at 750 hp. Three variants were rated at 825 hp: the R-1535-94, R-1535-96, and R-1535-SB4-G.

Perhaps the single most notable use of the R-1535 was by Howard Hughes, who used it to power his H-1 race plane and set a world landplane speed record of 352.39 mph in September 1935. In US Navy applications, the Twin Wasp Junior powered 112 Vought SB2U Vindicator scout bombers and 54 Grumman F3F-1 biplane fighters. For subsequent F3F variants, Grumman chose the Wright R-1820 Cyclone that carried over into its F4F Wildcat monoplane fighter.

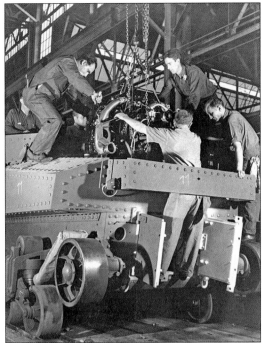

Alfred Palmer of the Office of War Information took this photo of workers lowering a 400-hp Wright R-975 Whirlwind engine into an M3 tank at the Chrysler tank arsenal. They are taking care to ensure that each fitting and connection may be made within a few seconds after the motor has been placed in the tank. (Photo Courtesy Library of Congress)

The US Army's Chrysler-built M3 Lee medium tank was powered by an R-975 radial engine. This Lee was photographed by Alfred Palmer during training exercises at Fort Knox, Kentucky, in June 1942. (Photo Courtesy Library of Congress)

Wright's R-975 Whirlwind

Wright's 9-cylinder Model J-6-9, with the military designation R-975 (introduced in Chapter 1), was produced in larger numbers than any other Whirlwind radial. As noted at the beginning of this chapter, between 1929 and 1953, Wright Aeronautical built more than 7,000, but according to Wright's own *Historical Engine Summary*, Continental added another 53,418 license-built R-975EC-series tank engines to the total between January 1938 and June 1945.

R-975 variants included the basic R-975, which delivered 300 hp at 2,000 rpm, and the R-975E, which delivered 330 hp thanks to an enhanced cylinder head design. In turn, the R-975E-1 brought the rating to 365 hp at 2,100 rpm due to a higher compression ratio.

The R-975E-3 of 1935 produced up to 450 hp at 2,250 rpm for takeoff. The general specifications for the R-975E-3, as detailed in its FAA-type certificate data sheet note a specific displacement of 972 ci, a length 43 inches, a diameter of 45 inches, and a dry weight of 675 pounds. This engine had direct-drive gearing and a gear-driven supercharger, and it featured a stroke and bore of 5.5 inches and 5 inches, respectively. The R-975E-3's valvetrain had two pushrod-actuated valves in each cylinder.

The R-975E-3 was rated at 450 hp at 2,250 rpm for takeoff and 420 hp at 2,200 rpm up to 1,400 feet. The R-975E was rated at 330 hp at 2,000 rpm, and the R-975E-1 was rated at 365 hp at 2,100 rpm.

In the 1930s, Wright found a modest commercial market for the R-975. This included 58 Douglas Dolphin flying boats and 785 Beechcraft Staggerwing biplanes. During World War II, important military aircraft applications for the R-975 were in some of the most widely produced USAAF basic trainers.

As noted earlier in this chapter, both the North American Yale and Vultee Valiant were produced in parallel variants with alternate designations depending upon engine type—even though the airframes were essentially the same. There were 266 North American Aviation BT-9 Yales produced with 400-hp R-975-7 Whirlwinds, and 251 Yales were built under the BT-14 designation with 450-hp Pratt & Whitney R-985 Wasp Juniors.

Likewise, 1,693 Vultee Valiants were produced under the BT-15 designation with 450-hp Wright R-975-11 Whirlwinds, while 7,832 Valiants were produced with Pratt & Whitney R-985-25 and R-985-AN-1 Wasp Juniors.

As with Continental's R-670 engines, the major wartime application of the R-975 was in armored vehicles. In 1939, given that Continental was already producing its own engines for tracked land vehicles, the US Army contracted with Continental to build the larger R-975 under license from Wright. The result was the Continental-built R-975EC (or R-975E-C), which was rated at 400 hp at 2,400 rpm.

It was in the production of these engines that Continental rolled out 53,418 R-975 Whirlwinds, which was more than 7 times the number built by Wright themselves.

While the Continental R-670 had been used in the M3 Stuart light tank, the fan-cooled R-975 Whirlwind was specified for the M3 medium tank, which became operational in 1941.

The M3 was produced in two variants that were named after Civil War generals Robert E. Lee and Ulysses S. Grant. The chassis and engines were the same, but the Lee had an American-designed turret, while the Grant's turret was based on a British design. Both the Lee and Grant served with both the British and American armies during the campaigns against the German Afrika Korps in North

Men work on the engine wiring subassemblies for M3 medium tanks at the Chrysler tank arsenal in Detroit. Visible in the immediate background are the 9-cylinder, 400-hp Wright R-975 Whirlwind aviation-type engines that powered these tanks. (Photo Courtesy Library of Congress)

The R-975 Whirlwind engine of a British Army Grant tank is removed for overhaul by the mechanics of a light recovery section of the Royal Army Ordnance Corps in June 1942. (Photo Courtesy Imperial War Museum, Public Domain)

American troops of the 60th Infantry Division advance through a Belgian town under the protection of an M4 Sherman tank on September 9, 1944. (Photo Courtesy US Army)

destroyer. The latter had a highway speed of 55 mph and was the fastest tracked, armored vehicle in the American arsenal during World War II and for decades thereafter.

After the war, the R-975 was used in the Piaseki helicopter that was designated as HUP-1 and HUP-2 by the US Navy and was designated as H-25 by the US Army. It was also produced under license in Brazil by Fabrica Nationale de Motores and in Spain by Hispano-Suiza. The irony of the latter arrangement is that back in the World War I era, a big part of the business of both Wright-Martin and Dayton-Wright (Wright Aeronautical's predecessors) was building engines under a license from Hispano-Suiza.

Africa in 1942 and 1943, but they were thereafter superseded by the M4 Sherman medium tank.

There were 6,250 M3 medium tanks produced by the time that production ended in December 1942. Of these, 2,887 were sent to the British Army and 1,386 were Lend Leased to the Soviet Army—although, a third of those never arrived because the ships carrying them were sunk by German U-Boats.

The M4 Sherman, which was introduced in 1942 and used in every major campaign thereafter, was the definitive American medium tank of World War II. It was produced in larger numbers, nearly 50,000, than any other American tank ever. With a chassis based on that of the M3 Lee/Grant series, it had a lower overall profile and many improved features. The basic M4 had a turret-mounted 75-mm gun, but later variants mounted 76-mm or even 105-mm guns.

Fan-cooled Continental R-975 Whirlwinds powered 6,748 M4s; 1,641 M4(105)s; 6,281 M4A1s; and 3,426 M4A1(76)s. Later Shermans switched to inline diesel engines. The M4A2s were powered by General Motors diesels, the M4A3s had Ford diesels, and the M4A4s were powered by Chrysler diesel engines.

Other armored vehicles using the R-975 included the M7 Priest self-propelled gun and the Buick M18 Hellcat tank

An M4 Sherman tank of the British Army's 8th Armoured Brigade advances through Kevelaer, Germany, on March 4, 1945. Later Sherman variants were powered by inline engines. (Photo Courtesy Imperial War Museum, Public Domain)

Chapter 7

THE WASP AND THE TEXAN

Pratt & Whitney's R-1340 Wasp was an engine with many lives, as it was a prominent powerplant in repeated chapters of 20th-century aviation history. In this book, it was first introduced in Chapter 2 as Faye Belden Rentschler and Evelyn Mead were passing out turkeys at the Pratt factory on Christmas Eve in 1925. Financier Edward Deeds had promised a holiday fowl for all members of the team that had gotten the Wasp up and running by that date, and the team had done it.

Before being used in the singular aircraft that is the subject of this chapter, the R-1340 had a notable tenure with earlier military aircraft. As discussed in Chapter 2, it was Boeing's choice for its great interwar fighters, including the P-12, F4B, and P-26 Peashooter.

Pratt & Whitney records list the total R-1340 production through the years at 34,966, although USAAF Materiel Command records note that the Jacobs Aircraft Engine Company of Pottstown, Pennsylvania, also produced 11,614 R-1340s under license through August 1945. The American Society of Mechanical Engineers named the R-1340 as a "Historic Engineering Landmark" but not until 2016.

The R-1340 was a 9-cylinder, single-row, air-cooled radial engine displacing 1,344 ci. As typified by the R-1340-AN-1 that was used on

An "old hand" briefs some young Women Airforce Service Pilots (WASPs) on the North American AT-6 Texan. The aircraft's Pratt & Whitney R-1340 Wasp engine is prominently visible in this picture.

The Pratt & Whitney R-1340 Wasp single-row, 9-cylinder, air-cooled, radial engine was first run on December 29, 1925, and it remained in production through World War II, with nearly 35,000 produced. This example is preserved at the Smithsonian Institution's National Air and Space Museum in Washington, D.C. (Photo Courtesy Sanjay Acharya, Licensed under Creative Commons)

An armed Texan flies a training mission out of Buckingham Army Airfield in Florida, circa 1942. This is an early AT-6C built by North American in Dallas, Texas. (Photo Courtesy USAAF)

A pair of USAAF North American AT-6C-NT Texan trainers are shown in flight near Luke Field, Arizona, in 1943. (Photo Courtesy USAF)

wartime Texan trainers from the AT-6B through the AT-6G, it was 43 inches long with a diameter of 51.81 inches and a dry weight of 878 pounds. Its compression ratio was 6.03:1, and it had a stroke and bore of 5.75 inches.

The R-1340-AN-1 used a Bendix-Stromberg NA-Y9E1-511 float carburetor and was rated at 600 hp at 2,250 rpm for takeoff and 550 hp at 2,200 rpm at 5,000 feet.

In the early 1930s, Wasps had powered the Granville Brothers' Gee Bee Racers. There were just a few Gee Bees, but they were worth more than their weight in headlines. The Wasp was there to power the extended family of P-12s (mainly with 450-hp R-1340-7s) and F4Bs (mainly with 500-hp R-1340-16s) that made Boeing the king of American fighter aviation for a prominent interwar moment.

As the larger R-1830 Twin Wasp assumed its own prominence on Pratt & Whitney's production line and as the R-985 Wasp Junior filled the market for a smaller radial engine, it might have seemed that the venerable R-1340 had seen its day. But then there was North American Aviation's Texan.

The Texan was not only an airplane but also a sprawling family of airplanes as vast as the Lone Star State that was its namesake. It was certainly the best-known American advanced trainer family of World War II. The Navy designated it as SNJ, while the USAAF and its Air Corps predecessor designated it as AT-6. In 1948, when the USAAF became the independent US Air Force, the AT-6 became the T-6.

There were 15,495 members of this family. North American built more of them than it did P-51 Mustangs or B-25 Mitchell medium bombers. Yet, when talking about big numbers, let us not forget that this number accounted for only 33.3 percent of all the R-1340s that were produced.

The crankshaft of a Pratt & Whitney R-1340 Wasp engine is lowered into its rear power case (1943).

The Texan is included in this study of warbirds, not as a combat aircraft but because our modern perspective on the warbirds of World War II is profoundly incomplete without it. Dozens of these aircraft are still operational in the 21st century, constituting an important element within the warbird community.

The Texan was the result of a project that was North American's first all-new aircraft program, and it began seven long years after the company was created. Why did it take so long?

As introduced in Chapter 1, North American Aviation was formed in 1928 by investment banker Clement Melville Keys merely as an umbrella, a holding company, for the aviation businesses that he had been acquiring. A 70-percent stake in North American was owned by the Curtiss Aeroplane & Motor Company, which Keys then controlled. Ernest Breech, an accountant who later had a career as chairman of Ford Motor Company, was then brought in as North American's chairman. Unlike many early aircraft companies, Keys and Breech directed the fate of North American from the perspective of financiers—not engineers.

Although North American Aviation was founded in 1928, it was really not "born" until 1934, when Breech installed James Howard "Dutch" Kindelberger (a former chief engineer and vice president at

Douglas Aircraft) as North American's president and general manager. He moved the base of operations from Dundalk, Maryland, to Inglewood, California, and hired John Leland "Lee" Atwood as North American's chief engineer. The two of them transformed the company into being a major player in the industry.

Their first real project was the aircraft that was the Texan's predecessor. When Kindelberger and Atwood rolled up their sleeves, there was little ongoing business aside from some bits and pieces left over from the companies that the holding company held. Kindelberger had, however, managed to secure a contract for a new US Army Air Corps basic trainer, which was created as the North American Model NA-16. First flown in 1935, it spawned an extensive family of variants. These received a large number of separate North American Aviation model numbers that reached into the NA-60s but were intermingled with model numbers applied to the larger aircraft that became the Texan.

Many were built for export to countries from Brazil to Japan. The largest overseas delivery was the 138 Model 31s that were bought by neutral Sweden.

After World War II began, both Britain and France sought to tap the industrial might of America to acquire military hardware.

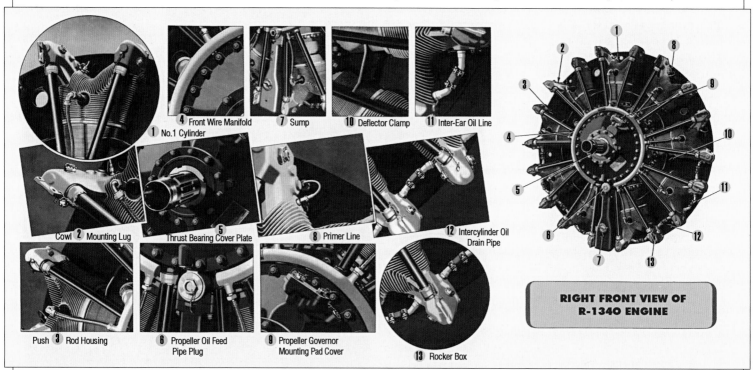

1 No.1 Cylinder
2 Mounting Lug
3 Rod Housing
4 Front Wire Manifold
5 Thrust Bearing Cover Plate
6 Propeller Oil Feed Pipe Plug
7 Sump
8 Primer Line
9 Propeller Governor Mounting Pad Cover
10 Deflector Clamp
11 Inter-Ear Oil Line
12 Intercylinder Oil Drain Pipe
13 Rocker Box

Cowl / Push

RIGHT FRONT VIEW OF R-1340 ENGINE

The details of a Pratt & Whitney R-1340 Wasp 9-cylinder radial engine are shown in this front view contained in a maintenance circular released by the USAAF Air Service Command in October 1943. (Photo Courtesy US Air Force)

Orders were placed by the New York–based Anglo-French Purchasing Board on a "cash-and-carry" basis because American neutrality laws prohibited military aid to warring parties. The French ordered 230 Model NA-64s from North American Aviation, but only 111 had been delivered before France was defeated by Germany in June 1940.

At this point, the Anglo-French Purchasing Board became the British Purchasing Commission, and the British Empire took over the orders that had previously been placed by France, including the 119 undelivered NA-64s. These were delivered to the Royal Canadian Air Force (RCAF) in the fall of 1940 for use in Canada under the British Commonwealth Air Training Plan. These aircraft were known as Yale Mk.I under the naming convention that had North American Aviation trainers designated with the names of American Ivy League colleges.

The US Army Air Corps bought two variants with separate designations based mainly on engine type. They were 266 Model NA-19s designated as BT-9 and powered by Wright R-975-7 Whirlwinds as well as 251 NA-64s built under the BT-14 designation with Pratt & Whitney R-985 Wasp Juniors. The name "Yale" was also applied to these.

The US Navy ordered 40 NA-28 (BT-9 equivalent) aircraft under the designation NJ-1, with "N" being the designator for "trainer,"

The crankshaft hydraulic puller bar is installed in a Pratt & Whitney R-1340 Wasp engine (1943).

The cylinder unit of the hydraulic puller is installed in a Pratt & Whitney R-1340 Wasp engine (1943).

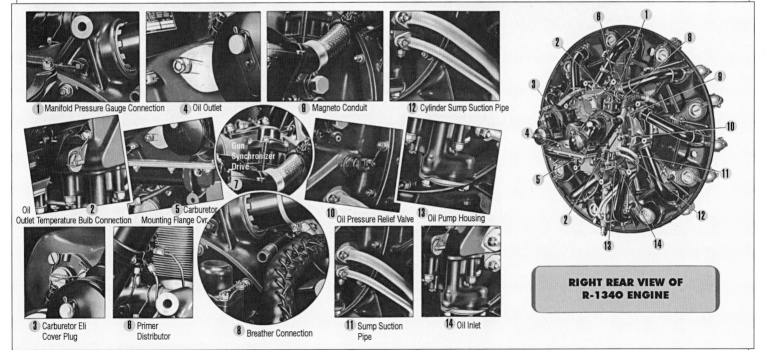

1 Manifold Pressure Gauge Connection
4 Oil Outlet
9 Magneto Conduit
12 Cylinder Sump Suction Pipe
2 Oil Outlet Temperature Bulb Connection
5 Carburetor Mounting Flange Cvr.
7 Gun Synchronizer Drive
10 Oil Pressure Relief Valve
13 Oil Pump Housing
3 Carburetor Eli Cover Plug
6 Primer Distributor
8 Breather Connection
11 Sump Suction Pipe
14 Oil Inlet

RIGHT REAR VIEW OF R-1340 ENGINE

The details of a Pratt & Whitney R-1340 Wasp 9-cylinder radial engine are shown in this rear view contained in a maintenance circular released by the USAAF Air Service Command in October 1943. (Photo Courtesy US Air Force)

and "J" being the manufacturer code for North American Aviation.

In the arc of the evolution from the original NA-16 to the Texan, the transition point came with the larger Model NA-36, 177 of which were acquired by the Army Air Corps under the "Basic Combat Trainer" designation BC-1. First delivered to the Air Corps in June 1937, it was powered by an R-1340-47, becoming the first member of the lineage to use the Wasp.

From the bigger BC-1 (with its more powerful engine, retractable landing gear, and other improvements) came the idea of adapting it as an advanced trainer. Indeed, nine aircraft on the BC-1 order became the first AT-6s. In the spring of 1939, an additional 85 AT-6s, also with R-1340-47 engines, were ordered under the AT-6 designation.

The US Navy acquired its AT-6 equivalent aircraft under the "Scout Trainer" designation prefix SNJ. There were 16 Model 52s that became SNJ-1s, 36 NA-65s that became SNJ-2s, and 25 NA-79s that also became SNJ-2s. The SNJ-2s were powered by R-1340-56 engines.

In the meantime, the British Royal Air Force (RAF) had placed orders for 400 of these aircraft under the model number NA-49 in December 1938 even before it acquired its Yales from the hand-me-down French order. The RCAF ordered 30 of these with

US Navy enlisted personnel hose down a North American SNJ Texan at Naval Air Station Jacksonville, circa 1944. (Photo Courtesy US Navy)

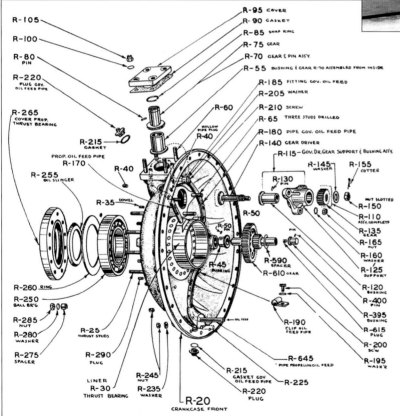

Here is an exploded view of the blower case in a Pratt & Whitney R-1340 Wasp engine (1943).

A detailed view is shown of the Bendix NA-Y9E1 float carburetor of the type used in Pratt & Whitney R-1340 Wasp engines.

North American model number NA-61 in May 1939. Under the Ivy League naming convention, the British and Canadians designated their NA-49s and NA-61s as Harvard Mk.Is. In November 1939, after World War II began, the British Purchasing Commission bought 1,275 aircraft (Models NA-66, NA-75, NA-76, and NA-81) for the RAF and RCAF as Harvard Mk.IIs.

The name "Harvard" was not shared by the American services, which had adopted the name "Texan." Indeed, the majority of them were built after 1941 at the new North American Aviation factory near Dallas, Texas.

In 1937, Australia acquired just two aircraft (a Model NA-32 and an NA-33) and a license by which the Commonwealth Aircraft Corporation (CAC) would build 755 of them, named Wirraway, in Melbourne. CAC also obtained a license from Pratt & Whitney to manufacture R-1340 engines in Australia.

A restored North American AT-6 Texan is shown in US Air Force markings (2013). (Photo Courtesy Bomberpilot, Licensed through Creative Commons)

This restored North American SNJ Texan is shown in US Marine Corps markings (2013). (Photo Courtesy John Murphy, Licensed through Creative Commons)

A technician tightens the pushrod housing nuts in a Pratt & Whitney R-1340 Wasp engine (1943).

US Navy mechanics work on the Pratt & Whitney R-1340-AN-1 engine of a North American SNJ trainer at Kingville Field, NATC Corpus Christi, Texas, in November 1942. (Photo Courtesy US Navy)

In 1941, on the eve of the United States entry into World War II as the Army Air Corps became the US Army Air Forces (USAAF), that service placed orders for 1,847 AT-6A Texans. Of these, 517 were built in Inglewood as AT-6A-NAs, and the rest were built in Texas as AT-6A-NTs. These were powered by R-1340-49 Wasps that were rated at 600 hp at 2,250 rpm for takeoff and 550 hp at 2,200 rpm at 5,000 feet.

The US Navy ordered 270 AT-6A-equivalent Texans as SNJ-3s, which were augmented by 298 AT-6A-NTs that were transferred from the USAAF and also designated as SNJ-3s. Meanwhile, Montreal-based Noorduyn Aviation received a license in 1942 to build AT-6A equivalents in Canada and produced 2,557 of them as Harvard IIBs with Pratt & Whitney R-1340-AN-1 engines.

Beginning with the AT-6B (NA-84), the R-1340-AN-1 engine became the standard Texan powerplant just as all production of Texans was now taking place in Texas. There were 400 AT-6Bs produced, and all were for the USAAF.

Orders for the AT-6C variant (NA-88) began in 1941, continued into 1942, and totaled 2,970 aircraft. Of these, 747 were lend-leased to the RAF and RCAF, where they were designated as Harvard IIAs. The Navy equivalent was the SNJ-4, of which 2,400 were produced.

The largest single Texan variant was the AT-6D (NA-88 and NA-121), of which 4,388 were built. The first deliveries were in June 1943. Many of these were transferred to the US Navy as SNJ-5s. John Andrade put the number at 1,573, while Dan Hagedorn, in his

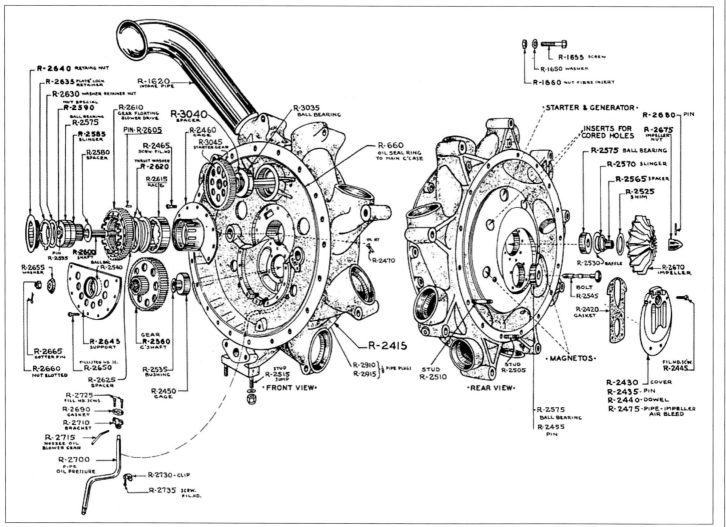

This is an exploded view of the nose section of a Pratt & Whitney R-1340 Wasp engine (1943).

After World War II, North American AT-6 Texans, mainly surplus American aircraft, served with more than 60 air forces around the world. Seen here in 1960 are Texans of the Austrian Air Force (Österreichische Luftstreitkräfte) at Langenlebarn (later Brumowski) Air Base. (Photo Courtesy Bundesheer Fotos, Licensed through Creative Commons)

definitive book on the Texan, gave a total of 1,987 SNJ-5s.

There were 956 examples of the AT-6F (NA-121) with transfers to the Navy as SNJ-6s numbering 411.

In 1948, after the USAAF became the independent US Air Force, the AT-6s were redesignated as T-6s, as it standardized its designation prefix for all trainers as "T." In 1949, the service ordered the remanufacturing of more than 2,000 earlier Texans under the designation T-6G (NA-168). These were rebuilt with their original R-1340-AN-1

During the Korean War, the US Air Force North American T-6 Texans were deployed into combat as forward air control aircraft. Here, one such Texan is seen at an American base in Korea armed with underwing phosphor rockets, which were used to visually mark targets for strike aircraft. Air Force personnel in the field fabricated rocket rails to attach custom-made rockets made from 2.36-inch white phosphorus bazooka warheads attached to the front of a 2.25-inch aircraft practice rocket. (Photo Courtesy US Air Force)

engines. The Navy also brought many of its earlier Texans up to T-6G standard as SNJ-7s.

The aircraft also remained in production. In Canada, Canadian Car & Foundry, which acquired Noorduyn Aviation in 1946, went on to produce 285 North American Model NA-186s as the Harvard IV and another 270 that were designated as the Harvard 4 by the RCAF. Many of the postwar T-6s as well as Harvard IVs were disseminated by the US government to countries in the North Atlantic Treaty Organization (NATO) as well as to small air forces around the world under the Military Assistance Program (MAP) and the Mutual Defense Assistance Program (MDAP).

Some postwar T-6 Texans used the R-1340-S1H1-G (R-1340-36) Wasp with a geared drivetrain. It was 44.2 inches long with a diameter of 51.5 inches and a dry weight of 877 pounds. Its compression ratio was 6:1, and it had a stroke and bore of 5.75 inches. The

A North American T-6G Texan is shown with the markings of the Spanish Air Force (Ejército del Aire) in 2012. (Photo Courtesy José A. Montes, Licensed under Creative Commons)

This restored Royal Australian Air Force Harvard II (AT-6A equivalent) is seen here in 2005 in Royal Air Force desert camouflage colors at the Australian International Airshow at Avalon Airport near Melbourne. (Photo Courtesy GSL, Licensed under Creative Commons)

A restored North American AT-6 Texan is on display at the Cavanaugh Flight Museum at Addison Airport in Addison, Texas. (Photo Courtesy Michael Barera, Licensed through Creative Commons)

R-1340-S1H1-G used a Bendix-Stromberg NA-Y9J-3 carburetor. The engine was rated at 600 hp at 2,250 rpm for takeoff and 550 hp at 2,200 rpm at 5,000 feet, which was the same as for the R-1340-AN-1.

As a military aircraft, the Texan's front-line career in American service, which began in the 1930s, defined flight training during World War II and extended into the 1960s. It served with American services as a liaison aircraft and forward air control platform from the Korean War through the Vietnam War era. With five dozen military services, it served as a trainer and even as a light attack aircraft. Adapted for the latter, it served Britain, France, Spain, and Portugal in counter-insurgency operations in Africa and with the Hellenic Air Force in Europe.

Today, a few decades into another century, this aircraft (as the Texan or Harvard) is widely found in civilian use and is ubiquitous on the air show circuit.

This shows the Pratt & Whitney R-1340-AN-1 Wasp powering this T-6G Texan on display at the Museo del Aire at Cuatro Vientos near Madrid, Spain. (Photo Courtesy Barcex, Licensed under Creative Commons)

Chapter 8

THE WRIGHT TWIN CYCLONE IN TWIN-ENGINE BOMBERS

On the road map of wartime round engines, Wright's R-2600 is analogous to the parallel Pratt & Whitney R-2800 in the way that the Wright R-1820 parallels Pratt & Whitney's R-1830. They were comparable and competing power-plants that achieved prominence in parallel aircraft types.

The 14-cylinder Wright R-2600 Twin Cyclone originated in 1935 as a company effort to develop a more powerful twin-row companion to the R-1820 Cyclone. Destined to become a commercial success, it came on the shoulders of some experimental twin-row efforts that Wright made a few years earlier as extensions of its smaller Whirlwind family.

The records of Wright Aeronautical show that the company produced 76,488 R-2600s for military use at its factories in Patterson, New Jersey, and Lockland, Ohio, on the north side of Cincinnati.

A Douglas technician examines the left Wright R-2600 Twin Cyclone of a DB-7 at Long Beach on July 12, 1940. This was one of more than a hundred such aircraft that was produced under a French contract issued prior to the fall of France to Germany a month earlier. They were turned over to the UK and served the RAF as Boston Mk.Is.

The 14-cylinder Whirlwind R-1510 of 1933 actually had a displacement of 1,512 ci, while the R-1670 of 1934 displaced the indicated 1,670 inches. The respective weights of the two engines were 1,025 and 1,236 pounds. The R-1510 had a rating of 600 hp at 2,100 rpm, while its larger sibling delivered 800 hp at 2,500 rpm.

These two prototype Whirlwinds were overshadowed by the R-760 and R-975 Whirlwinds. Only two R-1670s were built, and company records report just 33 R-1510s.

Although the R-2600, which actually displaced 2,603 ci, was installed almost exclusively in military combat aircraft, it was first used as a commercial engine. Pan American Airways had been offering airline service throughout the Americas and the Caribbean since 1931 using Sikorsky flying boats and had started trans-Pacific service using Marin M-130s in 1935. When Pan Am let it be known that it wanted a larger-capacity and longer-range flying boat for both Pacific and Atlantic service, Boeing responded with its Model 314 Clipper flying boat and won the contract in July 1936.

For the Model 314, Boeing initially chose the Pratt & Whitney R-1830 Twin Wasp, but Wright suggested the R-2600. Boeing made the switch from Pratt to Wright, and the Model 314A variant went into service. Used in the Boeing Clipper, the 14-cylinder GR-2600A Twin Cyclone of 1937 was rated at 1,600 hp at 2,400 rpm and had a dry weight of 1,935 pounds. It had a stroke of 6.3125 inches and bore of 6.125 inches. Wright promoted its geared-drivetrain GR-2600A as "the most powerful air-cooled aircraft engine developed up to this time."

Using the Model 314, Pan Am initiated luxury class service from San Francisco to Manila and Hong Kong via Honolulu, Wake Island, and Guam. Flights across the Atlantic to Southampton and Lisbon had just begun when World War II started in 1939. For a program that produced only a dozen aircraft, the Model 314 made an immense impression on the world of commercial air travel, but because of the war, the great commercial potential of the Boeing Clipper to revolutionize air travel was never realized.

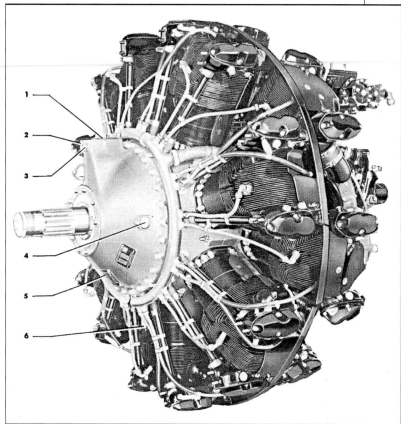

For Wright and its R-2600, however, World War II offered an immense opportunity. In this chapter, the story of the R-2600 is told within the context of twin-engine bombers. The main focus is on the Douglas Boston/Havoc family and the North American Aviation B-25 Mitchell, but not to be forgotten are the Martin Mariner and Martin Baltimore with which the chapter is rounded out.

This is the Wright R-2600 Twin Cyclone (also called the Cyclone 14) twin-row, 14-cylinder radial aircraft engine. It was first run in 1935, and more than 50,000 were built at plants in Paterson, New Jersey, and Cincinnati, Ohio. (Photo Courtesy Kogo, Licensed under the GNU Free Documentation License)

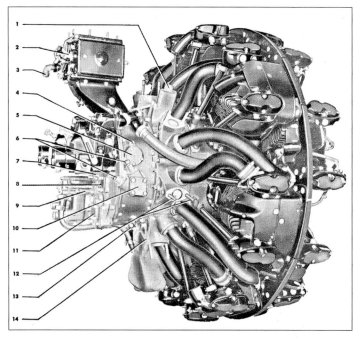

Above is a three-quarter left front view of a Wright R-2600 Twin Cyclone (May 1943).

1. Propeller Governor Drive
2. Hydro High Oil Gauge Connection
3. Hydro Low Oil Gauge Connection
4. Timing Hole Plug
5. Engine Data Plate
6. Crankcase Front Section Oil Drain

On the left is a three-quarter right rear view of a Wright R-2600 Twin Cyclone (May 1943).

1. Crankcase Breather Vent, Right Connection
2. Throttle lever
3. Fuel Inlet Connection
4. Accessory Oil Return Connection, Right
5. Gun Synchronizer Drive Substituting Cover, Right
6. Tachometer Drives, Mechanical
7. Starter Mounting Pad
8. Accessory Drive, Upper
9. Supercharger Clutch Control Valve
10. Fuel Pump Drive
11. Accessory Drive, lower
12. Dynamic Type Mount Attaching Studs
13. Supercharger Drain Valve
14. Plain Type Mount Bolt Holes

A crew at the Douglas Aircraft Company plant in Long Beach works on a Wright R-2600 Cyclone 14-cylinder engine of a Douglas A-20 Havoc twin-engine bomber. The markings on the propeller state that it was installed on October 2, 1942. (Photo Courtesy Library of Congress)

Launching the Douglas DB-7/A-20 Program

One of the first major military applications of the R-2600 Twin Cyclone was for the Douglas DB-7/A-20 family of bombers. This series, which began as the Douglas Model DB-7 bomber for export to France, was produced in greater numbers than any other Douglas warplane ever. Company records show that 7,477 were built, including 999 A-20A-DLs built in Long Beach; 808 A-20C-DOss built in Santa Monica; and 2,850 A-20G-DOs that were also built in Santa Monica. The aircraft was exported to Britain as the Boston and adapted by the USAAF as a night fighter under the P-70 designation.

When the DB-7 program began (with orders from Belgium and France before the United States entered World War II), Douglas used the Pratt & Whitney R-1830-SC3G Twin Wasp.

The Wright R-2600 entered the picture in 1939 when the US Army Air Corps ordered its first 63 A-20 Havocs with R-2600-7s, and France ordered 100 DB-7A aircraft to be powered by 1,275-hp GR-2600-A5Bs.

In Europe, events overtook the DB-7 program. The German assault on the West began in May 1940, and only 64 DB-7s reached French squadrons. Belgium and France were defeated on May 28 and June 25, respectively.

As with the Martin Model 167 Marylands that France ordered, many of the DB-7s on order or in the pipeline at the time were diverted to Britain's Royal Air Force. The first 121 DB-7s from continental orders were designated by the RAF as Boston Mk.Is, while the DB-7As were among those that became Boston Mk.IIs. Some of the Bostons were converted to night-fighter configuration and named Havoc Mk.Is and Havoc Mk.IIs, using the name assigned by the Americans to their aircraft.

The DB-7C was another export variant that was ordered after the defeat of France and the low countries. Unlike those of Belgium and France, the government of the Netherlands went into exile in Britain and continued to function. The Dutch were in a peculiar position of having their homeland under German occupation, while the Dutch East Indies, a colony 46 times larger than the home country, remained unoccupied and with a Dutch colonial government in place—albeit fearful of a Japanese invasion that did eventually come. In October 1941, to defend this colony, the Netherlands government ordered 48 DB-7Cs, of which roughly half had been delivered when the Japanese attacked three months later.

With its Wright R-2600 Twin Cyclone engines installed, this A-20 Havoc bomber rolls out of the Douglas Aircraft Company plant in Long Beach, California. (Photo Courtesy National Archives)

Beginning in 1939, the US Army Air Corps acquired 63 A-20 Havocs and 143 A-20A Havocs from Douglas, both of which were powered by R-2600 Twin Cyclones. The A-20 used the supercharged R-2600-7, while the A-20A used the R-2600-3. In October 1940, 999 A-20Bs with self-sealing fuel tanks and upgraded armament were added to the order books. The powerplant for the A-20B was the R-2600-11 Twin Cyclone.

Early R-2600s for Early Douglas Havocs

Of the three Twin Cyclones used in early variant A-20-series aircraft, the R-2600-3 entered production in April 1939 and remained on the assembly line until February 1940. Only 164 were built. The R-2600-7 appeared a month later, and production of 217 engines continued to September 1941. This overlapped the R-2600-11, which was in production from February 1940 through November 1942 with 3,258 engines manufactured.

The R-2600-3 was rated at 1,600 hp at 2,200 rpm for takeoff and at 1,275 hp at 12,000 feet. It had a compression ratio of 6.9:1 and a supercharger ratio of up to 10:1. The R-2600-7 was rated at 1,700 hp at 2,500 rpm for takeoff and at 1,700 hp at 20,000 feet. It had a compression ratio of 6.85:1 and a supercharger ratio of 7.06:1. The R-2600-11 was rated at 1,600 hp at 2,300 rpm for takeoff and at 1,275 hp at 11,500 feet. It had a compression ratio of 4.9:1 and a supercharger ratio of up to 10:1.

The stroke and bore of all three engines were 6.312 inches and 6.125 inches respectively, but other specifications differed from engine to engine.

The R-2600-3 weighed 1,940 pounds and was 65 inches long with a diameter of 55 inches. The R-2600-7 weighed 1,965 pounds and was 63.1 inches long with a diameter of 54.26 inches. The R-2600-11 weighed 1,940 pounds and was 65 inches long with a diameter of 55 inches.

Expanding Boston/Havoc Production

In March 1941, as the war raged in Europe, President Roosevelt signed the Lend Lease Act, a pet project of his that was a means of aiding Britain by "leasing," rather than selling or giving war materiel. A month later, the first aircraft orders under the Lend Lease scheme were issued to Douglas Aircraft under Contract DA2. The specific type covered by this contact was the latest variant of an ongoing program: the A-20C.

Against the backdrop of Lend Lease, production of Boston and Havoc aircraft mushroomed. The initial contract called for 375 A-20C-DO aircraft to be built at Santa Monica, most of which would be leased to the British as Boston Mk.IIIAs, but this was only the beginning. Contract DA934 increased the number of A-20C-DOs by 433 to 808.

Meanwhile, the Materiel Command's program of multisource acquisition came into play. Contract DA1 called for Douglas to license production to Boeing so that an additional 140 A-20C-BO Havocs could be built in Seattle. This was at the same time that Douglas was building Boeing B-17s at Long Beach.

In addition to these numbers, a review of tail numbers reveals 780 Boston Mk.IIIs that went directly to the RAF without having

A USAAF ground crew services a Douglas A-20C Havoc and its Wright R-2600-23 Twin Cyclone engines at Langley Field, Virginia in July 1942. (Photo Courtesy Library of Congress)

been assigned USAAF numbers, while 200 USAAF A-20Cs went to the RAF as Boston Mk.IIIAs. Another 56 Boston Mk.IIIs Lend Leased directly to the Soviet Union with Soviet tail numbers.

The next Havoc production variants, the A-20G and A-20H, were distinguished by having solid noses rather than the "greenhouse" nose configuration of the earlier types. This nose contained a variety of forward-firing armament, including an arrangement of four 20-mm cannons plus machine guns.

Beginning in 1942 and extending into 1943, the USAAF acquired a total of 2,850 A-20Gs, making it the largest Havoc variant. These were ordered in 10 production blocks, all of which were produced at Santa Monica.

Also made in Santa Monica, the 412 A-20H Havocs were essentially a nearly identical continuation of the A-20G series that were ordered in 1944. The main difference was a dissimilar engine variant. While the A-20C and A-20G aircraft were all powered by the R-2600-23, the A-20H was fitted with R-2600-29 engines.

The next production variant of the Havoc was the A-20J, of which 450 were built, including 169 that were delivered to the RAF as Boston Mk.IVs. These were similar to the A-20G and A-20H, but 7 inches longer to accommodate a frameless, single-piece Plexiglas nose containing a bombardier position and a Norden bombsight. As with the A-20G, the A-20J was powered with R-2600-23 engines.

Douglas workers are shown at Long Beach in a lighter moment as they pretend to rotate the propeller of a P-70, the night fighter variant of the A-20.

The final Havoc production variant was the A-20K, of which 413 were made, including 90 that joined the RAF as Boston Mk.Vs. The A-20K was essentially an A-20H airframe, including the R-2600-29 engines, but with the bombardier nose of the A-20J.

Another solid-nose, heavily armed derivative of the Havoc family was the P-70 night fighter. All 270 of the P-70s were conversions from A-20s of various types. At this time, the Airborne Intercept (AI) radar systems were quite large and needed a dedicated operator, so larger twin-engine aircraft were necessary.

The early P-70s were equipped with the Mk.V system developed by EMI in Britain as a development of the Mk.VI radar that had been successfully used by RAF night fighters since November 1940. The P-70B variant, converted from A-20Gs and A-20Js, used the widely installed Western Electric SCR-720 system, or SCR-729 (AN/APN-2) "Rebecca" transponding radar.

The P-70 was also equipped with a powerful "turbinlight" searchlight that was to be turned on when the Havoc got close to its target.

R-2600-23 R-2600-29 Twin Cyclones for Later Havoc Variants

As noted above, the great preponderance of Havoc and Boston aircraft were powered by Wright R-2600-23 or R-2600-29 engines. The records of Wright Aeronautical note that 10,342 R-2600-23s were built between March 1942 and November 1944. There was considerable overlap with the R-2600-29, of which 18,784 were produced between June 1943 and July 1945. The latter engine was also used in the North American Aviation B-25J.

Douglas workers mount a Wright R-2600 Twin Cyclone in the left engine nacelle of an A-20 Havoc at Long Beach.

Both the later Douglas A-20Gs and the A-20Hs had four .50-caliber guns installed in the nose and a powered top turret. The A-20G was powered by a pair of Wright R-2600-23 Cyclones; the A-20H by R-2600-29s. These Havocs are returning to bases in England after a 1944 mission over the continent.

The R-2600-23 was rated at 1,600 hp at 2,400 rpm for takeoff and at 1,350 hp at 2,300 rpm in flight. It had a compression ratio of 6.3:1 and a supercharger ratio of up to 10:1. The R-2600-23 weighed 1,969 pounds and was 58.32 inches long with a diameter of 55.1 inches.

The R-2600-29 was rated at 1,700 hp at 2,800 rpm for takeoff and at 1,500 hp at 2,400 rpm in flight. It had a compression ratio of 6.9:1 and a supercharger ratio of up to 10.06:1. The R-2600-29 weighed 2,000 pounds and was 63.1 inches long with a diameter of 54.26 inches.

As with earlier Twin Cyclones, the stroke and bore of both engines were 6.312 inches and 6.125 inches, respectively.

The North American Aviation B-25 Mitchell

As the Douglas A-20 was designated as an "attack," or "light," bomber, the Mitchell was identified as a "medium" bomber. However, they were both twin-engine aircraft quite similar in size and capability. B-25G was 51 feet long with a wingspan of 67 feet 7 inches compared to 48 feet and 61 feet 3.5 inches for the A-20G. The B-25G Mitchell had a gross weight of 33,500 pounds, while the A-20G Havoc weighed 21,971 pounds. The typical bomb load of each was around 2 tons depending on the mission and configuration, and they each had a ferry range of around 2,000 miles depending on various factors.

Both had variants with "glass" noses and bombardiers for conventional high-altitude bombing, and both had variants with solid noses filled with guns for low-level ground-attack operations.

Both Havoc and Mitchell were powered by variants of the Wright R-2600 Twin Cyclone. However, when the prototype of the Mitchell (the company-owned NA-40) first flew on February 10, 1939, it was powered by Pratt & Whitney R-1830-S6C3-G Wasps. North American Aviation switched out the Twin Wasps for GR-2600-A71s before presenting the aircraft to the Air Corps as the NA-40B.

Having accepted the NA-40B for production, the Air Corps assigned the B-25 designation and ordered two dozen with Wright R-2600-9 engines. These were followed by an order for 160 B-25As with crew armor installed. In the fall of 1941, after 40 B-25As had been delivered, the USAAF decided to add a Bendix top turret, and the last 120 were delivered as B-25Bs. At the time that the United States entered World War II in December 1941, all but 30 of the B-25A/B-25B order had been delivered—all with R-2600-9 engines. Of these, the RAF was Lend Leased 23 B-25Bs, which were designated as Mitchell Mk.Is.

Production of the B-25C, the first large-scale production variant, began in January 1942, and 1,625 were produced through May 1943 in seven production blocks. Powered by the R-2600-13 Twin Cyclone, they were all produced at North American's headquarters

Compare this left side view of a Wright R-2600 Twin Cyclone engine to the nearby image highlighting components. (Photo Courtesy Dsdugan, Licensed under Creative Commons)

plant in Inglewood, California, adjacent to Mines Field, the future Los Angeles International Airport (LAX).

In the meantime, the government factory in Kansas City that was earmarked for North American came online in February 1942, and production began of the B-25D, which was analogous to the California-produced B-25C, complete with R-2600-13s. As production unfolded through the coming months, the incremental block changes in the production of both variants were made in parallel. There were 2,290 B-25Ds built in 9 blocks. From this total, the RAF received 571 B-25C and B-25D aircraft, which were designated as Mitchell Mk.IIs. The US Navy received 50 B-25Cs and 152 B-25Ds from USAAF orders, designating them as PBJ-1Cs and PBJ-1Ds.

With the B-25E and B-25F designations going to single B-25C conversions used as deicing testbeds, the next production Mitchell variant was the B-25G. A total of 400 of these were built in 3 blocks in Inglewood.

Powered by the R-2600-13, the B-25G was similar to the B-25C but with a completely redesigned nose. While all previous Mitchells had a greenhouse nose with a bombardier's station, the B-25G had a shortened, solid nose filled with guns for ground attack. Most notably, one of these guns was an M4 75-mm cannon of the type used both in tanks and by ground troops as an anti-tank gun.

The B-25H retained the solid nose of the B-25G, in which were installed various configurations of .50-caliber machine guns as well as an Oldsmobile-built M6/T13E1 75-mm cannon. There were 1,000 B-25Hs built in 3 blocks at Inglewood between July 1943 and July 1944. Of these, 248 were transferred to the US Nat as PBJ-1Hs.

The largest number of Mitchells of any variant were the B-25Js, which was the final production variant. There were 4,318 B-25Js produced in 13 blocks. All were built at Kansas City, and all of them were powered by R-2600-29s. The RAF received USAAF 316 B-25Js, which were designated as Mitchell Mk.IIIs, while the US Navy got 255 as PBJ-1Js.

The B-25J marked a return to the greenhouse nose of earlier variants, although the B-25J-27-NC and B-25J-32-NC blocks had solid noses with eight .50-caliber machine guns.

In addition to the armament noted above, the B-25H and B-25J aircraft (except the first B-25H block) had a pair of forward-firing

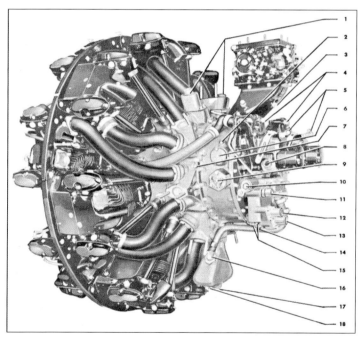

This is a three-quarter left rear view of a Wright R-2600 Twin Cyclone (May 1943).

1. Crankcase Breather Vents
2. Accessory Oil Return Connection, Left
3. Exhaust Heater Connection
4. Booster Magneto Terminals
5. Magneto Ground Terminals
6. Gun Synchronizer Drive Substituting Cover, Left
7. Manifold Pressure Gauge Connection
8. Magneto Blast Tube Connection, Left
9. Oil Filter
10. Oil Pump Check Valve
11. Oil Pump Pressure Relief Valve
12. Oil Inlet Connection
13. Oil Outlet Connection
14. Oil Out Thermometer Connection
15. Oil in Thermometer Connection
16. External Oil Scavenge Line
17. Oil Sump Strainer
18. Oil Sump Magnetic Drain Plug

A Wright R-2600 Cyclone engine is mounted in a North American B-25 Mitchell bomber at the North American Aviation plant in Inglewood, California. (Photo Courtesy Library of Congress)

North American Aviation's "Sunshine Assembly Line" at Inglewood took advantage of the Southern California weather, which allowed final assembly activities to take place outdoors. The Wright R-2600 engines have already been hung on these B-25 Mitchell bombers. (Photo Courtesy Library of Congress)

One of the early North American B-25C Mitchell bombers flies over Southern California in 1942. Like previous variant Mitchells, the B-25C sported a glass bombardier nose. The B-25Cs were powered by Wright R-2600-13 Cyclones. (Photo Courtesy Library of Congress)

Here, the cowling and control rods are added to Wright R-2600 engines as they move down the assembly line in 1942. The completed engines would soon be hung on B-25 Mitchell bombers here at the North American Aviation plant in Inglewood, California. (Photo Courtesy Library of Congress)

.50-calinber machine guns mounted in external "fuselage packages" on each side of the fuselage near the flight deck. This same package was retrofitted to many B-25C and B-25D aircraft.

Twin Cyclones for the Mitchell

As noted above, while the original preproduction prototype NA-40 was powered by a Pratt & Whitney R-1830-S6C3-G Wasp, all subsequent Mitchells used variants of the Wright R-2600 Twin Cyclone.

Through the B-25B, the engine was the R-2600-9, of which Wright produced a total of 522 for various aircraft. This engine was rated at 1,700 hp at 2,600 rpm for takeoff and 1,350 hp at 13,000 feet. It had a compression ratio of 6.9:1 and a supercharger ratio of 7.06:1 to 10.06:1. The R-2600-9 weighed 1,980 pounds and was 63.1 inches long with a diameter of 54.25 inches.

The B-25C through B-25H variants were powered by the R-2600-13, of which Wright Aeronautical produced 13,494 units between April 1941 and January 1944. The R-2600-13 was rated at 1,700 hp at 2,600 rpm for takeoff and at 1,450 hp at 12,000 feet. It had a compression ratio of 6.9:1 and a supercharger ratio of 7.06:1 to 10.06:1. The R-2600-13 weighed 2,000 pounds and was 63.1 inches long with a diameter of 54.26 inches.

The final Mitchell production variant, the B-25J, was powered by the R-2600-29, the same engine as used in the A-20H. As noted above, 18,784 were produced between June 1943 and July 1945. This engine was rated at 1,700 hp at 2,800 rpm for takeoff and at 1,500 hp at 2,400 rpm in flight. It had a compression ratio of 6.9:1 and a supercharger ratio of up to 10.06:1. The R-2600-29 weighed 2,000 pounds and was 63.1 inches long with a diameter of 54.26 inches. Also as noted previously, Twin Cyclones had a stroke and bore of 6.312 inches and 6.125 inches, respectively.

The Martin Mariner

Among US Navy twin-engine patrol bombers, the Martin PBM Mariner flying boat also used the Twin Cyclone. The XPBM-1 prototype made its debut in February 1939 powered by two R-2600-6s, and the same engine type powered the initial batch of 20 PBM-1s that were delivered between September 1940 and March 1942.

With the single XPBM-2 being an increased fuel capacity testbed, the PBM-3 series was the first Mariner in large-scale production. The early sub-variants of this series were powered by the R-2600-12, while the PBM-1D of 1943 was equipped with the R-2600-22.

Delivered in 1942, the 50 PBM-1Rs were unarmed transports, while the 274 PBM-1Cs had powered gun turrets on top and in the bow with additional gun positions in the waist and tail. The PBM-1S, of which 95 were built between July and October 1943, was an anti-submarine variant of the PBM-3C in which the powered turrets were deleted to save weight for the sake of range.

John Andrade listed 32 Mariners with the PBM-3B designation that were Lend Leased to Britain and redesignated as Mariner GR.Is, of which six were returned. Aviation historian Ray Wagner noted 54 Mariners were allocated to Britain in 1943 and a dozen PBM-3Ss that went to Australia.

There were 201 PBM-3Ds, the variant with the R-2600-22, that were delivered through June 1943.

The PBM-5 series, of which 670 were built through the end of 1945, was powered by the Pratt & Whitney R-2800, whose application in multi-engine aircraft is the subject of Chapter 11.

Twin Cyclones for the Mariner

For the XPBM-1, PBM-1, and most of the PBM-3 subvariants, Martin selected the Wright 2600-9, the same engine chosen by North American Aviation for the early B-25 Mitchell variants. This engine was rated at 1,700 hp at 2,600 rpm for takeoff and 1,350 hp at 13,000 feet. It had a compression ratio of 6.9:1 and a supercharger

Switch boxes are assembled on the firewalls inside the engine nacelles of B-25 bombers at the North American Aviation factory in Inglewood, California. (Photo Courtesy Library of Congress)

Workers make wiring assemblies at a junction box on the fire wall for the right engine of a B-25 bomber at North American Aviation in Inglewood, California. Forward of this wall, one of the two Wright R-2600 engines would be installed.

ratio of 7.06:1 to 10.06:1. The R-2600-9 weighed 1,980 pounds and was 63.1 inches long with a diameter of 54.25 inches.

For the PBM-3D, the powerplant was the R-2600-22 driving 4-blade propellers. This engine was rated at 1,900 hp at 2,800 rpm for takeoff and at 1,350 hp at 15,400 feet. It had a compression ratio of 6.9:1 and a supercharger ratio of 7.06:1 to 10.06:1. The R-2600-22 weighed 1,056 pounds and was 66.08 inches long with a diameter of 54.08 inches.

The Martin Baltimore

Overshadowed by so many other aircraft, and never operational with an American unit during World War II, the Baltimore is one of the overlooked warbirds of World War II. Nevertheless, it deserves a place in history for having been produced in larger numbers (1,575) than any other aircraft in the history of the Glenn L. Martin Company of Baltimore, Maryland, except the B-26 Marauder (see Chapter 11).

A contemporary of the Douglas DB-7/Boston/Havoc family, the Martin Model 187 Baltimore was part of the early interwar generation of early all-metal, twin-engine, monoplane bombers. Martin produced several such designs ahead of the Baltimore.

First was a family of similar bombers that included the B-10 (Model 139), which entered service in November 1934 and was briefly the front-line bomber for the US Army Air Corps. This family began with the private venture Model 123 that first flew in February 1932 and also included the B-12 and B-14 as well as Model 139 and Model 166 export variants. There were 348 aircraft under this umbrella, including 153 B-10/B-12s, 121 exports to the Netherlands, and 61 exports to other foreign customers.

A solid-nose North American B-25G-10-NA bomber takes its delivery flight out of Inglewood. It wears the "red outline" national insignia that was used on US military aircraft for just a brief time in the middle of 1943. Thereafter, a solid blue outline was introduced.

Next came the Model 167 Maryland, which first flew in March 1939. One of these was designated as XA-22 by the Air Corps and evaluated, but the Douglas Havoc was chosen instead. However, the remainder of the 450 Model 167 Marylands found a place on the export market, where the France was an early customer. However, France was defeated by Germany in June 1940 before all the Marylands were deliv-

A group of Mitchell bombers are on the ramp at Fairfax Field north of Kansas City, Kansas. The USAAF built a plant here that was used both as a modification center, and by North American to build bombardier-nose B-25Ds and B-25Js.

ered. As was also the case with Douglas DB-7s that France had ordered, the undelivered Marylands were diverted to the British.

The Model 187 Baltimore was very similar to but slightly larger than the Maryland. In early 1940, before Baltimore's first flight, France placed an order for 400 aircraft through the Anglo-French Purchasing Commission. When France was defeated in June 1940, this order, like similar orders for the Douglas DB-7, was diverted to the British.

By the time that the Baltimore made its debut flight in June 1941, the business of ordering warplanes from the still-neutral United States had changed. Under the Lend Lease Act of March 1941, the United States aided Britain through the "leasing" of warplanes

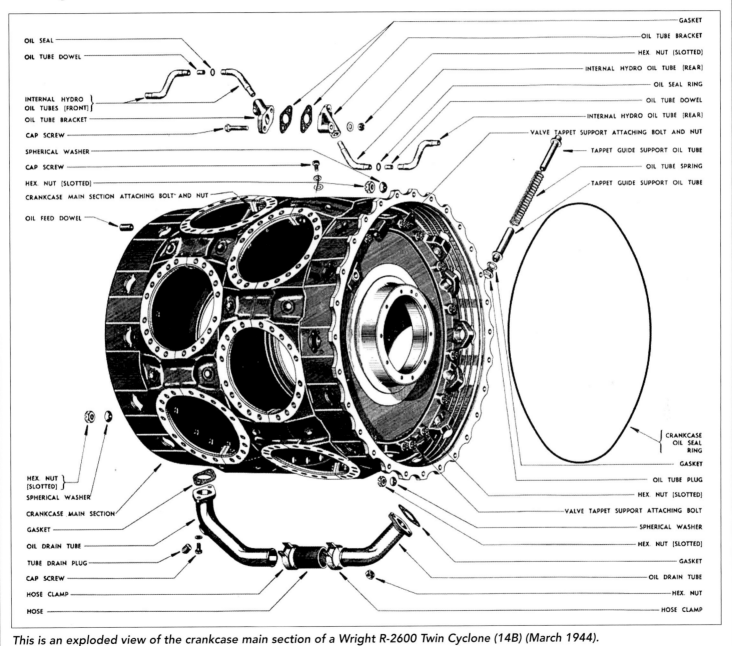

This is an exploded view of the crankcase main section of a Wright R-2600 Twin Cyclone (14B) (March 1944).

rather than sales. After the first 400 aircraft (Baltimore Mk.I, Mk.II, and Mk.III) from the original order were shipped, additional aircraft would be acquired by the USAAF under the designation A-30. These USAAF-owned and designated aircraft would then be Lend Leased to Britain without ever having been used by American crews in combat.

Delivery of the first batch was completed in June 1942, and deliveries of 281 A-30/Mk.IV Baltimores began in August. In turn, 894 were delivered between July 1943 and May 1944.

While Martin chose the Pratt & Whitney R-1830-SC3G Twin Wasp for the Maryland, the Wright Twin Cyclone was the engine of choice for the Baltimore.

Beginning with the Baltimore Mk.Is, the pre–Lend Lease aircraft were powered by engines with the commercial designation GR-2600-A5B-5. These were the equivalent of US military R-2600-19s. These engines were also carried forward in the A-30/Mk.IV Baltimores. Wright built 639 of these engines between July 1942 and December 1943.

The first 50 Martin PBM-3 Mariners were completed as PBM-3R transport aircraft and were powered with Wright R-2600-12 Twin Cyclones.

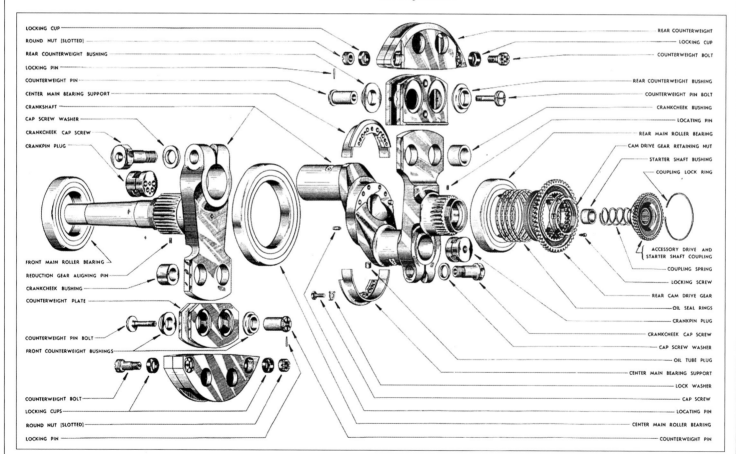

An exploded view is shown of the crankshaft of a Wright R-2600 Twin Cyclone (14B) (March 1944).

The Martin PBM-3C was powered by Wright R-2600-12 Twin Cyclones and equipped with radar for anti-submarine operations.

The Martin Mariner GR.I, seen here in August 1943, was the British equivalent of the US Navy's PBM-3B. It was powered Wright R-2600-22 Twin Cyclones and had four-blade props.

PBM-1 Mariners with Wright R-2600-6 engines take shape on the factory floor at Martin's Middle River plant in Baltimore in May 1940.

The Martin Model 187 light bomber was used primarily by the RAF, powered with Wright GR-2600-A5B Twin Cyclone engines under the name Baltimore. As they were Lend Leased from US Army contracts, they carried the designation A-30.

The GR-2600-A5B-5/R-2600-19 was rated at 1,350 hp at 2,300 rpm for takeoff and at 1,400 hp at 10,000 feet. It had a compression ratio of 6.3:1 and a supercharger ratio of 7.14:1 to 10:1. This engine weighed 1,969 pounds and was 62.2 inches long with a diameter of 55.1 inches.

The A-30A/Mk.V Baltimores were powered by the GR-2600-B655, which went by the military designation R-2600-29 because they were acquired by the USAAF on behalf of the RAF. Wright produced 18,784 of these engines between June 1943 and July 1945, and they were also used to power the Douglas A-20H and A-20K as well as the North American Aviation B-25J.

The GR-2600-B655/R-2600-29 was rated at 1,700 hp at 2,800 rpm for takeoff and at 1,500 hp at 2,400 rpm in flight. It had a compression ratio of 6.9:1 and a supercharger ratio of up to 10.06:1. The R-2600-29 weighed 2,000 pounds and was 63.1 inches long with a diameter of 54.26 inches. As with all Twin Cyclones, the stroke and bore were 6.312 inches and 6.125 inches, respectively.

The Maryland and Baltimore were widely used by the RAF in the Mediterranean Theater and in North Africa during the war as well as by the RAF in postwar colonial operations until 1948. They were also used by the Royal Australian Air Force, the Royal South African Air Force, and the Free French forces. When Italy switched sides in 1943 and formed an air force to fight alongside the Allies, they were given Baltimores. They remained in use in Italian service until 1947.

Martin Baltimores destined for the RAF take shape on the company's Middle River Plant on September 11, 1942. The Wright GR-2600-A5B geared radial engines have already been installed.

Chapter 9

THE WRIGHT TWIN CYCLONE IN SINGLE-ENGINE BOMBERS

A s was the case in Chapter 8, this chapter focuses on two well-known American warbirds and one more obscure American-made aircraft that spent its career with foreign air forces.

The R-2600 was selected as the powerplant for the aircraft that were two of the US Navy's most important carrier-based bombers of the late war period: the TBF/TBM Avenger and the SB2C Helldiver. The engine was also specified for the Vultee Vengeance, which spent most of its career with Allied air forces, mainly those of the British Commonwealth.

The Grumman Avenger

The Grumman Iron Works in Bethpage, Long Island (see Chapter 3), earned this appellation for the durability of its products, aircraft that were ubiquitous on the decks of the US Navy's carriers throughout World War II. Grumman dominated the Navy's fighting squadrons at the beginning of the war with the R-1830-powered F4F Wildcat and at the end of the war with the R-2800-powered F6F Hellcat. With the carrier torpedo squadrons, the record of the Grumman Avenger was exemplary—although 70 percent of the Avengers were not produced at a Grumman plant.

The Avenger program was initiated in April 1940, aimed at developing a successor to the Douglas TBD Devastator, which was growing obsolescent. The TBD's notoriously poor performance in the Battle of Midway was still two years in the future, but the Navy's Bureau of Aeronautics was aware in advance of its shortcomings.

So urgent was a new torpedo bomber to Navy planning that 286 TBF-1 production aircraft were ordered in December 1940, four months before the first flight of the XTBF-1 prototype. Deliveries of the first TBF-1 came in January 1942, and by the end of 1943, Grumman had produced 2,289.

Throughout the 1930s, aircraft companies struggled for business to fill their factories. With World War II, this turned around completely, and nowhere was this reversal more apparent than at Grumman. They company was running full bore with production of its F4F Wildcat—and now the Avenger. Then, on January 7, 1942, just as Avenger production began, the company received a production contract for the promising F6F-1 Hellcat (see Chapter 10). It was an embarrassment of riches in Bethpage. Grumman was suddenly stretched too thin to meet demands for its products. Something had to be done.

Both the Avenger and Hellcat were vitally important for the Navy, so the massive production capacity and expertise of the American auto industry was brought in to handle some of the load of

Lugging his parachute pack, a gunner climbs into the rear seat of the Grumman TBF-1 Avenger as the pilot revs up the 1,700-hp Wright R-2600-8 Twin Cyclone.

The blue and white insignia dates this photo of a Wright R-2600-8 Twin Cyclone–powered TBF-1 Avenger to 1942 or early 1943.

Wildcat and Avenger production so that Grumman could give its first priority to Hellcats.

Eastern Aircraft

As noted in Chapter 4, the Ford Motor Company bomber plant at Willow Run, Michigan, that turned out 6,792 B-24 Liberators is considered the exemplar of wartime aircraft manufacturing being taken over by the automotive industry, However, in terms of numbers of airframes, General Motors produced more than twice as many warplanes at two factories in New Jersey than Ford did at Willow Run.

As Ford had offered its expertise to build aircraft at a new purpose-built factory, GM came to the table with five existing factories on the East Coast. With civilian automobile production cur-

The supercharger rear housing cover is installed in a Wright R-2600 Twin Cyclone (May 1943).

tailed for the duration of the war, the company created its Eastern Aircraft Division early in 1942.

As had been the case at Willow Run, there was a steep learning curve as auto factory managers learned an entirely different business model and scrambled for workers. With the war on, much of the former automotive workforce was now in uniform and off to the services, so there was a scramble for new men and women to take their places and be trained for industrial factory work.

The GM plant in Linden, New Jersey, which opened in 1937 for Buick, Oldsmobile, and Pontiac production, was now reinvented for Eastern's Wildcat production contract. The first Eastern FM-1 Wildcat, the analog of the Grumman-built F4F-4, was flown in August 1942. Grumman built 1,169 F4F-4s to Eastern's 1,060 FM-1s, but when it came to the FM-2, Eastern built 4,127 after Grumman produced only a pair of samples.

Meanwhile, the former GM factory in Trenton, New Jersey, became the Eastern Aircraft facility tasked with building Avengers. After the completion of 2,291 TBF-1s, Bethpage thereafter conducted only modification work of existing Avengers, having created templates for Eastern TBM–series Avengers built at Trenton.

Beginning in November 1942, the Trenton plant turned out 550 TBM-1s, the analog of the TBF-1, and 2,336 TBM-1Cs, which were like the TBM-1 but with increased fuel capacity and provision for

The rear cam and rear cam gears of a Wright R-2600 Twin Cyclone show the proper position of the marked teeth (May 1943).

.50-caliber wing guns. The largest Avenger production variant was the TBM-3, which had provisions for wing tanks and aerial rockets. A look at a list of tail numbers indicated that there were 4,657 TBM-3 Avengers produced between April 1944 and September 1945. There were also a number of postproduction TBM-3 conversions, including those retrofitted with airborne radar. A production series of 2,141 TBM-4s with factory-installed radar was planned, but the order was canceled as the war neared its end.

Both aviation historian Ray Wagner and John Andrade, in his detailed tail number roster, agree that there were 9,839 Avengers produced, of which 7,546 were built by Eastern. However, a USAAF Materiel Command overview records that Eastern produced 7,522 TBMs. Using the latter number and adding it to 5,926 FM Wildcats that the Material Command credits Eastern with producing at Linden, General Motors produced 1.98 times as many warplanes as Ford.

R-2600 Twin Cyclones for the Avengers

The R-2600-8 variant of the 14-cylinder Wright Twin Cyclone was the engine of choice for all the first-generation Avengers from both Grumman and Eastern, including the 5,179 aircraft of the XTBF-1, TBF-1, TBM-1, and TBM-1C variants. Wright produced 11,410 examples of this engine between April 1940 and May 1944.

This color photo shows a Wright R-2600-8 Twin Cyclone–powered TBF-1 Avenger in standard US Navy markings, circa 1942 or 1943 when the type first found itself in the tick of the Pacific air war.

This is a flight of operational US Navy TBF-1 Avenger torpedo bombers with Wright R-2600-8 Twin Cyclones.

This postwar photo shows Eastern Aircraft–built TBM-3Cs of Anti-Submarine Squadron VS-23. The TBM-3 Avengers were powered by Wright R-2600-20 Twin Cyclones.

The R-2600-8 was rated at 1,700 hp at 2,500 rpm for takeoff and 1,450 hp at 12,000 feet. It had a compression ratio of 6.9:1 and a supercharger ratio of 7.06:1/10:1. The R-2600-8 weighed 1,995 pounds and was 54.91 inches long with a diameter of 54.26 inches.

The TBM-3 series, totaling 4,657 Avengers, was powered by the R-2600-20, which was in production from February 1942 until October 1945. Wright produced 14,620 of these engines, more than any other Twin Cyclone variant.

The first prototype Curtiss XSB2C-1 Helldiver made its debut flight on December 18, 1940, powered by a Wright R-2600-8 Twin Cyclone. (Photo Courtesy US Navy)

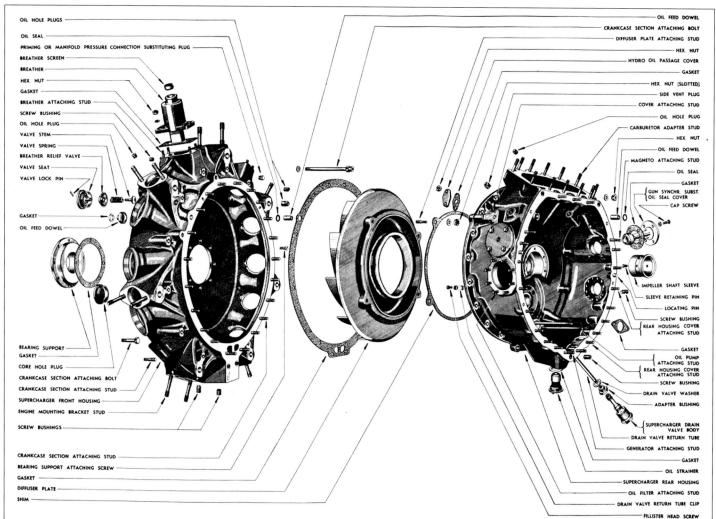

This exploded view displays the supercharger housings and diffuser plate of a Wright R-2600 Twin Cyclone (14B) (March 1944).

This restored Curtiss SB2C-5 Helldiver flying with the Commemorative Air Force was photographed at the 2015 Arsenal of Democracy Flyover to celebrate the 70th Anniversary of VE Day at Culpeper Regional Airport in Virginia in May 2015. (Photo Courtesy Alan Wilson, Licensed under Creative Commons)

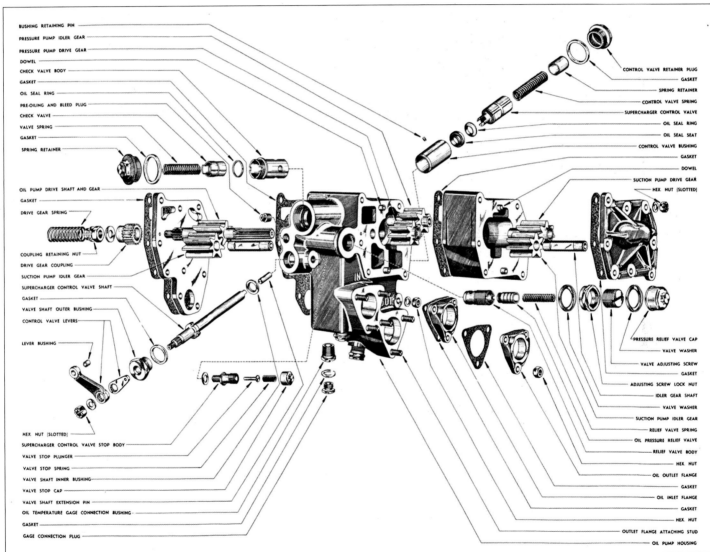

BUSHING RETAINING PIN
PRESSURE PUMP IDLER GEAR
PRESSURE PUMP DRIVE GEAR
DOWEL
CHECK VALVE BODY
GASKET
OIL SEAL RING
PRE-OILING AND BLEED PLUG
CHECK VALVE
VALVE SPRING
GASKET
SPRING RETAINER
OIL PUMP DRIVE SHAFT AND GEAR
GASKET
DRIVE GEAR SPRING
COUPLING RETAINING NUT
DRIVE GEAR COUPLING
SUCTION PUMP IDLER GEAR
SUPERCHARGER CONTROL VALVE SHAFT
GASKET
VALVE SHAFT OUTER BUSHING
CONTROL VALVE LEVERS
LEVER BUSHING

HEX NUT (SLOTTED)
SUPERCHARGER CONTROL VALVE STOP BODY
VALVE STOP PLUNGER
VALVE STOP SPRING
VALVE SHAFT INNER BUSHING
VALVE STOP CAP
VALVE SHAFT EXTENSION PIN
OIL TEMPERATURE GAGE CONNECTION BUSHING
GASKET
GAGE CONNECTION PLUG

CONTROL VALVE RETAINER PLUG
GASKET
SPRING RETAINER
CONTROL VALVE SPRING
SUPERCHARGER CONTROL VALVE
OIL SEAL RING
OIL SEAL SEAT
CONTROL VALVE BUSHING
GASKET
DOWEL
SUCTION PUMP DRIVE GEAR
HEX NUT (SLOTTED)

PRESSURE RELIEF VALVE CAP
VALVE WASHER
VALVE ADJUSTING SCREW
GASKET
ADJUSTING SCREW LOCK NUT
IDLER GEAR SHAFT
VALVE WASHER
SUCTION PUMP IDLER GEAR
RELIEF VALVE SPRING
OIL PRESSURE RELIEF VALVE
RELIEF VALVE BODY
HEX NUT
OIL OUTLET FLANGE
GASKET
OIL INLET FLANGE
GASKET
HEX NUT
OUTLET FLANGE ATTACHING STUD
OIL PUMP HOUSING

An exploded view is shown of the oil pump from a Wright R-2600 Twin Cyclone (14B) (March 1944).

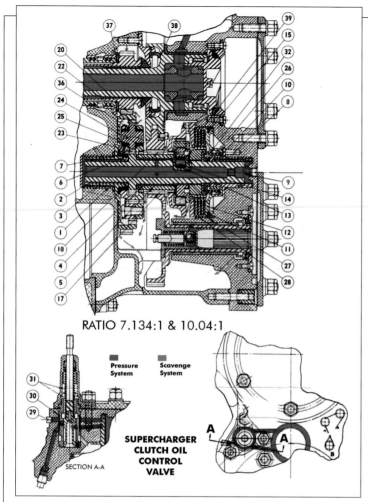

RATIO 7.134:1 & 10.04:1

Pressure System   Scavenge System

SUPERCHARGER
CLUTCH OIL
CONTROL
VALVE

SECTION A-A

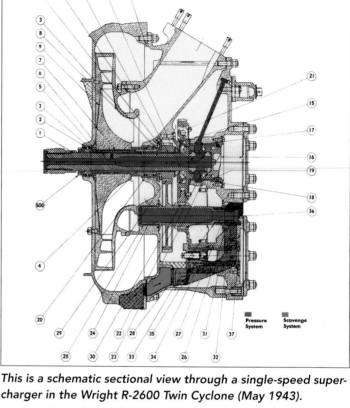

Pressure System   Scavenge System

This is a schematic sectional view through a single-speed super-charger in the Wright R-2600 Twin Cyclone (May 1943).

1. Accessory Drive and Starter Shaft and Coupling
2. Supercharger Front Housing Sleeve and Housing
3. Impeller Shaft Front and Rear Sleeve Oil Seal Ring
4. Impeller Shaft Front and Rear Sleeve Oil Seal Ring Gap
5. Accessory Drive and Starter Shaft and Impeller Driveshaft Front Bushing
6. Impeller Driveshaft Front and Rear Bushing and Shaft
7. Involute Spline Impeller and Impeller Shaft
8. Impeller and Impeller Shroud Plate
9. Impeller and Diffuser Plate
10. Impeller Shroud Plate and Rear Supercharger Housing
11. Supercharger Rear Housing and Front Housing
12. Impeller Driveshaft Gear
13. Accessory Drive and Starter Shaft and Impeller Driveshaft Rear Bushing
14. Impeller Shaft Retainer Oil Seal Ring Gap
15. Impeller Shaft Retainer and Ring
16. Starter Coupling Locating Dimension
17. Accessory Drive and Starter Shaft
18. Starter Shaft Bushing and Supercharger Rear Cover
19. Accessory Drive and Starter Shaft and Accessory Drive and Starter Shaft Bushing
20. Supercharger Rear Housing Sleeve and Housing
21. Accessory Drive Gear Spring Wire
22. Accessory Drive and Starter Shaft and Starter Coupling
23. Starter Coupling and Spacer
24. Intermediate Impeller Driveshaft Propeller End Bushing and Supercharger Rear Housing
25. Supercharger Intermediate Gear Shaft and Intermediate Impeller Driveshaft Propeller End Bushing
26. Supercharger Rear Cover and Impeller Driveshaft Bushing
27. Intermediate Impeller Driveshaft and Rear Bushing
28. Supercharger Intermediate Gear Shaft End
29. Impeller Driveshaft Gear and Intermediate Gear Shaft
30. Intermediate Supercharger Gear Shaft and Accessory Drive Gear Backlash
31. Generator Gear Bushing and Supercharger Rear Cover
32. Generator Gear and Bushing
33. Generator Gear Oil Seal Spring Wire
34. Generator Gear Spring Retainer and Pin
35. Generator Gear and Spring Retainer
36. Intermediate Impeller Drive Gear and Pinion and Generator Gear Backlash
37. Generator Gear and Generator Drive Oil Seal Collar
500. Impeller Driveshaft Gear Nut

This is a schematic view of the 2-speed, roller-clutch type super-charger in the Wright R-2600 Twin Cyclone (May 1943).

1. Impeller Shaft Drive Gear and Bushing
2. Intermediate Impeller Driveshaft and Front Bushing
3. Impeller Shaft Drive Gear and Intermediate Driveshaft Front Bushing
4. Intermediate Impeller Driveshaft and Intermediate Impeller Drive Gear Bushing
5. Intermediate Impeller Drive Gear and Bushing
6. Impeller Shaft Drive Gear and Intermediate Impeller Drive Pinion Cage (Front) Bushing
7. Intermediate Impeller Driveshaft Pinion Cage (Front) and Bushing
8. Intermediate Impeller Driveshaft and Rear Bushing
9. Intermediate Impeller Driveshaft
10. Impeller Drive Multi-Plate Clutch Piston and Intermediate Impeller Driveshaft Bushing (Rear)
11. Impeller Drive Multi-Plate Clutch Piston and Oil Seal
12. Impeller Drive Multi-Plate Clutch Piston Oil Seal
13. Clutch Roller Cage and Roller
14. Clutch Roller Cage and Roller
15. Impeller Low Speed Drive Clutch Cam and Bushing
16. Intermediate Impeller Driveshaft and Pinion Backlash
17. Intermediate Impeller Drive Gear and Generator Gear Backlash
18. Intermediate Impeller Drive Gear and Accessory Drive Gear Backlash
19. Impeller Shaft Drive Gear and Intermediate Impeller Drive Pinion Backlash
20. Impeller Shaft Drive Gear and Impeller Driveshaft Gear Backlash
21. Intermediate Impeller Driveshaft Pinion Cage (Front) and Pinion Shaft
22. Impeller Shaft Drive Gear and Intermediate Impeller Drive Pinion Backlash
23. Intermediate Impeller Driveshaft and Pinion Backlash

A US Navy Curtiss SB2C-3 Helldiver, powered by a Wright R-2600-20 Twin Cyclone, of Bombing Squadron VB-7 is shown from the aircraft carrier USS Hancock. The photo was taken during the September 1944 to January 1945 deployment that included the Battle of Leyte Gulf in October 1944. (Photo Courtesy US Navy)

It was rated at 1,900 hp at 2,800 rpm for takeoff and at 1,450 hp at 15,000 feet. It had a compression ratio of 6.3:1 and a supercharger ratio of 7.14:1/10:1. The R-2600-20 weighed 2,045 pounds and was 66.08 inches long with a diameter of 54.08 inches.

As with all Twin Cyclones, the stroke and bore for both of these Avenger powerplants were 6.312 inches and 6.125 inches, respectively.

The Curtiss Helldiver

Complementing the torpedo bombers among the offensive aircraft on US Navy carriers were the dive bombers, designated in Navy nomenclature as "scout" bombers. Complementing the Avenger as the standard torpedo bomber in 1944 and 1945 was the Curtiss SB2C Helldiver. Its use of the same R-2600 engine as the Avenger simplified the parts and supply chain.

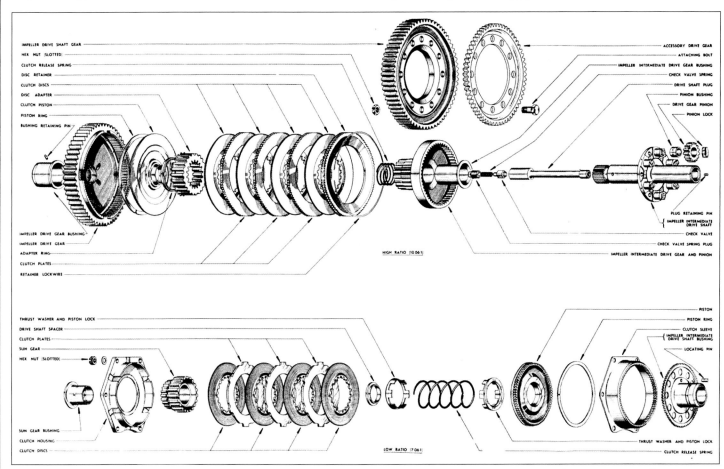

An exploded view shows the two-speed plate, clutch-type impeller drive of a Wright R-2600 Twin Cyclone (14B) (March 1944).

The SB2C was not the first Curtiss Helldiver. A decade earlier, 257 SBC Helldiver biplane bombers had been delivered. Earlier than that, in the 1920s, variants of the Curtiss F8C and O2C Falcon biplane family had been called Helldivers when used as dive bombers by the Marine Corps and aboard Navy carriers. These aircraft also "starred" in the 1932 Clark Gable heroic aviator film entitled *Hell Divers*.

The SB2C was ordered in May 1939 and first flown in December 1940. Intended to enter production at the end of 1941, SB2C development lagged, and the first SB2C-1 Helldiver was not flight testing until June 1942. Although the Helldiver was heavily promoted in Curtiss advertising, production was off to a bad start.

Meanwhile, Senator (and later President) Harry Truman, had empaneled the Senate Special Committee to Investigate the National Defense Program, which was tasked with looking into waste and inefficiency in wartime production. In April 1943, having looked at Curtiss, Truman concluded that the Helldiver program was "hopelessly behind schedule," as the company "had not succeeded in producing a single SB2C usable as a combat airplane." Indeed, the Helldiver did not enter combat until November 1943. Fortunately, in the meantime, the Douglas SBD Dauntless (see Chapter 5) proved to be a very effective dive bomber.

Thereafter, though, things moved quickly. By March 1944, 1,178 Helldivers had been rolled out at the Curtiss plant in Columbus, Ohio. The first 200 were SB2C-1s with 4 .50-caliber wing guns, and the balance were similar SB2C-1Cs in which the machine guns were replaced with 20-mm cannons. These quickly became standard equipment aboard the US Navy carriers.

These deliveries overlapped the advent of three higher-production

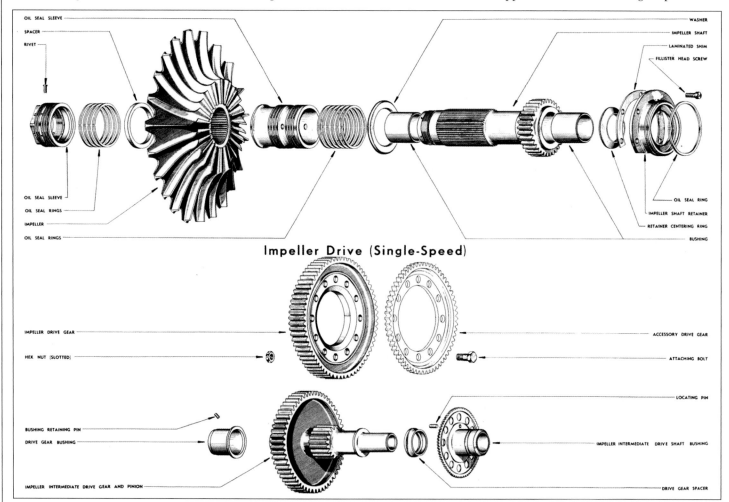

This is an exploded view of the Impeller and Impeller Shaft of a Wright R-2600 Twin Cyclone (14B) (March 1944).

variants, including the SB2C-3 with its more powerful R-2600-20 Twin Cyclone. Of this variant, 1,112 were produced, beginning in January 1944. The SB2C-4, of which 2,045 began reaching the fleet in June 1944, had provisions for underwing ground-attack rockets, and its bomb capacity was increased by half a ton.

First appearing in February 1945, 970 examples of the SB2C-5 (the final production variant) were fitted with the Philco AN/APS-4 ground search radar.

The USAAF, meanwhile, had taken a parallel interest in dive bombers. As stated in the attack aircraft page on the Air Force Museum website, the success of the German Stuka dive bomber in the early years of the war led to the USAAF acquiring variants of Navy dive bombers. These included the Douglas A-24 Dauntless and the Helldiver, which was given the designation A-25A and named "Shrike."

The first 100 Shrikes were SB2C-1As transferred from the Navy and were followed by an order for 900 A-25As. Built at an assembly line that Curtiss established at St. Louis, Missouri, these were first delivered in December 1942. In combat, however, the USAAF found dive bombers to be so vulnerable to enemy fighter action that they were withdrawn from front-line service. Many Shrikes were passed on to the Royal Australian Air Force, and 270 were transferred to the US Navy.

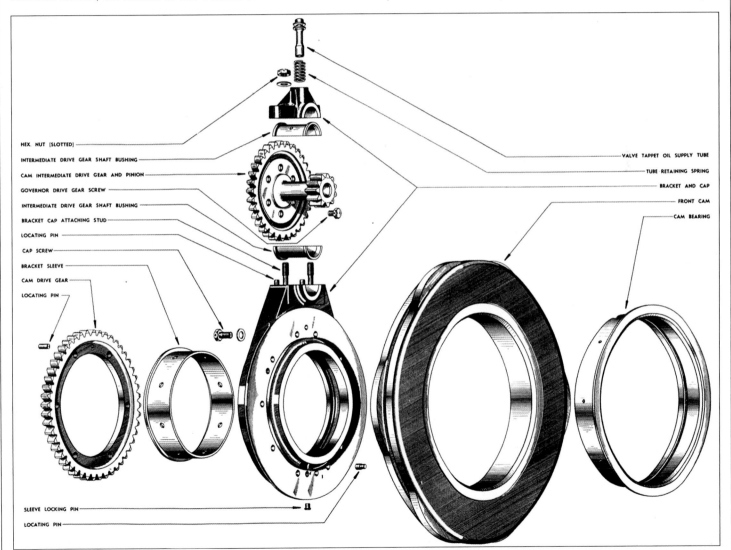

An exploded view is shown of the front cam and cam drive of a Wright R-2600 Twin Cyclone (14B) (March 1944).

R-2600 Twin Cyclones for the Helldivers

Curtiss Wright products themselves, the SB2C-1 Helldivers were each equipped with Wright R-2600-8 radials. The same engine that was used in the first-generation TBF-1 and TBM-1 Avengers being built by Grumman and Eastern, the R-2600-8 was in production from April 1940 and May 1944. It was rated at 1,700 hp at 2,500 rpm for takeoff and 1,450 hp at 12,000 feet. It had a compression ratio of 6.9:1 and a supercharger ratio of 7.06:1/10:1. The R-2600-8 weighed 1,995 pounds and was 54.91 inches long with a diameter of 54.26 inches.

With the SB2C-3, as with the TBM-3 series, the engine of choice was the more powerful Wright R-2600-20 with four-blade propellers. Having the same engine installed in both the Avenger and Helldiver aboard the carriers (where space was at a premium) certainly eased the maintenance situation, as parts were interchangeable. The R-2600-20 was rated at 1,900 hp at 2,800 rpm for takeoff and at 1,450 hp at 15,000 feet. It had a compression ratio of 6.3:1 and a supercharger ratio of 7.14:1/10:1. The R-2600-20 weighed 2,045 pounds and was 66.08 inches long with a diameter of 54.08 inches.

The Vultee Vengeance

In the previous chapter, two famous aircraft were profiled, and a third, lesser-known aircraft that played a much larger role than is generally remembered was added.

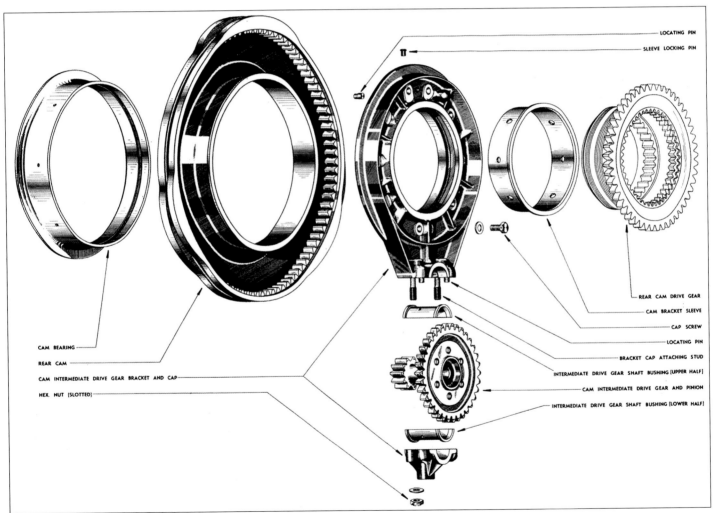

This exploded view shows the rear cam and cam drive of a Wright R-2600 Twin Cyclone (14B) (March 1944).

The Vengeance was a product of the Vultee Aircraft Corporation of Downey, California, the smaller component of Consolidated-Vultee (see Chapter 4). The company was founded in 1938 as a successor to the Airplane Development Corporation started in 1932 by Gerard Freebairn "Jerry" Vultee, a promising young engineer whose Model V-1 airliner was of great interest to American Airlines. The industrial empire builder Errett Lobban Cord was an early investor, and Vultee's company was folded into his Aviation Corporation (AVCO) in 1936. Jerry Vultee himself was killed in a plane crash in 1938, and Vultee Aircraft was merged with Consolidated in 1943.

Wartime Vultee products included a small number of Vanguard fighters that were built for Sweden but mostly exported to China as well as the small Valiant basic training aircraft, which was powered by the Pratt & Whitney R-985 Wasp Junior and is discussed in Chapter 6.

The Vengeance (Vultee Model V-72) dive bomber first flew in March 1941, with the program having originated in 1940 with an order from France that was transferred to Britain as the Vengeance Mk.I when France fell to the Germans. This order included 700 aircraft, most of them built by Vultee in Downey with 200 Vengeance Mk.IAs made by Northrop, 15 miles to the west in Hawthorne because Vultee was impacted with orders for Valiants at Downey. Vengeances were also built at a former Stinson factory in Nashville, Tennessee, that AVCO had inherited.

Deliveries of this first batch of 700 continued to August 1942. In June 1941, 600 more were ordered, including another 200 from Northrop. As this was under Lend Lease contract, requiring the US government to buy them and lease them, the USAAF assigned the designation A-31. Deliveries of the Vengeance Mk.IIs concluded in August 1943.

Changes to the A-31 originating in July 1942 included a redesigned wing with an increased angle of incidence as well as improved USAAF standard armament. There were 99 (some say 100) of these delivered under the designation A-35A Vultee Model V-88 and known to the British as the Vengeance Mk.III. There were 831 of the final A-35B/Vengeance Mk.IV variant delivered between May 1943 and June 1944. This variant was like the A-35A/Mk.III but with 6 .50-caliber machine guns.

While two-thirds of the Vengeances went to the RAF, the aircraft also served with the air forces of Australia, Brazil, and India, as well as with the Free French. The USAAF deployed a few into combat in Europe but used them mainly for training. Total production topped out at 1,931.

Powering the Vengeance

The Vultee V-72 prototype and the Vengeance Mk.Is were powered by the GR-2600-A5B military export variant of the Twin Cyclone. This engine was rated at 1,600 hp at 2,400 rpm for takeoff and at 1,350 hp at 2,300 rpm at cruising speed. It had a compression ratio of 6.3:1 and a supercharger ratio of 7.14:1/10:1. The GR-2600-A5B weighed 1,950 pounds and was 62.04 inches long with a diameter of 55 inches.

The Vultee A-1 and A-35A, ordered under USAAF contract were powered by the R-2600-19, of which the export variant was the GR-2600-A5B-5, which was the same engine used in the exported Martin Baltimore Mk.I. It was rated at 1,350 hp at 2,300 rpm for takeoff and at 1,400 hp at 10,000 feet. It had a compression ratio of 6.3:1 and a supercharger ratio of 7.14:1 to 10:1. This engine weighed 1,969 pounds and was 62.2 inches long with a diameter of 55.1 inches.

The A-35B/Vengeanvce Mk.IV was powered by the R-2600-13, of which the export variant was designated as GR-2600-B-655. The R-2600-13 was rated at 1,700 hp at 2,600 rpm for takeoff and at 1,450 hp at 12,000 feet. It had a compression ratio of 6.9:1 and a supercharger ratio of 7.06:1 to 10.06:1. The R-2600-13 weighed 2,000 pounds and was 63.1 inches long with a diameter of 54.26 inches.

Chapter 10

SINGLE-ENGINE FIGHTERS AND THE DOUBLE WASP

Having a displacement of 2,800 ci, the 18-cylinder Pratt & Whitney R-2800 Double Wasp was a twin-row radial that literally doubled the earlier R-1830 Twin Wasp in number of cylinders, if not displacement. As noted in Chapter 8, within the "House of Pratt," the R-2800 was to the earlier R-1830 what the R-2600 Twin Cyclone was to the earlier R-1820 Cyclone at Wright Aeronautical.

With more than 125,000 engines built, the R-2800 powered what can be called the three most important radial-engine American fighter aircraft of World War II: the Republic P-47 Thunderbolt, the Grumman F6F Hellcat, and the Vought F4U Corsair.

Grumman and Its Hellcat

Leroy Randle Grumman enlisted as an ensign in the US Naval Reserve in 1916, and he became a pilot and studied aeronautical engineering at the Massachusetts Institute of Technology. In 1920, Grumman became general manager at Loening Aeronautical Engineering and remained until the company was sold to Keystone in 1929. With the help of fellow Loening alums Bill Schwendler and Leon "Jake" Swirbul, Grumman started Grumman Aeronautical Engineering. The company was located at several places on Long Island before settling into a permanent home at Bethpage in 1937.

For the US Navy, the Grumman Company designed the first practical floats with retractable landing gear, and thereafter Navy contracts flowed in large numbers. During World War II, Grumman built more combat aircraft for the Navy than anyone. The aircraft were so solid and sturdy that the company was referred to as the "Grumman Iron Works."

The name and reputation of the Iron Works were almost synonymous with US naval carrier aviation for 40 of aviation's first 70 years. Grumman's great TBF Avenger was discussed in Chapter 9. The Iron Works reputation was also solidly grounded in the line of

A Grumman F6F-3 Hellcat, powered by a water-injected Pratt & Whitney R-2800-10W Double Wasp, is shown in flight during the summer of 1943. Grumman delivered 2,545 Hellcats that year.

radial engine fighters built since the early 1930s. The first monoplane among them was the F4F Wildcat (see Chapter 3), which entered service early in 1940 with the US Navy as well as with the British Royal Navy and Royal Air Force, who designated it as Martlet I.

When the United States entered World War II, the F4F Wildcat was the Navy's standard carrier-based fighter, and it was also in service in the Southwest Pacific Theater with US Marine Corps units. The process of designing the Wildcat's successor, the F6F Hellcat, was underway at the Iron Works as the United States entered the war, and the first flight of the XF6F-1 prototype occurred in June 1942.

While Grumman picked the Wright R-2600-16 Cyclone for the first Hellcat prototype, the second XF6F-1 was completed with a Pratt & Whitney R-2800-10 Double Wasp and first flown on July 8, 1942. Thereafter, Grumman never looked back. A single XF6F-2 was completed as a single XF6F-3, and on the basis of this, the F6F-3 series went into production.

The Hellcat line began with a June 1941 order for two XF6F-1s to be powered by Pratt & Whitney R-2800-10 Double Wasps, which first flew in June 1942. Note the large prop spinner.

Only 10 F6F-3s were delivered by the end of 1942, but production quickly ramped up with 2,545 of a total of 4,402 F6F-3s reaching the fleet in 1943. It was during 1943 that the Navy had sufficient Hellcats to equip all of the fighting squadrons aboard all of its fast carriers. In addition, the Navy took delivery of 18 F6F-3Es with AN/APS-4 ground search radar, and 205 F6F-3N night fighters with AN/APS-6 lightweight air-to-air/air-to-surface search radar.

The next, and largest volume, Hellcat variant was the F6F-5, of which 9,629 were built, including 1,529 F6F-5N night fighters with AN/APS-6 radar.

Beginning in May 1943, Britain's Royal Navy received 332 F6F-3s as Hellcat Mk.Is and 850 F6F-5s (including 80 F6F-5Ns) as Hellcat Mk.IIs.

As Ray Wagner pointed out, Hellcat pilots scored 5,156 of the 9,282 aerial victories scored by US Navy and US Marine Corps aviators during World War II.

The Bearcat

The Hellcat's lasting legacy was in its designated successor, the Grumman F8F Bearcat, which made its first flight in August 1944. Various problems, including horizontal stability issues were encountered and eventually resolved, but this delayed the first deliveries to May 1945. Bearcats were en route to the Pacific Theater when the war ended in August.

The US Navy had placed orders for 2,023 F8F-1 Bearcats from Grumman and 1,876 from General Motors under the designation F3M-1. When the war ended, the former contract was cut to 770, and the latter contract was canceled. However, The Navy considered the Bearcat as its first postwar fighter and added 126 examples of the F8F-1B variant with 4 20-mm cannons superseding the 6 .50-caliber machine guns of earlier Bearcats.

The F8F-2 Bearcat, with 4 20-mm cannons and various other improvements, was first flown in October 1947. Through May 1949, 317 of this variant, including 24 F8F-2N night fighters with AN/APS-19 radar, were delivered, keeping the Bearcat in production until 1949.

The Bearcat remained in US Navy service until 1952 and was the aircraft of the Blue Angels demonstration team from 1946 to 1950. Bearcats exported to the French were used in combat in Indochina

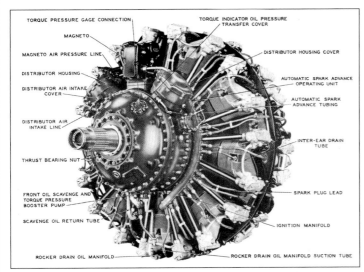

This is a front left three-quarter view of a Pratt & Whitney R-2800 Double Wasp 18-cylinder engine.

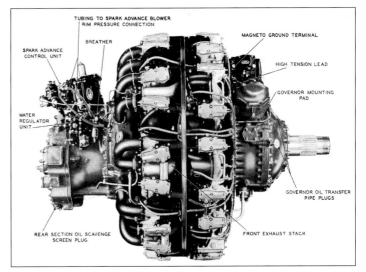

A right-side view is shown of a Pratt & Whitney R-2800 Double Wasp twin-row, 18-cylinder engine.

between 1950 and 1954, and with the South Vietnam Air Force until 1960.

The Bearcat excelled on the air race circuit in the late 20th century and was a fixture in many a winner's circle. In 1964, a modified Bearcat flown by Mira Slovik won the first-annual Reno Air Race, which is officially the National Championship Air Races.

Most notable among the Bearcats on the racing circuit was *Rare Bear*, an F8F-2 that was discovered as a wreck by Lyle Shelton, restored, and first raced in 1969—albeit re-engined with a Wright R-3350 Duplex Cyclone engine (see Chapter 13).

Rare Bear went on to dominate air racing for decades, scoring 5 Unlimited Class victories from 1969 to 1975, and 11 more between 1980 and 2015. In 1989, the aircraft set a long-standing World Unlimited Class Speed Record of 528.33 mph.

Double Wasps for Hellcats and Bearcats

With the first of two XF6F-1 prototypes having been powered by the Wright R-2600-16 Twin Cyclone and the second by a Pratt & Whitney R-2800-10 Double Wasp, Grumman standardized the supercharged and water-injected R-2800-10W Double Wasp for all of its F6F-3 and F6F-5 production Hellcats. It had a compression ratio of 5.65:1 and used Stromberg PT13G-series carburetors. The engines weighed 2,450 pounds and were 88.47 inches long with a diameter of 52.5 inches.

With their water-injected Pratt & Whitney R-2800-10W Double Wasps ready for takeoff, Grumman F6F-3 Hellcats of Carrier Air Group 5 aboard the aircraft carrier USS Yorktown prepare for a mission over Marcus Island in August 1943. (Photo Courtesy US Navy)

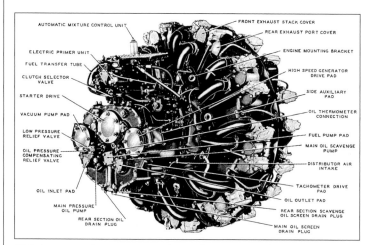

This is a rear three-quarter view of a Pratt & Whitney R-2800 Double Wasp twin-row, 18-cylinder engine.

The two XF8F-1 Bearcats were equipped with water-injected R-2800-22Ws with four-blade propellers, while the F8F-1 production aircraft used the R-2800-34, and the F8F-2s were powered by R-2800-30W engines.

The R-2800-22W was rated at 2,100 hp at 2,800 rpm for takeoff, and at 1,600 hp at 2,800 rpm at 16,000 feet. It had a compression ratio of 6.75:1 and used a Stromberg PT58E-1 carburetor. The R-2800-22W weighed 2,359 pounds and was 78.134 inches long with a diameter of 52.8 inches.

The R-2800-34W was rated at 2,100 hp at 2,500 rpm for takeoff and at 1,700 hp at 2,800 rpm at 15,000 feet. It had a compression ratio of 6.75:1 and used a Stromberg PR58E1 or PR58E2 carburetor. The R-2800-34W weighed 2,358.5 pounds and was 78.134 inches long with a diameter of 52.8 inches.

The R-2800-30W was rated at 2,300 hp at 2,800 rpm for takeoff and at 1,800 hp at 2,700 rpm at 19,500 feet. It had a compression ratio of 5.75:1 and used a Chandler-Evans 64CPC2-1 carburetor. The engine weighed 2,585 pounds and was 93.5 inches long with a diameter of 52.6 inches.

Republic's Thunderbolt

In the hierarchy of great USAAF fighters of World War II, the P-47 Thunderbolt resides in the top tier alongside the inline-engine North

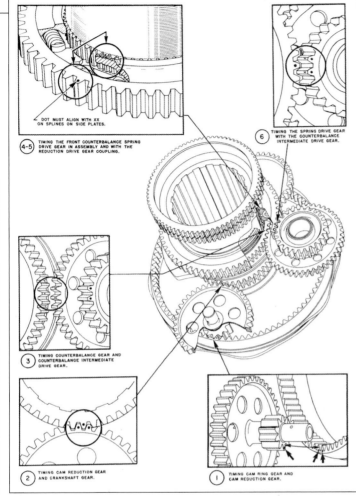

This shows the timing of the front cam and counterbalance geartrains in a Pratt & Whitney R-2800 Double Wasp engine (1943).

Timing of the rear cam and counterbalance geartrains is shown in a Pratt & Whitney R-2800 Double Wasp engine (1943).

American Aviation P-51 Mustang and Lockheed P-38 Lightning.

Republic Aviation Corporation, located in East Farmingdale, Long Island, only five miles east of the Grumman Iron Works, also had an interesting story. In 1931, it was started by (and originally named for) the most unlikely of American aviation pioneers—a Russian nobleman. Alexander Procofiev de Seversky was born in 1894, became a pilot with the navy of Tsar Nicholas II, and during World War I, he became a fighter ace. He was sent to the United States as an air attaché in 1917, and when the Russian Revolution occurred, he decided to stay. He became a citizen in 1927 and started the Seversky Aircraft Corporation in 1931.

His early designs included amphibians, but he is best remembered for his P-35 radial-engine monoplane fighter of the late 1930s. He built 76 for the US Army Air Corps and 60 for Sweden.

Despite these small military contracts, the company was never profitable, so Seversky's investors voted him out in 1939 and reorganized the company as Republic Aviation. The reorganized company developed an improvement on the P-35 that was known as the P-43 Lancer, and the US Army Air Corps ordered nearly 150 of them in 1940 and 1941.

By the time that the United States entered the war, Republic was concentrating on an evolution of the Lancer design that the USAAF ordered as the P-47 Thunderbolt. The XP-47 and XP-47A existed only on paper, so the first Thunderbolt to take flight was the XP-47B, which made its debut on May 6, 1941. While the Lancer was powered by a Pratt & Whitney R-1830-57, the Thunderbolt used Pratt's still-experimental XR-2800-21. It was the largest single-engine fighter yet built, yet it was able to achieve 412 mph.

The spinning prop of this Pratt & Whitney R-2800 Double Wasp engine forms condensation rings as this F6F-3 Hellcat from VF-5 rolls toward a takeoff from the USS Yorktown. (Photo Courtesy US Navy)

One of two US Navy Grumman XF8F-1 Bearcat prototypes is shown at the NACA (later NASA) Langley Research Center on February 5, 1945. The first XF8F-1 flew in August 1944, powered by a Pratt & Whitney R-2800-22W Double Wasp. (Photo Courtesy NASA)

A pair of preserved F8F-2 Bearcats fly during the October 2019 Wings over Houston Airshow at Ellington Airport in Texas. F8F-2s were delivered with Pratt & Whitney R-2800-34W Double Wasps. The top Bearcat was operated by the Commemorative Air Force; the lower one was by Lewis Air Legends. (Photo Courtesy Alan Wilson, Licensed under Creative Commons)

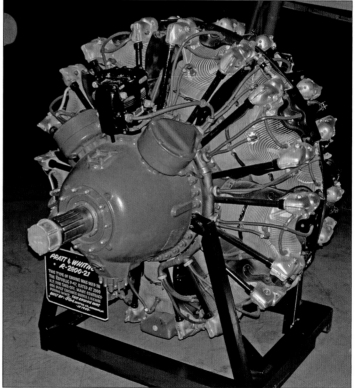

This Pratt & Whitney R-2800-21 engine is displayed at the National Museum of the US Air Force at Wright-Patterson Air Force Base in Ohio. The R-2800-21 Double Wasp variant powered both the P-47B and P-47C Thunderbolts. (Photo Courtesy Highflier, Licensed under the GNU Documentation License)

On May 6, 1941, two days after this photo was taken, the Republic XP-47B became the first of the Thunderbolt lineage to take to the air. It was powered by a Pratt & Whitney XR-2800-2 Double Wasp. The production P-47Bs as well as the P-47Cs were powered by the Pratt & Whitney R-2800-21.

A Block 11 Republic P-47D with a "razorback" canopy winds up its Pratt & Whitney R-2800-16 Double Wasp at the Republic Aviation Corporation airfield at Farmingdale, Long Island, New York. The man on the tarmac is Alexander Kartveli, the company's aeronautical genius, who is said to have designed the Thunderbolt on a single sheet of paper.

Deliveries of the first of 170 production P-47Bs began in December 1941, and the first of 602 P-47Cs, built in four production blocks, rolled out at Farmingdale in September 1942.

Even as this was ongoing, the USAAF had committed to very large orders for the P-47D variant, which was to become the definitive Thunderbolt. To support this production, Republic opened a second production facility at Evansville, Indiana, over 700 miles west of Farmingdale.

There were 6,510 P-47D-REs manufactured in 17 production blocks at Farmingdale and 6,093 P-47D-RAs built in 17 parallel production blocks at Evansville. This volume reduced unit cost. The P-47s cost $113,246 apiece, but by 1944, as they were swarming off the assembly lines, the price was a more manageable $85,578.

The first P-47Ds, like the earlier Thunderbolts, had a tall rear fuselage with no direct rear view from the cockpit and were nicknamed "Razorbacks." After April 1944, most P-47Ds, as well as the subsequent P-47M and P-47N, had bubble canopies.

The high-speed, supercharged P-47M interceptor variant was adapted from Farmingdale-built P-47Ds beginning in September 1944 at Block 30. These were originally created to intercept V-1 cruise missiles.

The ground-attack P-47N incorporated zero-length rocket launchers. There were 1,667 P-47N-REs built in five production blocks at Farmingdale and 149 P-47N-RAs in two production blocks at Evansville.

According to official USAAF Materiel Command wartime production data, Republic Aviation built a total of 9,006 Thunderbolts in Farmingdale and 6,225 at Evansville.

To spread the work around, the USAAF also brought Curtiss into the Thunderbolt production pool, and it built 354 of them at the

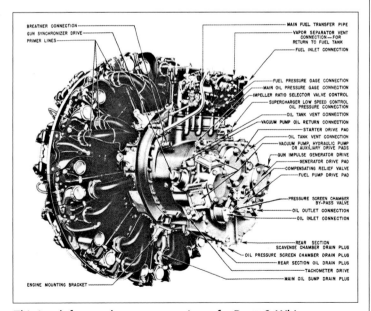

This is a left rear three-quarter view of a Pratt & Whitney R-2800 Double Wasp twin-row, 18-cylinder engine with a dual vacuum pump adaptor (1943).

An Eighth Air Force P-47D Thunderbolt is parked on a Marsten Matting runway, circa 1943. The white cowling and tail band suggest that it belonged to the 56th Fighter Group that was known as Zemke's Wolf Pack for its famous commander, Colonel Hubert "Hub" Zemke, who led the unit between January and August 1944.

Francis Stanley "Gabby" Gabreski, the highest-scoring USAAF ace in the European Theater of World War II, scored 28 aerial victories while flying Thunderbolts with the 56th Fighter Group of the USAAF Eighth Air Force. Here, Gabby Gabreski rolls across the ramp at the base at Boxted, England, in his P-47D. (Photo Courtesy National Archives)

Buffalo plant, where P-40 production tapered off late in World War II. These were essentially the same as the Republic-built P-47D but were designated as P-47G.

Most Thunderbolts served with the USAAF, but they also were delivered to the Royal Air Force (mainly in India), the Soviet Air Force, the Free French Air Force, the Brazilian Air Force (which flew combat missions in Italy), and the Mexican Air Force (which flew combat missions in the Philippines).

Powering the Thunderbolt

As the XP-47B was powered by a Pratt & Whitney XR-2800-21, most production-series P-47Bs and P-47Cs were equipped with production-series R-2800-21 engines. As with all Double Wasp engines installed in Thunderbolts, it drove a four-blade propeller.

Many P-47D aircraft were equipped with Curtiss Electric C542S constant-speed props with a 13-foot diameter.

To achieve war emergency power, including capability for a 2,300-hp war emergency rating at 27,500 feet, water injection was made available in part of the P-47D production to increase power output for short durations. Water injection was provided in kit form as well as on the Thunderbolt assembly lines from Block 4 in Evansville and Block 5 at Farmingdale. When water injection was factory installed, the R-2800-63 designation was used for the engine.

The R-2800-21 was rated at 2,000 hp at 2,500 rpm for takeoff and the same at 25,000 feet. It

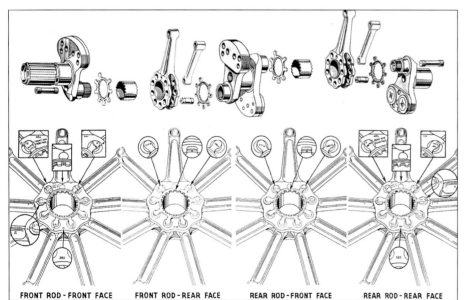

FRONT ROD - FRONT FACE   **FRONT ROD - REAR FACE**   **REAR ROD - FRONT FACE**   **REAR ROD - REAR FACE**

The components of the crankshaft and master rod assembly are shown in a Pratt & Whitney R-2800 Double Wasp engine (1943).

had a compression ratio of 6.65:1 and used a Stromberg PT13G1-13 carburetor. The engine weighed 2,265 pounds and was 75.72 inches long with a diameter of 52.5 inches.

Although there were exceptions, most P-47D aircraft were equipped with the R-2800-59 or R-2800-63 Double Wasps. These two engines were manufactured both by Pratt & Whitney and by the Ford Motor Company. They were equipped with General Electric CH-5 high-altitude turbosuperchargers.

This is one of the first Block 1 Republic P-47N Thunderbolts, circa September 1944. The last Thunderbolt production variant, the P-47N, was powered by the Pratt & Whitney R-2800-77 Twin Cyclone.

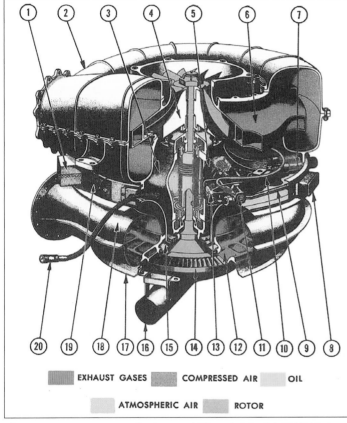

EXHAUST GASES   COMPRESSED AIR   OIL

ATMOSPHERIC AIR   ROTOR

This is a cutaway view of a General Electric Model CH-5 Turbo-supercharger, such as was used in the Pratt & Whitney R-2800 Double Wasps Installed in Republic P-47 Thunderbolts.

1. Cooling-Shroud Air Inlet
2. Compressor Casing
3. Bearing and Pump Casing
4. Impeller
5. Oil Pump
6. Diffuser
7. Oil Lines
8. Terminal Box*
9. Conduit
10. Grease Line**
11. Right-Angle Adapter**
12. Diaphragm
13. Speed-Control Generator
14. Bucket Wheel
15. Sealing-Plate Assembly
16. Cooling Cap
17. Z-Ring
18. Nozzlebox
19. Cooling Shroud
20. Flexible Tachometer Shaft**
*Early CH-5-A1s only. Later CH-5s had recessed terminal boxes.
**Model CH-5-A1 only. Not installed on later variants.

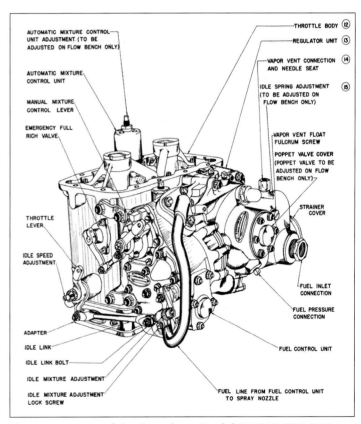

The components of the Stromberg Model PT13F1 (PT-13F1) injection carburetor are shown with the fuel head enrichment valve as was installed in Pratt & Whitney R-2800 Double Wasp engines (1943).

The R-2800-59 was rated at 2,000 hp at 2,700 rpm for takeoff and at 2,000 hp at 2,500 rpm at 25,000 feet. It had a compression ratio of 6.55:1 and used a Stromberg PT13G5-13 carburetor. The engine weighed 2,290 pounds and was 75.72 inches long with a diameter of 52.5 inches.

The water-injected R-2800-63, meanwhile, delivered 2,000 hp at 2,700 rpm for takeoff and the same at 25,000 feet using the CH-5 turbosupercharger. It had a compression ratio of 6.65:1 and used a Stromberg PT13G5-13 carburetor. The engine weighed 2,265 pounds and was 75.72 inches long with a diameter of 52.5 inches.

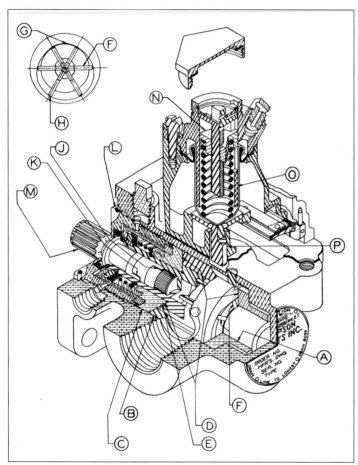

The Thompson Model TFD-Series fuel pump is shown as installed in Pratt & Whitney R-2800 Double Wasp Engines (1943).

A. Bearing Bore to Rotor Hub
D. Liner Length to Blade Length
E. Liner Length to Rotor Length
F. Rotor Slot to Blade
H. Liner Bore to Blade End

J. Coupling Link Tang to Slot
K. Driver Shaft Tang to Slot
M. Driver Shaft Spline Tooth
N. Valve Adjustment Nut to Guide
P. Valve Stem to Guide

Other Double Wasps used in various Thunderbolt production blocks, notably the P-47M and P-47N variants, included the R-2800-57, R-2800-73, and R-2800-77.

Built by both Pratt & Whitney and the Chevrolet Division of General Motors, the R-2800-57s were rated at 2,100 hp at 2,800 rpm for takeoff and at 2,000 hp at 2,800 rpm at 25,000 feet with the CH-5 turbosupercharger. They each had a compression ratio of 6.75:1 and used Stromberg PR58E2-2 carburetors. The engines weighed 2,515 pounds and were 78.39 inches long with a diameter of 52.8 inches.

Manufactured by Chevrolet, the R-2800-73 was rated at 2,100 hp at 2,800 rpm for takeoff and at 1,600 hp at 2,700 rpm at 26,500 feet. It had a compression ratio of 6.75:1 and used a Stromberg PR58E2-2 carburetor. The engine weighed 2,351 pounds and was 78.394 inches long with a diameter of 52.8 inches.

The R-2800-77 delivered 2,100 hp at 2,600 rpm for takeoff and at 2,100 hp at 2,800 rpm at 25,500 feet. It had a compression ratio of 6.75:1 and used a Stromberg PR58E2-2 carburetor. The engine weighed 2,321 pounds and was 75.3 inches long with a diameter of 52.5 inches. These engines were made only by the Chevrolet Division of General Motors.

The Vought Corsair

Chauncey Milton "Chance" Vought, first introduced in Chapter 2, began his career as an engineer with Orville Wright and operated a series of companies on his own until his untimely death in 1930. Notable among his creations was the Vought O2U-1 Corsair two-place observation biplane that was introduced in 1926. Two years later, the company became part of United Aircraft and Transport Corporation (UATC) along with Boeing, Sikorsky, and Pratt & Whitney. After UATC was broken up in 1934, the Vought, Pratt & Whitney, and Sikorsky components, all based in Connecticut, remained part of the entity called United Aircraft (United Technologies after 1975), from which Vought was spun off in 1954.

In the lead-up to World War II, Vought's most important product was the O2SU Kingfisher, an observation floatplane for the US Navy, of which 1,519 were built. The company's most important wartime program was the F4U (the fourth of five Vought aircraft to wear the "Corsair" name), of which 12,571 were built.

The prototype XF4U-1 first flew on May 29, 1941, and the production-series F4U-1 was ordered a month later. Vought delivered its first of 758 F4U-1s in June 1942, and two other manufacturers were brought into the Corsair manufacturing pool to produce aircraft analogous to the F4U-1. Beginning in April 1943, the Goodyear Aircraft Company produced 1,704 such aircraft as FG-1s in Akron, Ohio, while Brewster Aeronautical Corporation began

The Vought Corsair, with its long nose, was designed around the powerful Pratt & Whitney Double Wasp. The first production variant, the F4U-1 was powered by the R-2800-8 Double Wasp. When the Corsair entered service in early 1943, it was found to be less well suited for carrier operations than the F6F Hellcat because of visibility issues associated with the F4U-1's "birdcage" canopy. However, the Marines, operating from land bases on South Pacific islands found that its performance allowed them to achieve air superiority in their contests with the Japanese. (Photo Courtesy US Navy)

A blown-Plexiglas canopy replaced the Corsair's "birdcage" canopy on the production line in 1943 with the Vought F4U-1A and the license-built Goodyear FG-1D variants.

delivering 735 F3A-1 Corsairs in June 1943 from its plant in Johnsville, Pennsylvania.

Corsairs were designed with "gull" wings that bent downward for the main landing gear to allow adequate ground clearance for the massive Hamilton Standard Hydromatic three-blade propeller. With a diameter of 13 feet 4 inches, it was the largest prop yet hung on a US Navy fighter. The engine/prop combination had a great deal of torque that required special handling on takeoff.

As the wings were designed to accommodate the propeller, the fuselage was literally built *around* the R-2800 Double Wasp. Corsairs had about half of their fuselage length forward of the cockpit. This was partly because of the massive engine (more than 7 feet in length) and partly because of the insertion of large fuel tanks. The latter had to be moved out of the wing because wing armament increased over the original specs from four to six .50-caliber machine guns. The downside of the massive assembly of engine and propeller was reduced forward visibility during takeoffs and landings. This initially complicated the use of the Corsair aboard aircraft carriers.

Because of these problems, the US Navy decided late in 1942 to restrict the Corsair to land-based operations until techniques for carrier operations were figured out, and the aircraft, which was most promising in all other respects, was passed off to the US Marine Corps.

In service with the Marines in the Solomon Islands campaign, the Corsair turned out to be the right aircraft at the right time. It was fast. It was the second American fighter (after the USAAF's P-38 Lightning) to be capable of cruising faster than 400 mph, making it roughly 100 mph faster than the Grumman Wildcat and nearly twice as fast as the Mitsubishi Zero used by the Imperial Japanese Navy. Four of the

Marine Corps F4U-1 Corsairs are shown on the flight line at Vella Lavella's Barakoma airfield in the South Pacific, which began operations in September 1943. (Photo Courtesy USMC)

five top-scoring Marine aces of World War II (Robert "Butcher Bob" Hanson, Gregory "Pappy" Boyington, Ken Walsh, and Don Aldrich) scored their victories in Corsairs.

Beginning in November 1943 with 95 F4U-1s, Corsairs were Lend Leased to Britain for use by the Royal Navy aboard its carrier fleet. The British played a key role in developing modifications, such as raising the pilot's seat and enlarging the canopy, to address the compromised visibility in the F4U-1.

In American production, design changes, such as replacing the faceted "birdcage" canopy of the F4U-1 with a one-piece "blown Plexiglas" bubble canopy to aid pilot visibility, appeared in the

Vought F4U-1A and F4U-1D variants and in the parallel Goodyear FG-1D.

Although these later subvariants began appearing during the summer of 1944, Corsairs were not used aboard American aircraft carriers until January 1945, and these were piloted by Marine Corps pilots.

Vought built 2,066 F4U-1As and 1,375 F4U-1Ds with the "D" that designated those Corsairs that were fitted with underwing attachments for launching aerial rockets. Goodyear built 2,302 FG-1Ds, and Brewster built 96 F3A-1Ds. Vought also built 200 F4U-1Cs that were armed with 20-mm cannons rather than .50-caliber machine

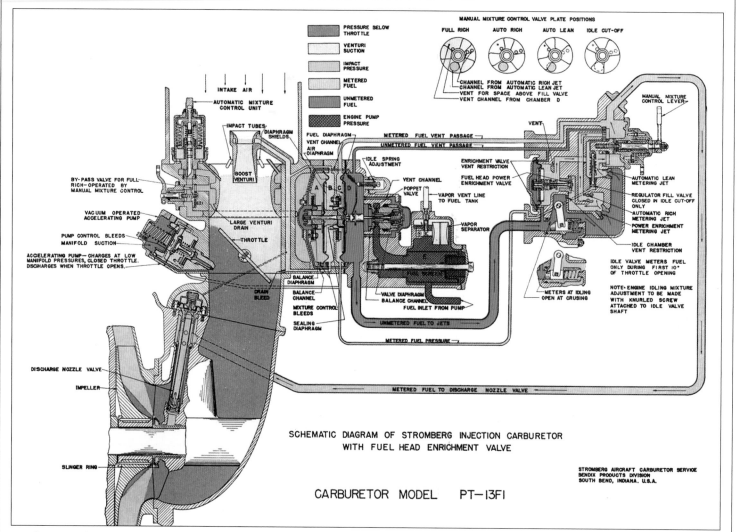

A schematic drawing of the operation of the Stromberg Model PT13F1 (PT-13F1) shows the injection carburetor with fuel head enrichment valve as installed in Pratt & Whitney R-2800 Double Wasp engines (1943).

guns. The F4U-2 designation went to a dozen F4U-1s that were equipped with radar for use as night fighters.

Those F4U-1s of both Vought subvariants with the new higher-visibility canopy were designated as Corsair Mk.IIs in British service. The Corsair Mk.III designation went to all 430 F3A-1 and F3A-1D Corsairs coming from Brewster, and the Corsair Mk.IV designation went to FG-1/FG-1D aircraft built by Goodyear. A total of 2,012 Corsairs went to the Royal Navy, where many were used by the British Pacific Fleet onward from April 1944.

The Royal New Zealand Air Force began receiving a total of 437 Corsairs in March 1944, and eventually operated 10 fighter squadrons equipped with the aircraft.

In aerial combat, especially with the US Marine Corps, the Corsair established a significant record, downing 1,140 enemy aircraft to just 189 losses, a kill ratio of 11 to 1.

US Navy and Marine Corsairs were also widely used in the ground attack role in the Pacific during World War II, a function with which they were later tasked during the Korean War. For the latter conflict, 111 Corsairs were retrofitted with cannons modified to carry aerial rockets and more than 2 tons of bombs and were redesignated as AU-1 attack aircraft. Some were fitted with radar for night-attack missions.

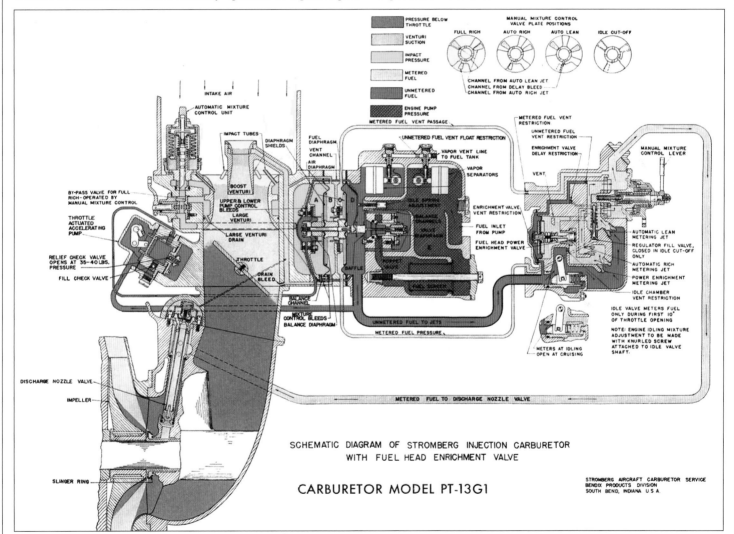

This is a schematic drawing of the operation of the Stromberg Model PT13G1 (PT-13G1) injection carburetor with fuel head enrichment valve as installed in Pratt & Whitney R-2800 Double Wasp engines (1943).

The last F4U variant was the F4U-7, of which 94 were for the French Navy and delivered in the latter half of 1952 under the Military Assistance Program. These, along with 69 recently modified AU-1s were used in combat operations from Indochina to North Africa through 1964. The Honduran Air Force obtained 19 Corsairs and used them in combat against El Salvador. The last three Corsair aerial victories were scored by Honduras against El Salvador in 1969.

Today, the Corsair is widely seen on the air show and air race circuit. There are a scattering of flyable Corsairs from New Zealand to Europe and Latin America and more than a dozen flying (and nearly as many under restoration) in the United States.

The Double Wasp and Its Corsair

As noted above, the Corsair was designed around the power of Pratt & Whitney's R-2800-8 Double Wasp—the tail that wagged the dog, so to speak. In the early days, only the single prototype differed, with the XF4U-1 being powered by the 1,850-hp XR-2800-4.

In November 1943, as F4U-1 aircraft No. 1,551 came down the line, Vought began installing the water-injected R-2800-8W, which boosted takeoff horsepower from 2,000 to 2,250.

The R-2800-8W was rated at 1,800 hp at 2,700 rpm at 15,500 feet. It had a compression ratio of 6.65:1 and used a Stromberg PT13D5-6 carburetor. The engine weighed 2,480 pounds and was 88.47 inches long with a diameter of 52.5 inches.

In May 1944, Vought began deliveries of F4U-4 Corsairs powered by the R-2800-18W with a four-bladed propeller. The R-2800-18W was also used in the F4U-7, which was built specifically for the French Navy in 1952. The R-2800-18W was rated at 2,100 hp at 2,800 rpm for takeoff and at 2,000 hp at 2,700 rpm at 25,000 feet. It had a compression ratio of 6.75:1 and used a Stromberg PR5812-31 carburetor. The engine weighed 2,560 pounds and was 93.77 inches long with a diameter of 52.8 inches.

Vought had delivered 1,859 F4U-4s by war's end, but the US Navy considered the aircraft sufficiently important to its postwar needs that production continued through April 1946.

The postwar F4U-5, in production from November 1947 to September 1951, was powered by the R-2800-32W, which was rated at 2,300 hp at 2,800 rpm for takeoff and at 1,800 hp at 2,600 rpm at 30,000 feet. It had a compression ratio of 6.75:1 and used a Chandler-Evans 54CPC8-2 carburetor. The engine weighed 2,715 pounds with its torque meter, dual auxiliary blower, and variable-speed impellers installed. The water-injection equipment weighed 10 pounds. The R-2800-32W was 96.5 inches long and had a diameter of 52.8 inches.

POWER *in action*

Commanding 2,000 Pratt & Whitney horsepower packed into a single engine, Marine Corsair pilots have rolled up a victory ratio of better than five to one. Like the Republic Thunderbolt and Grumman Hellcat fighters, also built around the Double Wasp, the Vought Corsair has proved in action, "There's no substitute for supe."

Pratt & Whitney engines now power these great fighters: Corsair, Hellcat, Thunderbolt, Black Widow, Wildcat.

PRATT & WHITNEY AIRCRAFT
EAST HARTFORD, CONNECTICUT
ONE OF THE FOUR DIVISIONS OF UNITED AIRCRAFT CORPORATION

This wartime magazine advertisement placed by Pratt & Whitney celebrates the use of the R-2800 Twin Wasp in the Vought F4U Corsair as well as in the Grumman Hellcat and Republic Thunderbolt.

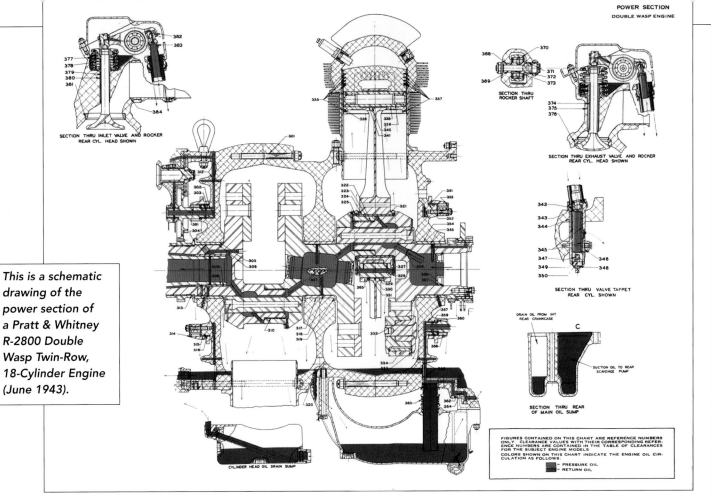

This is a schematic drawing of the power section of a Pratt & Whitney R-2800 Double Wasp Twin-Row, 18-Cylinder Engine (June 1943).

POWER SECTION
DOUBLE WASP ENGINE

SECTION THRU INLET VALVE AND ROCKER
REAR CYL. HEAD SHOWN

SECTION THRU EXHAUST VALVE AND ROCKER
REAR CYL. HEAD SHOWN

SECTION THRU
ROCKER SHAFT

SECTION THRU VALVE TAPPET
REAR CYL. SHOWN

DRAIN OIL FROM INT
REAR CRANKCASE

C

SUCTION OIL TO REAR
SCAVENGE PUMP

SECTION THRU REAR
OF MAIN OIL SUMP

CYLINDER HEAD OIL DRAIN SUMP

FIGURES CONTAINED ON THIS CHART ARE REFERENCE NUMBERS
ONLY. CLEARANCE VALUES WITH THEIR CORRESPONDING REFER-
ENCE NUMBERS ARE CONTAINED IN THE TABLE OF CLEARANCES
FOR THE SUBJECT ENGINE MODELS
COLORS SHOWN ON THIS CHART INDICATE THE ENGINE OIL CIR-
CULATION AS FOLLOWS:
= PRESSURE OIL
= RETURN OIL

301. Studs, Main Crankcase
302. Bearing, Front Cam Reduction Shaft Rear (Shaft)
303. Bearing, Front Cam Reduction Shaft Rear (Crankcase)
304. End Play, Crankshaft
305. Bearing, Crankshaft Front Main
306. Bearing, Crankshaft Front Main Crankshaft
307. Lock, Crankshaft Center Main Bearing
307. Lock, Crankshaft Center Main Bearing (Crankcase)
308. Bearing, Propeller Shaft Rear (Shaft)
309. Bearing, Propeller Shaft Rear (Crankshaft)
310. Splines, (Crankshaft, Front Section)
312. Pipe, Front Tappet Oil Feed Crankcase, Front Maul
313. Gear, Front Crankshaft
314. End Clearance, Cam, Front
315. Bearing, Front Cam (Cam)
316. Bearing, Front Cam (Crankcase)
317. Pinch, Bearing, Crankshaft Center Main (Crankcase)
318. Bearing, Crankshaft Center Main (Crankshaft)

319. End Fit, Bearing, Crankshaft Center Main (Crankcase)
320. Spring, Main Oil Sump Drain
321. Plate, Master Rod Bearing
322. Splines, Crankshaft, Center Section
323. Bearing, Master Rod (Crankshaft)
324. Bearing, Master Rod (Rod)
325. Assembly, Master Rod and Bearing Plate
326. Pipe, Crankshaft Rear Section (Crankshaft)
327. Pin, Floating Knuckle (Plates, Master Rod Bearing)
328. Pin, Floating Knuckle (Plate, Master Rod Bearing)
329. Bushing, Link Rod (Rod)
330. Bushing, Link Rod (Pin, Floating Knuckle)
331. Rod, Link (Rod, Master)
332. Flyweight, Outer
333. Liner, Flyweight (Flyweight)
334. Liner, Flyweight (Crankshaft, Rear Section)
335. Side Clearance, Piston Rings
337. End Clearance, Piston Rings
338. Piston (Pin, Piston)
339. Plug, Piston Pin (Pin)
340. Bushing, Piston Pin (Rod, Master and Link)
341. Bushing, Piston Pin (Pin)

342. Socket, Push Rod Ball (Tappet, Valve)
343. Ball End, Push Rod (Socket)
344. Guide, Valve Tappet (Crankcase, Rear Main)
345. Tappet, Valve (Guide, Valve Tappet)
346. Guide, Valve Tappet (Crankcase, Rear Main)
347. Roller, Valve Tappet (Guide)
348. Roller, Valve Tappet (Tappet)
349. Pin, Valve Tappet Roller (Tappet)
350. Pin, Valve Tappet Roller (Roller)
351. Bearing, Rear Cam (Cam)
352. Bearing, Rear Cam (Crankcase)
353. Cam, Rear
354. Bearing, Crankshaft Rear Main
355. Bearing, Crankshaft Rear Main (Crankshaft)
356. Pipe, Rear Cam Oil Transfer (Crankcase, Rear Main)
357. Bearing, Rear Cam Reduction Shaft Front (Crankcase, Rear Main)
358. Backlash (Cam, Rear, Gear, Cam Reduction)
359. Bearing, Rear Cam Reduction Shaft Front
360. End Clearance (Gear, Rear Cam Reduction)
361. Backlash (Cam, Front, Gear, Cam Reduction)
362. Pipe, Rear Cam Oil Transfer

363. Spring, Main Oil Sump Drain (Large)
364. Pipe, Rear Cam Oil Transfer (Crankcase, Blower)
365. Pin, Link Rod (Rod, Master)
366. Side Clearance (Ring, Accessory Shaft Front, Oil Seal Retainer)
367. Seal, Accessory Shaft Front Oil
368. Bushing, Valve Rocker Shaft Small (Head, Cylinder)
369. Bushing, Valve Rocker Shaft Small (Shaft)
370. Bearing, Rocker Arm (Rocker, Valve)
371. Bushing, Valve Rocker Shaft Large (Head, Cylinder)
372. Bushing, Valve Rocker Shaft Large (Shaft)
373. Bearing, Rocker Arm (Shaft, Valve Rocker)
374. Guide, Exhaust Valve (Valve)
375. Guide, Exhaust Valve (Head, Cylinder)
376. Seat, Exhaust Valve (Head, Cylinder)
377. Spring, (Outside) Inlet and Exhaust Valve
378. Spring, (Inside) Inlet and Exhaust Valve
379. Guide, Inlet Valve (Valve)
380. Guide, Inlet Valve (Head, Cylinder)
381. Seat, Inlet Valve (Head, Cylinder)
382. Cup, Rocker Push Rod Ball (Rocker, Valve)
383. Ball End, Push Rod (Push Rod)
384. Coupling, Intake Pipe (Head, Cylinder)

Chapter 11

THE DOUBLE WASP IN TWIN-ENGINE BOMBERS

In addition to its use in the hottest of America's round-engine fighters, the R-2800 was also used in two important twin-engine bombers for the USAAF: the Douglas A-26 Invader and the Martin B-26 Marauder.

The Douglas Invader

First flown in July 1942, the Douglas Invader was like North American Aviation's Mustang in that it was an example of an aircraft developed entirely during the war that can be included among the technological and tactical best war-time aircraft of its type. The Invader was one of the early creations of Edward "Ed" Henry Heinemann, one of the greatest American military aircraft designers of the 20th century. His career as Douglas chief engineer spanned the years from 1936 to 1960. In the Invader program, Heinemann was aided by Robert Donovan and Ted Smith, and the laminar flow airfoil of the wing was designed by Apollo Milton Olin Smith (no relation), who left Douglas in 1942 to help create the Aerojet company.

The Douglas XA-26 made its first flight at El Segundo, California, in July 1942 powered by a pair of Pratt & Whitney R-2800-27 Double Wasp twin-row radial engines.

The idea behind the Invader was to create an aircraft that was larger and faster than the Douglas A-20 Havoc attack bomber—and with twice the payload capacity. As Douglas had previously chosen the Wright R-2600 for its Havoc, Heinemann and his team picked the parallel-developed Pratt & Whitney R-2800 for the A-26.

As had been the case with the A-20, production would be divided between aircraft with blown-Plexiglas "bombardier" noses and aircraft with solid noses bristling with guns.

The prototypes were built at the Douglas plant in El Segundo, California: the XB-26 with a Plexiglas nose, the XB-26A with a solid nose, and the XB-26B with a solid nose plus a forward-firing 75-mm cannon.

The B-26B became the first production series, with 1,174 built by Douglas at Long Beach and another 205 produced by Douglas in Tulsa, Oklahoma. In the A-26B, the 75-mm gun of the XA-26B was superseded by .50-caliber machine guns. Initially, there were 6 such weapons, but the number was increased to 8 beginning with the Block 50 A-26B aircraft.

Various modifications occurred at various blocks during the production run, which continued seamlessly into the A-26C series. The early-production A-26Cs differed from the later A-26Bs only in the substitution of a Plexiglas nose for the solid nose. Of the A-26C, 1,091 were built, all but five in Tulsa.

Beginning in 1945, around 150 USAAF "B" and "C" variant Invaders were transferred to the US Navy under the JD-1 designation. These included 140 that had been earmarked for the Royal Air Force as Invader Mk.Is but not delivered.

After World War II, large numbers of surplus USAAF Invaders served with the air forces of Brazil and France. Other air forces operating at least one squadron of Invaders included those of Chile, Columbia, Indonesia, Nicaragua, Peru, Portugal (in Angola operations), and Saudi Arabia. The CIA also used them in support of the ill-fated Bay of Pigs invasion of Cuba in 1961.

This is a close-up view of the large prop spinner on the left Pratt & Whitney R-2800-27 Double Wasp of the first XA-26. The photo was taken four days before the first flight on July 10, 1942.

A Pratt & Whitney R-2800 Double Wasp twin-row, 18-cylinder engine is shown on display at the Museum of Aviation at Robins Air Force Base in Georgia. (Photo Courtesy Dsdugan, Licensed under Creative Commons)

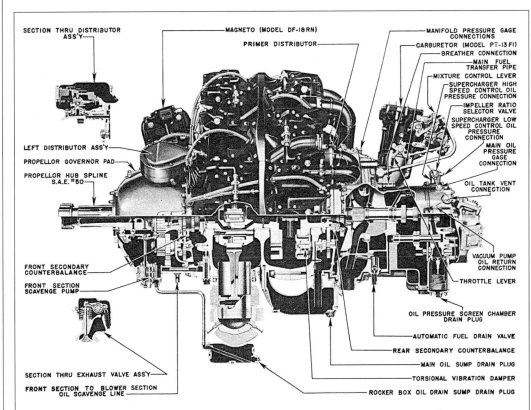

This is a cutaway view of a Pratt & Whitney R-2800 Double Wasp twin-row, 18-cylinder engine.

When the USAAF became the independent US Air Force in 1947, the sizable number of Invaders that were still in the inventory were redesignated as B-26s. Naturally, this created some confusion for those familiar with the Martin B-26, but by that time, all the Martin Marauders had been retired.

The B-26 Invader went on to a long postwar career with the US Air Force. It was used extensively in Korea but was gradually phased out in the late 1950s. In the 1960s, however, as the United States became involved in the war in Southeast Asia, the US Air Force 1st Air Command Group adopted the Invader for counterinsurgency operations.

In 1964, when the 1st Air Command Group began suffering technical issues leading to aircraft loss, the Air Force contracted with On Mark Engineering of Van Nuys, California, to upgrade the Invaders. The result was a batch of 41 B-26s being rebuilt and re-engined as B-26K (including a YB-26K) Counter Invader aircraft. Assigned to the 609th Special Operations Squadron, these were redesignated in 1966 as A-26A for political reasons. Thailand, where they were based, did not like the "B for Bomber" designation. On Mark also converted a number of Invaders into executive transports under the Marksman brand name.

Into the 21st century, there were still around two dozen flyable Invaders operating around the world, mainly in the United States. Some were on the air show circuit, and some were aerial fire-fighting tankers.

A Block 5 Douglas A-26B Invader powered by Pratt & Whitney RE-2800-27 engines is shown on the ramp in Long Beach in September 1943. A small number of early production A-26Bs carried the 755-mm cannon in the nose (seen here) that was first tested on the XA-24B. Later, A-26Bs retained the solid nose but were fitted with a grouping of machine guns.

This is a sectional view of the Type 1359 Model 6 Automatic Engine Control, circa 1948. Manufactured in Teterboro, New Jersey, by the Eclipse-Pioneer Division of the Bendix Aviation Corporation, it was installed in Pratt & Whitney R-2800 Double Wasp engines.

1. Rear Pilot's Shaft
2. Manual Control Arm
3. Throttle Linkage Arm
4. Walking Beam
5. Manual Control Shaft
6. Operating Piston Assembly
7. Follow-up Valve Spring
8. Follow-up Valve Piston
9. Push Rod
10. Follow-up Arm
11. Follow-up Arm Support
12. Follow-up Arm Adjusting Screw
13. Flow Regulating Valve Body
14. Flow Regulating Valve Plunger
15. Flow Regulating Valve Spring
16. Bottom Cover
17. Pressure Reducing Valve Adjusting Screw
18. Pressure Reducing Valve Spring
19. Pressure Reducing Valve Piston
20. Pressure Reducing Valve Body
21. Manual Control Piston
22. Manual Control Piston Spring
23. Mounting Flange
24. Manual Control Piston Rod
25. Throttle Shaft
26. Throttle Lever
27. Carburetor Rod
28. Rod End

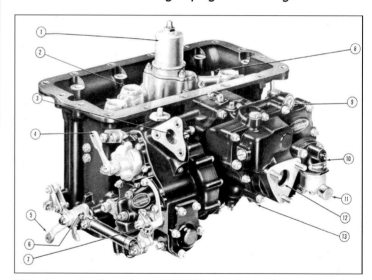

This shows the Stromberg PR58E5 injection carburetor as installed in later Pratt & Whitney R-2800 Double Wasp engines.

1. Automatic Mixture Control Unit
2. Boost Venturi Tube
3. Fuel Transfer Tube Mounting Flange
4. Manual Mixture Control Lever
5. Throttle Lever
6. Idle Speed Adjustment
7. Idle Mixture Adjustment
8. Impact Tube
9. Vapor Vent Connection
10. Primer Valve Fuel Line Connection
11. Primer Valve Electrical Connection
12. Fuel Inlet
13. Fuel Pressure Gauge Connection

Powering the Invader Across Three Decades

In 1942, the original XA-26, XA-26A, and XA-26B prototypes, as well as the early A-26B production aircraft were powered by the R-2800-27 built by Pratt & Whitney or by the analogous R-2800-71, which was built by the Ford Motor Company under license from Pratt. For the latter, Ford used its famous River Rouge Complex in Michigan, which was once the largest automobile factory in the

A Tulsa-built Douglas A-26C-20-DT Invader powered by Pratt & Whitney R-2800-79 engines is shown on a European Theater combat mission, circa 1945. While the A-26B had a solid "gun" nose, the A-26C had a glass "bombardier" nose. This aircraft was assigned to the 416th Bombardment Group of the USAAF Ninth Air Force and was delivered in November 1944 when the 416th was based at Melun airfield in France.

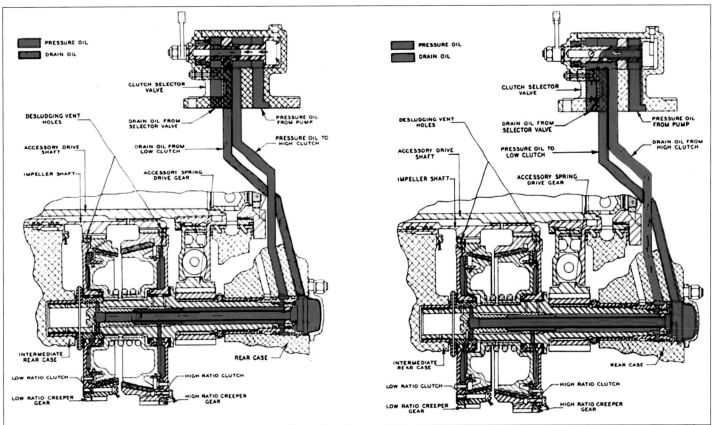

This schematic view shows the rear section of a Pratt & Whitney R-2800 Double Wasp twin-row, 18-cylinder engine (1948). On the left, the selector valve and clutch are in the high position. On the right, they are in the low position.

A Douglas A-26B Invader of the USAAF Ninth Air Force drops bombs on the Siegfried Line, circa 1944. The Ninth operated Invaders in five bomb groups. (Photo Courtesy USAF)

said that the engine change affected only the Block 50 through Block 65 Long Beach deliveries of A-26Bs, while Ray Wagner included Block 66, which was the last Long Beach production block. In any event, the R-2800-79 was the powerplant was used throughout A-26C production at Tulsa.

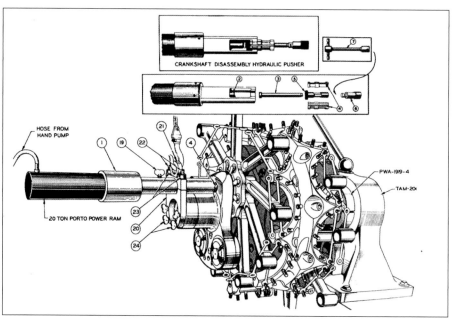

Crankcase through-bolts are removed from the front section of a Pratt & Whitney R-2800 Double Wasp engine (1943).

world. It still operates today, building F-150 pickups.

The R-2800-27 was rated at 2,000 hp at 2,700 rpm for takeoff and at 1,600 hp at 2,600 rpm at 13,500 feet. It had a compression ratio of 6.65:1 and used a Stromberg PT-13G1-9 carburetor. The engine weighed 2,300 pounds and was 75.72 inches long with a diameter of 52.5 inches.

The R-2800-71, like the R-2800-27, was rated at 2,000 hp at 2,700 rpm for takeoff and at 1,600 hp at 2,700 rpm at 13,500 feet. It had a compression ratio of 6.65:1 and used a Stromberg PT13G1-9 carburetor. The engine weighed 2,325 pounds and was 75.72 inches long with a diameter of 52.5 inches.

The engine installation later shifted to Ford-built R-2800-79s. Rene Francillon, in his book about Douglas aircraft, notes that this began with the Block 45 Invaders coming off the Long Beach line (A-26B-45-DL). John Andrade, in his exhaustive block-by-block production overview,

This overview of the crankcase rear section shows its removal from a Pratt & Whitney R-2800 Double Wasp engine (1943).

The R-2800-79 was rated at 2,000 hp at 2,700 rpm for takeoff and at 1,600 hp at 2,700 rpm at 13,500 feet. It had a compression ratio of 6.65:1 and used a Stromberg PT-13G5 carburetor. The engine weighed 2,325 pounds and was 75.72 inches long with a diameter of 52.5 inches.

Beginning in 1962, the Invaders that were rebuilt and upgraded by On Mark Engineering used a variety of engines. The YB-26K was powered by the Double Wasp. The production-series B-26K (later A-26A) used the water-injected R-2800-52W. On Mark's later Marksman executive transports were powered by R-2800-83AM3 and R-2800-83AM4 commercial engines.

The R-2800-27W was rated at 2,500 hp at 2,800 rpm for takeoff when "wet" and 2,200 hp at 2,800 rpm for takeoff when "dry." Like other Invader engines, it delivered 1,600 hp at 2,700 rpm at

A restored A-26 flies in 2016, marked with the "Invasion Stripes" that were painted on Allied aircraft for Operation Overlord in June 1944. (Photo Courtesy Ragnhild and Neil Crawford, Licensed under Creative Commons)

An Invader sits on the ramp at the Royal Thai Air Force Base at Korat, circa 1963. A veteran of three wars, the invader was redesignated as B-26 after the retirement of the Martin B-26 and served as such in Korea and Southeast Asia. This R-2800-powered B-26B was assigned to the 1st Air Commando Wing for Operation Farm Gate, which was part of the early American involvement it Southeast Asia.

The first Martin B-26 Marauder is shown on the ramp at Martin's Middle River plant near Baltimore in November 1940. The 201 aircraft of this first Marauder variant were powered by Pratt & Whitney R-2800-5 Double Wasps.

Crankcase cross sections are shown in a Pratt & Whitney R-2800 Double Wasp twin-row, 18-cylinder engine (1948).

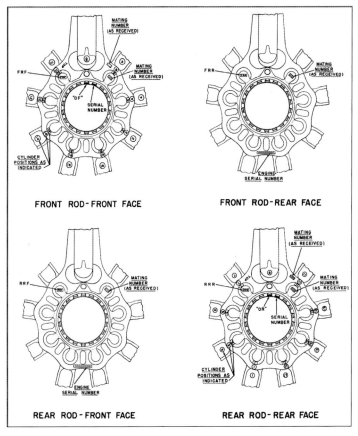

FRONT ROD-FRONT FACE

FRONT ROD-REAR FACE

REAR ROD-FRONT FACE

REAR ROD-REAR FACE

13,500 feet. It had a compression ratio of 6.75:1 and used a Stromberg PR58E5-13 or PR58E5-16 carburetor. The engine weighed 2,390 pounds and was 81.5 inches long with a diameter of 53 inches.

A Martin B-26B-15-MA Marauder flies over England, circa 1944. The variant was produced in the largest numbers. The Pratt & Whitney R-2800-41 was installed through Block 3 of this variant, with the R-2800-43 used thereafter.

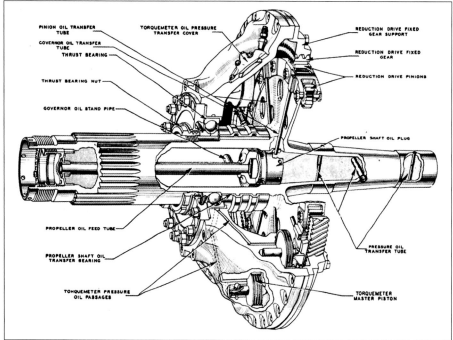

The R-2800-52W was rated at 2,500 hp at 2,800 rpm for takeoff, and at 1,700 hp at 2,500 rpm at 14,500 feet. It had a compression ratio of 6.75:1 and used a Stromberg PR58E5-13 or PR58E5-16 carburetor. The engine weighed 2,390 pounds, was 81.5 inches long, and had a diameter of 53 inches.

The R-2800-83W was rated at 2,100 hp at 2,800 rpm for takeoff and at 1,700 hp at 2,500 rpm at 16,000 feet. It had a compression ratio of 6.75:1 and used a Stromberg PR58E2-2 carburetor. The engine weighed 2,384 pounds, including the torquemeter, General Electric ignition equipment, manifold pressure regulator, and other equipment. It was 73.15 inches long and had a diameter of 52.8 inches.

The Martin Marauder

The Glenn Martin Company, the second oldest of America's major existing planemakers, divided its World War II production at its facility near Baltimore between flying boats for the US Navy and medium bombers for the USAAF. The principal flying boat type was the PBM Mariner patrol bomber, of which early variants (see Chapter 8) were powered by the Wright R-2600 Twin Cyclone. Although, the later PBM-5 variant used the Pratt & Whitney R-2800-34 Double Wasp.

Martin's principal production aircraft during World War II was the B-26 Marauder medium bomber (Martin Model 179), which made its first flight on November 25, 1940.

The Marauder was developed by the US Army Air Corps in parallel with the North American Aviation B-25 Mitchell (see Chapter 8), which first flew in August 1940. With their similar size and identical intended combat role, the two are often compared. However, the Marauder is often maligned for the negative reputation it developed in its early days for its high accident rate. Often called the "Widowmaker," "Martin Murderer," "Flying Coffin," or "Baltimore Whore" (no visible means of support), it was unforgiving of inexact approach and landing speeds—especially in the hands of inexperienced pilots. The high loading of the small wing area resulted in slow-speed stalling and crashing. This, and

This is a cutaway view of the front section of a Pratt & Whitney R-2800 Double Wasp twin-row, 18-cylinder engine (1948). The engine continued to be used in postwar aircraft, including the Douglas B-26 (ex-A-26).

USAAF Ninth Air Force maintenance crews are at work on the left Pratt & Whitney R-2800-43 Double Wasp of this Martin B-26B at a base in England in 1944.

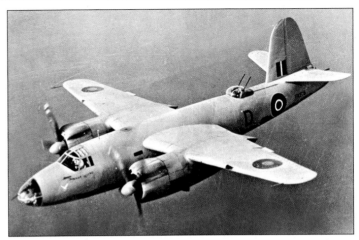

This British Marauder IA was one of 19 B-26B aircraft delivered to the Royal Air Force.

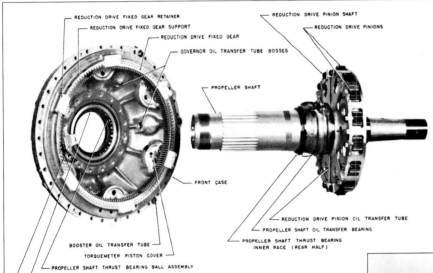

The front case and reduction gear assembly of a Pratt & Whitney R-2800 Double Wasp twin-row, 18-cylinder engine is shown (1948). The engine continued to be used in postwar aircraft, including the Douglas B-26 (formerly the A-26).

This was the first Block 15 B-26G Marauder on the ramp at Martin's Middle River plant in Baltimore on August 17, 1944. It retained the Pratt & Whitney R-2800-43 that had been used as a powerplant in the B-26C, B-26F, and most B-36Bs.

higher production costs, meant that nearly twice as many Mitchells were built than Marauders.

However, it did not start out that way. As aviation historian Ray Wagner recalled, the Marauder looked better "on paper" than the Mitchell, leading the Air Corps to take "a large risk on an untested aircraft" by ordering 201 B-26s and 139 B-26As with increased fuel capacity before the first flight. When the United States entered the war in December 1941, the USAAF had just managed to equip the 22nd Bomb Group, its first Marauder unit.

The largest production variant was the B-26B, of which 1,883 aircraft were delivered from the Baltimore plant, beginning in May 1942. Numerous changes were made over the course of 15 production blocks, including several engine changes (see below). Martin also produced 208 AT-23A gunnery trainer variants of the B-26B, which were also used for towing aerial targets.

Gradually, the causes of the early high accident rate were deduced and rectified by such things as a larger wing, taller tail, and the installation of a dorsal turret to balance the weight. Beginning with B-26B aircraft number 642 and continuing through the entire B-26C production, the wingspan increased from 65 to 71 feet, and the wing area increased from 602 to 658 square feet. The height was raised from 19 feet, 10 inches to 21 feet, 6 inches.

The first B-26C was first delivered in August 1942 as B-26B production was going strong. There were 1,210 B-26Cs built, all of them at Martin's new operation in Omaha. Also built at Omaha were 375 AT-23Bs, the trainer variant of the B-26C.

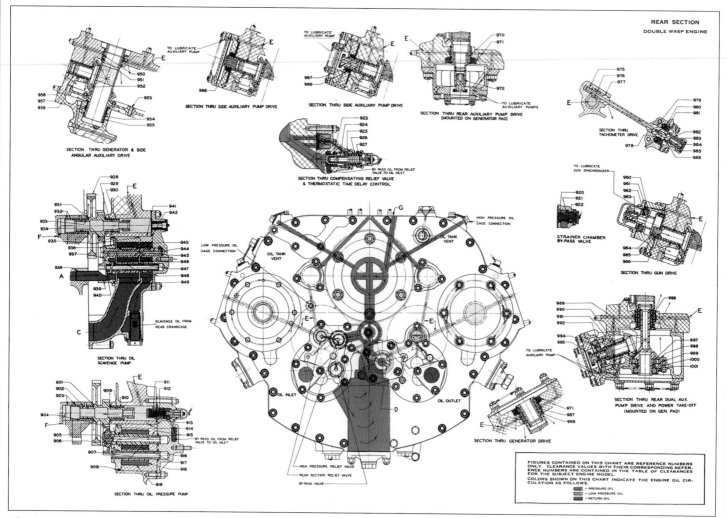

This is a schematic drawing of the rear section of a Pratt & Whitney R-2800 Double Wasp Twin-Row, 18-cylinder engine (June 1943).

901. End Clearance (Gear, Accessory Intermediate)
902. Bearing, Accessory Intermediate Driveshaft Front (Shaft)
903. Bearing, Accessory Intermediate Driveshaft Front (Plate, Bearing Support)
904. Backlash (Gear, Oil Pressure Pump Drive)
905. Splines (Shaft, Oil Pressure Pump Drive, Gear, Drive)
906. Shaft, Oil Pressure Pump Idler (Plate, Cover)
907. Shaft, Oil Pressure Pump Idler (Gear)
908. Side Clearance (Rings, Pressure Pump Body Oil Seal)
909. Bearing, Accessory Intermediate Driveshaft Rear (Crankcase, Rear)
910. Bearing, Accessory Intermediate Driveshaft Rear (Shaft)
911. Housing, Low Oil Pressure Relief (Valve)
912. Spring (Low Oil Pressure Relief)
913. Cover, Oil Pressure Pump (Body)
914. Body and Cover Plate, Oil Pressure Pump (Crankcase, Rear)
915. Shaft, Oil Pressure Pump Drive (Body and Cover Plate)
916. Backlash (Gears, Oil Pressure Pump)
917. Shaft, Oil Pressure Pump Idler (Body)
918. End Clearance (Gears, Oil Pressure Pump)
919. Diametrical Clearance (Gears, Oil Pressure Pump)
920. Body, Strainer Bypass (Cover, Oil Pressure Pump)
921. Plunger, Strainer Bypass (Body)
922. Spring (Strainer Bypass)

Continued on page 151

923. Plunger, Compensating Relief Valve (Body)

924. Piston, Compensating (Relief Valve Housing, Small End)

925. Housing, Compensating Relief Valve (Cover, Oil Pressure Pump

926. Piston, Compensating (Relief Valve Housing, Large End)

927. Spring (Compensating Relief Valve)

928. Backlash (Gear, Accessory Intermediate Drive, Floating Accessory Drive)

929. Bearing, Accessory Intermediate Driveshaft Rear (Shaft)

930. Bearing, Accessory Intermediate Driveshaft Rear (Crankcase, Rear)

931. End Clearance (Gear, Accessory Intermediate Drive)

932. Bearing, Accessory Intermediate Driveshaft Front (Plate, Bearing Support)

933. Bearing, Accessory Intermediate Driveshaft Front (Shaft)

934. Backlash (Gear, Oil Scavenge Pump Drive, Gear, Accessory Intermediate Drive)

935. Side Clearance (Rings, Scavenge Pump Body Oil Seal)

936. End Clearance (Gears, Oil Scavenge Pump Bodies)

937. End Clearance (Gear, Oil Scavenge Pump Drive)

938. Pipe, Intermediate Case to Suction Pump (Crankcase, Inter-Rear)

939. Pipe, Intermediate Crankcase to Suction Pump (Plate, Cover)

940. Shaft, Oil Scavenge Pump Idler (Plate, Cover)

941. Bodies and Cover Plate, Oil Scavenge Pump (Crankcase Rear)

942. Cover, Oil Scavenge Pump (Body)

943. Keys (Gears, Oil Scavenge Pump)

943. Keys (Shaft, Drive)

944. Shaft, Oil Scavenge Pump Drive (Bodies)

945. Shaft, Oil Scavenge Pump Drive (Gears)

946. Backlash (Gears, Oil Scavenge Pump)

947. Shaft, Oil Scavenge Pump Idler (Bodies)

948. Shaft, Oil Scavenge Pump Idler (Gears)

949. Diametrical Clearance (Gears, Oil Scavenge Pump, Bodies, Pump)

950. Bearing, Generator Intermediate Driveshaft (Shaft)

951. Bearing, Generator Intermediate Driveshaft Rear (Crankcase, Rear)

952. Backlash (Gears, Auxiliary Drive)

953. Backlash (Gear, Generator Intermediate Drive Gear, Accessory Intermediate Drive)

954. Bearing, Generator Intermediate Driveshaft Front (Shaft)

955. Bearing, Generator Intermediate Driveshaft Front (Crankcase, Intermediate Rear)

956. Bearing, Auxiliary Driveshaft (Shaft)

957. Bearing, Auxiliary Driveshaft (Crankcase, Rear)

958. Clearance (Gear, Generator Intermediate Drive Crankcase Rear)

960. Cage, Gun Generator Ball Bearing (Adapter, Gun Generator Drive)

961. Bearing, Gun Generator Driveshaft Ball (Cage)

962. Bearing, Gun Generator Driveshaft, Ball (Shaft)

963. Splines Gear, Gun Control (Shaft, Gun Generator Drive)

964. Backlash Gear, Gun Generator Intermediate Drive Gear, Gun Generator Drive)

965. Bearing, Gun Generator Driveshaft (Shaft)

966. Bearing, Gun Generator Driveshaft (Adapter, Gun Generator Drive)

967. Splines Adapter, Auxiliary Pump Drive (Shaft, Auxiliary Drive)

968. Seal, Auxiliary Pump Drive Oil Retainer)

970. Splines (Shaft, Generator Intermediate Drive Adapter, Auxiliary Pump Drive)

971. Seal, Generator Intermediate Drive Oil (Crankcase Rear)

972. Splines (Adapters, Auxiliary Pump Drive)

975. Shaft, Tachometer Drive (Crankcase, Rear, Inner

End, Small)

976. Backlash Gear, Accessory Intermediate Drive (Gear, Tachometer Drive)

977. Shaft, Tachometer Drive (Crankcase, Rear, Inner End, Large)

978. End Clearance (Shaft, Tachometer Drive)

979. Shaft, Tachometer Drive (Crankcase, Rear, Outer End)

980. Liner, Tachometer Shaft Oil Seal (Crankcase, Rear)

981. Seal, Tachometer Driveshaft Oil (Liner)

982. Bearing, Tachometer Driveshaft Adapter (Housing, Tachometer Shaft Adapter)

983. Bearing, Tachometer Driveshaft Adapter

984. Insert, Tachometer Driveshaft Adapter

985. Shaft, Tachometer Drive (Adapter)

986. End Play (Adapter, Tachometer Driveshaft)

987. Splines (Shaft, Generator Intermediate Drive Adapter, Generator Drive)

988. Splines (Gear, Generator Drive (Generator),

989. Backlash Gear, Auxiliary Pump Driver (Gear, Auxiliary Pump Drive)

990. Bearing, Auxiliary Pump Driveshaft (Shaft)

991. Bearing, Auxiliary Pump Driveshaft (Housing, Auxiliary Pump Drive)

992. Housing, Auxiliary Pump Drive (Cage, Auxiliary Pump Oil Seal)

994. Seal, Auxiliary Pump Driveshaft Oil (Cage)

995. Splines (Shaft, Auxiliary Pump Drive, Adapter, Auxiliary Pump Drive)

996. Splines (Gear, Auxiliary Pump Driver, Adapter, Generator Drive)

997. Bearing, Auxiliary Pump Driver Shaft Ball (Shaft)

998. Clamp (Bearing, Auxiliary Pump Driver Shaft Ball)

999. Bearing, Auxiliary Pump Driver Shaft Ball (Housing, Auxiliary Pump Drive)

1000. Retainer, Auxiliary Drive Baring, Oil Seal (Housing, Auxiliary Pump Drive)

1001. Seal, Auxiliary Pump Drive Oil (Retainer)

Operationally, the Marauder received high marks from combat crews, especially with the early teething troubles fading from the institutional memory surrounding the aircraft.

With the XB-26D designation going to a single conversion and the B-26E being an unproduced variant, the next production variant was the B-26F, of which 300 were delivered from Baltimore beginning in February 1944.

The final Marauder variants were 893 Baltimore-built B-26G bombers and 104 TB-26 trainers, with deliveries coming to an end on March 26, 1945.

The US Navy received 225 AT-23B and 47 TB-26G Marauders from the US Air Force, designating them as JM-1 and JM-2, respectively. The Royal Air Force was Lend Leased 52 B-26As as Marauder Mk.Is, 19 B-26Bs as Marauder Mk.IAs, 123 B-26Cs as Marauder Mk.IIs, and 350 B-26Fs and B-26Gs as Marauder Mk.IIIs. Many of these aircraft were passed on to the South African Air Force.

Powerplants for Marauders

The prototype Marauder flew with a pair of Pratt & Whitney R-1830-5 Wasps, but the production aircraft moved up to the R-2800 Double Wasp. Thereafter, changes in Double Wasp variants did not coincide with the changes in Marauder variants. Rather, engine types were switched in the midst of variant production runs.

All 201 B-26s and the first 30 B-26As were powered by the Pratt & Whitney R-2800-5, some of which were built by the Ford Motor Company. It was rated at 1,850 hp at 2,600 rpm for takeoff and at 1,500 hp at 2,500 rpm at 14,000 feet. It had a compression ratio of 6.65:1 and used a Stromberg PT13F1-12 carburetor. The engine weighed 2,270 pounds, was 75.72 inches long, and had a diameter of 52.06 inches.

Most B-26As, a total of 159, were delivered with the R-2800-39, as were the first 307 B-26Bs. This engine was rated at 1,850 hp at 2,600 rpm for takeoff and at 1,500 hp at 2,600 rpm at 14,000 feet. It had a compression ratio of 6.63:1 and used a Stromberg PT13F1-12 carburetor. The engine weighed 2,300 pounds, was 75.72 inches long, and had a diameter of 52.06 inches.

After 307 B-26Bs were built with the R-2800-39, the R-2800-41 was installed in just 95 B-26-Bs before the switch was made to the R-2800-43. Thereafter, the R-2800-43 became standard equipment for the entire production run of the B-26C, B-26F, and B-26G.

The R-2800-41 and R-2800-43 were both rated at 2,000 hp at 2,700 rpm for takeoff and at 1,600 hp at 2,700 rpm at 14,000 feet. Each had a compression ratio of 5.55:1 and used Stromberg PT13G-1 carburetors. The engines each weighed 2,300 pounds, were 75.72 inches long, and had a diameter of 52.5 inches.

Powered by R-2800-43 Double Wasps, this B-26B-55-MA Marauder was assigned to the 596th Bombardment Squadron of the 397th Bombardment Group of the USAAF Ninth Air Force. The fading D-Day "Invasion Stripes" date this photo to late summer 1944, around the time that the 397th relocated from a base in England to a forward airfield in France. (Photo Courtesy USAF)

Martin powered its early variant PBM Mariners with Wright R-2600s, but for the PBM-5 variant, introduced in 1944, the company changed engine suppliers and began installing the R-2800-34 variant of the Pratt & Whitney Double Wasp.

Here is a cutaway view of the torquemeter system of a Pratt & Whitney R-2800 Double Wasp twin-row, 18-cylinder engine (1948). The engine continued to be used in postwar aircraft, including the Douglas B-26 (ex-A-26).

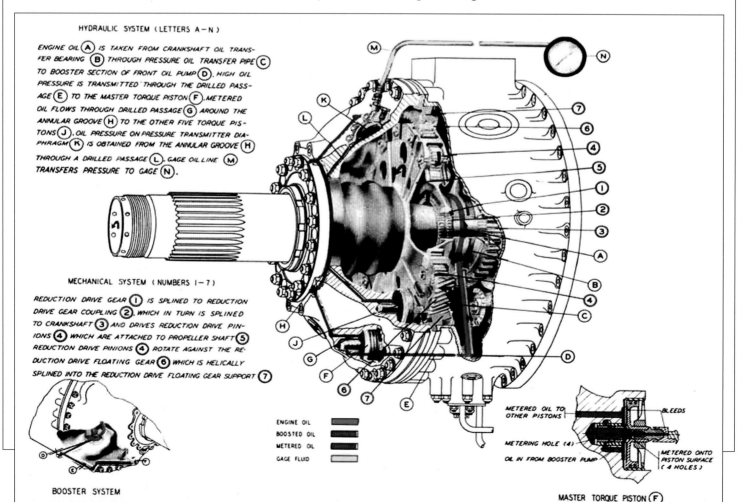

HYDRAULIC SYSTEM (LETTERS A-N)

ENGINE OIL (A) IS TAKEN FROM CRANKSHAFT OIL TRANSFER BEARING (B) THROUGH PRESSURE OIL TRANSFER PIPE (C) TO BOOSTER SECTION OF FRONT OIL PUMP (D). HIGH OIL PRESSURE IS TRANSMITTED THROUGH THE DRILLED PASSAGE (E) TO THE MASTER TORQUE PISTON (F). METERED OIL FLOWS THROUGH DRILLED PASSAGE (G) AROUND THE ANNULAR GROOVE (H) TO THE OTHER FIVE TORQUE PISTONS (J). OIL PRESSURE ON PRESSURE TRANSMITTER DIAPHRAGM (K) IS OBTAINED FROM THE ANNULAR GROOVE (H) THROUGH A DRILLED PASSAGE (L). GAGE OIL LINE (M) TRANSFERS PRESSURE TO GAGE (N).

MECHANICAL SYSTEM (NUMBERS 1-7)

REDUCTION DRIVE GEAR (1) IS SPLINED TO REDUCTION DRIVE GEAR COUPLING (2), WHICH IN TURN IS SPLINED TO CRANKSHAFT (3) AND DRIVES REDUCTION DRIVE PINIONS (4) WHICH ARE ATTACHED TO PROPELLER SHAFT (5). REDUCTION DRIVE PINIONS (4) ROTATE AGAINST THE REDUCTION DRIVE FLOATING GEAR (6) WHICH IS HELICALLY SPLINED INTO THE REDUCTION DRIVE FLOATING GEAR SUPPORT (7).

ENGINE OIL
BOOSTED OIL
METERED OIL
GAGE FLUID

BOOSTER SYSTEM

METERED OIL TO OTHER PISTONS
BLEEDS
METERING HOLE (4)
OIL IN FROM BOOSTER PUMP
METERED ONTO PISTON SURFACE (4 HOLES)

MASTER TORQUE PISTON (F)

Chapter 12

THE SUPERFORTRESS AND THE DUPLEX CYCLONE

The Boeing B-29 Superfortress (Boeing Model 345) was the ultimate strategic bomber of World War II. It had payload, range, and altitude capabilities that were unmatched by any other operational bomber of that era. A true secret weapon, the Boeing B-29 Superfortress embodied all the principles of long-range strategic air power that had been theorized before the war and proven during the war by aircraft such as Boeing's own B-17 Flying Fortress.

Strategically, the Superfortress was in a class unto itself. The war-winning potential of such an aircraft was such that theater commanders throughout the world coveted it for themselves. However, General Henry H. "Hap" Arnold, the commanding general of the USAAF took the unprecedented step of releasing the Superfortress to *none* of the theater commanders. Rather, he retained command of the B-29 force for himself—directly from his seat as a member of the Joint Chiefs of Staff.

When the Superfortress fleet was ready for combat in mid-1944, Arnold decided to concentrate the entire force against Japan rather than to use some against Germany. Arnold set up an all-new Air Force, the 20th, to manage the B-29 armada. It would contain two operational Bomber Commands: XX and XXI.

While the Superfortress offered unprecedented range, Japan was still far away from the nearest American base in the Pacific. With this in mind, Arnold was forced to inaugurate XX Bomber Command missions against Japan in June 1944 by flying from Chengdu, deep inside China at the end of a long and tenuous supply route.

By August 1944, the Pacific islands of Guam, Saipan, and Tinian were recaptured from the Japanese, so the 20th Air Force could begin operations from bases here that could easily be supplied by sea.

Boeing's XB-29s of 1942 were powered with Wright R-3350-13s, while the YB-29s (seen here) a year later were equipped with R-3350-21s. The Wichita-built YB-29s, like the three Seattle-built XB-29s, were painted olive drab. Thereafter, Superfortresses were left in natural metal finish.

Anticipating the Superfortress

Prior to World War II, the US Army Air Corps had devoted considerable behind-the-scenes planning effort to the idea of a very long-range strategic bomber. Especially keen on the theory of strategic airpower was Hap Arnold, who became Air Corps chief in 1938, a post he retained through the war as commanding general of the USAAF.

These projects included Project A of 1934 and the parallel Project D that called for an aircraft with the "maximum feasible range into the future." Out of the projects came two huge prototypes: the Boeing XB-15 (Boeing Model 294) and Douglas XB-19—along with a lot of theoretical prep work. Among the projects spun off from this work was the Boeing Model 316, to which the Air Corps assigned the designation XB-20. This was never built, but it was a bridge to the Model 341, itself a stepping stone toward the Model 345, which became the B-29.

Edmund T. "Eddie" Allen's legendary career as a test pilot began during World War I. He went on to fly for almost every American aircraft manufacturer, making the first flight of numerous important aircraft. In 1942, he was first to fly the Superfortress but later lost his life in the devastating crash of the second XB-29 on February 18, 1943.

In January 1940, four months after the start of World War II in Europe, Arnold and the Air Corps issued the R40-B request for data. This top-secret document solicited design proposals from aircraft builders for a "Hemisphere Defense" aircraft with a range of 5,333 miles—a bomber that could carry a full bomb load 2,000 miles from its base. Boeing put together a team of designers that included Ed Wells, the engineer who had proved himself so well in the design of the B-17.

Boeing dusted off and refined its Model 341 idea into the Model 345, submitting a proposal based on this aircraft in June 1940. The Air Corps assigned the XB-29 designation to the Boeing proposal, which came in along with three others: the Lockheed XB-30, the Douglas XB-31, and the Consolidated XB-32. In September, contracts were

This is a front three-quarter view of a Wright R-3350 Duplex Cyclone engine (1945).

1. Ignition Spark Plug Lead
2. High Tension Lead to Distributor Connection
3. Rocker Lubricating Tube
2. Crankcase Front Section
3. Front Oil Pump and Sump
4. Ignition System, Distributors, Ignition Cables, etc.
5. Distributor and Governor Drive and Torque Indicator Booster Pump
6. Propeller Shaft Reduction Gear
7. Front Cam, Vibration Balancer, and Drive
8. Crankshaft
9. Front Connecting Rods
10. Crankcase Main Section
11. Rear Connecting Rods
12. Cylinder and Piston
13. Valve Mechanism

14. Supercharger Front Housing
15. Supercharger Rear Housing, Diffuser Plate, and Shroud Plate
16. Rear Cam, Vibration Balancer, and Drive
17. Impeller and Impeller Shaft
18. Rear Oil Sump
19. Generator Drives
20. Tachometer and Fuel Pump Drives
21. Oil Strainer
22. Carburetor
23. Magneto Drive
24. Accessory Drive and Starter Shaft
25. Magneto
26. Rear Oil Pump
27. Supercharger Rear Cover Accessory Drives
28. Supercharger Rear Cover

A Superfortress emerges from the Boeing Wichita factory on a moody, rainy night. There were 1,620 B-29s built here.

With victory having been declared in the "Battle of Kansas," Boeing ramped up for full-scale production of B-29s with R-3350-23As in Wichita and B-29As with R-3350-57s in Renton.

issued to Boeing and Consolidated for two prototypes each, with a third added to Boeing's order.

The XB-29 Superfortress included many entirely new features, including the remarkable Boeing Model 117 wing design, which greatly increased efficiency and performance. Computers were introduced, as the Superfortress would have a computerized, remote-control gun-aiming system. There was also the innovative "three bubble" system of pressurization for the crew spaces. The flight deck and the waist gunner's sections were pressurized, and the two compartments were connected by a pressurized tunnel. The tail gunner's area was pressurized independently. Pressurization would allow the B-29 to operate at much higher altitudes than previous bombers (such as the B-17), which were not pressurized.

Wright's R-3350 Duplex Cyclone

The almost impossibly complex and ambitious development program that led to the B-29 required the development of an equally advanced and powerful engine. The one selected was the Wright

This in-flight photo shows a B-29A-5-BN, one of the first of 1,119 out of Renton. The Renton-built Superfortresses were powered by Wright R-3350-57s.

B-29Bs take shape on the Bell Aircraft assembly line in Marietta, Georgia, circa 1945. Note the Wright R-3350-51 Duplex Cyclones on the factory floor in the right foreground.

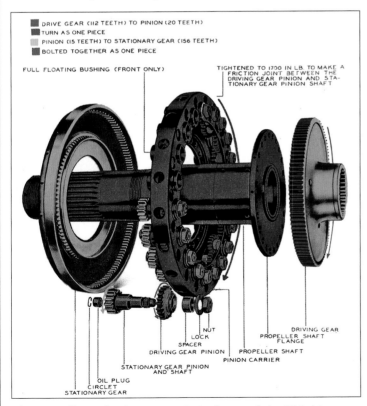

The propeller reduction geartrain is shown of the Wright R-3350 Duplex Cyclone engine (1943).

This is the B-29 assembly line at the Glenn L. Martin Company factory in Omaha, Nebraska, on April 11, 1945. Like the Wichita-built B-29s, the Omaha-built Superfortresses were powered by Wright R-3350-23A engines.

R-3350 Duplex Cyclone, which was a twin-row, 18-cylinder, super-charged radial that displaced 3,356 ci.

The design work on the huge R-3350 began at Wright Aeronautical in January 1936, nine months before the company had run its R-2600 Twin Cyclone, but work on the R-2600 took precedence at Wright, and the exceedingly complex R-3350 was not first run until May 1937. The engine passed through its test phase by January 1938 and entered limited production two months later.

Although it had an additional 4 cylinders, the R-3350 had clear and apparent roots in the earlier R-2600. For example, according to company data, the R-3350 shared the same stroke and bore as the R-2600, this being 6.312 inches and 6.125 inches respectively.

The R-3350 was first flown in May 1939 as the powerplant for the Consolidated XP4Y-1 flying boat, and it was later used in the one-of-a-kind Douglas XB-19, the largest aircraft ever built for the USAAF when it first flew in June 1941.

For Boeing, the Superfortress had the stamp of being the highest of USAAF priorities. Orders were mounting, including 14 service test YB-29s in June 1941, 250 B-29s in September 1941, and 500 more B-29s in January 1942. The parallel urgency of R-3350 development had meanwhile engulfed Wright. The company found itself pushing to get the R-3350-13 variant ready, but only a handful were delivered in 1941.

The first flight of the XB-29 finally came on September 21, 1942, with Boeing's top test pilot, Edmund T. "Eddie" Allen, at the controls.

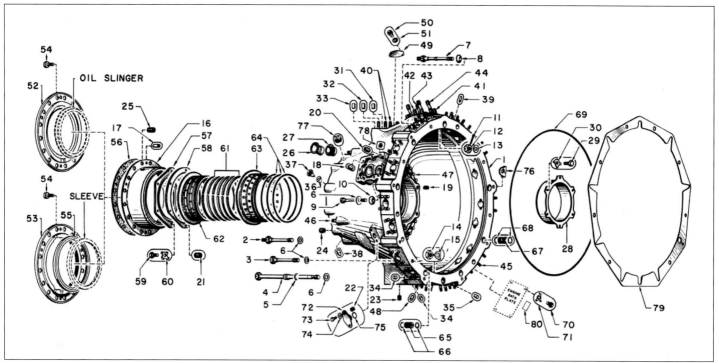

This is the crankcase front section of the Wright R-3350 Duplex Cyclone engine.

1. Crankcase	17–18. Pins	51. Washer	66. Ring
2–4. Screws	19–27. Bushings	52. Flange	67. Dowel
5. Ring	28. Bearing	53. Flange Assembly	68–69. Rings
6. Washer	29. Bolt	54. Bolt	70. Bolt
7. Screw	30. Washer	55. Seal	71. Washer
8. Washer	31–35. Pins	56. Gasket	72. Flange
9. Screw	36. Washer	57. Ring	73. Bolt
10. Washer	37. Plug	58. Lock	74. Washer
11. Cotter Pin	38. Plug	59. Bolt	75. Ring
12. Nut	39. Pin	60. Washer	76. Lug Assembly
13. Washer	40–47. Studs	61. Ring	77–78. Plugs
14. Nut	48. Pin	62–63. Sleeves	79. Shim
15. Washer	49. Plate	64. Ring	80. Decal
16. Liner	50. Screw	65. Dowel	

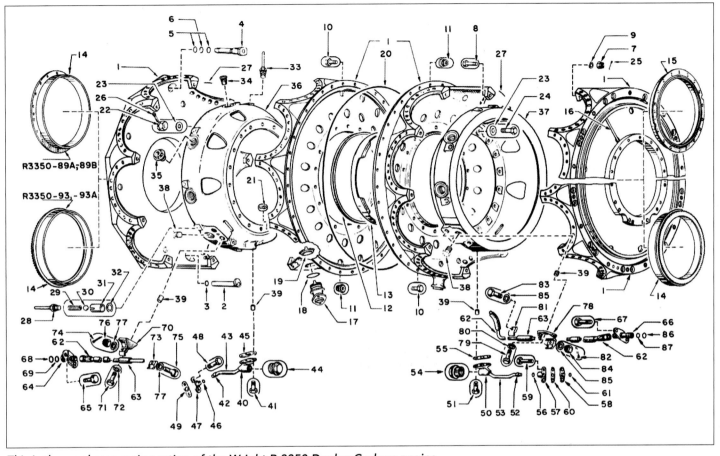

This is the crankcase main section of the Wright R-3350 Duplex Cyclone engine.

1. Crankcase Assembly
2. Bolt
3. Ring
4. Bolt
5. Packing
6. Circlet
7. Nut
8. Bolt
9. Washer
10. Bolt
11. Nut
12–15. Rings
16. Tube
17. Connector
18. Packing
19. Nut
20. Ring
21. Pin
22. Nut

23. Washer
24. Bolt
25–26. Cotter Pins
27. Packing
28. Nozzle
29. Spring
30. Ball
31. Seat
32. Ring
33. Nozzle
34–38. Plugs
39. Bushing
40. Tube Assembly
41. Bolt
42. Nozzle
43. Tube
44. Plug
45. Gasket
46. Ring

47. Flange
48. Screw
49. Gasket
50. Tube Assembly
51. Bolt
52. Nozzle
53. Tube
54. Plug
55. Gasket
56. Ring
57–58. Flanges
59. Screw
60. Gasket
61. Ring
62. Hose Assembly
63. Sleeve
64. Adapter
65. Screw
66. Connector

67. Screw
68–69. Rings
70. Support
71. Bolt
72. Washer
73. Clamp
74. Cotter Pin
75. Bolt
76. Nut
77. Washer
78. Support
79. Bolt
80. Washer
81. Clamp
82. Cotter Pin
83. Bolt
84. Nut
85. Washer
86–87. Rings

A Troubled Pair

With both the B-29 and R-3350 program schedules having been pushed and accelerated, the flight test program exposed an avalanche of engine-related problems. There were oil leaks, vibration problems, cracking, incorrectly installed gears, and serious overheating—especially in the rear row of cylinders.

Most problematic, especially in light of the overheating was that the crankcase was made of magnesium (to save weight), but magnesium is *combustible* at high temperatures! Having caught fire, it is virtually impossible to extinguish, and it burns hot enough (up to 5,600 degrees Fahrenheit) to cause catastrophic wing failure.

Both the B-29 and the R-3350 were pushed harder and faster than they should have been for their own good, but with the war on and all eyes on them as some of the magic bullets of ultimate victory, the almost reckless momentum became a fact of life—and death.

On February 18, 1943, the frantic pace caught up with the program. Eddie Allen took off from Boeing Field in Seattle in the second prototype XB-29 with a crew of 11. At 12:16 p.m., just 5 minutes into the flight, Allen reported a fire in the number-one engine nacelle. He feathered the prop and reported that he was returning to the field. At 12:21, as he reported that the engine was on fire and requested crash equipment to stand by, another crewmember could be heard in the background exclaiming "Allen, better get this thing down in a hurry—the wing spar's burning badly!"

The aircraft was at 1,200 feet over downtown Seattle and losing altitude when Allen reported that he was "coming in with a wing on fire."

Two men bailed out as the XB-29 struck the top of the five-story Frye meat packing plant but did not survive.

W.J. Yenne, a welder working at the nearby Todd Shipyards was at work in the forward end of the USS *Fletcher* Class destroyer when the power suddenly went out. He recalled, "Without waiting a second, I

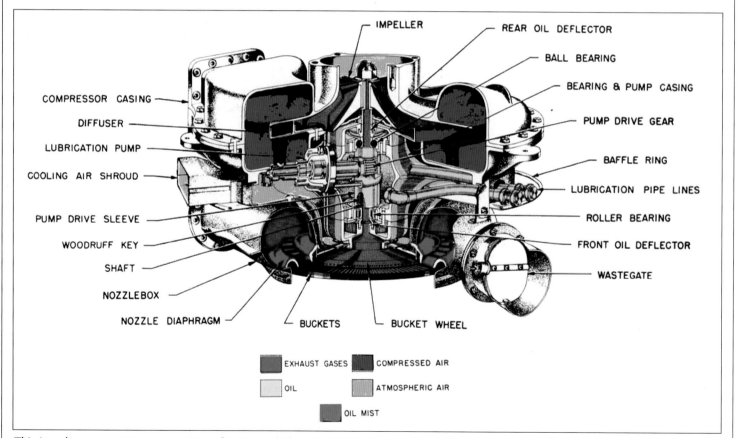

This is a three-quarter cutaway view of a General Electric B-11 turbosupercharger such as was installed in Wright R-3350 Duplex Cyclone engines (1943).

went up to the main deck. A couple of fellows at the top of the stairs immediately pointed out the Frye Packing Company building across the waterway where the plane had crashed a few seconds before. It rested on the packing plant's roof like a hen sitting on her nest.

"Even though the building was very large, both ends of the plane extended a small distance past the sides of the building. All of us wondered at first if it might be a passenger plane because of its bare aluminum color. Since this was Seattle, where Boeing had been producing the familiar B-17 for some time, everyone was familiar with the lines [shape] of that plane. The plane we were looking at was similar, although it was longer and more slender appearing. It was only a matter of minutes before every window became a fire-red square. Soon, the building was swallowed by billowing black smoke."

The deadly crash, immediately blamed on the overheating of the problematic R-3350, resulted in the grounding of the Superfortress and all other aircraft equipped with the engine. An investigation that traced the problem to a fuel line failure, rather than to the engine, was a first step in getting the dual programs back on track.

The first flight of the third XB-29 prototype at Boeing Field, as well as the first flight of a service test YB-29 from the Boeing facility at Wichita, Kansas, both came in June 1943. Although hundreds of changes were introduced through the ensuing months of 1943, the program was under a cloud for the remainder of the year. By the end of 1943, fewer than 100 of the nearly 2,000 Superfortresses were on order, and fewer than 1,000 R-3350s had been delivered.

Industrial Expansion

As was the case with both the B-17 and B-24, the USAAF Materiel Command decided that the Superfortress was to be manufactured at multiple locations. In fact, *four* brand-new aircraft factories and two engine plants would be constructed to manufacture Superfortresses, and these factories were being built even as the first prototypes were being tested.

Boeing had built the three XB-29 prototypes in Seattle, but to not interfere with ongoing B-17 production at Seattle's Plant 2 plant, the company shifted Superfortress production to two other facilities. One was at Renton, Washington, just a few minutes flying time from Boeing Field. This factory, located at the foot of Lake Washington, had been financed by the US Navy for the production of the PBB-1 Sea Ranger flying boat, but this program had been terminated after only one R-3350-powered prototype.

The other Boeing facility was at Wichita, Kansas, where Boeing already operated the former Stearman facilities, building Kaydet trainers.

While Boeing operated these two factories, Buffalo-based Bell Aircraft built a new Superfortress factory near Atlanta, Georgia, and

The end play is checked between the main accessory drive gear and supercharger rear housing unit in a Wright R-3350 Duplex Cyclone engine (1943).

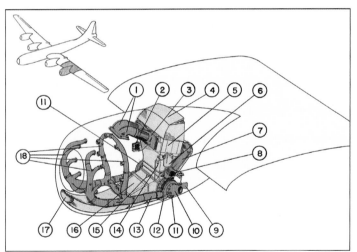

This shows the installation of a General Electric Model B-11 turbosupercharger in a B-29 engine nacelle.

1. Air-Induction Ducting from Air Filter to Carburetor
2. Pressuretrol
3. Carburetor Air Filter
4. Intercooler Door
5. Intercooler
6. Turbosupercharger Oil-Supply Tank
7. Air-Induction Ducting from Turbosupercharger to Intercooler
8. Wastegate Motor
9. Wastepipe
10. Exhaust Hood
11. Turbosupercharger
12. Cooling Cap, Cooling Air Duct
13. Engine Exhaust Stack to Nozzlebox Inlet
14. Turbosupercharger Oil Filter
15. Turbosupercharger Oil-Supply Lines
16. Servicing Door in Ducting
17. Induction and Cooling-Air Scoop
18. Exhaust Manifold Collector Rings

the Baltimore-based Glenn L. Martin Company built a new facility in Omaha, Nebraska, that also produced the Martin B-26C. Boeing built 1,620 B-29-BWs at Wichita, Bell produced 357 B-29-BAs in Atlanta, and Martin built 204 B-29-MOs in Omaha. In addition, 1,119 B-29A-BNs would be built by Boeing at Renton and 310 B-29B-BAs would be built in Atlanta by Bell.

For engine production, Wright switched its Cincinnati factory entirely to R-3350 work and added a new factory in Woodbridge, New Jersey. At these two facilities, Wright built 13,800 R-3350s.

Meanwhile, the Chrysler Corporation hired the eminent automotive factory architect Albert Kahn to design a factory in Chicago so that Chrysler's Dodge Division could build R-3350s under license. Ground was broken on the 82-acre facility in June 1942, and the first engines were rolling out by the spring of 1943.

It was always a dramatic moment at Boeing's Renton plant when the huge overhead crane brought forth a B-29A wing section and lowered it delicately into a fuselage midsection. The pressurized tunnel at the top of the fuselage leading between fore and aft crew sections is clearly visible.

B-29A Superfortresses, with their Wright R-3350-57 engines are on the assembly line at Boeing's factory in Renton in December 1944.

The clearance of the rear master rod assembly is measured in a Wright R-3350 Duplex Cyclone engine (1943).

During the war, Dodge Chicago built 18,413 R-3350s, operating at such a volume as to drive the unit cost down from nearly $26,000 in 1942 to around $12,000 in 1945. With its auto industry experience, Dodge managed a galaxy of hundreds of subcontractors, but the factory did magnesium casting at the plant and operated a forging line that turned out enough cylinders in-house for around 90 percent of the Dodge R-3350s.

The Battle of Kansas

On January 11, 1944, General Hap Arnold visited the Boeing plant in Wichita, where the largest number of Superfortresses were expected to be built. Arnold had earlier made it clear that he wanted to begin Superfortress operations out of China by April—and he had promised this to Allied leaders. However, he found Wichita production moving at a snail's pace. The factory had finished fewer than 100 aircraft, and only 16 could be considered ready for action. The rest were languishing at modification centers around the county. As with B-17 and B-24 production, the task of getting bombers ready for combat happened at the modification centers.

"I was appalled at what I found," Arnold wrote in his memoirs. "There were shortages in all kinds and classes of equipment. The engines were not fitted with the latest gadgets; the planes were not ready to go. It would be impossible to get them anywhere near China by the 15th of April unless some drastic measures were taken."

Arnold walked down the line of unfinished aircraft to fuselage No. 179, scrawled his name on it and said he wanted all the aircraft through this one on its way to China by March 1.

He then called in Materiel Command production expert Brigadier General Bennett E. "Benny" Meyers and put him in charge of overseeing the program, and as the field commander in what would be known as the "Battle of Kansas."

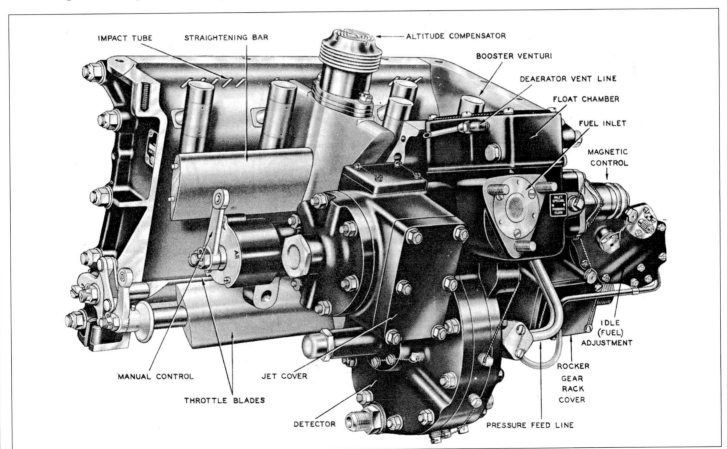

Here is a cutaway view of a MGA58A4 master control unit that was mounted on the rear of the Wright R-3350 Duplex Cyclone engine to control the amount of gasoline delivered by the injection pumps to the engine.

Arnold said of Meyers that he was "a pusher, a driver; he got things done."

By early April 1944, Superfortresses were passing through India on their way across the Himalayas to China, where they finally first arrived at Chengdu on April 24. After initial raids on targets closer at hand, such as Japanese-occupied Bangkok, the first mission against Japan struck Yawata on June 15, 1944.

As noted above, American forces had recaptured the Pacific Islands of Guam, Saipan, and Tinian from the Japanese in August 1944. As these islands were located 1,500 miles from Tokyo, they had

long since been earmarked as bases from which the 20th Air Force could conduct strategic operations. They were also easy to resupply by sea. Airfields were constructed, and the XXI began operations in November that would continue through the end of the war.

By February 1945, a sufficient number of aircraft had been delivered to the point that the XXI Bomber Command could launch missions involving more than 250 Superfortresses. By May, 400-plane missions were not uncommon, and in August, the Superfortress became the first aircraft to drop nuclear weapons in wartime.

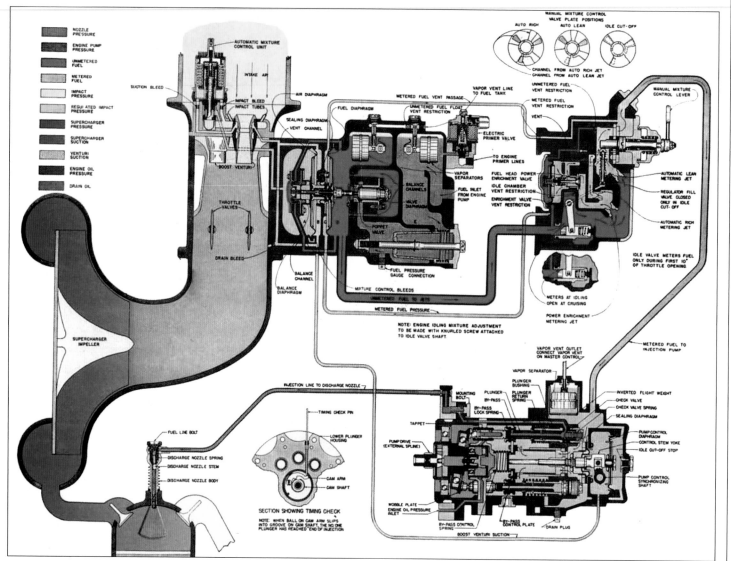

This schematic diagram shows the Stromberg direct fuel-injection system in the Wright R-3350 Duplex Cyclone engine (1944).

The Model 58-18-A2B gasoline injection system, manufactured by the American Bosch Corporation of Springfield, Massachusetts, is shown as installed in the Wright R-3350 Duplex Cyclone engine (1944).

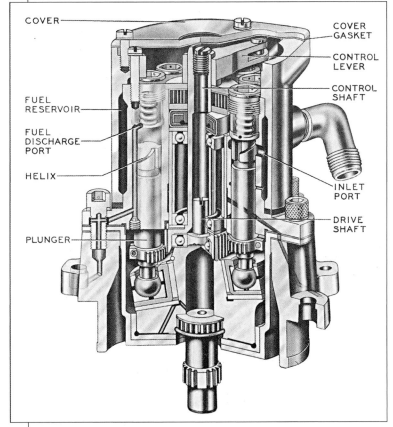

This cutaway view shows the PGA9100A3 gasoline injection pump installed in the Wright R-3350 Duplex Cyclone engine.

Duplex Cyclones for Superfortresses

The first post-prototype Duplex Cyclone variants were a pair of R-3350-1s built between in March and April 1938, and a single R-3350-2 built in April 1938. Both types were rated at 1,800

A low-angle view shows a B-29 nearing completion on the assembly line at the Glenn L. Martin Company factory in Omaha. The Wright R-3350-23A engines await the installation of their propellers.

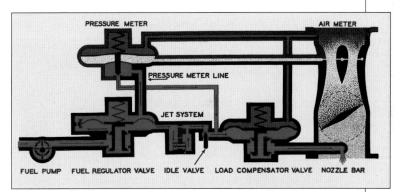

This is a schematic drawing of a basic hydro-metering carburetor. As noted in the Chandler-Evans documentation, "the object of all carburetion is to mix with the air going into the engine the proper amount of fuel for all operating conditions in accordance with a predetermined mixture formula or curve . . . The amount of gasoline mixed with the air delivered to the engine is controlled by the fuel metering system, which operates as a function of the pressure differential obtained from the air meter . . . In the hydro-metering carburetor, the quantity of fuel delivered to the engine is controlled, varying the pressure drop through a system of fixed orifices set between two pressure control valves."

hp at 2,200 rpm for takeoff and had a compression ratio of 6.8:1. The supercharger ratio of the former was 6.42:1/8.86:1, and of the latter 6.41:1. Both engines weighed 2,500 pounds. The R-3350-1 was 71.5 inches long with a diameter of 55-15 inches. The R-3350-2 was 77.25 inches long with a diameter of 54 inches.

The Duplex Cyclone program moved slowly and methodically with just seven R-3350-4 engines produced between May 1939 and November 1940. The R-3350-4 was rated at 2,000 hp at 2,400 rpm for takeoff. It had a compression ratio of 6.85:1 and a supercharger ratio of 6.42:1/8.86:1. The engine weighed 2,460 pounds and was 71.5 inches long with a diameter of 55.12 inches.

The first Duplex Cyclone built in double-digit numbers was the R-3350-13, which powered the three XB-29s. Fifty of these engines were produced between January 1942 and July 1943. The R-3350-13 was rated at 2,200 hp at 2,800 rpm for takeoff and 2,200 hp at 25,000 feet. It had a compression ratio of 6.85:1 and a supercharger ratio of 6.06:1. The engine weighed 2,668 pounds and was 76.26 inches long with a diameter of 55.78 inches.

The 14 service-test YB-29 Superfortresses were powered by the R-3350-21, of which 147 were built between November 1942 and April 1944. The R-3350-21 was rated at 2,200 hp at 2,200 rpm for takeoff and at 2,000 hp at 2,400 rpm in normal flight. It had a compression ratio of 6.85:1 and a supercharger ratio of 6.06:1. The engine weighed 2,646 pounds and was 76.26 inches long with a diameter of 55.78 inches.

Initial production-series B-29 aircraft were powered with the R-3350-23, of which 1,265 were built between February 1942 and March 1943. The R-3350-23 was rated at 2,200 hp at 2,200 rpm for takeoff and at 2,000 hp at 2,400 rpm in normal flight, which was the same as the R-3350-21. It also had the same compression ratio and supercharger ratio as its predecessor. It was a lighter engine, weighing 2,646 pounds but had the same overall dimensions.

The R-3350-23 was an engine that was so problematic during the opening weeks of the Battle of Kansas that the engines continued to overheat and even catch fire. Troubleshooting narrowed down causes, and fixes were developed. Cowl flaps were redesigned, and the engines themselves were redesigned, pulled out, and rebuilt

with new rocker arms, new exhaust valves, new casings, new sumps, and provisions to increase airflow to the cylinders. The result was the R-3350-23A.

The R-3350-23A was produced in far larger numbers than any other Duplex Cyclone, with 22,486 being manufactured between January 1944 and September 1945. The R-3350-23A was rated at 2,200 hp at 2,800 rpm for takeoff. It had a compression ratio of 6.85:1 and a supercharger ratio of 6.06:1. The engine weighed 2,646 pounds and was 76.26 inches long with a diameter of 55.78 inches.

The official General Electric supercharger documentation (dated May 1944 and updated in August 1945) specified the GE Model B-11 Turbosupercharger to be used for the R-3350 engines that were used in the Superfortress, although General Electric noted that the later GE Model B-31 Turbosupercharger was also compatible with R-3350 variants used in B-29s. The B-31 was to be the standard turbosupercharger in the Consolidated B-32.

The B-11 had a weight flow of 120 pounds per minute at 28,000 feet, at which altitude both the B-11 and B-31 were rated with a rotor speed of 24,000 rpm, although they could be operated at 26,400 rpm for 15 minutes. The B-11 weighed 144 pounds and was similar in design to the B-2 and B-22 turbosuperchargers found in Boeing's Flying Fortress.

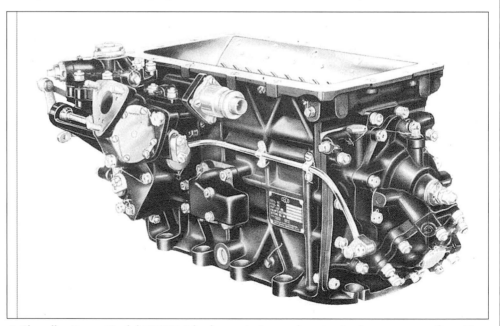

A Chandler-Evans Model 58CPB-4 hydro-metering carburetor is shown as seen from the pressure meter end. The Model 58CPB-4 superseded the Bendix-Stromberg carburetors that were initially installed in the Wright R-3350 Duplex Cyclone engines of B-29 Superfortresses.

According to the 1945 Service Instructions manual, the fuel system used Bendix-Stromberg or American Bosch fuel injection pumps, Bendix-Stromberg PR58P1, or American Bosch MGA58A4 master controls. The Bendix-Stromberg carburetors initially installed the R-3350s of the Superfortresses were superseded early on by the Chandler-Evans Model 58CPB-4 carburetor (see following subsection).

The R-3350-57 was rated at 2,200 hp at 2,800 rpm for takeoff and at 2,000 hp at 2,400 rpm in what Wright literature describes as normal flight. It had a compression ratio of 6.06:1 and a supercharger ratio of 4.06:1 with its two General Electric turbosuperchargers.

The R-3350-57 was the engine of choice for the B-29A, of which 1,119 were built by Boeing in Renton. The airframe was essentially the same as the B-29, except for the center wing structure. The engine was the second most widely produced member of the Duplex Cyclone family (after the R-3350-23A) with 6,958 built between January 1944 and November 1945. An additional 407 R-3350-57A engines were produced between January and September 1945.

The R-3350-57 weighed 2,753 pounds and was 76.25 inches long with a diameter of 55.78 inches. The specifications for the R-3350-57A were the same as those of the R-3350-57 except that this engine weighed 2,757 pounds and was 55.2 inches in diameter.

Throughout the stellar combat career of the Superfortress in the final eight months of World War II, the problems with overheating that had dogged the R-3350 in its early days continued. By 1945, though, they had been ameliorated by the work of the participants in the Battle of Kansas, and later by maintenance crews who came to understand the whims of this very particular engine.

The Model 58CPB-4 Carburetor

The Chandler-Evans (CECO) Model 58CPB-4 Carburetor was a fully automatic hydro-metering type of pressure carburetor. It was designed so that it could be divided into units and the units subsequently disassembled individually. There were five major units to this carburetor: the fuel metering unit, the fuel end plate unit, the pressure meter unit, the accelerating pump unit, and the main body unit.

The fuel metering unit was attached to the rear of the carburetor. It contained the fuel inlet cut-off valve assembly, which was operated by a link connecting the cut-off valve arm to the mixture control. Its function was to completely shut off the supply of fuel at the carburetor inlet when the mixture control was placed in the cut-off position.

The fuel inlet chamber was provided with a strainer that was attached to a plug below the primer. A vapor trap was also built into this chamber. A circular casting on the top of the fuel meter contained the pressure regulator valve. Directly below the pressure

The components of a Chandler-Evans Model 58CPB-4 Hydro-Metering carburetor are shown as installed in Wright R-3350 Duplex Cyclone engines.

1. Housing Assembly (Fuel Meter)
2–5. Studs
6. Tube, Fuel Pick, Lip
7. Plug, Drive
8. Fitting, Pipe
9. Seal
10. Gasket
11. Guide Assembly, Vapor Trap Valve

12. Gasket
13. Cover, Vapor Trap
14. Screw, Aircraft Fill Head, Drilled, Coarse Thread
15. Valve, Vapor Trap
16. Float Assembly, Vapor Trap
17. Gasket
18. Screw, Vapor Trap Float Fulcrum

19. Strainer Assembly, Fuel, Complete
20. Gasket, Fuel Strainer Plug
21. Primer Assembly, Complete
22. Strainer, Primer
23. Gasket, Primer Pad Cover
24. Washer, Plain
25. Nut, Engine, Plain
26. Lock Nut

regulator valve was the housing that contained the jets. The mixture control valve was contained in a housing that was mounted on the extreme left side of the fuel meter housing. The mixture control valve was a disc-type selector valve driven directly by the mixture control lever.

CECO noted in its literature that the 58CPB-4 was "non-icing to the extent that it had no inherent tendency to create an icing condition."

Other Engines for the Superfortress

Through the development of the Superfortress, there were ongoing discussions of alternate powerplants, and several such scenarios were flight tested. Two of these warranted the application of a new USAAF designator. The XB-39 Superfortress began life as one of the YB-29 service test aircraft. In November 1943, it was selected to help evaluate the use of a liquid-cooled inline engine to power

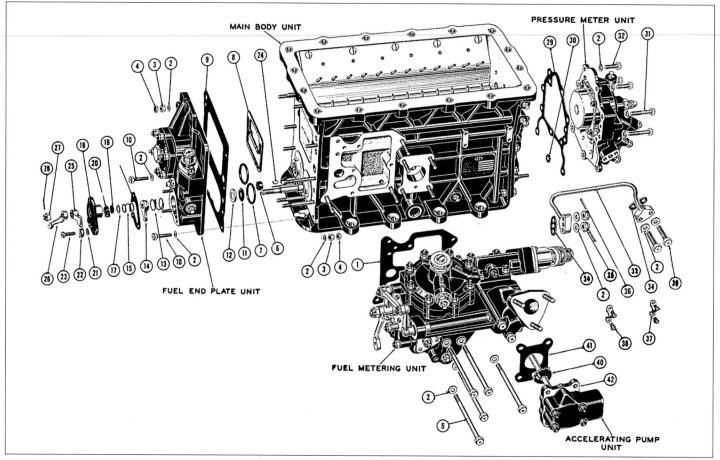

This exploded view of a Chandler-Evans Model 58CPB-4 hydro-metering carburetor shows how it could be disassembled into units.

1. Gasket-Fuel Meter Housing
2. Washer-Plain
3. Nut-Engine-Plain
4. Lock Nut
5. Bolt-Aircraft Drilled Head
6. Seal-Nozzle Bar
7. Seal
8. Seal-Venturi End
9. Gasket-Fuel End Plate
10. Bolt-Aircraft Drilled Head
11. Seal

12. Washer
13. Spring
14. Lever Assembly-Idle Control
15. Spring
16. Seal-Throttle Shaft Lever End, Outer
17. Washer
18. Gasket-Throttle Shaft Bracket
19. Bracket Assembly Throttle
20. Bushing
21. Washer-Lock External and Internal Teeth
22. Stop-Throttle

23. Screw-Fillister Head
24. Key-Woodruff
25. Lever-Throttle Stop
26. Lever-Throttle
27. Nut-Aircraft-Castle
28. Cotter Pin
29. Gasket-Pressure Meter Body
30. Gasket
31–32. Bolt-Aircraft Drilled Head
33. Nut-Aircraft-Castle
34. Gasket-Pressure Meter Connection

35. Nut-Aircraft-Castle
36. Pin-Cotter
37. Clamp-Pressure Meter Connection
38. Screw-Fill, Head Drilled or Plain Head, Coarse Thread
39. Bolt-Hex Head
40. Strainer-Accelerating Pump
41. Gasket-Accelerating Pump
42. Pump Assembly-Accelerating

A Wichita-built Boeing B-29-90-BW is shown on its delivery flight in 1945. Note the black undersurface paint scheme that was added as camouflage for night operations over Japan.

production Superfortresses.

The specific engine was the 24-cylinder V-3420-11 (known commercially as the V-3420-A18R) from the Allison Engine Company, a component of General Motors. The V-3420-11 engine was an experimental powerplant on which development began in 1937. This had involved combining two 12-cylinder "Vee-type" V-1710 engines that were geared together and driving a common driveshaft. The V-1710 was the engine that powered the Lockheed P-38 and Curtiss P-40 fighters, among other aircraft.

The V-3420-11 was rated at 2,600 hp at 3,300 rpm for takeoff and 3,000 hp at 3,000 rpm at 28,000 feet. It had a compression ratio of 6.65:1 and a supercharger ratio of 6.9:1. The engine weighed 2,655 pounds and was 97.7 inches long with height of 38.7 inches and a width of 60 inches. It had one overhead camshaft for each of 4 6-cylinder blocks, 2 intake and 2 exhaust valves per cylinder, and sodium-cooled exhaust valves. It was equipped with a single-speed, 1-stage gear-driven supercharger, and a Stromberg PR58-B3 3-barrel injection-type carburetor.

The performance of the XB-39 was superior to that of the B-29 but only slightly. Meanwhile, the V-3420 had been earmarked for the Fisher P-75 Eagle, a remarkably promising high-performance fighter that was being developed by the Fisher Body Division of General Motors. The promise was never delivered. Only 14 P-75s were built, as the Materiel Command decided in 1944 to limit the number of new aircraft types under development. Only around 150 V-3420s were built.

The XB-44 was the second new designation to be assigned to a re-engined Superfortress. It was a single B-29A re-engined with the Pratt & Whitney R-4360 Wasp Major, an engine that is the subject of Chapter 14. Unlike the XB-39, the XB-44 evolved into a production aircraft. A redesigned Superfortress airframe with a tail taller than the conventional B-29 and powered by R-4360s was developed as the B-29D. It entered production after World War II as the B-50 Superfortress and is discussed in Chapter 14.

The last Superfortress to be built by Martin in Omaha, this B-29-60-MO reached the end of the production line on July 19, 1945.

Chapter 13

MILITARY R-3350s: BEYOND THE SUPERFORTRESS

The development of Wright Aeronautical's 18-cylinder R-3350 Duplex Cyclone and Boeing's B-29 Superfortress were thoroughly intertwined, but the engine was adapted for several other important airframes. Despite the problems detailed at length in Chapter 12, this powerful engine was deemed too promising and too potentially significant to abandon (as were many other troubled projects).

Two "could-have-been" bombers of note were intended to be powered by it—had the B-30 and B-33 actually been built. Lockheed considered it for the four-engine XB-30, its own candidate for the USAAF "super bomber" program that earned contracts for the Boeing B-29 and the Consolidated B-32 (discussed in the following subsection). Martin also specified it for the twin-engine XB-33 "Super Marauder" but reverted to the Wright R-2600 for the reimagined four-engine XB-33A Super Marauder, which was ordered in quantity but never built.

The Dominator and Its Duplex Cyclones

In June 1940, as development work on the B-29 was progressing at Boeing, the Army Air Corps considered the complexities of this advanced aircraft and requested that the Consolidated Aircraft Company undertake parallel development of a similar "superbomber" as a potential backup in case the Superfortress proved to be a dud. Consolidated, which was then building the B-24 Liberator and PB2Y Coronado, had the most experience with four-engine bombers of any American company aside from Boeing, so this was a logical choice.

Originally known as the "Terminator," the first prototype XB-32 made its initial flight on September 7, 1942, two weeks before Boeing's B-29. It was similar in design to the B-24, complete with the twin tail configuration that was standard on the Liberator, although this would be changed to a single tail for the production series. Also in the production series, the aircraft name was changed from "Terminator" to "Dominator."

As with the XB-29, the XB-32 was powered by the R-3350-13 variant, of which Wright built 50 between January 1942 and July 1943. As noted in Chapter 12, this engine delivered 2,200 hp at 2,800 rpm for takeoff, and 2,200 hp at 25,000 feet. It had a compression ratio of 6.85:1 and a supercharger ratio of 6.06:1. The R-3350-13 weighed 2,668 pounds and was 76.26 inches long with a diameter of 55.78 inches. The engines were equipped with the General Electric B-31 Turbosupercharger, rated with a rotor speed of 24,000 rpm at 28,000 feet.

The problems with overheating and oil leaks suffered during XB-32 flight testing mirrored the issues that Boeing was going through with the XB-29. Just as the second prototype XB-29 crashed in spectacular fashion in February 1943, the first XB-32 was lost three months later. Both programs continued, however, as the USAAF had put such a high priority on its superbombers. Indeed, the service had

The Lockheed RC-121D (later designated as EC-121D) was the US Air Force equivalent of the US Navy's WV-2. Although they were superseded by the Boeing E-3 Sentry AWACS in the late 1970s, the Air Force operated EC-121s from 1954 to 1978.

ordered 300 production-series B-32s in March 1943, four months before the second XB-32 entered flight testing.

After this, though, the B-32 program amassed its own set of unique problems even as the B-29 program was sorting though its myriad of issues. Two of the main difficulties for the B-32 program

With Wright R-3350-23s installed, production-series B-32 Dominators take shape on Consolidated's Fort Worth Assembly line, circa late 1944. Only 74 were built as bombers, the final 40 were completed as TB-32 crew trainers.

The second prototype Consolidated XB-32 Terminator made its debut flight on July 2, 1943, with Wright R-3350-13 engines. Only the first two prototypes had twin tails.

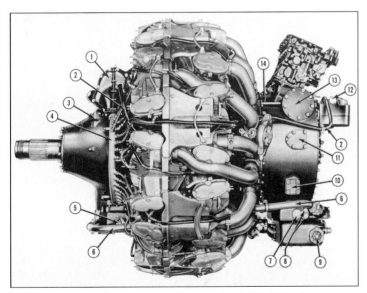

This shows the left side view of a Wright R-3350 Duplex Cyclone engine (1945).

1. Left Distributor
2. Left High-Tension Lead
3. Torque Meter Oil Separator
4. Ignition Cable Left Side Manifold
5. External Oil-out Tube to Front Oil Pump Connection
6. External Oil-in Tube
7. Rear Oil Pump Strainer
8. Oil-in Thermometer Connection
9. Rear Oil Pump and Sump Strainer
10. Alternate Fuel Pump Drive Substituting Cover
11. Left Gun Synchronizer Drive Substituting Cover
12. Magneto Optional Air Blast Tube
13. Left Fuel Injection Pump Substituting Cover
14. Supercharger Front to Rear Housing Left Vent Tube

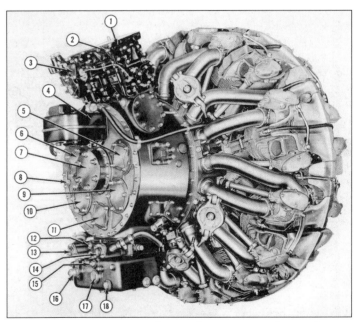

A rear three-quarter view of a Wright R-3350 Duplex Cyclone engine (1945) is shown.

1. Carburetor
2. De-Icing Fluid or Static Air Scoop Pressure Connection
3. Fuel Inlet Connection
4. Magneto
5. Hydraulic Pump Substituting Cover
6. Vacuum Pump Substituting Cover
7. Starter Substituting Cover
8. Low Pressure Oil for External Line Connection
9. Right Generator Substituting Cover
10. Left Generator Substituting Cover
11. Spare Accessory Substituting Cover
12. Optional Oil Pressure Gage
13. Oil-in Connection
14. Oil-out Connection
15. Pre-Oiling Drain Connection
16. Oil Pressure Relief Valve
17. Check Valve
18. Alternate Oil Tank Vent Connection

A Consolidated Block 25 B-32 Dominator, powered by a Wright R-3350-23, is shown in its delivery flight in 1944. The Dominators saw action with the 312th Bomb Group of the Fifth Air Force in the Pacific. They ended their combat career flying armed reconnaissance over Japan in August 1945.

were that neither the remote-control gun turrets nor the aircraft pressurization system worked properly. Because the B-29 program was on track, the USAAF decided that the B-32 was no longer needed as a backup, so both problematic systems were simply deleted from the production aircraft. They were unpressurized and had manual gun turrets like the B-17 or B-24.

Nevertheless, by the time that the first production B-32 Dominator was rolled out in September 1944, USAAF orders had increased to 1,500 aircraft.

As noted in Chapter 12, USAAF Commanding General Hap Arnold had decided to retain direct command of the B-29 force from his seat on the Joint Chiefs of Staff rather than relinquish control to theater commanders. One such theater commander was General Douglas MacArthur, who very much wanted to have B-29s in his operational arsenal, as did his air boss, General George Kenney. As commander of the Far East Air Forces (FEAF) command, Kenney controlled the Fifth, Seventh, and Thirteenth—the second largest concentration of USAAF air assets in the world (after the "mighty" Eighth Air Force in Europe). MacArthur and Kenney also had immense distances to cover across the vastness of the Pacific. The long range of the B-29 had been very appealing.

After pleading his case to Arnold personally, Kenney was given the "next best thing," the B-32 Dominator. Kenney's FEAF became the only organization to be operational with this aircraft. Operations finally began in May 1945 with a campaign against the Japanese synthetic petroleum industry, which was centered on the island of Formosa (now Taiwan, China), where the fuel was refined from sugar cane. In July 1945, FEAF B-32s relocated to Okinawa, from which they flew reconnaissance missions over Japan itself through August 28.

Out of the vast numbers of Dominators that were ordered, only 74 B-32 bombers and 40 TB-32 conversion trainers were built. The two XB-32s were built in San Diego, and the rest were manufactured in 11 production blocks by Consolidated in Fort Worth ending in

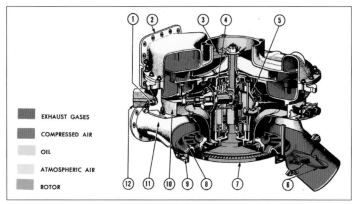

EXHAUST GASES

COMPRESSED AIR

OIL

ATMOSPHERIC AIR

ROTOR

This is a cutaway view of a General Electric Model B-31 turbo-supercharger as used in the Consolidated B-32 Dominator as well as in some Boeing B-29s.

1. Tachometer Driveshaft
2. Compressor Casing
3. Impeller
4. Oil Pump
5. Bearing and Pump Casing
6. Wastegate
7. Bucket Wheel
8. Nozzle Diaphragm
9. Exhaust-Hood Mounting Ring
10. Cooling Shroud
11. Nozzlebox
12. Cooling-Shroud Air Inlet

The first Douglas XBT2D-1 Destroyer II made its debut flight on March 18, 1945. XBT2D-1 prototypes were powered with Wright R-3350-24W water-injected engines. The "Bomber-Torpedo" designation was changed to "A for Attack," and production aircraft were designated as AD and named "Skyraiders."

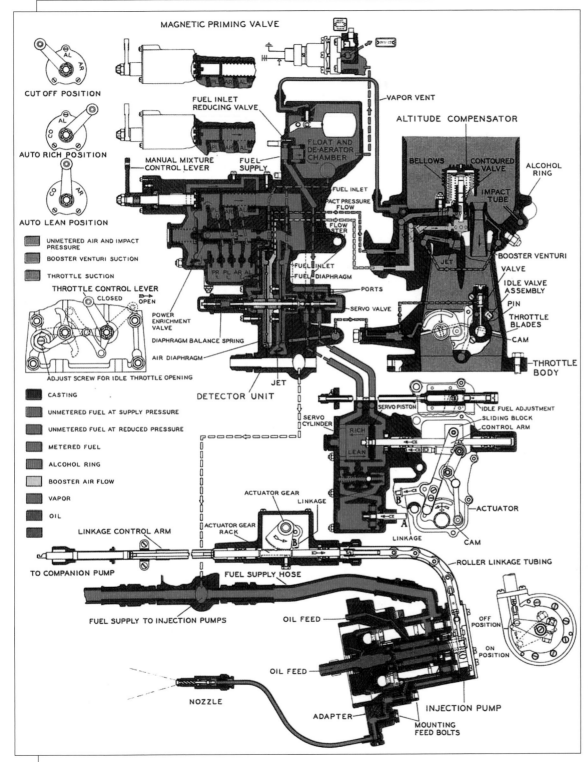

MAGNETIC PRIMING VALVE

CUT OFF POSITION

AUTO RICH POSITION

AUTO LEAN POSITION

UNMETERED AIR AND IMPACT PRESSURE

BOOSTER VENTURI SUCTION

THROTTLE SUCTION

THROTTLE CONTROL LEVER

CLOSED — OPEN

ADJUST SCREW FOR IDLE THROTTLE OPENING

CASTING

UNMETERED FUEL AT SUPPLY PRESSURE

UNMETERED FUEL AT REDUCED PRESSURE

METERED FUEL

ALCOHOL RING

BOOSTER AIR FLOW

VAPOR

OIL

FUEL INLET REDUCING VALVE

MANUAL MIXTURE CONTROL LEVER

FUEL SUPPLY

FLOAT AND DE-AERATOR CHAMBER

FUEL INLET

IMPACT PRESSURE FLOW

FLOW BOOSTER

FUEL INLET

FUEL DIAPHRAGM

PORTS

POWER ENRICHMENT VALVE

DIAPHRAGM BALANCE SPRING

AIR DIAPHRAGM

SERVO VALVE

JET

DETECTOR UNIT

SERVO CYLINDER

RICH

LEAN

ACTUATOR GEAR

LINKAGE

ACTUATOR GEAR RACK

LINKAGE CONTROL ARM

TO COMPANION PUMP

FUEL SUPPLY HOSE

FUEL SUPPLY TO INJECTION PUMPS

NOZZLE

ADAPTER

OIL FEED

OIL FEED

MOUNTING FEED BOLTS

INJECTION PUMP

OFF POSITION

ON POSITION

ROLLER LINKAGE TUBING

CAM

LINKAGE

ACTUATOR

SERVO PISTON

IDLE FUEL ADJUSTMENT

SLIDING BLOCK

CONTROL ARM

VAPOR VENT

ALTITUDE COMPENSATOR

BELLOWS

CONTOURED VALVE

ALCOHOL RING

IMPACT TUBE

JET

BOOSTER VENTURI VALVE

IDLE VALVE ASSEMBLY

PIN

THROTTLE BLADES

CAM

THROTTLE BODY

September 1945.

The 114 production Dominators were powered by the R-3350-23A, the same engine that was developed on the factory floor during the Battle of Kansas in early 1944, when the original Wright R-3350-23 proved to be so dangerously problematic as to threaten the very existence of the B-29 program. The B-32 program benefited from this and was able to absorb a small number of the 22,486 R-3350-23As that were produced between January 1944 and September 1945.

As noted in Chapter 12, this engine produced 2,200 hp at 2,800 rpm for takeoff. It had a compression ratio of 6.85:1 and a supercharger ratio of 6.06:1. The engine weighed 2,646 pounds and was 76.26 inches long with a diameter of 55.78 inches.

The Douglas Skyraider

In the story of the great aircraft of the World War II era that arrived too late for combat, the Douglas Skyraider deserves a place alongside such aircraft as the Grumman F8F Bearcat and the Lockheed P-80 jet fighter. However, the Skyraider did go on to play a significant role in combat operations in Korea and Vietnam.

The Skyraider originated in early 1944 as part of a Douglas effort to regain its late prewar

A schematic drawing shows the fuel injection system of a Wright R-3350 Duplex Cyclone engine.

A US Navy "Hunter-Killer" team of Douglas AD-6 (top) and AD-5W (bottom) is shown. These aircraft were powered by subvariants of the water-injected Wright R-3350-24W Duplex Cyclone engine.

Built at Boeing's Renton, Washington, plant, the XPBB-1 Sea Ranger was a prototype twin-engine flying boat patrol bomber. It took off from nearby Lake Washington (seen here in the background) for its first flight on July 9, 1942, powered by a pair of Wright R-3350-8 Duplex Cyclones. (Photo Courtesy US Navy)

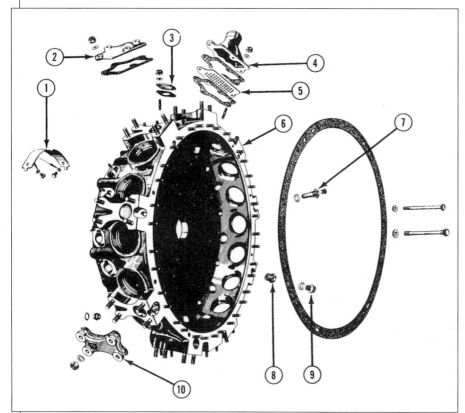

single-engine, carrier-based strike aircraft. It was in that category with the TBD Devastator and SBD Dauntless but was losing to the Grumman TBF Avenger and Curtiss SB2C Helldiver.

The first such attempt had been with the gull-wing, single-engine, single-seat XSB2D-1 Destroyer, a proposed successor to the Dauntless. Redesignated as XBTD-1, it served a dual role as a bomber and torpedo bomber. It first flew in April 1943, proved to be faster than the Dauntless, and had a greater payload capacity. However, it was heavier and more complex, so only 28 were built, and they never saw action before the program was terminated in 1944.

The front housing of the General Electric supercharger in a Wright R-3350 Duplex Cyclone Engine (1945) is shown.

1. Supercharger Front Housing Breather Baffle
2. Supercharger Front Housing Breather Substituting Cover
3. Rear Cam Drive Intermediate Gear and Balanceweight Support Lubricating Tube Flange
4. Supercharger Front Housing Breather
5. Supercharger Front Housing Breather Screen
6. Supercharger Front Housing
7. Supercharger Front Housing Primer Jet
8. Heater Intake Connection Bushing
9. Heater Intake Connection Substituting Plug
10. Engine Mounting Bracket Substituting Cover

The six Martin Mars transports were built with a single tail. Five were built as JRM-1 and one as a JRM-2 with a higher gross weight, although all were brought up to JRM-2 standard. After the Navy took them out of service in 1956, they had careers in the private sector. This aircraft, named Hawaii Mars, is seen on California's Lake Shasta while operating as a forest firefighting tanker in August 2008. (Bill Yenne Photo)

changed to "Skyraider." After the 25 XBT2D-1 development aircraft, the production Skyraiders were redesignated from BT2D-1 to AD-1 (for "Attack, Douglas, First"). With the war over, the quantity went down to 242 AD-1 attack bombers and 35 AD-1Q electronic countermeasure variants.

The XBTD-1 as well as the AD-1 were powered by the water-injected Wright R-3350-24W, of which 644 were produced between April 1945 and January 1948. This engine produced 2,500 hp at 2,900 rpm for takeoff and 2,200 hp at 11,500 feet. It had a compression ratio of 6.5:1 and a supercharger ratio of 6.46/8.67:1. The engine weighed 2,822 pounds and was 80.58 inches long with a diameter of 54.13 inches.

Douglas records show that there were 178 AD-2s and 194 AD-3s. Both were powered by the water-injected Wright R-3350-26W, of which 304 were produced between January 1947 and April 1948. This engine produced 2,700 hp at 2,900 rpm for takeoff and 2,100 hp at 2,400 rpm normally. It had a compression ratio of 6.7:1 and a supercharger ratio of 6.46/8.67:1. As with the R-3350-24W, this

Undaunted, a team led by Douglas Chief Engineer (and future aviation legend) Ed Heinemann went back to the drawing board and came up with another single-engine, single-seat design that impressed the US Navy Bureau of Aeronautics and earned a July 1944 contract for 25 development aircraft under the XBT2D-1 designation. The aircraft, initially called "Destroyer II," made its first flight in March 1945, and 548 production BT2D-1s were ordered two months later.

When the war ended, the US Navy decided to develop the aircraft for its postwar inventory, although in 1946, the name was

This Douglas AD-5 Skyraider of US Navy attack squadron VA-45 is loaded with training rockets. VA-45, the "Blackbirds," operated AD-2 Skyraiders during the Korean War and received their AD-5s later.

The huge Martin XPB2M-1 Mars, created as a flying boat patrol bomber for the US Navy, made its first flight in July 1942 powered by four Wright R-3350-18 Duplex Cyclones. It was the largest Allied flying boat to enter production, although only five were produced—and these as JRM-1 transports.

The first production Martin P5M-1 Marlin, powered by a Wright R-3350-30W engine, is shown on its delivery flight in July 1951.

This tall-tail Martin P5M-2S Martin, seen here in 1959 powered by a Wright R-3350-32WA, was originally delivered to the US Coast Guard but later transferred to the US Navy.

engine weighed 2,822 pounds and was 80.58 inches long with a diameter of 54.13 inches.

The Skyraider variant produced in the largest numbers was the AD-4, of which 1,051 were built, according to Douglas records. These included AD-4Qs, AD-4W early-warning aircraft, and AD-4N night-attack aircraft. Most of this production occurred during the Korean War.

The AD-4s, as well as most of the 670 AD-5s were powered by the water-injected Wright R-3350-WA, of which 3,446 were produced between July 1948 and November 1956. This engine produced 2,700

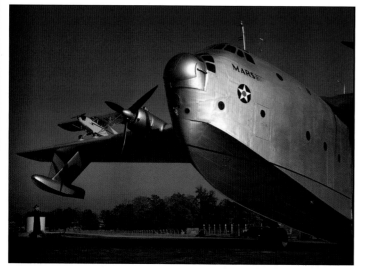

hp at 2,900 rpm for takeoff and 2,100 hp at 14,500 feet. It had a compression ratio of 6.7:1 and a supercharger ratio of 6.46/8.67:1. The engine weighed 2,848 pounds and was 80.81 inches long with a diameter of 55.62 inches.

These were followed by 713 AD-6s. The 3,180th and final Skyraider, the last of 72 AD-7s, was completed by Douglas in El Segundo in January 1957.

Both the AD-6 and AD-7 Skyraiders were powered by the water-injected Wright R-3350-26WB, of which 559 were produced between March 1950 and December 1951. This engine produced 2,700 hp at 2,900 rpm for takeoff and 2,100 hp at 14,000 feet. It had a compression ratio of 6.7:1, and a supercharger ratio of 6.46/8.67:1. The engine weighed 2,953 pounds and was 81.23 inches long with a diameter of 55.62 inches.

In 1962, when Army, Navy, and Air Force nomenclature was merged, the AD designation changed to an "A for attack" designation and the Skyraider became the A-1. The existing AD-5s became A-1Es, A-1Fs, and A-1Gs. The AD-6s became A-1Hs, and AD-7s became A-1Js.

During the Vietnam War, the US Air Force, as well as the air force of South Vietnam, joined the US Navy in using the Skyraider in service extensively, especially in a close air support role.

This US Navy publicity photo compares the scale of the Martin XPB2M-1 Mars as compared to a Piper J-3 Cub light aircraft. Even the Wright R-3350-18 overshadows the Cub, with its Continental A-65 air-cooled horizontally opposed 4-cylinder engine.

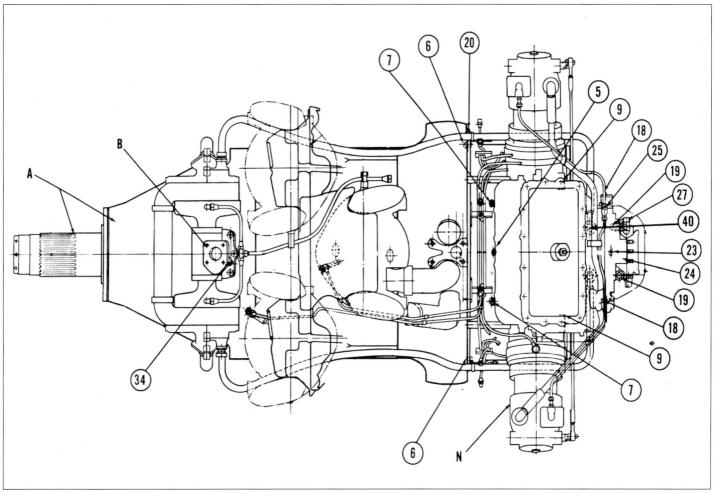

This is the specification diagram for the Wright R-3350 Duplex Cyclone engine (top view).

The components specified in the three adjacent specification diagrams for the Wright R-3350 are as follows:

A. Propeller Shaft and Engine Nose
B. Governor 12-Tooth Spline
C. Fuel Pump 12-Tooth Spline
D. Mechanical Tachometer
E. Electrical Tachometer
F. Vacuum Pump 12-Tooth Spline
G. Hydraulic Pump 12-Tooth Spline
H. Generator (May Be Used for Accessory) 16-Tooth Spline
J. Starter-12 Tooth Spline
K. Accessory (May Be Used for Generator)
M. Accessory; 12-Tooth Spline
N. Cover Plates
P. Gun Synchronizer-Provision for 16-Tooth Spline

R. Magneto
T. Carburetor
1. Crankcase Breather
2. Oil Thermometer-Oil in
3. Oil Thermometer-Oil out
4. Oil Pressure Gauge-Rear
5. Mixture Thermometer
6. Heater Inlet-Combustion Type
7. Heater Exhaust-Combustion Type
8. Starter Oil Drain
9. Oil Tank Vent
10. Manifold Pressure Gauge
11. Manifold Pressure Gauge (Optional)
12. Pressure Oil for External Line (Low Pressure)

13. Supercharger Drain
14. Pre-Starting Check (on Engines so Equipped)
15. Pre-Starting Oil Drain
16. Oil out
17. Ignition Distributor Housing Ventilator
18. Magneto Air Blast Tube
19. External Ground
20. Alternate Primer
21. Oil in
22. Mixture Control Lever
23. Fuel Pressure Gauge
24. Fuel Inlet
25. Vapor Separator Return to Tank
26. De-icing Fluid or Static Air Scoop Pressure

27. Electric Primer Cable
28. Throttle Lever
29. Torque Indicator (When so equipped)
30. Oil Pressure Gauge, Front
31. Magneto Supercharged Air Inlet
32. Accessory Drain
33. Alternate Oil Tank Vent
34. Propeller Low Pressure
35. Pressure Oil-Unfiltered
36. Oil Pressure Gauge (Optional)
37. Accessory Drain
38. Two-Speed Supercharger Clutch Control
39. Primer Inlet (Special Fuel)
40. Primer Outlet

Big Navy Flying Boats

The R-3350-8 variant of Wright's Duplex Cyclone played its role in two aircraft that were produced in negligible numbers but which nevertheless occupy an important footnote of the history of round-engine warbirds. This engine produced 2,400 hp at 2,600 rpm for takeoff and 1,800 hp at 13,600 feet. It had a compression ratio of 6.5:1 and a supercharger ratio of 6.46:1/8.67:1. The R-3350-8 weighed 2,796 pounds and was 54.12 inches long with a diameter of 77.6 inches.

With the R-3350 so closely intertwined with Boeing's most high-profile program, that of the Superfortress, it was only natural that the company should specify the engine for its promising XPBB-1 Sea Ranger, the largest of American twin-engine flying boat patrol bombers.

The program got underway in June 1940, just as the Superfortress program was beginning, but by the time that the single prototype XPBB-1 made its first flight in July 1942, the US Navy decided that landplanes provided better performance for land-range operations.

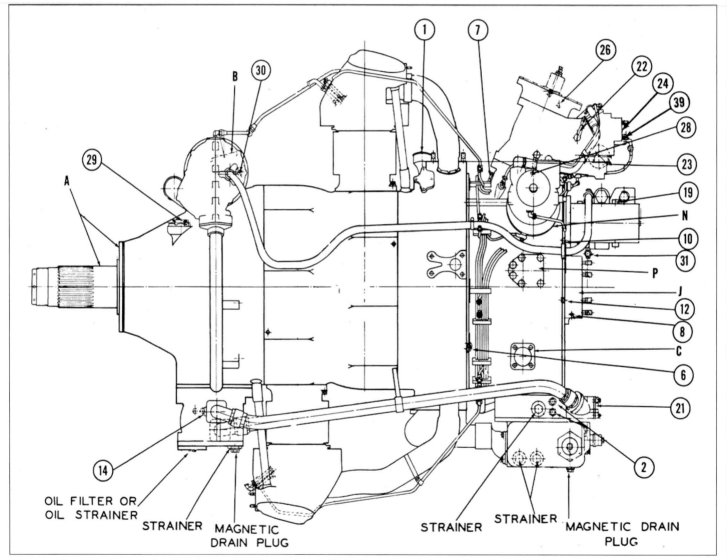

OIL FILTER OR OIL STRAINER

STRAINER   MAGNETIC DRAIN PLUG

STRAINER   STRAINER   MAGNETIC DRAIN PLUG

The specification diagram for the Wright R-3350 Duplex Cyclone engine is shown (left side view).

In the meantime, the PBB had seemed like such a good idea that the US Navy had financed a huge factory complex in Renton (near Seattle) at the foot of Lake Washington, an ideal place for a flying boat factory. With the PBB cancellation, Boeing already had a use for the factory. This, of course, was the plant that would build the B-29A Superfortress. Today, the site still operates and has been the center of Model 737 jetliner production for more than half a century.

The great Martin Mars was another flying boat powered by the R-3350. The largest of American wartime flying boats, it was ordered as a patrol bomber under the designation XPB2M-1 and made its first flight as such on July 3, 1942 (just two days ahead of the debut of the Boeing XPBB-1), powered by a Wright R-3350-18. This aircraft was converted to freighter configuration, and the Navy decided to continue production in this form rather than as a patrol bomber.

There were 20 Mars transports ordered under the designation JRM-1, although none were delivered until June 1945, so only six were built. They differed from the XPB2M-1 in that they had single (rather than double) tails. They were also delivered with water-injected Wright R-3350-24W engines, except one that was delivered as a higher gross weight JRM-2 powered by a Pratt & Whitney R-4360-4 engine.

Two of the Mars freighters were lost in 1947 and 1950, but the other four remained in service across the Pacific until 1956. They were named for Pacific island chains: *Caroline Mars*, *Hawaii Mars*, *Marianas Mars*, and *Philippine Mars*. In 1959, they were all sold to Forest Industries Flying Tankers of British Columbia as aerial water tankers. Two of these, *Hawaii Mars* and *Philippine Mars*, continued to fight forest fires into the 21st century. They were sold to Coulson Aviation in 2007.

The P5M Marlin, one of the last long-range flying boats for the US Navy and Martin's last great piston-powered flying boat, flew with a Pratt & Whitney Duplex Cyclone. Designed to supersede the Martin PBM Mariner flying boat, the Marlin had a similar gull-wing configuration.

The XP5M-1 first flew on May 30, 1948, and production P5M-1 Marlins were being delivered by the summer of 1951. There were 160 P5M-1s produced for the US Navy as maritime patrol and anti-submarine aircraft, while seven went to the US Coast Guard as air-sea rescue aircraft. The improved P5M-2 Marlin followed, with 103 produced for the US Navy and 12 for the French Navy.

Redesignated as SP-5B in 1962, the US Navy Marlins were active during the Vietnam War, operating from seaplane tenders and interdicting boats supplying the Viet Cong in the Mekong Delta. The last US Navy Marlin was retired in 1967.

The P5M-1 was powered by a pair of Wright R-3350-30Ws, while the P5M-2 (SP-5B) used a pair of R-3350-32WAs. The latter was rated at 3,700 hp at 2,900 rpm for takeoff and had a normal rating of 2,600 hp at 2,400 rpm. The engine weighed 3,560 pounds and was 91.8 inches long with a diameter of 56.59 inches.

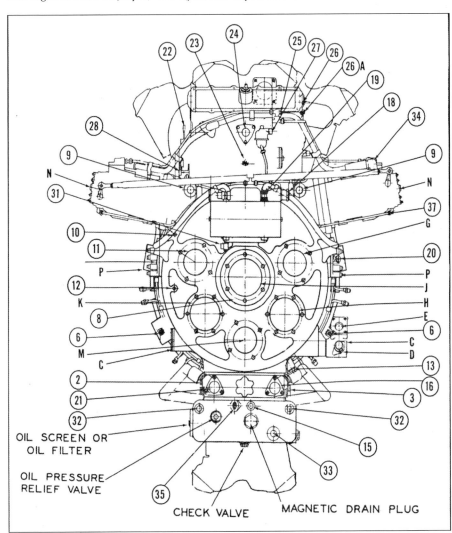

OIL SCREEN OR OIL FILTER

OIL PRESSURE RELIEF VALVE

CHECK VALVE

MAGNETIC DRAIN PLUG

This is the specification diagram for the Wright R-3350 Duplex Cyclone engine (rear view).

A Lockheed P2V-4 Neptune flies along the California coastline under the power of a pair of water-injected Wright R-3350-30W engines. The P2V-4 was similar in appearance to earlier variants but with the addition of tip tanks.

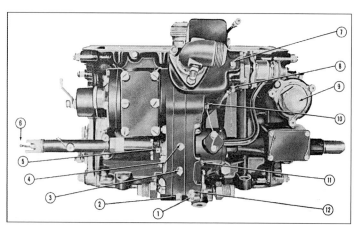

Here is the American Bosch fuel system master control installed in the Wright R-3350 Duplex Cyclone engine (1944).

1. Impact Fuel Chamber Drain
2. Metered Fuel Chamber Drain
3. Metered Fuel Pressure
4. Boost Suction
5. Impact Pressure
6. Cross Rack Blades
7. Special Priming Fluid "in"
8. Primer "out"
9. Idle Adjustment Protection Nut
10. Inlet Fuel Pressure
11. Unmetered Fuel Pressure
12. Boost Chamber Drain

The Navy's Last Great Piston-Engine Patrol Landplane

Lockheed's remarkable P2V Neptune was produced against the backdrop of the company's substantial legacy in twin-engine patrol aircraft. Leading up to World War II, Lockheed owned a slice of the niche market for small twin-engine commercial aircraft with the likes of its Model 10 Electra, Model 14 Super Electra, and Model 18 Lodestar. The Model 14 was also adapted as the Hudson light bomber, which served especially (but not exclusively) with British Commonwealth air forces.

Likewise, the Model 18 was adapted as the Ventura bomber, which served with the RAF as well as in USAAF anti-submarine operations as the B-34. In 1942, as the USAAF handed anti-submarine patrols over to the Navy, the latter service began acquiring the Pratt & Whitney R-2800-powered Ventura under the PV-1 designation. Lockheed produced 1,600 PV-1s and then handed production off to its Vega subsidiary.

The Vega PV-2 Harpoon was substantially improved over the Ventura, with a larger wing and tail and increased armament, although it retained the R-2800 engines. There were 470 basic PV-2s, 65 PV-2C and PV-2D Harpoons, and more than 100 Lend Lease Venturas sent to Canada.

In February 1943, when the US Navy decided to develop an eventual successor to its Consolidated PB4Y Privateer as a long-range

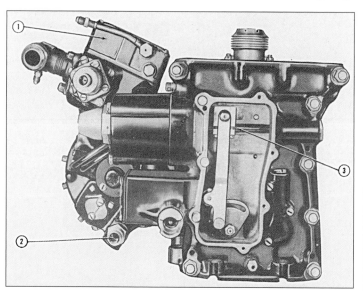

The American Bosch fuel system master control installed in the Wright R-3350 Duplex Cyclone engine (1944) shows the vapor separator (1), fuel outlets (2), and the actuator piston shaft (3) in the rich position.

landplane patrol bomber, it entertained proposals from Martin and Lockheed. Martin's P4M-1 Mecator is discussed in Chapter 14, but here we look at the Lockheed Neptune.

The Navy commissioned Lockheed to build two prototypes of the twin-engine XP2V-1 Neptune as a very long-range anti-submarine patrol aircraft with orders climbing to 166 production aircraft by December 1944. The specified engine was the Wright R-3350-8, the same Cyclone variant used in the Martin Mars and Boeing Jet Ranger.

Although it was a Lockheed aircraft, the Navy designated the Neptune as P2V, using the "V for Vega" manufacturer's suffix designator rather than the usual "O for Lockheed." In 1950, the Navy replaced the "O" designator with "V" for all Lockheed aircraft, and so it remained for most of the Neptune's production run.

The production-series P2V-1 Neptunes were first delivered in September 1946, one year after the war had ended. On September 29, a Neptune named *The Truculent Turtle* famously took off from Australia and flew 11,236.6 miles to Columbus, Ohio, without refueling. This 55-hour flight set a world absolute distance record that eclipsed those recently set by B-29s. The record stood until 1962 when it was surpassed by a B-52 Stratofortress.

While the operational range of production Neptunes was substantially less, the aircraft certainly established the long-range operational capabilities of the aircraft and gave the Navy a strategic bomber.

After just 17 P2V-1s (including two XP2V-1 prototypes), Lockheed built 80 P2V-2s and began delivery of 53 P2V-3 Neptunes in July 1948. The P2V-2 was powered by the water-injected R-3350-24W, while the P2V-3 was upgraded to the R-3350-26W engines that the Navy was also acquiring for the Skyraider program. Wright Aeronautical records indicated a combined total of 948 of the two engine types being manufactured through April 1948.

The R-3350-24W was rated with 2,700 hp at 2,900 rpm for takeoff and 2,200 hp at 11,500 feet. The R-3350-26W had the same takeoff horsepower rating and 2,100 hp at 2,400 rpm normally. Both engines had a compression ratio of 6.7:1 and a supercharger ratio of 6.46/8.67:1. They both weighed 2,822 pounds and were 80.58 inches long with a diameter of 54.13 inches.

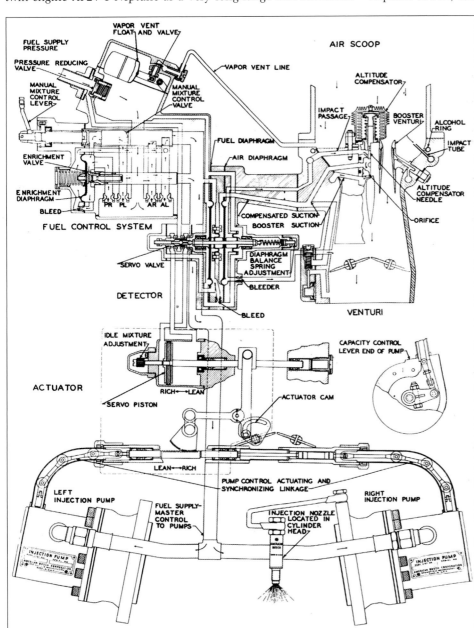

This is a schematic diagram of the American Bosch Model 58-18A1B fuel injection system for the Wright R-3350 Duplex Cyclone engine (1944).

In 1953, the power of the two Wright R-3350 piston engines of a P2V-5 Neptune were experimentally augmented by the addition of two Westinghouse J34 turbojets. With this experiment being a success, the addition of J34-WE-36 turbojets became standard in the P2V-6 and P2V-7 variants.

There were 83 P2V-3s introduced in July 1948. Of these, 30 were equipped with an AN/APS-20 search radar radome and designated as P2V-3W. These were followed by 52 P2V-4s that were introduced in September 1949, which also had the AN/APS-20 radome as well as wingtip fuel tanks.

The P2V-4 was powered by water-injected Wright R-3350-30W engines, of which 559 were produced through December 1951. This engine was rated at 3,250 hp at 2,900 rpm for takeoff and 2,600 hp at 2,600 rpm normally. It had a compression ratio of 6.7:1 and a supercharger ratio of 6.46/8.67:1. The engine weighed 3,408 pounds and was 91.8 inches long with a diameter of 56.59 inches.

The largest volume Neptune variant was the P2V-5, which accounted for 422 aircraft delivered between April 1951 and September 1954 on the wave of the Korean War–era military buildup. Of these, 52 went to the RAF Coastal Command, 20 to Australia, and 12 to the Netherlands.

Most P2V-5s were powered by the water-injected Wright R-3350-30WA, of which 1,348 were produced between November 1951 and March 1954. This engine produced 3,500 hp at 2,900 rpm for takeoff and 2,550 hp at 15,400 feet. It weighed 3,520 pounds and had the same outside dimensions as the R-3350-30W. The compression ratio and supercharger ratio of the two engines were also the same.

The P2V-6, also powered by the R-3350-30WA, was the mine-laying variant of the Neptune. Of the 83 production P2V-6s that were delivered from November 1953, 16 were P2V-6Bs equipped

The impeller-drive planetary system is superimposed on the accessory drive geartrain in a Wright R-3350 Duplex Cyclone engine (1945).

P2V-2 Neptunes are shown on the Lockheed assembly line in 1947. Deliveries of this variant, powered by R-3350-24Ws, began in June 1947. Deliveries of the succeeding P2V-3 began in July 1948.

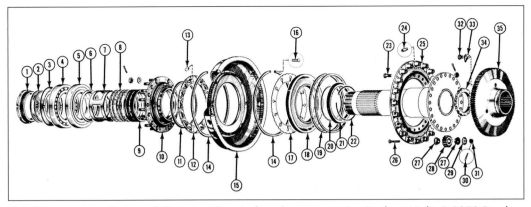

This is an exploded view of the propeller shaft reduction gearing in the Wright R-3350 Duplex Cyclone engine (1945).

1. Propeller Shaft Thrust Bearing Nut
2. Propeller Shaft Thrust Hearing Nut Oil Seal Rings
3. Propeller Shaft Thrust Hearing Oil Slinger
4. Propeller Shaft Thrust Ball Bearing
5. Propeller Shaft Roller Bearing
6. Propeller Shaft Thrust Bearing Spacer
7. Propeller Shaft Oil Seal Spacer
8. Propeller Shaft Oil Seal Sleeve Rings
9. Propeller Shaft Oil Seal Sleeve
10. Stationary Reduction Gear Support
11. Stationary Reduction Gear Support Oil Seal Ring
12. Torque Meter Roller Cage
13. Torque Meter Roller
14. Stationary Reduction Gear Adapter Lock Ring
15. Stationary Reduction Gear and Adapter Assembly
16. Stationary Reduction Gear Adapter Lock Ring Rivet
17. Stationary Reduction Gear Adapter Spacer
18. Torque Meter Piston
19. Torque Meter Oil Seal Rings
20. Stationary Reduction Gear Support Oil Seal Ring
21. Torque Meter Piston Retaining Nut
22. Torque Meter Piston Retaining Nut Lock Ring
23. Reduction Gear Pinion Carrier to Propeller Shaft Bolt
24. Reduction Gear Pinion Oil Jet
25. Reduction Gear Pinion Carrier
26. Reduction Gear Pinion Retaining Bolt
27. Reduction Gear Pinion Bushing
28. Reduction Gear Pinion
29. Reduction Gear Pinion Retaining Washer
30. Reduction Gear Pinion Bolt Taper Lock Pin
31. Reduction Gear Pinion Retaining Nut
32. Reduction Driving Gear Nut Lock Bolt
33. Reduction Driving Gear Nut Lock
34. Reduction Driving Gear Nut
35. Reduction Driving Gear

to fire Fairchild AUM-N-2 (AQM-41A after 1962) Petrel anti-submarine guided missiles. There were also 26 P2V-6Bs delivered to France.

The final Neptune production variant was the P2V-7, of which the US Navy acquired 212 between April 1954 and September 1962. In addition, the US Air Force received 7 under the RB-69A designation for electronic countermeasures missions, 16 were sold to Japan, and 76 were acquired by the US government to be given away under the Military Assistance Program (MAP). Recipients included Australia, Canada, France, the Netherlands, and Brazil.

The P2V-7 was powered by a pair of after-injected R-3350-32Ws as well as a pair of Westinghouse J34-WE-36 turbojets to augment the piston power. There were 1,316 R-3350-32Ws produced between August 1953 and mid-1961. This engine was rated at 3,700 hp at 2,900 rpm for takeoff and 2,400 hp at 18,000 feet. It had a compression

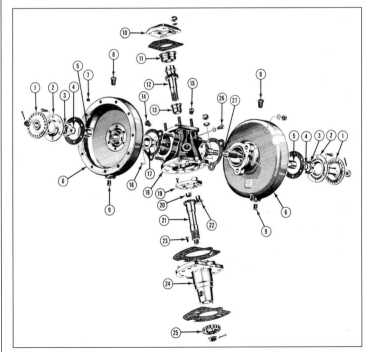

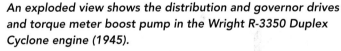

An exploded view shows the distribution and governor drives and torque meter boost pump in the Wright R-3350 Duplex Cyclone engine (1945).

1. Distributor Driveshaft Coupling
2. Distributor Driveshaft Adapter
3. Distributor Driveshaft Oil Seal
4. Distributor Driveshaft Coupling Oil Seal Ring
5. Distributor Driveshaft Hushing
6. Distributor Drive Housing
7. Distributor Housing Cover Screw and Bushing
8. Distributor Drive Housing Ventilating Plug
9. Distributor Drive Housing Moisture Drain Plug
10. Governor Substituting Cover
11. Governor Drive Adapter
12. Governor and Distributor Driveshaft
13. Governor and Distributor Driveshaft Gear Bushing
14. Governor and Distributor and Torque Meter Booster Pump Upper Housing Oil Line Hole Plug
15. Governor and Distributor and Torque Meter Booster Pump Upper Housing Oil Line Hole Plug
16. Distributor Driveshaft Bushing Retaining Pin
17. Distributor Driveshaft Bushing
18. Governor and Distributor Drive and Torque Meter Booster Pump Upper Housing
19. Governor and Distributor Drive and Torque Meter Booster Pump Lower Housing Cover
20. Governor and Distributor Drive and Torque Meter Booster Pump Drive Gear Shaft Screen
21. Governor and Distributor Drive and Torque Meter Booster Pump Drive Gear Shaft
22. Torque Meter Booster Pump Driven Gear
23. Torque Meter Booster Pump Lower Housing Cover to Housing Screw
24. Governor and Distributor Drive and Torque Meter Booster Pump Lower Housing
25. Governor Drive Pinion
26. Governor Drive Adapter Retaining Screw
27. Distributor Driveshaft

ratio of 6.7:1 and a supercharger ratio of 6.46/8.67:1. The engine weighed 3,540 pounds and was 91.8 inches long with a diameter of 56.59 inches. These were the same dimensions as the R-3350-30W and -30WA.

The Neptunes were widely used worldwide by the US Navy for more than two decades as patrol aircraft and in Vietnam for a variety of roles, including as gunships. Both Navy P2Vs and US Air Force RB-69As were also used for clandestine missions in Southeast Asia as well as on covert missions into Chinese air space with Taiwan, China crews of the Black Bat Squadron through 1966. Neptunes in Argentine service, including those from third-party arms sales, served in the 1978 war with Chile and against Britain in the Falklands War in 1982.

In 1962, US Navy Neptunes still in service received new designations under tri-service nomenclature that included P-2D (formerly P2V-4), P-2E (formerly P2V-5), P-2F/P-2G (formerly P2V-6), and P-2H (formerly P2V-7).

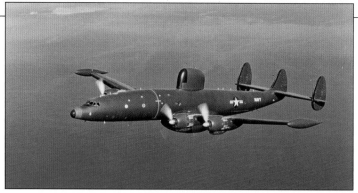

The US Navy's Lockheed WV-2 (PO-2W until 1954 and EC-121K after 1962) Warning Star Airborne Early Warning (AEW) aircraft were powered by Wright R-3350-34 engines and based on the popular Lockheed L-1049 Constellation commercial airliner. Entering service in 1953, Warning Stars remained operational in various forms until the 1980s.

The Constellation

In parallel with its use in military aircraft, the Wright R-3350 family of engines had a long career in the last great four-engine American propliners, including the Douglas DC-7 and the Lockheed Constellation. While these aircraft are outside the scope of the present book, we briefly consider military variants of the Constellation, which were used not only as transports but also as reconnaissance and electronic warfare platforms. The DC-7, meanwhile, had no military variant.

The catalyst for the Constellation program had been Transcontinental and Western Airlines (TWA), then controlled by Howard Hughes (see Chapter 14), who ordered 40 Model 49 (L-049) Constellations in 1940. Pan American also ordered 40. The first Constellation, part of the TWA order, made its debut flight on January 9, 1943, by which time commercial orders had been taken over as military orders, and the aircraft was drafted into the USAAF as the first of 23 C-69s.

After the war, Lockheed delivered 73 L-049s, offering customers a choice of Pratt & Whitney R-2800-series engines or Wright R-3350s. These began service early in 1946 and were followed by the commercial L-649 and L-749 variants, which were in service by 1947. The much larger L-1049 Super Constellation, with accommodations for more than

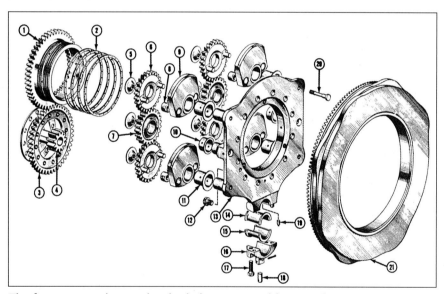

The front cam and second order balancer assemblies are shown in a Wright R-3350 Duplex Cyclone engine (1945).

1. Front Cam Drive Gear
2. Front Cam Drive Gear Oil Seal Rings
3. Intermediate Front Can Drive Gear
4. Intermediate Front Cam Drive Pinion
5. Balanceweight Gear and Intermediate Balanceweight Gear Retaining Nut
6. Balanceweight Gear
7. Intermediate Balanceweight Gear
8. Balanceweight Bushing
9. Balanceweight
10. Intermediate Balanceweight Gear Bushing
11. Balanceweight and Balanceweight Gear Bushing
12. Intermediate Cam Drive Gear and Balanceweight Support to Crankcase Front Main Section Screw
13. Intermediate Cam Drive Gear and Balanceweight Support
14. Intermediate Cam Drive Gear and Pinion Upper Bushing
15. Intermediate Cam Drive Gear and Pinion Lower Housing
16. Intermediate Cam Drive Gear and Balanceweight Support Cap
17. Intermediate Cam Drive Gear and Balanceweight Support Cap to Support Screw
18. Front Intermediate Cam Drive Gear and Balanceweight Support Cap Plug
19. Front Intermediate Cam Drive Gear and Pinion Lower Bushing Retaining Pin
20. Intermediate Balanceweight and Balanceweight Drive Gear Retaining Bolt
21. Front Cam (Intake and Exhaust)

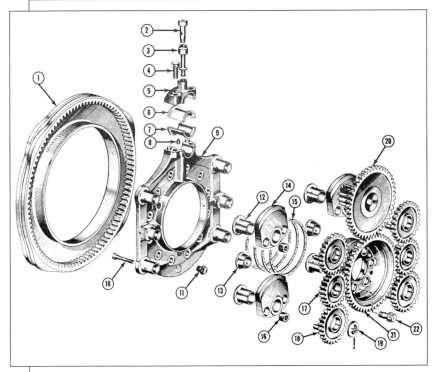

100 passengers, entered service in 1951 and soon became the standard of luxury air travel. Nearly 250 entered service by 1956. The ultimate member of the commercial Constellation family was the L-1649 Starliner, of which 44 were delivered, beginning in 1957.

While the USAAF had made limited use of its small number of C-69s, the postwar US Air Force took an extensive interest in the L-749 and L-1049 Super Constellation, ordering many variants under the basic C-121 designation. The US Navy did likewise under several designations.

After 10 L-749s for the Air Force and 2 for the Navy, all of the postwar military Constellations were based on the L-1049 Super Constellation airframe.

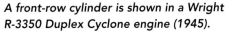

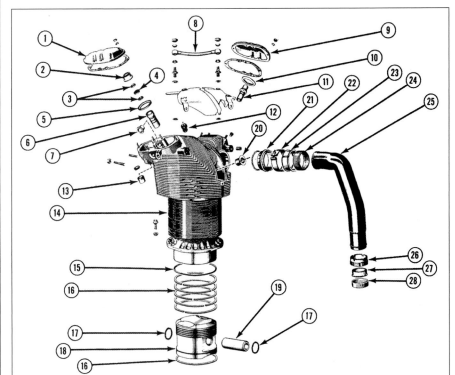

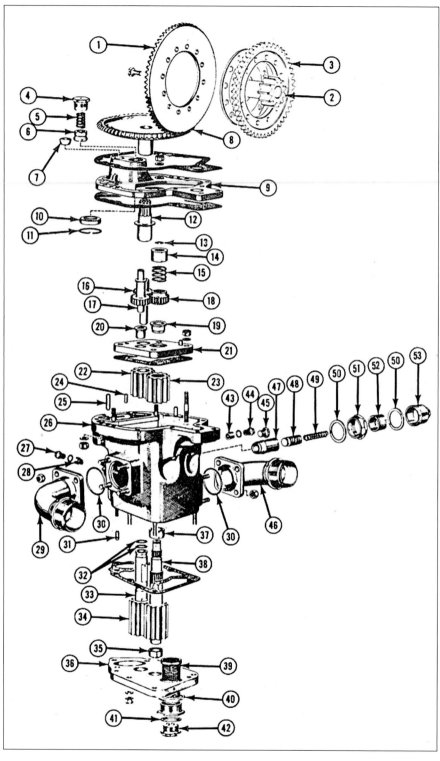

A Type III Front Oil Pump and Sump from a Wright R-3350 Duplex Cyclone engine (1945) are shown.

1. Front Oil Pump Intermediate Drive Gear
2. Intermediate Front Cam Drive Pinion
3. Intermediate Front Cam Drive Gear
4. Front Oil Pump Oil Check Valve Retainer
5. Front Oil Pump Oil Check Valve Spring
6. Front Oil Pump Oil Check Valve
7. Front Oil Pump Housing Feed Tube Packing Ring
8. Front Oil Pump Drive Gear
9. Front Oil Pump Adapter
10. Front Oil Pump Oil Check Valve Seat
11. Front Oil Pump Oil Check Valve Seat Retaining Circlet
12. Front Oil Pump Driveshaft Coupling
13. Front Oil Pump Drive Gear Spring Retaining Circlet
14. Front Oil Pump Drive Gear Spring Retainer
15. Front Oil Pump Drive Gear Spring
16. Front Oil Pump Driveshaft Gear
17. Front Oil Pump Idler Shaft Gear
18. Front Oil Pump Drive Gear
19. Front Oil Pump Driveshaft Gear Bushing
20. Front Oil Pump Idler Gear Shaft Bushing
21. Front Oil Pump and Sump End Plate
22. Front Oil Pump Pressure Driven Gear
23. Front Oil Pump Pressure Drive Gear
24. Front Oil Pump and Sump Body to End Plate Locating Pin
25. Front Oil Pump and Sump Through Adapter to Crankcase Front Section Locating Pin
26. Front Oil Pump and Sump Body
27. Front Oil Pump Pre-Oiling Vent Plug
28. Front Oil Pump and Sump Body Pre-Oiling Vent Plug Screw Bushing
29. Front Oil Pump Oil Inlet Elbow
30. Inlet and Outlet Elbow Flange to Oil Pump and Sump Body Packing Ring
31. Front Oil Pump and Sump Body to Cover Locating Pin
32. Front Oil Pump Driven Gear Shaft Packing Rings
33. Front Oil Pump Driven Gear Shaft
34. Front Oil Pump Scavenge Driven Gear
35. Front Oil Pump Drive Gear Shaft Bushing
36. Front Oil Pump and Sump Cover
37. Front Oil Pump Drive Gear Shaft Bushing
38. Front Oil Pump Driveshaft and Scavenge Drive Gear
39. Front Oil Sump Strainer
40. Front Oil Sump Strainer Gasket
41. Front Oil Sump Strainer Magnetic Drain Plug Gasket
42. Front Oil Sump Strainer Magnetic Drain Plug
43. Front Oil Pump and Sump Body Pre-Oiling Vent Plug, Screw Bushing
44. Front Oil Pump Pre-Oiling Vent Plug
45. Front Oil Pump Pressure Gauge Hole Plug
46. Front Oil Pump External Oil Outlet Elbow
47. Oil Pressure Relief Valve Body 48. Oil Pressure Relief Valve
49. Oil Pressure Relief Valve Spring
50. Oil Pressure Relief Valve Adjusting Screw Lock and Cap Washer
51. Oil Pressure Relief Valve Adjusting Screw Lock Nut
52. Oil Pressure Relief Valve Adjusting Screw
53. Oil Pressure Relief Valve Cap

The first postwar Air Force Constellations included L-749/VC-121As that served as executive transports for Generals Douglas MacArthur and Dwight Eisenhower. An L-1049/VC-121E later served as *Columbine III*, which was Eisenhower's "Air Force One," while he was president.

The first two Navy Constellations were L-749s first flown in 1949 under the designation PO-1W for "Patrol, Lockheed, First Airborne Early Warning." The Navy also acquired 11 L-1049 Super Constellations as transport aircraft under the designation R7O. In 1950, the Navy changed the Lockheed manufacturer's designator from "O" to "V," so an additional 40 L-1049 transports were designated as R7Vs.

An L-1049 in configuration similar to the PO-1W was designated as PO-2W, but the Navy changed the aircraft's primary role from "Patrol" to "Airborne Early Warning" and assigned the new designation WV-2. This aircraft type, of which 124 were built, was given the name "Warning Star." An additional eight WV-3 weather reconnaissance Warning Stars were also built.

The Warning Stars were notable for their huge radomes above and below the center fuselage. The dorsal radome was initially equipped with an AN/APS-45 height finder (altitude measuring) system. This was later upgraded to the AN/APS-103 radar. The ventral search radar radome contained an AN/APS-20 system that was later upgraded to AN/APS-95 radar.

The US Air Force, which used C-121 Super Constellations analogous to the WV-2s as well as others in similar roles used both the "R for Reconnaissance" or "E for Electronic installation" designation prefixes with some aircraft redesignated from one to the other. Lockheed built 82 L-1049 Super Constellations for the Air Force with

A US Navy Martin SP-5B (formerly P5M-2) Marlin, powered by Wright R-3350-32WA Duplex Cyclones, lands in San Diego Bay. Assigned to Patrol Squadron VP-40, the "Fighting Marlins," it is completing the last-ever operational Marlin flight on November 6, 1967. The aircraft is now on display at the National Museum of Naval Aviation in Pensacola, Florida. (Photo Courtesy US Navy)

radomes and radar systems like those of the WV-2. These included 10 RC-121Cs (later EC-121Cs) without wingtip fuel tanks and 72 RC-121Ds (later EC-121Ds) with them.

After 1962, when US Army, Navy, and Air Force designation nomenclature was merged into the tri-service system, the Navy's WV-2s were redesignated as EC-121Ks, and its WV-3s as WC-121Ns.

These aircraft were used in an early-warning role over the North Atlantic and the Pacific from the early 1950s through the mid-1960s. The US Air Force used them over Southeast Asia between 1964 and 1974 in numerous operations, including Big Eye, College Eye, Kingpin, and Rivet Top.

The largest numbers of these Super Constellation-derived recon/electronic military aircraft were the 124 WV-2/EC-121Ks for the US Navy that were followed by 72 US Air Force RC-121D/EC-121Ds and 42 US Air Force EC-21Hs. Many of the Navy and Air Force EC/RC-121s underwent special conversions and were given new designations. Examples include the Air Force EC-121R Batcat aircraft that were used over Vietnam to electronically monitor enemy troop movements under Operation Igloo White.

Most of the reconnaissance/electronics Super Constellations, especially the WV-2 and EC-121D aircraft, were powered by the Wright R-3350-34 engine, of which 1,640 were produced between June 1952 and September 1957. This engine produced 3,250 hp at 2,900 rpm for takeoff and 2,600 hp at 2,600 rpm normally. It had a compression ratio of 6.7:1 and a supercharger ratio of 6.46/8.67:1. The engine weighed 3,641 pounds and was 89.53 inches long with a diameter of 56.59 inches.

The R-3350-powered Lockheed EC-121R Batcats were EC-121Rs operated by the US Air Force 553d Reconnaissance Wing between 1967 and 1970 out of Korat Royal Thai Air Force Base as a part of Operation Igloo White. Their mission was to monitor ground sensors detecting enemy troop movements along the Ho Chi Minh Trail.

THE WASP MAJOR:
THE ULTIMATE ROUND ENGINE

The R-4360, which can be seen as the ultimate American round engine of the World War II era, did not actually see combat service during the war. In turn, it became the powerplant for many advanced aircraft which, like it, would have made an important impact on the war but arrived afterward. Among these aircraft are the early postwar strategic bombers with roots in wartime development programs, such as the Consolidated B-36 and the Boeing B-50.

R-4360 Development

The natural progression of piston-engine technology through the first half of the 20th century was toward larger and more capable powerplants. Multiple rows of pistons permitted an increase of total displacement without increasing its frontal area of an engine. For example, Wright Aeronautical's 14-cylinder R-2600 Twin Cyclone had 2 rows of 7 cylinders, while Pratt & Whitney's 18-cylinder R-2800 Double Wasp had 2 rows of 9. For its own largest wartime engine, Wright also gave its 18-cylinder R-3350 Duplex Cyclone 2 rows of 9 cylinders.

The apogee of Pratt & Whitney piston engine development was the 28-cylinder R-4360 Wasp Major, which had *4* rows of 7 cylinders. The engine's appearance, with its four rows of pistons, led it to be described as a "corncob."

Actually displacing 4,362.5 ci, the R-4360 was the largest American piston engine ever to enter large-scale mass production. According to the Aircraft Engine Historical Society, citing Pratt & Whitney records, the company produced 18,679 R-4360s between 1943 and 1955. However, of these, only 152 were produced through 1945. The peak years of production were 1952 (2,923 engines), 1953 (3,910 engines), and 1954 (2,942 engines), years in which the totals included licensed as well as in-house production.

Although the R-4360 was the largest among production engines, it should be noted that in the evolving quest for larger piston engines, the largest American piston aircraft engine was the Lycoming XR-7755. It was a 5,000-hp, *9-row*, 36-cylinder behemoth displacing 7,750 ci. Lycoming began work on the project in 1944 at its Williamsport, Pennsylvania, plant on behalf of the USAAF with the idea that such a huge engine could be available for extremely large future

The Consolidated B-36 Peacemaker was America's largest strategic bomber and the largest piston-engine aircraft ever mass produced. Powered by six Pratt & Whitney R-4360-25 28-cylander Wasp Majors, the single XB-36 prototype (seen here) made its debut flight on August 8, 1946, one year after the end of World War II.

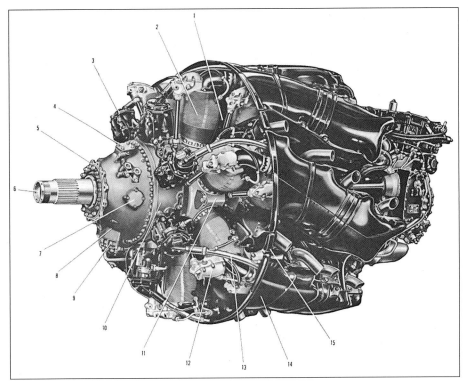

A three-quarter left front view is shown of a Pratt & Whitney R-4360 28-cylinder, four-row Wasp Major engine.

1. Cylinder Deflector
2. No. 7 Cylinder
3. No.1 Magneto
4. Governor Pad Cover
5. Thrust Cover
6. Propeller Shaft
7. Accessory Pod Cover
8. Propeller Shaft Case
9. Front Oil Pump
10. Magneto Drive Case
11. Front Crankcase
12. Rocker Box Cover
13. Ignition Manifold Assembly
14. Front Hood
15. Intermediate Hood

aircraft, such as intercontinental bombers like the B-36. Two XR-7755s were completed and tested in 1946, but with the R-4360 coming online and jet propulsion seen in the future, the project was canceled.

By comparison, those who envisioned the R-4360 seem almost modest in their ambitions. Those doing the envisioning included Andy Willgoos (see Chapters 1 and 2), as well as Leonard "Luke" Hobbs (see Chapter 4), whom Pratt & Whitney noted as having assumed "complete direction of all Pratt & Whitney engineering" when George Mead left the post of chief engineer in 1935.

While Hobbs was in charge, a key man on his team was Assistant Project Engineer G.E. Armbruster. It was Armbruster who kept the project notes and in 1946 compiled Pratt & Whitney's official history of the R-4360 development process.

As Armbruster pointed out, Pratt & Whitney did not originally consider a radial engine as the

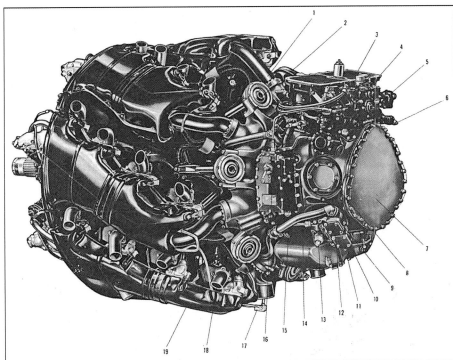

A three-quarter left rear view is shown of a 28-cylinder, four-row Pratt & Whitney R-4360 Wasp Major engine.

1. Intake Manifold
2. Mount
3. Carburetor
4. Magneto Pump
5. Tachometer Drive Adopter Housing
6. Water Injection Regulator Solenoid
7. Accessory Drive Case Cover
8. No. 5 Accessory Pad Cover*
9. Rear Oil Pump
10. Sump
11. Oil Inlet Cover
12. Oil Outlet Cover
13. Rear Oil Pump Pressure Relief Valve
14. Oil Line from Rocker Drain System
15. Oil Line from Blower Case
16. Automatic Engine Control Unit (Optional)
17. Rocker Box Oil Drain Manifold
18. Exhaust Pipe
19. Rear Hood
*A vacuum-pump drive adapter, starter, or generator might be installed on No. 5 pad.

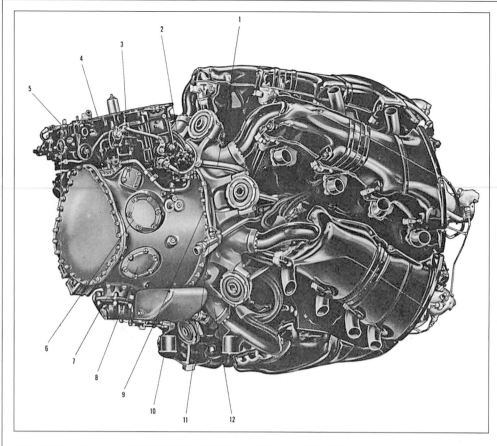

front-runner candidate for the ultimate mega-powerplant. He wrote that the company "experimented with various types of liquid-cooled aircraft engines varying from diesel or gasoline to sleeve-valve or poppet-valve arrangements. In the period from 1938 to 1940, efforts were directed primarily to the development of 2 sizes of 24-cylinder liquid-cooled sleeve-valve "H" type engines."

These included the XH-3130 and the XH-3730, both of which were sponsored by the US Navy.

He went on to write that "several innovations in the method of injecting the fuel brought about by integral multistage supercharging and intercooling created unusual and difficult problems in the induction and carburetion systems of these engines."

A 28-cylinder, four-row Pratt & Whitney R-4360 Wasp Major engine is on display at the Museum of Aviation at Robins Air Force Base. (Photo Courtesy Dsdugan, Licensed under Creative Commons)

Citing problems with "the design and manufacture of durable sleeve valves, reduction gears, and crankcases that are not inherent with radial air-cooled engines and with which the majority of personnel at Pratt and Whitney Aircraft had little or no experience."

All of this led the company back to where it had begun, and "it was felt that by reverting to designs with which we were familiar and also a design which was readily adaptable to our tools and manufacturing procedure, we could do a much better job in favor of a 28-cylinder air-cooled 4-row radial engine. Therefore, it was decided (with the consent of both Army and Navy) to abandon development of [inline] engines."

The Consolidated B-36A production aircraft made its first flight in August 1947, and the first B-36As started arriving in US Air Force squadrons between June and November 1948. The greenhouse canopy was completely redesigned from the prototype aircraft's flight deck configuration. Like the XB-36 and YB-36, the B-36A was powered by six Pratt & Whitney R-4360-25 Wasp Majors.

The Lycoming XR-7755, built in 1944 for possible use in the B-36, was the largest piston aircraft engine ever completed in the United States. It had 36 cylinders and delivered 5,000 hp. Only two were built before the project was terminated. (Photo Courtesy Sanjay Acharya, Licensed under Creative Commons)

Looking a bit like the product of a high school shop class, the Vought V-326 made is first flight on June 18, 1943. It was created for Pratt & Whitney explicitly as a high-altitude test bed for its then-experimental XR-4360 Wasp Major engine. A second V-326 followed in 1944 but was used only once.

Pratt & Whitney management gave a green light to design work on November 11, 1940, and the prototype of the new, large R-4360-precursor was first run five months later on April 28, 1941.

The first engine was, as Armbruster recalled, "made up largely of salvaged XH-3130 reduction gear, R-2180 rods, R-2800 front-bank cylinders and R-2800 rear, a cast steel crankshaft, and hurriedly manufactured crankcases."

Adding more technical detail, he noted that "the fourth engine was the first to operate with forged heads. However, the intake pipes were located in the position now occupied by the exhaust. This was the only engine operated in this manner, it being found more

This Consolidated B-36B was originally ordered as a B-36C with the intention of being powered by six R-4360-51 variable discharge turbine (VDT) engines. As a B-36B, it was powered by R-4360-41s. However, in 1949, it was one of several that were retrofitted with four General Electric J47-GE-19 turbojets and brought up to B-36D standard.

The slogan "six turning and four burning," was a slogan that referenced six R-4360-41s and four General Electric J47-GE-19 turbojets, as seen in this B-36D (delivered as an RB-36D reconnaissance variant).

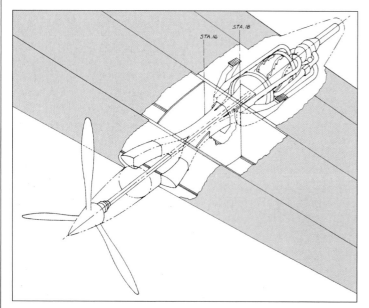

A cutaway view shows the proposed installation of the controversial R-4360-51 variable discharge turbine (VDT) engine that was planned for the B-36C. The propeller was connected to the engine by a long shaft. As Meyers Jacobsen pointed out, there was a "major problem with mating the engine to the VDT supercharger."

B-36 Peacemakers take shape on the same assembly line at the Convair plant in Fort Worth where the company had produced B-24s and B-32s in its previous incarnation as Consolidated Vultee.

The B-36J was the ultimate Peacemaker. As with the B-36F and B-36H, its six piston engines were Pratt & Whitney R-4360-53 Wasp Majors. This B-36J is preserved at the Pima Air and Space Museum in Arizona. (Photo Courtesy Mike LaChance, Licensed under Creative Commons)

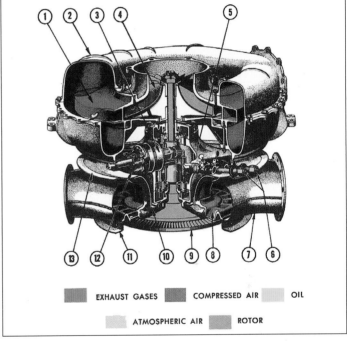

EXHAUST GASES   COMPRESSED AIR   OIL

ATMOSPHERIC AIR   ROTOR

This is a cutaway view of a General Electric Model BH-1 turbosupercharger as used in the Pratt & Whitney R-4360 Wasp Major engine.

1. Diffuser
2. Compressor Casing
3. Oil Pump
4. Impeller
5. Bearing and Pump Casing
6. Oil Lines
7. Nozzlebox
8. Diaphragm
9. Bucket Wheel
10. Sealing Plate Assembly
11. Mounting Ring
12. Filter Lines
13. Baffle Ring

A close-up view shows the Pratt & Whitney R-4360-53 Wasp Majors in their engine nacelles in the Convair RB-36H Peacemaker that is preserved at the Castle Air Museum in California. (Bill Yenne Photo)

The Northrop XB-35, with its unique "flying wing" configuration made its debut flight out of Hawthorne, California, on June 25, 1946. The XB-35 was powered by two variants of the Pratt & Whitney Wasp Major. Mounted left and right outboard were two R-4360-17s with eight-blade contra-rotating props. Mounted left and right inboard were two R-4360-21s with eight-blade contra-rotating props.

With the propellers yet to be hung, this is a good view of the Pratt & Whitney R-4360-35 Wasp Majors nestled in their nacelles on the first Boeing B-50A on the factory floor in Renton, Washington, in June 1947.

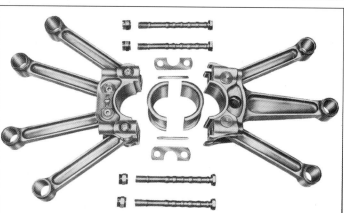

This is the master rod assembly for the Pratt & Whitney R-4360 Wasp Major engine.

A Boeing B-50B Superfortress, powered by Pratt & Whitney R-4360-35 Wasp Majors, displays full Strategic Air Command markings.

This photo of a Boeing Block 70 B-50D provides a good color view of the Pratt & Whitney R-4360-35 Wasp Majors that powered the B-50 family of Superfortresses.

Here is a good top view of the first Boeing B-50A rolling out of the Renton factory ahead of its first flight on June 25, 1947.

A Boeing B-50D-115-BN Superfortress is refueled by a Boeing KC-97A-BO Stratofreighter. Both of them are powered by subvariants of the Pratt & Whitney R-4360-35 Wasp Major.

efficient from a performance standpoint to operate with a top intake and side exhaust."

There was still much to be done before Pratt & Whitney arrived at a production-ready configuration. Armbruster admitted that throughout 1941: "three four-row engines and one single-row engine had been run, and parts for six engines had been fairly well machined. At the end of 1941, approximately one year after starting design, 500 hours of full scale operation plus 176 hours of single-row operation, and 1,412 hours of single-cylinder operation had been completed" before the R-4360 finally emerged.

In early 1942, as this work was ongoing, Pratt & Whitney was bringing in aircraft to be used as flying testbeds for the new engine. One of these was an adaptation of the Vultee A-31 Vengeance (Model V-72), which had been used for testing modified Wright R-3350 engines in 1942. Adapted and redesignated as Model V-85, these aircraft were used by both the R-3350 and R-4360 programs.

Another type used for the latter engine was the V-326. It was produced by Pratt & Whitney's sister company, Vought Aircraft, specifically as a high-altitude testbed. Loosely based on Vought's F4U Corsair, this pressurized aircraft had the ungainly appearance of something built by a high school shop class. Two were built, with the first flying with an R-4360 in June 1943.

The R-4360 itself had its debut in the Vultee aircraft. While some sources put the first flight of the XR-4360 in April 1942, Armbruster stated that this occurred on May 25, 1942, using the third XR-4360 engine to be built.

The prototype XR-4360 was also tested in a Vultee Model V-72 Vengeance that was redesignated as XA-31B for the tests.

The development of the engine moved slowly. Armbruster reported that when the engine was "released to semi-production" in 1942, "10 engines were delivered as experimental models" in 1943.

By early 1943, the USAAF had decided that two of its future generation of strategic bombers (the Consolidated B-36 and the Northrop B-35 "flying wing" bomber) use R-4360s in a "pusher"

Pratt & Whitney R-4360-59 Wasp Majors are being installed in a Boeing KC-97G Stratofreighter on the Seattle factory floor in April 1955. The aircraft at the left in the foreground is undergoing boom testing.

rather than "tractor" configuration with the powerplants installed on the trailing edges of the wings.

Meanwhile, Pratt & Whitney had found it more efficient from a performance standpoint to operate the R-4360 with a top intake and side exhaust. As Armbruster noted, "this method also allowed a very simple manifolding system to be used on both pusher and tractor engines without any other change to the cylinder being made other than to reverse it 180 degrees on the crankcase."

He went on to add that in the final designs of the R-4360 "it was possible to take any power section and convert it to a tractor or pusher model by changing only the cams, reversing the cylinders, and changing the intake pipes and baffles."

In his overview of the program, he wrote that "this same basic power section was used on all the multiplicity of models designed around the R-4360. A similar application was made to the rear section where converting from single to auxiliary stage involves little more than removing a rear cover plate and substituting the additional stages of parts, or a single-stage, single-speed rear section could be converted to a single-stage, variable-speed rear with a simple addition of parts."

Beyond the Vought and Vultee testbed aircraft of 1942–1943, the R-4360 was flown in several single-engine experimental aircraft in 1944. First, there was the Republic P-72, a high-altitude interceptor based on the Republic P-47 Thunderbolt. Only two XP-72s were built: one with an R-4360-13 that first flew on February 2, 1944 and the other, which made its debut on June 26, 1944, with an R-4360-19.

Meanwhile, a single Vultee Model V-90, designated as XA-41, made its first flight on February 11, 1944, with an R-4360-9. The Goodyear Aircraft Company, which produced around 4,000 Vought-designed Corsairs under the FG designation, went on to create an advanced, bubble-canopied variant under the F2G designation that was powered by the R-4360-4. After the first of these was converted from FG-1s, 15 were built as F2G-1 and F2G-2.

On November 27, 1944, Boeing first flew its XR-4360-10-powered XF8B-1 naval fighter. It was a prototype of a carrier-based, deep-penetration fighter to be used in operations against the Japanese home islands during Operation Downfall. Only three were built as the end of the war brought an end to the program.

One single-engine aircraft that made its debut with an R-4360 during World War II that went into production was the Martin Mauler. It made its first flight on August 26, 1944, under the bomber-torpedo designation XBTM-1 and was powered by an XR-3460-4. After two prototypes, it entered production, with 149 aircraft built under the AM-1 attack designation.

Enter the B-36 Peacemaker

The B-36 was born as an idea in the spring of 1941, even before the United States entered the war. It came about against the backdrop of strategic planning for a very large, very long-range bomber that could strike Berlin from bases in North America, should Britain be occupied by German forces.

On April 11, 1941, the US Army Air Corps issued a request to planemakers for the design of a strategic bomber with a range of 10,000 miles and 10,000-pound payload capacity. Several planemakers submitted proposals for this huge, almost larger-than-life aircraft. In November 1941, Consolidated and Northrop received contracts for what would be designated as the B-35 and B-36.

The Consolidated contract called for a pair of XB-36 prototypes and production of 100 B-36s by 1943. They would be powered by the also almost larger-than-life R-4360 that was then under development by Pratt & Whitney. Consolidated lengthened the runway at its Fort Worth plant to 8,200 feet and prepared to build the bomber there.

The ambitiousness of the Consolidated B-36 program rivaled that of the B-29, although as the development stretched out into 1943 and beyond, the B-36 program lost the wartime urgency afforded to that of the B-29. This was a function of its development being overtaken by events. As the months ticked by, it became obvious that bomber bases in Britain were secure from a German invasion, and existing USAAF strategic bombers would use these bases to reach Berlin. Likewise in the Pacific, the bomber bases in the Marianas would support routine USAAF B-29 missions to Tokyo.

Gradually, as the exigency of the B-36 project waned, the schedule slipped, and the B-32 Dominator (see Chapter 13) came to dominate the Fort Worth assembly line.

The Convair XB-36, powered by the R-4360-25 variant of the Wasp Major, made its first flight on August 8, 1946, a year after the end of the war. An initial order for 100 B-36 Peacemakers included 22 B-36As powered by the R-4360-25 and 78 B-36Bs powered by the R-4360-41. Both engines used the General Electric BH-1 turbosupercharger, which weighed about 192 pounds.

The BH-1 had a weight flow of 160 pounds per minute at 35,000 feet, where it was rated with a rotor speed of 22,500 rpm, although it could be operated at 24,750 for 15 minutes.

The first production variant, the B-36A, made its debut flight in August 1947, four months ahead of the R-4360-25 powered second prototype YB-36. The B-36B first flew in July 1948.

Time had marched on. The USAAF had become the independent US Air Force in September 1947, with the Strategic Air Command (SAC) within it as the manager of its strategic bomber fleet. The B-36A entered service with SAC in June 1948. The first B-36 unit was the 7th Bombardment Group, which was conveniently based at Carswell Air Force Base, across the runway from Convair's Fort Worth factory complex.

Internationally, June 1948 also marked the beginning of the Soviet blockade of Berlin and effectively the start of the Cold War. The B-36 was no longer a huge postwar anomaly but a high-visibility weapons system in the American strategic arsenal.

Based on the R-4360-5 of 1942, the R-4360-25 was rated at 3,000 hp at 2,700 rpm for takeoff and had a military rating of 3,000 hp at 2,700 rpm at 40,000 feet. It had a compression ratio of 7:1 and used a Bendix PR-100-B2-3 carburetor. The engine weighed 3,483 pounds and was 109.5 inches long with a diameter of 52.5 inches.

The B-36C was a substantial departure from the existing trajectory of the program. For this, Convair intended to use Pratt & Whitney R-4360-51 engines incorporating Variable Discharge Turbine (VDT) technology.

The three YC-97As were powered by Pratt & Whitney R-4360-35A Wasp Majors. The US Air Force retained this aircraft, the first of the three, at Wright Field for extensive testing through June 1949. It was then returned to Boeing, where it was used as a flying test bed for many types of aircraft technology that the company developed for the Air Force. It operated in this role until 1965.

The last of 952 KC-97G Stratofreighters flies under the power of its Pratt & Whitney R-4360-59 Wasp Majors.

The Notorious VDT

The variable discharge turbine (VDT) is a small footnote in the joint narrative of the B-36 and the R-4360, but without it, the story is incomplete. The VDT was a unique system that came and went with a small slice of the roster of Wasp Major variants. It was one of those concepts that "looked good at the time" but was not.

Meyers Jacobsen, in his extraordinary book about the program, *Convair B-36: A Comprehensive History of America's "Big Stick,"* explained that "the VDT engine had been proposed by the Air Force for the Boeing B-50, and it was placed into development. Convair knew this, and with Pratt & Whitney's encouragement, proposed the VDT engine for a new B-36 model that would be designated as B-36C. Convair and Pratt & Whitney estimated that with the new VDT engine, the B-36 could have a top speed of 410 mph, a service ceiling of 45,000 feet, and a 10,000-mile range carrying a 10,000-pound bomb load."

In his description of VDT technology, Meyers explains that within the engine itself, "exhaust gases from the engine would pass through a General Electric CHM-2 turbosupercharger with a clam-

One of the last KC-97L Stratofreighters in US Air Force markings arrives at Castle Air Force Base in 1980. The KC-97Ls were KC-97Gs whose R-4360s were augmented by General Electric J47-GE-23 turbojets. This aircraft was originally delivered as a KC-97G in July 1956. (Bill Yenne Photo)

shell nozzle that created jet thrust by varying the size of the turbine exit. The variable discharge nozzle was to be operated by automatic control [and] activated by a manifold pressure-sensing device. Cooling air would be ducted through wing leading edge inlets flanking the nacelle extension. It was a cumbersome and complex design change to say the least."

There was a major airframe issue inherent in a conversion to the VDT system for future Peacemakers. As Jacobsen noted, "to accommodate the VDT engine in the B-36, it would be necessary to change the propeller/engine configuration from the pusher type to the tractor type. Although the engine would remain aft of the wing spar, its position would have to be reversed to face forward. The propeller shaft would have to extend through the entire wing and then another 10 feet forward of the wing's leading edge. Such an arrangement would present a complex engineering challenge."

Although the VDT engine had originally been intended for the Boeing B-50, in a presentation to the Air Materiel Command (AMC) on March 25, 1947, Convair proposed it for a B-36C variant of the Peacemaker. This came nine months before the first production B-36A was delivered.

In June 1947, the Air Force assigned the designation R-4360-51 to Pratt & Whitney's VDT engine concept. The R-4360-51 was rated at 4,300 hp at 2,800 rpm for takeoff and had a compression ratio of 6.7:1. The R-4360-51 used a General Electric CHM-2 supercharger and a Bendix PR-100-28-A3 carburetor. The engine weighed 4,020 pounds and had a diameter of 55 inches. It was 91 inches long with the reduction gear unit being 36 inches long.

Although the Air Force had assigned a designation, there was little enthusiasm within the service for the idea. In fact, two months later, the Air Force Aircraft & Weapons Board explicitly rejected the VDT concept. But, the story did not end there.

In September 1947, Convair proposed retrofitting a B-36B to B-36C standard and delivering the last 34 aircraft on the existing B-36B order as B-36Cs with R-4360-51 VDT engines.

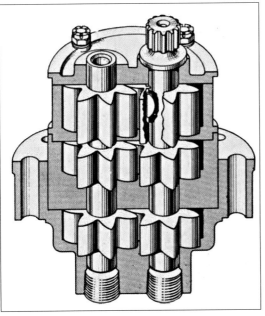

This is a sectional view of the front oil pump of the Pratt & Whitney R-4360 Wasp Major engine. The front oil pump housing consists of four sections bolted together to form three scavenge chambers. The pump was mounted in the bottom of the case and was secured to the studs in the mounting pad that project through the pump cover. The housing supports the oil pump driveshaft and the idler shaft. The three gears, which were keyed to the driveshaft, mesh with the three gears mounted on the idler shaft. The top idler gear was pinned to its shaft. Each pair of gears operates within one of the scavenge chambers of the pump.

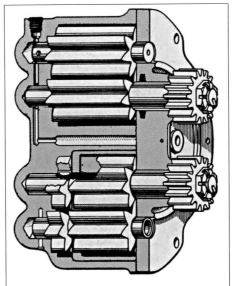

A sectional view is shown of the rear oil pump in a Pratt & Whitney R-4360 Wasp Major engine. The gears integral with these shafts mesh with the corresponding pressure and scavenge idler gears. These idler gears were mounted on the bronze idler shafts, each of which was pinned to its section of the pump body. The larger scavenge gears scavenge the main sump and were housed within the scavenge section, which separates the scavenge section of the pump into two chambers. The smaller of the two chambers, located between the scavenge section body and the pump body, houses the smaller scavenge gears that scavenge the rocker box drain oil system. One of the smaller scavenge gears was keyed to the outer end of the scavenge section driveshaft and meshes with the idler gear that was mounted on the outer end of the scavenge section idler shaft. The inner ends of all the pump shafts were supported by the rear oil pump body cover.

General Joseph McNarney, head of AMC, as well as Major General Lawrence Craigie, chief of Research and Development at AMC, supported the idea, though it was opposed by General George Kenney, the Commanding General of SAC. In December 1947, General Hoyt Vandenberg, vice chief of staff decided to give a go-ahead to the B-36C, this being welcome news for Convair because the end of the B-36B deliveries would have meant the end of the B-36 program, upon which the company depended financially.

Even as the VDT crept forward, problems crept in. The VDT was promoted as giving the B-36C a speed of 410 mph, but, as Jacobsen pointed out, when "analyses were made of the cooling problems, this was scaled down to 385 mph. Cooling difficulties would prove to be the 'Achilles heel' of the B-36C . . . The shortcomings

The US Navy's fifth Martin P4M-1 Mercator flies on January 11, 1950, under the power of both Pratt & Whitney R-4360-20 Wasp Majors and Allison J33-A-10A turbojets.

of the VDT fed the foremost objection to the B-36. It would cause the big bomber to be dangerously slow over the target . . . Ultimately, the attempt to mate the VDT engine to the B-36 became a failure."

In April, with no production Peacemaker of any variant yet delivered to SAC, McNarney recommended to the Chief of Staff of the Air Force, General Carl "Tooey" Spaatz, that the B-36C/VDT program be terminated. In his April 12 cancellation memo to Spaatz, McNarney wrote that "the B-36 engine installation is critically affected by increased cooling requirements due to location of the engines in the

rear portion of the wing and the high altitude at which the airplane is designed to operate."

McNarney suggested four possible scenarios of what to do next. These ranged from terminating the entire B-36 program after 22 B-36As to reverting the order for 34 not-yet-built B-36Cs back to their original place being on the B-36B roster and finishing the deliveries of 100 Peacemakers.

The latter option was picked, and after abandoning the discredited VDT system, the B-36 story would turn to an all-new page.

Six Turning and Four Burning

The problem of slow speed over a potential target, especially while armed with nuclear weapons, was finally resolved by augmenting the R-4360-41 Wasp Majors with jet engines. The concept was first test flown on March 28, 1949, in a B-36B retrofitted with four Allison J-35-19 turbojets, creating a 10-engine strategic bomber. The phrase "six turning and four burning" was coined.

The configuration went into production under the designation B-36D, and General Electric J47-GE-19 engines were chosen over the Allison type in production aircraft, which made their debut in August 1950. Aviation historian Ray Wagner noted 26 B-36Ds and 24 RB-36D reconnaissance subvariants, although other sources list different numbers. In addition, 59 B-36Bs were retrofitted by Convair with J47-GE-19 engines and redesignated as B-36Ds. Meanwhile, the YB-36 and 21 B-36As were also given J47-GE-19s, and these were designated as B-36Es.

A Martin P4M-1 Mercator runs up its Pratt & Whitney R-4360-20 Wasp Majors. These engines were each augmented by an Allison J33-A-10A turbojet in the same nacelle.

a compression ratio of 6.7:1. The R-4360-53 used a Bendix PR-100-28-A5 carburetor. The engine weighed 4,040 pounds with the deflector torquemeter, ignition system, and priming system. It was 117 inches long with a diameter of 55 inches.

The final Peacemaker was the B-36J, first flown on September 3, 1953. This series, which again used the R-4360-53/J47-GE-19 engine combination, included 333 B-36J bombers and no reconnaissance subvariants.

The R-4360-41 was rated at 3,000 hp at 2,700 rpm for takeoff and had a military rating of 3,000 hp at 2,700 rpm at 40,000 feet with the supercharger. It had a compression ratio of 6.7:1 and used a Bendix PR-100-B3 carburetor. The engine weighed 3,567 pounds, including the torquemeter and water injection equipment, and was 109.75 inches long with a diameter of 53.5 inches.

Beginning in November 1950, another factory-built, jet-augmented series appeared. This included 34 B-36Fs and 24 RB-36Fs. These retained the J47-GE-19 turbojets, but their Wasp Majors were the R-4360-53 variant. The same engine combination continued into the B-36H/RB-36H variant, which was first flown on April 5, 1952. It was the most numerous of all Peacemaker variants, with 83 B-36Hs and 73 RB-36H aircraft delivered through July 1953.

The R-4360-53 Wasp Major C-series engine was rated at 3,800 hp at 2,800 rpm for takeoff and had

Crews at Consolidated's Lindbergh Field plant in San Diego are seen here hanging the props of the big XC-99 transport. Like the B-36B and B-36D from which it was derived, the XC-99 was powered by Pratt & Whitney R-4360-41 Wasp Majors.

The huge Lockheed Constitution was an ambitious design with a double-deck, pressurized fuselage that was intended for both the military and airline market. Only two were built, however, both for the US Navy under the XR6O-1 (later XR6V-1) designation. The first one, seen here, flew in November 1946, powered by four Pratt & Whitney R-4360-22Ws.

The Northrop B-35

The distinction of having the most unusual appearance of any round-engine American bomber ever goes to the Northrop B-35 "flying wing." Like the Consolidated B-36, The B-35 was designed in response to the April 11, 1941, Air Corps request for the design of a strategic bomber with a range of 10,000 miles and 10,000-pound payload capacity. Both aircraft were to use the R-4360, which was then in development by Pratt & Whitney, and both aircraft used the engines in a pusher configuration. In both cases, the engines were enclosed within the wing with the shafts running through the nacelles to the propellers.

The two companies received contracts for a pair of prototypes. The initial plans called for production of the B-35 by the Glenn L. Martin Company at their plant at Omaha, but this production space was later allotted to the Martin-built B-29s. The B-29s had a higher priority because they would be available sooner than the B-35.

Both the B-35 and B-36 were planned to use the Pratt & Whitney R-4360, but in most other ways, they were as different as night and day. The B-35 had the same flying wing configuration as Jack Northrop's experimental N-1M of 1940, a design which was almost the stuff of science fiction. Indeed, flying wings appeared often on the covers of pulp science fiction periodicals of that era.

Northrop test flew the design with four one-third scale N-9M experimental aircraft and proceeded with the two XB-35 prototypes.

The first made its debut flight on June 25, 1946, which was six weeks before that of Consolidated's XB-36.

Explained by G.E. Armbruster in his 1946 summary of the R-4360

This view of the second Lockheed XR6O-1 (later R6V-1) Constitution ahead of its June 1948 debut flight provided a good look at its Pratt & Whitney R-4360-22W engines. Jack Real, the supervisor of testing for the Constitution, is standing far left.

program, the "XB-35 uses the R-4360-17 and -21 engines, their only difference being the length of the extension shaft. This is probably the most unusual engine model Pratt & Whitney have ever built and had required a more extensive outlay for testing facilities than any other engine. Originally, this engine had been scheduled to use a two-speed dual rotation reduction gear. However, this was abandoned because of its extreme complexity and weight. This engine has a turbo-type rear and a two-speed fan drive, also equipped with a fan break."

As Armbruster noted, a pair of two separate engine types were used to power the B-35 with the "only difference being the length of the extension shaft."

There were actually three pairs of engines used at various stages through the life of the program. These were the R-4360-7 and -11, the

R-4360-17 and -21, and finally the R-4360-45 and -47. The R-4360s used in the B-35 program were equipped with General Electric BH-1 Model B1, B2, C1, or C2 turbosuperchargers. All three combinations drove contra-rotating propellers.

The R-4360-7 and -11 were rated at 3,000 hp at 2,700 rpm for takeoff and had a military rating of 2,400 hp at 2,700 rpm at 13,500 feet or 2,000 hp at 2,700 rpm at 40,000 feet with turbosupercharger. They had compression ratios of 7:1. They used Bendix PR-100-A3-1 carburetors, and, as Wasp Major B-series engines, they had General Electric CH-1 turbosuperchargers. The engines each weighed 3,525 pounds without the torquemeter and had a diameter of 52.5 inches. The outboard direct-drive R-4360-7 was 114.25 inches long or 213.847 inches including the shaft to the propeller thrust-nut

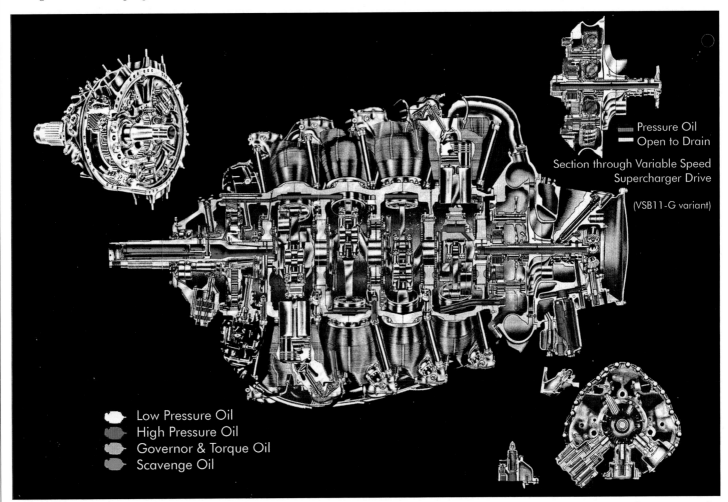

Pressure Oil
Open to Drain

Section through Variable Speed
Supercharger Drive

(VSB11-G variant)

Low Pressure Oil
High Pressure Oil
Governor & Torque Oil
Scavenge Oil

A sectional view of a Pratt & Whitney R-4360 Wasp Major 28-cylinder four-row radial piston aircraft engine shows the nuances of its oil system.

face. The inboard direct-drive R-4360-11 was 87 inches long or 326.4 inches including the shaft to the propeller thrust-nut face.

The R-4360-17 and -21 were rated at 3,000 hp at 2,700 rpm for takeoff and had a military rating of 3,000 hp at 2,700 rpm at 40,000 feet with supercharger. They had compression ratios of 7:1. They used Bendix PR-100-B2-3 carburetors, and, as Wasp Major B-series engines, they had General Electric CH-1 turbosuperchargers.

These two engine types each weighed 3,308 pounds without the torquemeter, reduction gear housing, and other equipment, which added 556 pounds. The extension shaft and coupler added 185 pounds to the R-4360-17, and 830 pounds to the R-4360-21.

The outboard direct-drive R-4360-17 was 87 inches long or 213.85 inches including the shaft to the propeller thrust-nut face. The inboard direct-drive R-4360-21 was 87 inches long or 326.4 inches including the shaft to the propeller thrust-nut face.

Finally, the R-4360-45 and -47 were rated at 3,000 hp at 2,700 rpm for takeoff and had a military rating of 2,500 hp at 2,550 rpm at 40,000 feet. They had compression ratios of 7:1 and used Bendix PR-100-B2-3 carburetors. The engines each weighed 3,308 pounds without the torquemeter, reduction gear housing, and other equipment. They had diameters of 52.5 inches. The outboard direct-drive R-4360-45 was 87 inches long or 213.85 inches including the shaft

to the propeller thrust-nut face. The inboard direct-drive R-4360-47 was 87 inches long or 326.4 inches including the shaft to the propeller thrust-nut face.

Eight YB-35 aircraft and five YB-35As were built. An order for 200 B-35As was canceled when the war ended. By this time, the USAAF (US Air Force after September 1947) was already looking ahead toward jet propulsion for its strategic bombers. They were not, however, ready to abandon Jack Northrop's flying wing concept.

On June 1, 1945, World War II still raged as the USAAF contracted with Northrop to re-engine two YB-35s with Allison J-35-A-15 turbojet engines. The first of these made its debut flight under the designation YB-49 on October 21, 1947, only 16 months after the first XB-35. A third YB-35 was converted with an Allison J-35-A-21 as YB-49A and flown in May 1950. A production series of 30 RB-49s was canceled.

Neither the YB-35 nor YB-49 moved beyond flight testing, and this was concluded for both programs by 1951.

Boeing and the Wasp Major

In the summer of 1944, the Boeing B-29 Superfortress had only just entered combat, and the Battle of Kansas, during which the trouble-plagued Wright R-3350 engine had nearly sunk the whole program, was still fresh in the memories of all concerned. With this memory indeed fresh both at Boeing and the USAAF, decision-makers had entertained thoughts of the R-4360 as an alternate powerplant for the Superfortress as early as July 1944.

To pursue this idea, a proof-of-concept aircraft was ordered under the designation XB-44. This aircraft was a B-29A that was turned over to Pratt & Whitney as a testbed for the concept. Redesignated as XB-44, it was re-engined with four R-4360-33s, and flight testing began in May 1945.

By this time, though, the B-29 had at last proven itself in combat and Boeing was moving toward a new, taller-tailed, R-4360-powered variant that was to have been designated as B-29D. When the war officially ended in September 1945, orders for 200 B-29Ds were cut to just 60. In December 1945, the USAAF redesignated the program as B-50A and touted it as not

Developed as a heavy-duty trans-ocean, airlifter for the USAAF, the Douglas C-74 Globemaster I first flew on September 5, 1945. The dual fighter-style bubble canopies of the first C-74, seen here, were a unique flight deck feature. The first C-74 flew with Pratt & Whitney R-4360-27 engines that were upgraded to R-4360-69s in later C-74s.

just another B-29 but a 75-percent *new* aircraft. The B-50 still retained the Boeing Model 345 designation, though.

Peter Bowers, in his book *Boeing Aircraft Since 1916*, called the redesignation "an outright military ruse to win appropriations for the procurement of an airplane that by its designation appeared to be merely a later version of an existing model [the B-29] that was being canceled wholesale, with many existing examples being put into cold storage."

If it was a ruse, it worked. The first of 79 B-50As made its debut flight on June 25, 1947. These were followed by 45 B-50Bs, 222 B-50Ds, and 24 TB-50H crew trainers—all with strengthened airframes. The last deliveries of the new-build B-50s came in March 1953, but there were numerous conversions of these aircraft to non-bomber roles. These included numerous RB-50 reconnaissance variants and around 300 conversions as KB-50 aerial refueling tankers. Of these, 112 had their R-4360 engines augmented by the addition of a pair of General Electric J-47 turbojets.

The basic powerplant for the new-build B-50s was the R-4360-35. It was rated at 3,500 hp at 2,700 rpm for takeoff and had a military rating of 2,400 hp at 2,700 rpm at 25,000 feet. It had a compression ratio of 6.7:1. The R-4360-35 used a Bendix PR-100-B3-4 carburetor. The engine weighed 3,490 pounds and was 96.75 inches long with a diameter of 54 inches.

The B-50C, later redesignated as the B-54, was to have had a longer fuselage, and was earmarked to be powered by a VDT engine (see VDT subsection above). Specifically, this was to have been the R-4360-43 VDT engine rather than the R-4360-51 VDT engine of the planned B-36C. However, when development of the VDT concept was terminated, effective April 1949, so too was the B-50C/B-54 program.

Another Boeing product lineage with roots in the B-29 program that began at the end of World War II was the Model 367/377 family of four-engine transports. The Model 367 Stratofreighter was a military transport, of which many variations were produced with the basic C-97 designation. The Model 377 Stratocruiser was Boeing's only postwar piston-engine propliner.

The XC-97 first flew in November 1944 powered by four Wright R-3350-23 Duplex Cyclones. The YC-97, appearing in March 1947, used R-3350-57A Duplex Cyclones, but the production-series Stratofreighters turned to variants of the R-4360. After 68 C-97A through C-97C transports (including three converted YC-97As), the vast majority of Stratofreighters, now being built with taller "B-50-type" tails, were delivered as aerial refueling aircraft. This included 60 KC-97Es, 159 KC-97Fs, and 592 KC-97Gs. The latter two variants were both powered by the R-4360-59B variant of the Wasp Major. A small number of KC-97Gs had their piston power augmented by

The Douglas C-124 Globemaster II, first flown on November 27, 1949, was the direct successor to the C-74. Seen here, the C-124A was powered by four Pratt & Whitney R-4360-20WA engines.

turbojet engines. These included KC-97J conversions with Pratt & Whitney YT43 engines and KC-97L conversions with General Electric J47s.

First flown on July 8, 1947, the tall-tailed Model 377 Stratocruiser used the R-4360-B6 Wasp Major commercial variant. There were 56 Stratocruisers produced, with the first entering service with Pan American World Airways in April 1949.

Martin, the Navy, and the Wasp Major

In the story of the Pratt & Whitney R-4360 Wasp Major and its military aircraft applications, much of the focus tends to be toward the US Air Force with its last great piston-engine strategic aircraft, such as the B-36, B-50, and KC-97. However, the engine also played a role at the Glenn L. Martin Company with its last large piston-engine aircraft for the US Navy.

In the years after World War II, the US Navy imagined that it also had a role in long-range strategic airpower, which flowed naturally from its earlier fleet of long-range land and sea-based aircraft. Among such postwar aircraft, there was the R-3350-powered Lockheed P2V Neptune, which is discussed in Chapter 13. Meanwhile, Martin developed another aircraft with a pair of R-4360s.

The Martin P4M-1 Mercator program originated during World War II as the US Navy was looking to develop a successor to its Consolidated PB4Y Privateer as a long-range patrol bomber and anti-submarine aircraft. The Lockheed P2V Neptune won the prize of the large production contract, but the Navy also ordered a small number of Mercators.

Ordered in July 1944, the XP4M-1 made its debut flight on September 20, 1946. The two prototypes were powered by a pair of R-4360-4s, but the 19 P4M-1 production Mercators used the R-4360-20. As with later Neptunes, the Mercator's piston power was augmented by turbojets. In the case of the prototypes, it was a pair of Allison J33-A-17s, while the P4M-1s used the Allison J33-A-23. While the Neptune's turbojets were hung on the wing outboard of the piston engines, the Mercator's were blended into the same nacelle.

The R-4360-20 was rated at 3,500 hp at 2,700 rpm for takeoff and had a military rating of 2,500 hp at 2,700 rpm at 17,000 feet. It had a compression ratio of 6.7:1. The R-4360-20 used a Bendix-Stromberg PR-100-B4 carburetor. The engine weighed 3,540 pounds and was 102 inches long with a diameter of 54 inches.

The Mercator remained in service until 1960, flying electronic surveillance missions in the Western Pacific off the coasts of China, North Korea, North Vietnam, and the Soviet Union.

Other Large-Airframe Wasp Major Applications

As World War II was nearing its climactic end in 1945, there were several very large aircraft (mainly transports) on the drawing boards and in the machine shops of planemakers around the United States. The engine of choice because of its size, power, and leading-edge technology was naturally the R-4360 Wasp Major.

While transports are beyond the scope of this book of warbirds, these aircraft are worth a brief mention. The largest of the transports, the Hughes HK-1/H-4, is discussed in the next subsection, but some of the others follow.

The Model 37 from Consolidated (now branding itself as Convair) was essentially a transport variant of the B-36. As the war was coming to an end, it was only natural for makers of large combat aircraft to consider the potential of military and commercial transport variations on these aircraft. Boeing had done this with its Stratocruiser, which was born with B-29 roots, just as Convair had proposed its Model 39 Liberator Liner based on the B-24 Liberator. Two Model 39s were built, but no airlines were interested.

The USAAF ordered a single Model 37 under the designation XC-99, and it first flew on November 23, 1947, utilizing the same wing as the B-36. As in the B-36, this wing spanned 230 feet and contained six R-4360-41 engines in pusher configuration. The world's largest landplane, the XC-99, was 186.5 feet long, which is 20 feet longer than the B-36, with a voluminous, double-deck fuselage. Used as a heavy lift transport, the XC-99 continued in service with the US

The Douglas C-124C Globemaster II, seen here in Military Air Transport Service markings, was distinguished by more powerful Pratt & Whitney R-4360-63A engines and the nose radome, which contained APS-42 weather radar. It also had wingtip-mounted combustion heaters to heat the cabin.

A pair of Douglas C-124C Globemaster II transports are shown. The one in the foreground was originally delivered as a C-124A with tail number 51-151. They flew in the markings of the 1501st Air Transport Wing, which operated C-124s between 1957 and 1963.

A Fairchild C-119B-10-FA Flying Boxcar powered by a pair of Pratt & Whitney R-4360-20 Wasp Majors. Seen over Korea in 1952, this aircraft served with the US Air Force 314th Troop Carrier Group, which participated in two major airborne operations: at Sunchon in October 1950 and at Munsan-ni in March 1951. It later transported supplies to Korea and evacuated prisoners of war. (Photo Courtesy USAF)

A Fairchild C-119C-17-FA Flying Boxcar, originally powered with R-4360-20 engines is now on display at the Castle Air Museum in Atwater, California, in 2016. After retirement from the US Air Force, it served with the US Forest Service. (Photo Courtesy Alan Wilson, Licensed under Creative Commons)

Air Force until March 1957. Lockheed, meanwhile, had its own huge four-engine Model 89 Constitution. This very large transport aircraft was on the back burner of the same metaphorical stove where the Constellation was being developed into the standard of excellence in postwar commercial transportation. In the meantime, there was a competition between the military services. Just as the Air Force would have the X-99, the US Navy would have its XR6O-1 (XR6V-1 after 1950) Constitution.

As with the Convair Model 37, the Lockheed Model 89 Constitution was created with more than just a casual glance ahead to postwar commercial applications. Indeed, though the big, double-decked aircraft had been ordered by the Navy, Lockheed and the Navy engineers were rubbing shoulders at Burbank with their opposite numbers from Pan American Airways as the big thing took form in 1942. Although its wingspan was 41 feet less than the X-99, it was 66 feet greater than that of a Constellation or Super Constellation. The first of just two Constitutions made its debut flight on November 9, 1946. Each flew with four water-injected Pratt & Whitney R-4360-22Ws, and the Constitutions operated with the US Navy until 1953. There was to be no airline order.

This Fairchild C-119G Flying Boxcar of the 817th Troop Carrier Squadron is returning to its home base at Ashiya Air Base in Japan after a 15-day temporary duty assignment at Kadena Air Base on Okinawa in March 1955. (Photo Courtesy Tequask, Licensed under Creative Commons)

The Douglas Aircraft Company had better postwar large transport marketing success than either Convair or Lockheed. Its Globemaster family of four-engine transports began with the C-74 Globemaster I and continued with the C-124 Globemaster II, both of which used the R-4360 Wasp Major. The C-17 Globemaster III was an F117-PW-100 turbofan-powered transport that would appear half a century in the future.

The Douglas C-74 was a contemporary of the Boeing C-97 (both were developed during World War II) but never saw wartime action. The first of 14 C-74s made its debut flight on September 5, 1945, powered by four R-4360-27s. With a wingspan of 173 feet, the Globemaster I was then the largest landplane to be produced in quantity, and they remained in service with the US Air Force even as the Globemaster II arrived on the scene.

The C-124 Globemaster II had roughly the same overall dimensions as the C-74, but its big double-deck fuselage enclosed a larger volume. The YC-124, a heavily modified C-74, made its first flight on November 27, 1949, with four R-4360-49s, an engine with which the C-74s had been re-engined. The first production C-124As, powered by R-4360-20WAs, were in service with the US Air Force when the Korean War began in June 1950.

Douglas delivered 204 C-124As and 243 C-124Cs, with the single YC-124B being an experiment with a Pratt & Whitney YT34-P-6 turboprop engine similar to that which would later be used for the Douglas C-133 Cargomaster. The C-124C, which remained in production until May 1955, was powered by four R-4360-63A Wasp Majors.

Fairchild Aircraft also used the R-4360 for its twin-engine C-119 Flying Boxcar, which first flew in November 1947 as the XC-119A with R-4360-20 engines. This aircraft was developed after World War II to address structural and performance issues that cropped up in the company's earlier C-82 Packet. Considered underpowered, the C-82 had used a pair of Pratt & Whitney R-2800-85s.

For the US Air Force, Fairchild built 55 C-119Bs with either

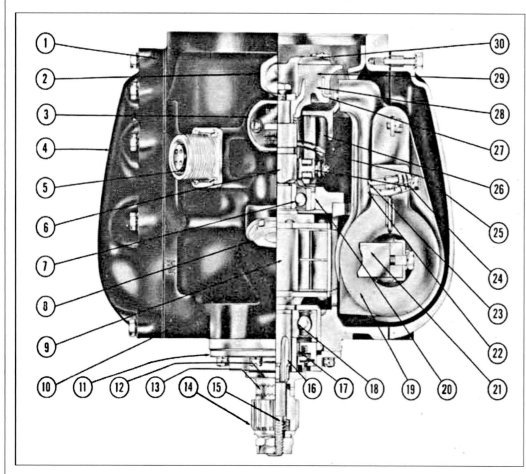

This is a sectional view of a magneto in a Pratt & Whitney R-4360 Wasp Major engine.

1. Coil Cover Gasket
2. Altitude Valve
3. Cam Identification Plate
4. Coil Cover
5. Ground Wire Terminal
6. Breaker Cam
7. Upper Magnet Ball Bearing
8. Condenser
9. Rotating Magnet
10. Magneto Housing
11. Ball Bearing Retainer
12. Lapped Washer
13. Timing Ratchet
14. Drive Coupling
15. Timing Ratchet Spring
16. Driveshaft Sleeve
17. Oil Seal
18. Lower Magnet Ball Bearing
19. Coil
20. Breaker Plate
21. Pole Shoe
22. Coil to Condenser Lead
23. Coil to Ground Wire Terminal lead
24. Cam Follower
25. Breaker to Condenser Lead
26. Distributor Insulating Cup
27. Coil High Tension Electrode
28. Distributor Finger Pick-Up Segment
29. Distributor Finger
30. Distributor Finger Segment

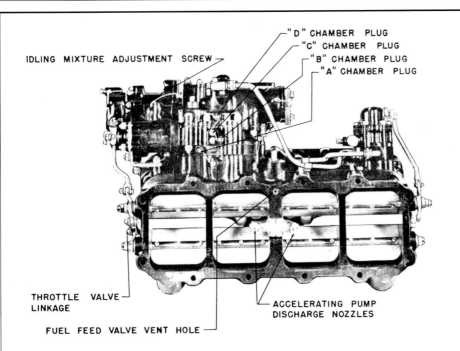

"D" CHAMBER PLUG
"C" CHAMBER PLUG
"B" CHAMBER PLUG
"A" CHAMBER PLUG

IDLING MIXTURE ADJUSTMENT SCREW

THROTTLE VALVE LINKAGE

FUEL FEED VALVE VENT HOLE

ACCELERATING PUMP DISCHARGE NOZZLES

Bottom View of Carburetor

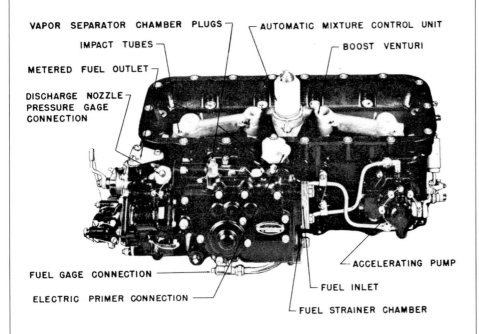

VAPOR SEPARATOR CHAMBER PLUGS
IMPACT TUBES
METERED FUEL OUTLET
DISCHARGE NOZZLE PRESSURE GAGE CONNECTION

AUTOMATIC MIXTURE CONTROL UNIT
BOOST VENTURI

FUEL GAGE CONNECTION
ELECTRIC PRIMER CONNECTION

ACCELERATING PUMP
FUEL INLET
FUEL STRAINER CHAMBER

Top View of Carburetor

These are some details of the Bendix-Stromberg PR-100 B-series carburetor that was used in many variants of the Pratt & Whitney R-4360 Wasp Major engine.

R-4360-20 or R-4360-20W engines. These were followed by 303 C-119Cs for the Air Force and 39 similar R4Q-1s for the US Marine Corps.

One of the C-119Bs was converted as a demonstrator for the concept of the aircraft having a removable cargo pod instead of a fuselage that would be filled with cargo. This modular approach, which became common in the rail and ground trucking industry in later years, seemed like a good idea, but only one such demonstrator was built. This aircraft, redesignated as XC-120 and named "Packplane," was widely tested and widely displayed at air shows, but the idea was abandoned.

The next Flying Boxcar production variant abandoned the Pratt & Whitney Wasp Major for Wright's Duplex Cyclone. Of these, there were 58 R4Q-2s with R-3350-35Ws for the Marines, 141 C-119Fs with R-3350-85s for the US Air Force, and 39 with R-3350-85s for the Royal Canadian Air Force. These were followed by an additional 480 aircraft that were redesignated as C-119G because they used substituted Aeroproducts propellers for the Hamilton Standard props used on the C-119Fs.

There actually was a combat variant of the Flying Boxcar. During the Vietnam War, 26 C-119Gs were retrofitted as ground attack gunships with four 7.62-mm waist guns. Redesignated as AC-119Gs, they were given the name "Shadow." The AC-119G Shadow gunships were later modified again, this time with the addition of two 20-mm cannons and a pair of General Electric J85-GE-17 underwing jet engine pods. They were then redesignated as AC-119K and named "Stinger."

Howard Hughes:
His Airplanes and Their R-4360s

Howard Hughes was the Elon Musk of his day: unconventional, brilliant, in the news, and very, very wealthy. Although he has gradually faded from his one-time household-word prominence in popular culture during recent years, his name still conjures up the image of the archetypical eccentric and reclusive billionaire. Indeed, he *was* at one time the world's richest man, and his private life, by all accounts of those who actually knew the details, was nearly as strange as it is described in urban legend.

Hughes started out with inherited wealth. Early in the 20th century, just as the American oil industry started to take off, his father, Howard Hughes, Sr., had invented an oil-drilling bit that revolutionized petroleum extraction and made him rich. In fact, the current successor company to the Hughes Tool Company (ToolCo), the Baker-Hughes Company, is still a world leader in the petroleum services industry.

The younger Howard added to his bequeathed fortune through shrewd business transactions, real estate dealing, and through what for others might be considered hobbies. In the 1920s, he became a Hollywood producer of Academy Award–winning movies. In the 1940s, he gradually took control of RKO Pictures, one of the "Big Five" Hollywood Studios. At one time, he owned more Las Vegas casinos than anyone.

Hughes was also a genuine aviation legend. In the 1930s, he earned the Collier Trophy and the Harmon Trophy (twice). He set records flying around the world in 1938 and designed the H-1 race

that put more trophies in his case. He took a controlling interest in Transcontinental and Western Airlines (TWA), later TransWorld Airlines (also TWA), and was the catalyst for TWA becoming the "launch customer" for the Lockheed Constellation.

He founded two often-confused aircraft companies. One was the Aircraft Division of the Hughes Tool Company, which made aircraft and eventually became Hughes Helicopters in 1976. The other was the postwar Hughes Aircraft Company, which made guided missiles and eventually spacecraft and a broad range of electronic and communications systems.

Hughes himself had little to do with the latter, but he used the former almost as Elon Musk uses SpaceX, albeit on a less-grandiose scale than Musk.

Operating from its plant in Culver City, California, the Hughes Tool Company Aircraft Division was one of the largest producers of flexible-feed ammunition chutes for aircraft in the USAAF supply chain during World War II. From ToolCo's Aircraft Division there also came two aircraft types that used the Pratt & Whitney Wasp Major. First was the Hughes XF-11 reconnaissance aircraft for the USAAF. Second was the Hughes H-4 Hercules, which has its small but prominent place in aviation history as the infamous "Spruce Goose."

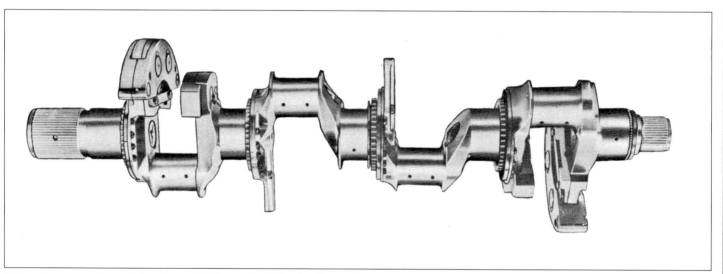

This is the crankshaft of the Pratt & Whitney R-4360 28-cylinder, four-row Wasp Major engine. The one-piece crankshaft was dynamically balanced and had four crankpins and five supporting bearing journals. The center journal had flanged ends that locate the crankshaft axially. Each crankpin was angularly positioned 192.857 degrees clockwise around the longitudinal axis of the shaft with reference to the crankpin behind it. The hollow crankshaft was fitted with plugs and tubes for conducting pressurized oil to the master rod bearings and crankshaft bearings. Nozzle-type oil slingers and small drilled holes adjacent to the crankpins provide oil squirts for improved cylinder wall lubrication. The accessory driveshaft coupling was splined into the rear end of the crankshaft and anchored to the crankshaft rear plug.

The twin-engine XF-11 was, along with the four-engine Republic XF-12 Rainbow, part of a 1943 USAAF effort to develop purpose-built, high-altitude reconnaissance aircraft. Until then, all of the "F for Photographic" aircraft in the USAAF inventory were adapted from existing bombers or fighters.

Both the XF-11 and XF-12 were powered by the R-4360-31 Wasp Major. It was rated at 3,000 hp at 2,700 rpm for takeoff and had a military rating of 3,000 hp at 2,700 rpm at 40,000 feet with the turbosupercharger. It had a compression ratio of 7:1. The R-4360-31 used a Bendix PR-100-B3-3 carburetor. The engine weighed 3,526 pounds with torquemeter installed. It was 114.25 inches long with a diameter of 52.5 inches. In the XF-11, the first prototype was fitted with contra-rotating propellers. Hughes used the General Electric BH-1 Model C3 or C4 turbosuperchargers for the R-4360s installed in the XF-11 aircraft.

An order for 100 production F-11s was issued but later canceled as neither it nor the XF-12 was available before the end of World War II. Only

With Howard Hughes himself at the controls, the Hughes H-4 taxis into San Pedro Bay for its first and only flight, which was on November 2, 1947. It was powered by eight Pratt & Whitney R-4360-4A Duplex Cyclones. At the time, it was the largest aircraft ever built, and until the 2019 first flight of the Scaled Composites Strato-launch, it had the broadest wingspan of any aircraft yet flown. (Photo Courtesy Federal Aviation Administration)

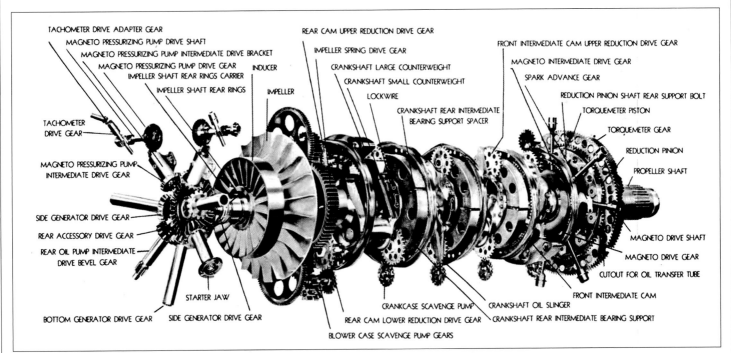

This is the geartrain assembly for the TSB3-G commercial variant of the Pratt & Whitney R-4360 Wasp Major engine.

two of each were built, with the XF-12 becoming the first to fly on February 4, 1946. Howard Hughes himself piloted the first flight in his XF-11, taking off from the ToolCo plant in Culver City on July 7, 1946. He was over Beverly Hills when the rear propeller on the starboard engine went into reverse pitch, subtly increasing drag and resulting in a nearly fatal crash. The extensive injuries suffered by Hughes led to a long convalescence, and ultimately to an addiction to pain medication that was with him for the rest of his life.

The eight-engine flying machine known as the "Spruce Goose" is perhaps the signature aircraft of Howard Hughes, though he despised this term. (It is made of birch, not spruce.) It remains the largest flying boat ever built, and its 321-foot wingspan was not exceeded by a landplane until the debut of the Scaled Composites Model 351 Stratolaunch with its 385-foot span in 2019.

The idea originated with California industrialist and builder Henry J. Kaiser, who built the Hoover Dam, as well as more than 500 ships during World War II. In 1942, dismayed by the losses to German U-Boats in the North Atlantic, Kaiser suggested that huge transport aircraft be built to fly *over* these dangerous waters.

Kaiser may have been churning out dozens of Liberty ships at his California shipyards, but he had no credibility in aviation, so the US Navy and the USAAF rejected his idea. Howard Hughes, meanwhile, liked the concept and entered into a partnership with Kaiser to build them. With an $18 million contract from the government Defense Plant Corporation, work began on three HK-1 Hercules prototype flying boats in Culver City.

The military services, still skeptical of the idea, insisted that the big aircraft not be made of war-critical materials, so Hughes turned to the Duramold process. This involved building structural components of thin plies of birch or poplar, impregnated with phenolic resin and laminated to form a material that is lighter than aluminum and at least as strong.

Power for the H-4 was supplied by eight R-4360-4As of the type that Hughes had originally specified for his XF-11 before going to the R-4360-31. The R-4360-4A was rated at 3,000 hp at 2,700 rpm for takeoff and had a military rating of 2,400 hp at 2,700 rpm at 13,500 feet. It had a compression ratio of 7:1 and used a Bendix PR-100-B3-3 carburetor. The R-4360-4A weighed 3,390 pounds, exclusive of the 20-pound torquemeter. It was 96.75 inches long with a diameter of 52.5 inches.

With Hughes in control of the project, Kaiser dropped out, and the Hercules was redesignated as the HFB-1 (Hughes Flying Boat) and

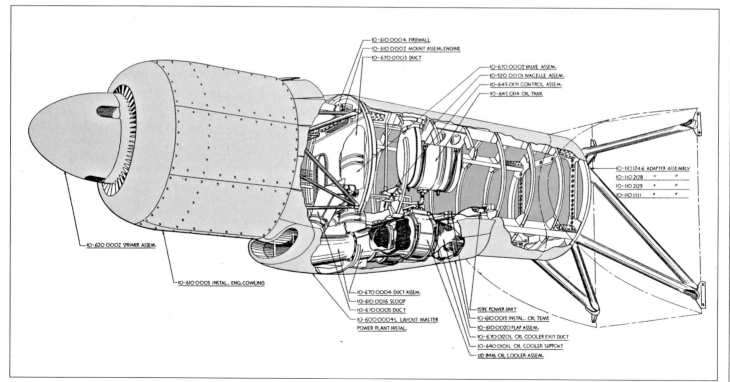

A cutaway view of a Pratt & Whitney R-4360-4A shows the engine in its nacelle as installed in the Hughes H-4 Hercules flying boat.

later as the Hughes H-4. The number to be built was reduced to just one. Constructed in Culver City, it was trucked to Long Beach in eight major sections in June 1946 for final assembly and flight testing.

After the war, the program, with its big never-flown prototype, came under the scrutiny of the Senate Special Committee to Investigate the National Defense Program. Originally chaired by Senator Harry Truman (before he became vice president and then president), the committee was looking into waste, inefficiency, and war profiteering. Hughes himself was called on the carpet in August 1947 for an $18 million program that failed to produce

a flying aircraft—although he had spent $17 million of his own money on it.

Hughes returned to California and ordered the H-4 to be readied for taxi tests. On November 2, 1947, with Hughes as the only pilot on the flight deck, the H-4 taxied into San Pedro Bay. Much to the surprise of the other 35 people aboard (Hughes's employees, invited guests, and reporters) Hughes accelerated to takeoff speed, climbed to about 70 feet, and flew for about a mile before touching down. He had proven that the H-4 could fly.

Hughes ordered the aircraft to be stored in a specially built, climate-controlled building to await a second flight that never came. After his death in 1976, his Summa Corporation holding company bought out full ownership of the H-4 from the federal government, which still claimed an interest in it. In 1980, it was acquired by the Aero Club of Southern California, which displayed it within a large dome in Long Beach Harbor until 1991, when the site was acquired by the Walt Disney Company and repurposed.

In 1992, the Aero Club was approached by Delford Smith, the founder of the Oregon-based, multi-faceted aviation holding company called Evergreen International Aviation, and his son, Air Force veteran Michael King Smith. They wanted to buy the H-4 from the Aero Club with installment payments and move it to Oregon.

To facilitate the negotiations, Del Smith brought aboard an aviation legend as the chairman of his museum in planning. Jack Garrett Real was a former Lockheed engineer and executive, who had served as personal aviation advisor to Howard Hughes from 1971 until Hughes died in 1976. Real then became president of Hughes Helicopters (McDonnell Douglas Helicopters after 1984), where he earned a Collier Trophy for his work on the AH-64 Apache helicopter program.

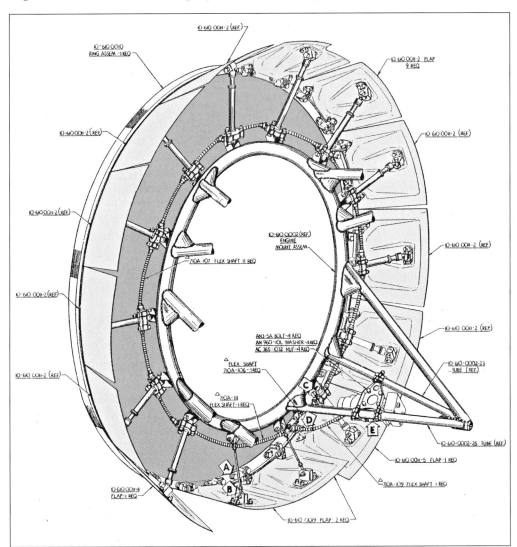

The engine cowling flap installation is shown for each of the eight Pratt & Whitney R-4360-4A engines installed in the Hughes H-4 Hercules flying boat.

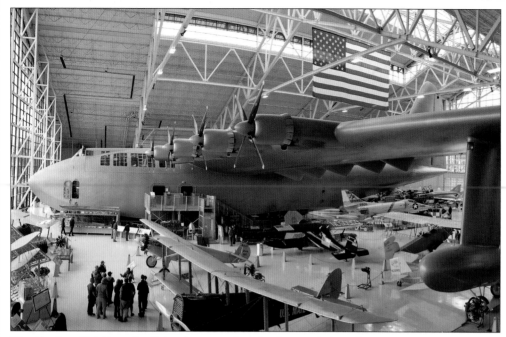

The Hughes H-4 Hercules flying boat was on display in 2019 at the Evergreen Aviation and Space Museum in McMinnville, Oregon. (Bill Yenne Photo)

The Pratt & Whitney R-4360-4A engines are shown installed on the left wing of the Hughes H-4 Hercules flying boat as displayed at the Evergreen Aviation and Space Museum in McMinnville, Oregon. (Bill Yenne Photo)

During the 1990s, I got to know Real quite well. I coauthored his autobiography and spent many hours with him in Oregon, but mainly in California, where both of us lived, discussing Hughes and looking through H-4 memorabilia he had collected. We also spent time poking around inside the H-4 itself and on the back roads of Yamhill County, Oregon, where Evergreen managed around 8,000 acres of agricultural land. It was here, in a metal barn amid the hazelnut trees that I first got my hands dirty examining the eight R-4360-4As with which the H-4 was equipped when Hughes put it into storage six decades earlier. Real left the company in 2001, the year that the museum was completed, and the H-4 finally went on display. He passed away in 2005.

As befitting the Hughes legacy, another twist in the story was to come. Although they were shared with me by Jack Real, the details of the agreement between Evergreen and the Aero Club were never fully disclosed publicly, and there was a widely held assumption that Evergreen owned the H-4 outright. The facts did not see the light of day until Evergreen International Aviation was tumbling into bankruptcy in late 2013. For an article published on December 11, 2013, Richard Read of Portland's *Oregonian* interviewed Museum director Larry Wood and Robert Lyon, an attorney for the Aero Club, to pull back the curtain of mystery.

Lyon told Read that Del Smith had "personally guaranteed a promissory note in 1992 backing purchase of the Spruce Goose. He said Evergreen recently made the last of 240 monthly payments—over 20 years—that totaled $500,000 for the plane."

Read went on to add that "the Aero Club is still due at least $50,000—a per-

Powered by a Pratt & Whitney R-4360-63, the Dreadnought is a Hawker T.20 Sea Fury that was built by the late Frank Sanders and sons Brian and Dennis. Dreadnought has taken home the Gold in the Unlimited Class at the National Championship Air Races several times, including 2018, 2019, and 2021. Dennis Sanders himself was at the controls in 2019 with a speed of 403.274 mph. (Photo Courtesy Tataquax, Licensed under Creative Commons)

centage of the museum's earnings, per the sales agreement—before ownership can be transferred to Evergreen through a complex stock-swap scheme."

"Who wrote the checks for the $500,000?" Read queried.

"Interesting you should ask," Lyon said. "They came from Evergreen Aviation [rather than from the museum]. Wood had previously explained to Read that the foundation that owned the museum was "entirely separate" from Evergreen International. Wood said that he had assured "anyone who asks that the museum owns the Spruce Goose free and clear. . . When I took this job in 2010, I didn't know anybody owed any money on it. I found out when I met Mr. Lyon in California at a meeting. I said, 'What?'"

By 2015, Evergreen International Aviation was gone and Del Smith himself had passed away. Many of the aircraft in the museum

A sense of the scale of the R-4360-4A engines and the nacelles of Hughes H-4 Hercules is revealed in this photograph of the author standing among them in September 2000. From 1993 until 2001, the engines and nacelles were in storage here in a metal barn in the midst of a hazelnut orchard in Yamhill County, Oregon. (Bill Yenne Photo Collection)

collection had been sold to satisfy museum debts, but the H-4 remained, and Robert Lyon told the Associated Press that an agreement had been reached for the museum "to take full ownership of the plane." The AP report added that "the details of the agreement were not disclosed."

The R-4360 Legacy

The R-4360, like the Spruce Goose, became a museum piece. In addition to being installed in displayed aircraft like the Hughes flying boat, more than two dozen of them are prominently displayed at museums around the United States and the world, where they may be seen up close.

But the R-4360 is not *only* a static artifact. Through the later decades of the 20th century and into the 21st, there are still KC-97s flying with them, and they have had a second life on the air race circuit. R-4360-powered former warbirds have been a fixture at Unlimited Class races, such as the National Championship Air Races at Reno, Nevada, for decades.

In Chapter 10, we introduced the Grumman F8F Bearcat, factory-equipped with Pratt & Whitney R-2800 Double Wasps, adding that the aircraft was later reborn as a racer. We highlighted Lyle Shelton's *Rare Bear*, which set a long-standing World Unlimited Class Speed Record of 528.33 mph in 1989. *Rare Bear* was still competing into the 21st century and remains one of the best known racers ever.

Among other Unlimited Class R-4360 racers have been Steve Hinton's famous F4U called *Super Corsair* and Lloyd Hamilton's Hawker Sea Fury known as *Furias*.

Of special note in the second decade of the 21st century is the R-4360-powered *Dreadnought*, a Hawker Sea Fury rebuilt with a Wasp Major by Frank Sanders and his sons Brian and Dennis and flown since the early 1980s. The *Dreadnaught* story is ongoing and thus is hard to summarize in a book such as this, but the aircraft was certainly on our minds as we were finishing this project. With its R-4360, the *Dreadnought* had just captured the Unlimited Class Gold at Reno in 2018, 2019, and 2021.

BIBLIOGRAPHY

Andrade, John. *US Military Aircraft Designations and Serials since 1909*. Hinckley, UK: Midland Counties Publications, 1979.

Armbruster, G.E. *History of the R-4360*. East Hartford, Connecticut: Pratt & Whitney, 1946.

Beatty, Lee M., *The Wright Whirlwind Engine Production Methods*. Warrendale, Pennsylvania: SAE Journal, 1927.

Bendix Corporation. *Instructions on Stromberg PD-12F8 and PD-12F12 Injection Carburetors*. Detroit: Bendix Corporation, 1945.

Boeing Historical Archives. *Pedigree of Champions: Boeing since 1916*. Seattle: Boeing Historical Archives, 1985.

Bowers, Peter M. and Gordon Swanborough. *United States Military Aircraft Since 1909*. Washington, DC: Smithsonian Institution Press, 1989.

Bowers, Peter M. *Boeing Aircraft Since 1916*. Annapolis: Naval Institute Press, 1989.

Buick Motor Division. *Instruction Manual, Pratt & Whitney Engines R1830-43 & -65 As Used in Consolidated-Vultee Liberators*. Detroit: Buick Motor Division, General Motors Corporation, 1943.

Buick Motor Division. *Parts Reference List, Pratt & Whitney Engines R1830-43 & -65*. Buick Motor Division, General Motors Corporation, 1944.

Champion, Lt. C.C. Jr., USN. *Recent Development in Aircraft Powerplants*. Warrendale, Pennsylvania: SAE Journal 1927.

Curtiss Wright Corporation. *Historical Engine Summary (Beginning 1930)*. Patterson, New Jersey: Curtiss Wright Corporation, 1983.

DeHaven, Ethel. *Case History of the VDT Engine*. Wright-Patterson AFB: Executive Secretariat of the Air Materiel Command, 1949.

Francillon, Rene. *Grumman Aircraft since 1929*. Annapolis: Naval Institute Press, 1989.

Francillon, Rene. *Lockheed Aircraft since 1913*. Annapolis: Naval Institute Press, 1982, 1989.

Francillon, Rene. *McDonnell Douglas Aircraft since 1920: Volume I*. Annapolis: Naval Institute Press, 1979, 1988.

Francillon, Rene. *McDonnell Douglas Aircraft since 1920: Volume II*. Annapolis: Naval Institute Press, 1979, 1990.

General Motors War Products Training Service. *Training Manual Model R-1830-43 Pratt and Whitney Aviation Engine*. Detroit: Chevrolet Motor Division, General Motors Corporation, 1943.

Green, William. *Famous Bombers of World War II, Volume Two*. Garden City, NY: Doubleday & Company, 1960.

Green, William. *Famous Bombers of World War II*. Garden City, NY: Hanover House, 1959.

Green, William. *Famous Fighters of World War II*. Garden City, NY: Hanover House, 1960.

Gunston, Bill. *Piston Aero Engines*. Sparkford, UK: Patrick Stephens Ltd., 1993.

Gunston, Bill. *The World Encyclopaedia of Aero Engines*. Sparkford, UK: Patrick Stephens Ltd., 1995.

Gunston, Bill. *The World Encyclopedia of Aero Engines: From the Pioneers to the Present Day. 5th edition*. Stroud, UK: Sutton, 2006.

Hagedorn, Dan. *North American NA-16/AT-6/SNJ*. North Branch, MN: Specialty Press, 1997.

Heron, S. D. *History of the Aircraft Piston Engine, a Brief Outline*. Detroit: Ethyl Corporation, 1961.

Hobbs, Leonard S. *The Wright Brothers' Engines and Their Design*. Washington, D.C.: Smithsonian Institution Press, 1971

Holley, Irving Brinton, Jr. *Buying Aircraft: Materiel Procurement for the Army Air Forces*. Washington, DC: Center of Military History, US Army, 1964.

Jacobsen, Meyers K. *Convair B-36: A Comprehensive History of America's "Big Stick."* Atglen, Pennsylvania: Schiffer Military History, 1997.

Jones, E. T. *The Development of the Wright Whirlwind Type J-5 Aircraft Engine*. Warrendale, Pennsylvania: SAE Journal, 1926.

Lawrance, Charles L. *Air-cooled Engine Development*. Warrendale, Pennsylvania: SAE Journal, 1922.

Materiel Command, USAAF. *Handbook of Overhaul Instructions for the Model R-2600-11 Engine and Associated Models*. Wright Field, Ohio: USAAF Materiel Command, 1942.

Materiel Command, USAAF. *Manual 02-35JA-3 Overhaul Instructions R-3350-18, -19, -21, -23, -23A, -35A, -41, -57, -59 Aircraft Engines*. Wright Field, Ohio: USAAF Materiel Command, 1945.

Materiel Command, USAAF. *Manual 03-10BF-1 Handbook of Instructions with Parts Catalog Hydro-Metering Carburetor Model 58CPB-4*. Wright Field, Ohio: USAAF Materiel Command, 1944.

Materiel Command, USAAF. *Manual Air Depot Progressive Overhaul Manual, Pratt & Whitney R-1340-AN1 Engine*. Wright Field, Ohio: USAAF Materiel Command, 1943.

Materiel Command, USAAF. *Manual AN 02-10CD-3 Overhaul Instructions for Aircraft Engines Models R-1830-33, -41, -43, -43A, -55, -61, -63, -65, -65A, -67, -90, -90B and -90C*. Wright Field, Ohio: USAAF Materiel Command, 1944.

Materiel Command, USAAF. *Manual AN 02-10GD-4 Parts Catalog for Aircraft Engines Model R-2800-18W*. Wright Field, Ohio: USAAF Materiel Command, 1945.

Materiel Command, USAAF. *Manual AN 02-35GD-2 Service Instructions for Aircraft Engines Models R-1820-56, -56W, -56WA, -62, -62A, -66, -72W, -72WA, -74W, -76*. Wright Field, Ohio: USAAF Materiel Command, 1946

Materiel Command, USAAF. *Manual AN 02-35JA-2 Service Instructions R-3350-13, -18, -19, -21, -23, -35, -41 Aircraft Engines*. Wright Field, Ohio: USAAF Materiel Command, 1944.

Materiel Command, USAAF. *Manual AN 02-35JA-2 Service Instructions R-3350-23, 23A, 35A, 57, 57A, 59, 59A*. Wright Field, Ohio: USAAF Materiel Command, 1945.

Materiel Command, USAAF. *Manual AN 02-35JA-3 Overhaul Instructions R-3350-13, -18, -21, -23, -33, -35 Aircraft Engines*. Wright Field, Ohio: USAAF Materiel Command, 1943.

Materiel Command, USAAF. *Manual AN 02-35JA-4 Parts Catalog for Aircraft Engines R3350-13, -21, -23, -23DW, -23A, -35, and -37*. Wright Field, Ohio: USAAF Materiel Command, 1944.

Materiel Command, USAAF. *Manual AN 02-35JA-4 Parts Catalog for Aircraft Engines R3350-13, -21, -23, -23DW, -23A, -35, and -37*. Wright Field, Ohio: USAAF Materiel Command, 1944, 1945.

Materiel Command, USAAF. *Manual AN 02-35JB-2 Handbook of Service Instructions for Aircraft Engines Models R-3350-8, -14, -24*. Wright Field, Ohio: USAAF Materiel Command, 1945.

Materiel Command, USAAF. *Manual AN 02A-10FC-3 (TO2R-R2000-23) Handbook Overhaul Instructions R-2000-4 Aircraft Engines*. Wright Field, Ohio: USAAF Materiel Command, 1950.

Materiel Command, USAAF. *Manual AN 03-10CA-1 Operation, Service, and Overhaul Instructions with Parts Catalog for Direct Fuel Injection System Models*. Wright Field, Ohio: USAAF Materiel Command, 1945.

Materiel Command, USAAF. *Manual AN 03-10CB-1 Operation, Service, and Overhaul Instructions with Parts Catalog for Gasoline Injection System Model 58-18-A2B*. Wright Field, Ohio: USAAF. Materiel Command, 1946.

Materiel Command, USAAF. *Manual TO No. 02-10CB-2 Service Instructions R-1830 Series Aircraft Engines*. 1942, 1943.

Materiel Command, USAAF. *Manual TO02-35HA-1 Handbook of Operation and Flight Instructions for the Model R-2600-11 Engine and Associated Models*. Wright Field, Ohio: USAAF, 1942.

Materiel Command, USAAF. *Manual TO2R-R2800-3 Handbook, Overhaul Instructions Models R-2800-27, -75, -79 Aircraft Engines*. Wright Field, Ohio: USAAF Materiel Command, 1949.

Materiel Command, USAAF. *Manual TO2R-R2800-43 Handbook, Overhaul Instructions Models R-2800-50, -52W, -54, -99W, -103W Aircraft Engines. AN 02A-10GH-3*. Wright Field, Ohio: USAAF Materiel Command, 1951.

Materiel Command, USAAF. *Manual TO2R-R2800-5 Overhaul Changes Appli-*

cable to Pratt & Whitney R-2800 Series Engines. Wright Field, Ohio: USAAF Materiel Command, 1953.

McFarland, Marvin W. (ed). *The Papers of Wilbur and Orville Wright.* New York: McGraw-Hill, 1953.

Mead, George J. *Some Aspects of Aircraft-Engine Development.* Warrendale, Pennsylvania: SAE Journal 1925.

Merkely, W.O. *The Variable Discharge Turbosupercharger (VDT).* Schenectady, New York: General Electric Company, 1947.

Page, Victor W. *Modern Aircraft.* New York: Norman W. Henley, 1928.

Pratt & Whitney. *Engine Parts List for Pratt & Whitney Engines Wasp Series A, B, C, Hornet Series A, A-1.* East Hartford, Connecticut: Pratt & Whitney, 1929.

Pratt & Whitney. *Engine Parts List for Pratt & Whitney Engines Wasp Series C, C-1, D-1, Wasp Junior Series A, Hornet Series A-1, A-2, B, B-1, C, C-1.* East Hartford, Connecticut: Pratt & Whitney, 1933.

Pratt & Whitney. *Engine Parts List for Pratt & Whitney Engines Wasp Series C, C-1, D-1, Wasp Junior Series A, B, Hornet Series A-2, B, B-1, C, C-1, D-1.* East Hartford, Connecticut: Pratt & Whitney, 1936.

Pratt & Whitney. *Maintenance Manual Wasp Major (R-4360) TSB3G and VSB11G Engines.* East Hartford, Connecticut: Pratt & Whitney, 1947.

Pratt & Whitney. *Maintenance Manual, Double Wasp (R-2800) CA Engines.* East Hartford, Connecticut: Pratt & Whitney, 1949.

Pratt & Whitney. *Maintenance Manual, Twin Wasp (R-1830) S1C3-G Engines.* East Hartford, Connecticut: Pratt & Whitney, 1946.

Pratt & Whitney. *Overhaul Manual Double Wasp (R-2800) CA Engines.* East Hartford, Connecticut: Pratt & Whitney, 1948.

Pratt & Whitney. *Overhaul Manual Double Wasp A and B Series Single Stage Engines (R-2800-5, -6, -21, -27, -31, -35, -39, -41, -43, -47, and -51).* East Hartford, Connecticut: Pratt & Whitney, 1943.

Pratt & Whitney. *Overhaul Manual Double Wasp B Series Engines (With Two-Stage Supercharger) First Edition.* East Hartford, Connecticut: Pratt & Whitney, 1942.

Pratt & Whitney. *Parts Catalog Double Wasp CA3, CA15, CA18, CB3, CB16 & CB17 Engines.* Pratt & Whitney, 1952.

Pratt & Whitney. *Pratt & Whitney Engines Disassembly Inspection Reassembly of R-1830-43 Engines; Shown in Complete Pictorial Form.* East Hartford, Connecticut: Pratt & Whitney, 1946

Pratt & Whitney. *Service Instructions R-1830-75 and -98.* East Hartford, Connecticut: Pratt & Whitney, 1945.

Pratt & Whitney. *The Aircraft Engine and its Operation; Installation Engineering.* East Hartford, Connecticut: Pratt & Whitney, 1952.

Pratt & Whitney. *The Pratt & Whitney Aircraft Story.* East Hartford, Connecticut: Pratt & Whitney, 1950.

Pratt & Whitney. *The Pratt & Whitney Aircraft Story.* Pratt & Whitney Division of United Aircraft Corporation, East Hartford, Connecticut, 1950.

Pratt & Whitney. *Twin Wasp (R-1830) C-Series Engines Overhaul Manual.* East Hartford, Connecticut: Pratt & Whitney Group, 1952.

Pratt & Whitney. *Twin Wasp 2SD1G R-2000-9 Engines.* East Hartford, Connecticut: Pratt & Whitney, 1947.

Pratt & Whitney. *Twin Wasp C3 and C4 Engines (R-1830-33, -42, -43, -45, -47, -49, -51, -53, -57, -61, -63, -65, -67, -82, -90, -90B, and -92).* East Hartford, Connecticut: Pratt & Whitney, 1944.

Pratt & Whitney. *Twin Wasp C3 Series Engines.* East Hartford, Connecticut: Pratt & Whitney, 1942.

Pratt & Whitney. *Twin Wasp C4 Series Engines.* East Hartford, Connecticut: Pratt & Whitney, 1942.

Pratt & Whitney. *Twin Wasp C7 Series Engines.* East Hartford, Connecticut: Pratt & Whitney, 1943.

Pratt & Whitney. *Twin Wasp C-Series Engines.* East Hartford, Connecticut: Pratt & Whitney, 1941.

Schlaifer, Robert, and S.D. Heron. *Development of Aircraft Engines and Fuels.* Boston: Graduate School of Business Administration, Harvard University, 1950.

Smith, Herschel. *A History of Aircraft Piston Engines.* Manhattan, Kansas: Sunflower University Press, 1986, 1993.

US Navy. *NavAer 02-10CW-3, Twin Wasp C3 and C4 Engines (R-1830-33, -41, -43, -45, -47, -49, -51, -53, -57, -61, -63, -65, -67, -82, -90, -90B and -92) First Edition.* Washington, DC: US Navy, 1943.

Wagner, Ray. *American Combat Planes, Third Enlarged Edition.* New York: Doubleday, 1982.

War Department. *TM1-405. Technical Manual of Aircraft Engines.* Washington, DC: War Department, 1941.

Wegg, John. *General Dynamics Aircraft and their Predecessors.* Annapolis: Naval Institute Press, 1990.

White, Graham. *Allied Aircraft Piston Engines of World War II.* Warrendale, Pennsylvania: SAE International, 1995.

White, Graham. *Allied Aircraft Piston Engines of World War II: History and Development of Frontline Aircraft Piston Engines Produced by Great Britain and the United States During World War II.* Warrendale, Pennsylvania: SAE International, 1995.

White, Graham. *R-2800: Pratt & Whitney's Dependable Masterpiece.* Shrewsbury, UK: Airlife Publishing, 2002.

White, Graham. *R-4360: Pratt & Whitney's Major Miracle.* North Branch, MN: Specialty Press, 2006.

Wilkinson, Paul H. *Aircraft Engines of the World.* London: Sir Isaac Pitman & Sons, 1946.

Wilson, Commander E. E., *U.S.N. Air-cooled Engines in Naval Aircraft.* Warrendale, Pennsylvania: SAE Journal, 1926.

Wright Aeronautical Corporation. *Instructions for the Installation, Inspection, and Maintenance of the New Wright Whirlwind Nine, Wright Whirlwind Seven, Wright Whirlwind Five Aviation Engines.* Patterson, New Jersey: Wright Aeronautical Corporation, 1930.

Wright Aeronautical Corporation. *Instructions for the Installation, Inspection, and Maintenance of the New Wright Whirlwind Nine, Wright Whirlwind Seven, Wright Whirlwind Five Aviation Engines.* Patterson, New Jersey: Wright Aeronautical Corporation, 1929.

Wright Aeronautical Corporation. *Instructions for the Installation, Inspection and Maintenance of the Wright Cyclone Aviation Engine Models R-1820-F and GR-1820-F. Wright Aeronautical Corporation.* Patterson, New Jersey: Wright Aeronautical Corporation, 1933.

Wright Aeronautical Corporation. *Instructions for the Installation, Inspection and Maintenance of the Wright Whirlwind Aviation Engine Models J-5A (A Series) J-5B (A Series) J-5A (B Series).* Patterson, New Jersey: Wright Aeronautical Corporation, 1929.

Wright Aeronautical Corporation. *Lubrication and Fuel Requirements of Aircraft Engines.* Patterson, New Jersey: Wright Aeronautical Corporation, 1930.

Wright Aeronautical Corporation. *Operation and Service Manual Wright Cyclone 9 Aircraft Engines Series C9GA, C9GB, C9GC.* Patterson, New Jersey: Wright Aeronautical Corporation, 1943.

Wright Aeronautical Corporation. *Overhaul Manual Wright Cyclone 14 Aircraft Engines Series A.* Patterson, New Jersey: Wright Aeronautical Corporation, 1943.

Wright Aeronautical Corporation. *Parts Catalog for Wright Whirlwind Engines Model J-5.* Patterson, New Jersey: Wright Aeronautical Corporation, 1928.

Wright Aeronautical Corporation. *Parts Reference Charts, Wright Aircraft Engines Cyclone 14BA.* Patterson, New Jersey: Wright Aeronautical Corporation, 1944.

Wright Aeronautical Corporation. *Parts Reference Charts, Wright Aircraft Engines Cyclone 18BA.* Wright Aeronautical Corporation, 1944.

Wright Aeronautical Corporation. *Wright Aircraft Engines Model 972TC18DA Parts Catalog.* Curtiss-Wright Corporation, Wright Aeronautical Division, 1954.

Yenne, Bill, with Curtis E. LeMay. *Superfortress: The B-29 and American Air Power.* New York: McGraw Hill, 1988; Yardley, Pennsylvania: Westholme, 2006.

Yenne, Bill, with Robert Redding. *Boeing: Planemaker to the World.* New York: Crown Publishers, 1983.

Yenne, Bill. *Building the B-17.* North Branch, Minnesota: Specialty, 2021.

Yenne, Bill. *Lockheed.* New York: Random House, 1987

Yenne, Bill. *McDonnell Douglas: A Tale of Two Giants.* New York: Random House, 1985

Yenne, Bill. *Rockwell: The Heritage of North American.* New York: Random House, 1989.

Yenne, Bill. *The 377 Stratocruiser & KC-97 Stratofreighter: Boeing's Great Post War Transports.* North Branch, MN: Specialty, 2014

Yenne, Bill. *The History of the US Air Force.* New York: Simon & Schuster, Exeter Books, 1984.

Yenne, Bill. *The Story of the Boeing Company.* San Francisco: AGS BookWorks, 2014.

Yenne, Bill with Jack Real. *The Asylum of Howard Hughes.* Bloomington, Indiana: XLibris Corporation, 2003.

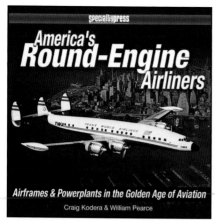

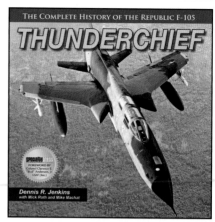

AMERICA'S ROUND-ENGINE AIRLINERS *Craig Kodera & William Pearce* The advancement and success of America's air transportation system can be linked directly to the concurrent growth of long-range, high-speed airliners and their revolutionary powerplants. This book tells the compelling story of aviation progress and development for the very first time. 10 x 10, 160 pages, 250 photos. Hardbound. *Item # SP257*

VIGILANTE!: A Pilot's Story of 1,200 Hours Flying the Ultimate US Navy Reconnaissance Aircraft *Robert Powell* Aviation enthusiasts will be fascinated with this complete study of the extraordinary RA-5C Vigilante. Easy-to-read historical facts and technical information is interspersed with personal stories from the pilot's point of view. 10 x 10, 192 pgs, 263 photos. Hdbd. ISBN 978-1-58007-261-8. *Item # SP261*

THUNDERCHIEF: The Complete History of the Republic F-105 *Dennis R. Jenkins* This book continues the story of Republic's Mach-2 F-105 Thunderchief where previous books on this aircraft left off. Author Dennis Jenkins uses rare archival air force documentation and original Republic factory material and photos never before seen by the public to tell the complete story of this legendary jet fighter-bomber. 10 x 10, 300 pages, 700 photos. Hardbound. *Item # SP259*

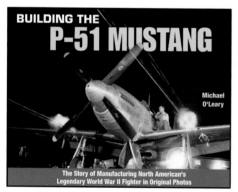

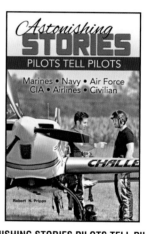

BUILDING THE P-51 MUSTANG: The Story of Manufacturing North American's Legendary World War II Fighter in Orginal Photos *Michael O'Leary* The author uses more than 300 original photos culled from his personal archive of offical North American and USAAF images, many of which have never before been seen in any publication whatsoever. This book provides a vital "missing link" in the saga of this famed World War II aircraft, and is sure to become a valued addition to libraries of P-51 modelers, historians, enthusiasts, and pilots in both the U.S. and England. 11 x 8-1/2, 240 pages, 300 b/w photos & 50 b/w illustrations. Softbound. *Item # SP190*

BUILDING THE B-17 FLYING FORTRESS: A Detailed Look at Manufacturing Boeing's Legendary World War II Bomber in Original Photos *Bill Yenne* This book features photos and manufacturing details of America's greatest multi-engine World War II combat aircraft and tells the compelling story of how more than 12,000 B-17s were built. 11 x 8-1/2, 240 pgs, 383 photos. Sftbd. ISBN 978-1-58007-271-7 *Item # SP271*

ASTONISHING STORIES PILOTS TELL PILOTS *Robert N. Pripps* Airplane pilots are notorious storytellers. As this collection of tales (mostly true) are revealed in this book, the reader, whether a pilot or not, can experience a sense of what it is like to be at the controls of everything from a puddle jumper to a Mach 3 jet. 8 x 5, 34 b/w photos, Sftbd. ISBN 978-1-58007-280-9. *Item # SP275*

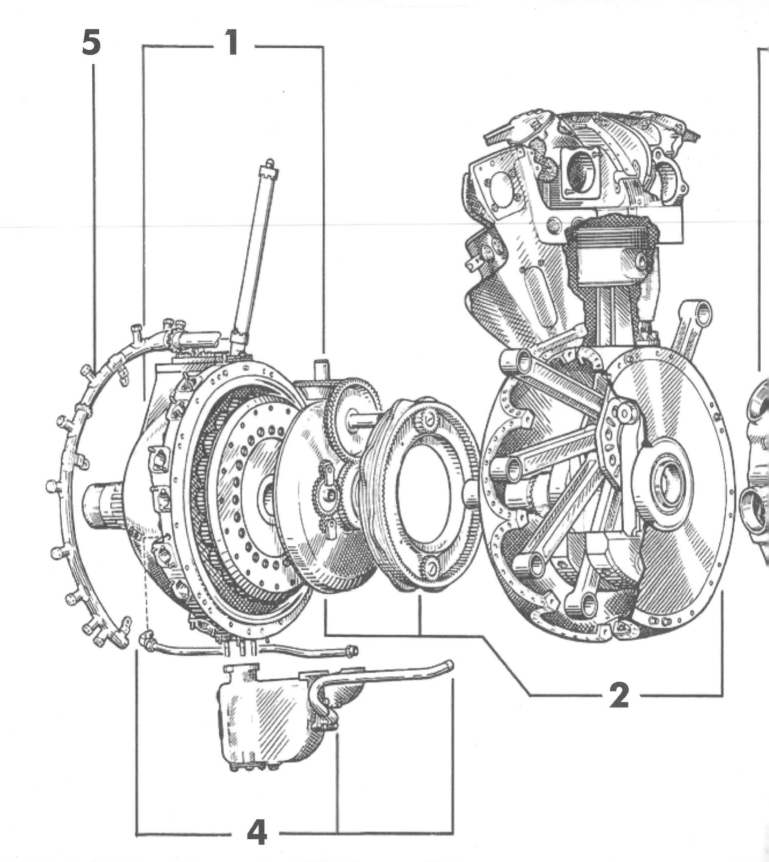